Debates, Controversies, and Prizes

Bloomsbury Studies in Modern German Philosophy

Series Editors:
Courtney D. Fugate, American University of Beirut, Lebanon
Anne Pollok, University of South Carolina, USA

Editorial Board:
Desmond Hogan (Princeton University, USA)
Ursula Goldenbaum (Emory University, USA)
Robert Clewis (Gwynedd Mercy University, USA)
Paul Guyer (Brown University, USA)
Brandon Look (University of Kentucky, USA)
Eric Watkins (University of California, San Diego, USA)
Corey W. Dyck (University of Western Ontario, Canada)
Stefanie Buchenau (University of Paris, France)
Paola Rumore (University of Turin, Italy)
Heiner Klemme (Martin-Luther-Universität Halle-Wittenberg, Germany)

Central and previously overlooked ideas and thinkers from the German Enlightenment Era are showcased in this series. Expanding research into areas that have been neglected particularly in English-language scholarship, it covers the work of lesser-known authors, previously untranslated texts, and issues that have suffered an undeserved life on the margins of current philosophical-historical discussion about eighteenth-century German thought.

By opening itself to a broad range of subjects and placing the role of women during this period center stage, the series not only advances our understanding about the German Enlightenment and its connection with the pan-European debates, but also contributes to debates about the reception of Newtonian science and the impact of Leibnizian, Kantian, and Wolffian philosophies.

Featuring edited collections and single-authored works, and overseen by an esteemed Editorial Board, the goal is to enrich current debates in the history of philosophy and to correct common misconceptions.

Titles in the series include:

Tetens's Writings on Method, Language, and Anthropology, edited by
Courtney D. Fugate, Curtis Sommerlatte, and Scott Stapleford

Kant's Rational Religion and the Radical Enlightenment, by Anna Tomaszewska

The Human Vocation in German Philosophy, edited by Anne Pollok and
Courtney D. Fugate

The Philosophy of Friedrich Heinrich Jacobi, by Birgit Sandkaulen

Hope and the Kantian Legacy, edited by Katerina Mihaylova and Anna Ezekiel

Kant and the Problem of Nothingness, by Ernesto Mayz Vallenilla and
translated by Addison Ellis

Debates, Controversies, and Prizes

Philosophy in the German Enlightenment

Edited by
Tinca Prunea-Bretonnet and Christian Leduc

BLOOMSBURY ACADEMIC
LONDON • NEW YORK • OXFORD • NEW DELHI • SYDNEY

BLOOMSBURY ACADEMIC
Bloomsbury Publishing Plc, 50 Bedford Square, London, WC1B 3DP, UK
Bloomsbury Publishing Inc, 1359 Broadway, 12th Floor, New York, NY 10018, USA
Bloomsbury Publishing Ireland, 29 Earlsfort Terrace, Dublin 2, D02 AY28, Ireland

BLOOMSBURY, BLOOMSBURY ACADEMIC and the Diana logo
are trademarks of Bloomsbury Publishing Plc

First published in Great Britain 2024
This paperback edition published 2026

Copyright © Tinca Prunea-Bretonnet, Christian Leduc and Contributors, 2024

Tinca Prunea-Bretonnet and Christian Leduc have asserted their right under the
Copyright, Designs and Patents Act, 1988, to be identified as Editors of this work.

For legal purposes the Acknowledgments on p. viii constitute
an extension of this copyright page.

Cover design by Louise Dugdale
Cover image: "Akademiesitzung um 1745. Zeichnung von Adolph Menzel"
in Kugler, Franz: Geschichte Friedrichs des Großen.
Mit Zeichnungen von Adolph Menzel, Leipzig 1840, p. 200.

All rights reserved. No part of this publication may be: i) reproduced or transmitted in any form, electronic or mechanical, including photocopying, recording or by means of any information storage or retrieval system without prior permission in writing from the publishers; or ii) used or reproduced in any way for the training, development or operation of artificial intelligence (AI) technologies, including generative AI technologies. The rights holders expressly reserve this publication from the text and data mining exception as per Article 4(3) of the Digital Single Market Directive (EU) 2019/790.

Bloomsbury Publishing Plc does not have any control over, or responsibility for, any third-party websites referred to or in this book. All internet addresses given in this book were correct at the time of going to press. The author and publisher regret any inconvenience caused if addresses have changed or sites have ceased to exist, but can accept no responsibility for any such changes.

A catalogue record for this book is available from the British Library.

Library of Congress Cataloging-in-Publication Data
Names: Prunea-Bretonnet, Tinca, editor. | Leduc, Christian, 1975- editor.
Title: Debates, controversies, and prizes : philosophy in the German Enlightenment / edited by Tinca Prunea-Bretonnet and Christian Leduc.
Description: 1. | London : Bloomsbury Academic, 2024. | Series: Bloomsbury studies in modern German philosophy | Includes bibliographical references and index. |
Summary: "This collection brings together a series of cutting-edge studies on the most significant controversies and prize essay contests of the German Enlightenment. Chapters address questions such as the condition of possibility of the debates, their institutional support and their aims, and introduce relatively unknown but key figures of the period. Set out into four parts, the essays provide new material on areas such as anthropology, the problem of language, colonialism and the origins of aesthetics for the wider study of 18th-century intellectual and philosophical life"– Provided by publisher.
Identifiers: LCCN 2023052712 (print) | LCCN 2023052713 (ebook) | ISBN 9781350348646 (hardback) | ISBN 9781350348684 (paperback) | ISBN 9781350348660 (epub) | ISBN 9781350348653 (ebook)
Subjects: LCSH: Philosophy, German–18th century.
Classification: LCC B2615 .D43 2024 (print) | LCC B2615 (ebook) | DDC 193–dc23/eng/20240429
LC record available at https://lccn.loc.gov/2023052712
LC ebook record available at https://lccn.loc.gov/2023052713

ISBN: HB: 978-1-3503-4864-6
PB: 978-1-3503-4868-4
ePDF: 978-1-3503-4865-3
eBook: 978-1-3503-4866-0

Series: Bloomsbury Studies in Modern German Philosophy

Typeset by Integra Software Services Pvt. Ltd.

For product safety related questions contact productsafety@bloomsbury.com

To find out more about our authors and books visit www.bloomsbury.com
and sign up for our newsletters.

Contents

Acknowledgments	viii
Introduction *Tinca Prunea-Bretonnet and Christian Leduc*	1

Part One Natural Law and History — 9

1	The Presumption of Goodness and the Controversy over Christian Wolff's Cosmopolitanism *Andreas Blank*	11
2	The Duties of the Historian—Raynal's Failed Prize Question *Gesa Wellmann*	31

Part Two Metaphysics — 49

3	A Negative Monadology: Condillac's Answer to the Berlin Academy Prize Competition *Christian Leduc*	51
4	Between Optimism and Anti-Optimism: Prémontval's "Middle Point" *Lloyd Strickland*	69
5	The *Public Debate* about the Abuse of Power by the Berlin Academy against Samuel König *Ursula Goldenbaum*	89
6	On Progress in Metaphysics: Responses to the Berlin Academy's 1792/1795 Prize Essay Question *Stephen Howard and Pavel Reichl*	113

Part Three Anthropology — 137

7	Aesthetics as Apolaustic: Baumgarten and the Controversy over Sensitive Pleasures *Alessandro Nannini*	139
8	Drives, Inclinations, and Perfectibility: Leonhard Cochius' Response to the 1768 Prize Question *Tinca Prunea-Bretonnet*	165
9	The Origin of Language as an Anthropological Topic: The 1769/1771 Prize Question of the Berlin Academy *Gualtiero Lorini*	183
10	The Philosophical Context of the 1773/1775 *Preisfrage*: Johann Georg Sulzer on Knowledge and Sensibility *Daniel Dumouchel*	207

Note on the Contributors	223
Index	226

Acknowledgments

This volume stems from a conference on "Controversies and *Preisfragen*: Shaping the Enlightenment between Wolff and Kant" held in May 2017 at New Europe College, Bucharest, and co-organized with the Research Institute of the University of Bucharest (Humanities division). We thank both institutions for their support. The volume was completed and is published within the frame of the research project "Between Truth and Freedom: Enlightenment Answers to *Thinking for Oneself*" (grant no. PN-III-P4-ID-PCE-2020-2579; funded by UEFISCDI-CNCS).

We thank the Social Sciences and Humanities Research Council of Canada for additional funding. Many thanks as well to Angelo Fata and Annelie Grosse for their help in the preparation of the text.

Introduction

Tinca Prunea-Bretonnet and Christian Leduc

Controversies have undoubtedly shaped the history of philosophy. Some have come to be quite renowned, such as the condemnation of Aristotelian propositions in 1277 by the Sorbonne and the subsequent disputes and argumentation that followed.[1] We now recognize that the condemnation had multiple theoretical and practical consequences for philosophy at the time, especially for Thomism, consequences that continue to resonate in philosophical discourse today. The early modern period is also notorious for having been the scene of important polemical engagements. One might recall here the aftermath of the published works of Descartes or Spinoza. The quarrel between Cartesians and Dutch theologians was particularly vivid, and it offered Descartes the opportunity to present details that allowed him to finesse his views.[2] The reception of Spinoza's metaphysics and political thought is also extensively documented and recently received significant attention.[3] It would be impossible to analyze the dissemination of their thought without considering the numerous theological, scientific, or speculative debates they engendered. What can reasonably be argued is that controversies and disputes are simply an inextricable feature of the history of the discipline of philosophy.

Although specific controversies have been studied at length, they rarely feature as the primary objects of examination. In contrast to the history of ideas, of sciences, or of literature, there seems to be an interpretative lacuna in the history of philosophy when it comes to addressing controversies, particularly for the early modern period—as if the thinkers of the early modern period had barely influenced the nature of the concepts, arguments, and the theories that were often the objects of disputes. Analyses have certainly been devoted to the method of controversies in general,[4] as well as the polemical style of individual philosophers, such as Pascal[5] and Leibniz.[6] However, controversies are seldom the main topic of research in the history of early modern philosophy. More recently, reflection on method in historiography has led to significant clarifications regarding the role of controversies. We should mention the historical perspectivism endorsed by Mogens Laerke here, according to whom contextualized and internal interpretations should be privileged.[7] We agree with Laerke that "determining the meaning of some text is [...] nothing but determining the role the text plays as a concrete intervention in some historical debate and situating the text in a complex network of intellectual positions actually at play at that time."[8] Therefore, the study of philosophical debates appears to be crucial for historiography as well as for the history of philosophy.

The present volume aims to fill such a gap by viewing the philosophy of eighteenth-century Germany through the prism of the central debates of the time, debates that were often taken up, if not generated, by essay competitions, that is, the famous academic prize questions. As with other significant periods within the history of philosophy, some of the early modern polemical exchanges are well known. The pantheism controversy likely remains the best known, one that was occasioned by Spinoza's metaphysics and involved major figures of the German intellectual milieu, including Lessing, Jacobi, Mendelssohn, and Kant.[9] Another renowned polemic centered around the *Fragmentenstreit* (fragments dispute) regarding Hermann Samuel Reimarus' views on revealed religion, which to a considerable extent shaped late eighteenth-century German philosophy and theology despite being less documented in Anglophone historiography.[10] To be sure, as with other intellectual contexts, very few of these Enlightenment controversies can be said to be purely philosophical in nature and their analysis requires prudent and detailed consideration. The theological, scientific, and even political elements of the polemics must often be taken into account for us sufficiently to appreciate the internal complexities of the debates. For instance, the analysis of the controversy about the principle of least action at the Berlin Academy cannot disregard the institutional and political framework in which it emerged.

Moreover, many controversies in the German Enlightenment took a particular direction for a very specific reason: debates and quarrels were often provoked, taken up, or intensified through prize competitions of the Berlin Academy. The controversies about monads, optimism, language, or history partly originate from and owe their prominence to *Preisfragen* (prize questions) that were organized by the Academy. We should emphasize that this situation was specific to the Prussian institution since it was the only academy that possessed a class of speculative philosophy at that time. Much like other learned societies, the Berlin Academy had classes of mathematics, natural sciences, and *belles-lettres*.[11] However, from 1744–1746 to the end of the eighteenth century, that is, throughout much of Frederick the Great's reign, the class of metaphysics, morals, and methods was very active. Many prize competitions of the period addressed philosophical issues and stemmed from the class of speculative philosophy, which typically published its questions every four years.[12]

Apart from prize competitions, the Berlin Academy was also the theater of important and sometimes fierce polemics, such as the controversy about the principle of least action,[13] but also of other disputes on specific aspects of the philosophies of Leibniz and Wolff, and particularly, the theory of monads.[14] It is our conviction that the German Enlightenment was significantly shaped by the dynamics between early modern controversies which in many cases revolved around the prize competitions. We should note that during this period, the numerous debates were particularly rich, passionate, and at times acrimonious. Thus, one can hardly over-emphasize the crucial role played by the Berlin Academy in these Enlightenment controversies, a role that not only owes itself to the Berlin Academy's organization of public and common sessions, to the debates it encouraged, and to the circulation of ideas it promoted, but also to the intrinsic philosophical value of the writings that were published by its members and correspondents. Not only did the institution truly belong to the *German* Enlightenment (despite a false, if familiar, narrative encouraged by Max Wundt who regards this institution as a foreign body within German philosophy),[15] but its philosophical activity, whether polemical or not, decisively enriched Prussian philosophical life through an erudite and lively discussion of European enlightened ideas. It is precisely this confrontation—that turned ardent and agonistic at times, as we will see—between the perspectives and specific viewpoints coming from French, Scottish, and English thinkers on the one hand, and the Leibnizian and Wolffian standpoints on the other, that shapes the controversies dealt with in this volume.

While recent studies of eighteenth-century German philosophy prior to Kant have considerably deepened our understanding of this period, they generally examine the German tradition with the aim of contextualizing specific aspects of Kant's philosophy.[16] Our collection does not endorse this teleological orientation, but instead focuses on controversies as a precondition and a means for the advancement of knowledge. In short, we examine the debates for themselves. The present chapters study significant prize essay contests and debates of the German Enlightenment in order to shed new light on the role of philosophical controversies and the practices arising from them. While addressing some broader themes in the study of eighteenth-century intellectual life, such as anthropology, the problem of language, colonialism, and the origins of aesthetics, they also examine specific questions, such as the condition of possibility of the debates, their institutional support, as well as their aims. The collection shows how the main outcome from these debates was not reconciliation as such, but the creation of a common territory, of a philosophical community where discussions and opposing arguments continued to nourish philosophical reflection. We hope that by introducing relatively unknown but significant figures and developments, the collection will strengthen our appreciation of the richness and complexity of the German Enlightenment.

In the first chapter, "The Presumption of Goodness and the Controversy over Christian Wolff's Cosmopolitanism," Andreas Blank argues that Wolff's cosmopolitanism did not, in fact, become influential due to the controversy about the concept of a world-encompassing citizenry (*civitas maxima*) in the 1750s following the publication of his *Law of Nature* in 1749. Wolff defined cosmopolitanism as the necessity to contribute as much as possible to the perfection of other peoples in order for a people to increase their own perfection. The controversy regarding this concept involved thinkers such as Emer de Vattel, Michael Christoph Hanov, and Hermann Friedrich Kahrel, all of whom debated the fictional character of the *civitas maxima*. Blank focuses on Wolff's views about the rationality of presumptions in order to show that the concept of cosmopolitanism is grounded on this issue, and much less on the role of fictions in natural law.

Gesa Wellmann's chapter on "The Duties of the Historian—Raynal's Failed Prize Question" focuses on the 1783 prize question regarding "the way to write history," proposed by Guillaume Raynal. She discusses his book *Histoire des deux Indes* (History of the Two Indies) from 1770 and analyzes Ewald Friedrich von Hertzberg's response to the Academy. While the prize was not awarded at all, the debate that resulted from the proposed topic was significant for broader debates that concerned the philosophy of history. This chapter reconstructs key aspects of the arguments defended by Raynal and Hertzberg.

Christian Leduc's chapter presents an analysis of Condillac's response to the famous prize question on monads. In "A Negative Monadology: Condillac's Answer to the Berlin Academy Prize Competition," Leduc compares Condillac's prize essay with Leibnizian and Wolffian metaphysics. He argues that Condillac ultimately defended aspects of Leibniz's metaphysical thought and elaborated what could be called a *negative monadology*. Leduc goes on to claim that this negative monadology, which maintains the unknowability of the essence of monads despite the proof of their existence offered by sensation, would prove to be significant for the debates concerning rational cosmology, including topics such as the divisibility of matter, the general order of things, and the reality of space and time.

Lloyd Strickland's "Between Optimism and Anti-optimism: Prémontval's 'Middle Point'" examines a famous prize question that was published during the 1750s and addressed the question of optimism. Strickland focuses on André-Pierre Le Guay de Prémontval's views concerning the topic, especially Prémontval's attempt to elaborate a "middle point" between positions that were generally favorable or opposed to optimism. The chapter examines several writings by Prémontval from 1754 and 1755, such as *Thoughts on Freedom, The Diogenes of d'Alembert, On Chance under the Rule of Providence*, as well as several later essays in order to assess Prémontval's contribution to the debates of his time. Strickland argues for the originality of Prémontval's standpoint on optimism.

In her "The *Public Debate* about the Abuse of Power by the Berlin Academy against Samuel König," Ursula Goldenbaum employs the "detective method" of historical analysis that she favors to propose a reconstruction of the public debate regarding Samuel König's thesis that Maupertuis' principle of least action was inspired by a letter from Leibniz. As König could not provide either the letter or a copy of it, with the support of Frederick II, the Academy concluded that this letter did not exist and therefore condemned König for forgery. Goldenbaum's chapter examines the public debate and the various reactions to this controversy not only in the German-speaking milieu, but also in France and the Netherlands. She argues that König successfully defended his reputation thanks to the reaction of the public and also managed to convince Voltaire to side with him.

Stephen Howard and Pavel Reichl in their chapter "On Progress in Metaphysics: Responses to the Berlin Academy's 1792/1795 Prize Essay Question" analyze the three essays that were awarded prizes in 1795 as well as Kant's drafts devoted to the 1792 prize question topic. After examining the essays of Johann Heinrich Abicht, Karl Leonhard Reinhold, and Johann Christoph Schwab, the authors compare the answers with drafts of Kant's position that can be retraced from his unfinished response to the prize question. Howard and Reichl offer an assessment of the respective views about the progress of metaphysics since Leibniz and Wolff that were defended by Abicht, Reinhold, and Schwab alongside an evaluation of the place that Kantian philosophy occupied during this period.

Alessandro Nannini's chapter is devoted to the controversy between Lutheran and Piestist thinkers that presided over the foundation of aesthetics. In "Aesthetics as Apolaustic: Baumgarten and the Controversy over Sensitive Pleasures," Nannini examines Alexander Baumgarten's essays and his psychological, moral, theological, and aesthetic writings on pleasure, arguing that Baumgarten's views not only transformed the period's approach to ethics, but also contributed to the birth of aesthetics as a discipline that focuses on sensitive pleasure in a manner that legitimizes it for philosophical reflection.

The eighth chapter, entitled "Drives, Inclinations, and Perfectibility: Leonhard Cochius' Response to the 1768 Prize Question" by Tinca Prunea-Bretonnet, analyzes Cochius' prize essay on inclinations. Prunea-Bretonnet argues for its inscription in the Leibnizian and Wolffian tradition and for its significant contribution to empirical psychology. While traditional concepts such as "the depth of the soul" or "drive" play an important role in the essay, Cochius redefines them within a perspective that departs from ethical and theological considerations. The "return to Leibniz" that Cochius promotes is thus more indebted to contemporary concerns about psychological issues and education than it is to positions that were defended during the early Enlightenment. Prunea-Bretonnet also holds that Cochius' relationship to Johann Georg Sulzer and Jean-Jacques Rousseau proves to be more complex than terminological similarities might otherwise suggest.

In the penultimate chapter, entitled "The Origin of Language as an Anthropological Topic: The 1769/1771 Prize Question of the Berlin Academy," Gualtiero Lorini first considers various theses and approaches that were proposed by anonymous responses to the 1769/1771 prize question. He then analyzes several common topics, such as language in animals, the existence of an original language, and above all, the relationship between words and thought in order to show that the problem of language, including its origin and its development, occupied a central place on the philosophical scene. The chapter goes on to examine other essays of the period devoted to the topic of language in order to elucidate the anthropological significance of the theoretical shifts that occurred throughout the early 1770s.

The final chapter by Daniel Dumouchel, "The Philosophical Context of the 1773/1775 *Preisfrage*: Johann Georg Sulzer on Knowledge and Sensibility," examines the philosophical background of the 1773/1775 prize question devoted to the faculties of the mind. Dumouchel focuses on Johann Georg Sulzer's academic essays in order to assess his contribution to empirical psychology, the theory of the mind, and metaphysics. The central argument maintains that Sulzer's endorsement and re-elaboration of the Wolffian standpoint regarding a single active force of the soul prove to have been particularly significant for the period.

Notes

1 See Piché 1999.
2 Verbeek 1992.
3 See, for example, Laerke 2021, chapter 2; see also Israel 2001 and Israel 2006.
4 Goldenbaum 2004; Dascal and Chang 2007; Lifschitz 2012; Rey and Tadié 2016.
5 Descotes 1993.

6 Dascal 2006; Laerke 2008.
7 See Laerke 2013.
8 Laerke 2013, 17. Contrast this approach with the "detective method" that Ursula Goldenbaum defends (Goldenbaum 2013, 71–90) and applies in her chapter in the present volume. She is interested in the (in her view, often deliberately concealed) "intention" of authors: "I simply ask for the intention of an author in the sense a detective asks for the motives of a wrongdoer […] Thus, as a detective would look for 'good reasons' some of the suspects might have had for committing the crime, I look for the 'good reasons' a philosopher might have had to take a particular stance in a controversy. […] All human actions are driven by intentions. Aren't philosophical texts actions as well?" (Goldenbaum 2013, 75).
9 Kinzel 2020.
10 One of the rare and recent studies in English examining the role of Elise Reimarus in this polemic is Winegar 2021.
11 On this, see Anstey 2022, 17–38.
12 See Prunea-Bretonnet and Anstey 2022; Duchesneau et al. 2022.
13 For details, see Lyssy 2022.
14 See Leduc's chapter in this volume.
15 On this, see Prunea-Bretonnet 2022.
16 Dyck and Wunderlich 2018; De Boer and Prunea-Bretonnet 2021.

Bibliography

Anstey, Peter R. 2022. "The Four Classes of the Berlin Academy." In *The Berlin Academy in the Reign of Frederick the Great: Philosophy and Science*, edited by Tinca Prunea-Bretonnet and Peter R. Anstey, Oxford University Studies in the Enlightenment, 17–38. Liverpool: Liverpool University Press.

Dascal, Marcelo (ed. and trans.). 2006. *Gottfried Wilhelm Leibniz. The Art of Controversies*. Dordrecht: Springer.

Dascal, Marcelo and Han-Liang Chang (eds.). 2007. *Traditions of Controversy*. Amsterdam: John Benjamins.

De Boer, Karin and Tinca Prunea-Bretonnet (eds.). 2021. *The Experiential Turn in Eighteenth-Century German Philosophy*. London: Routledge.

Descotes, Dominique. 1993. *L'argumentation chez Pascal*. Paris: PUF.

Duchesneau, François, Daniel Dumouchel, Angela Ferraro, and Christian Leduc (eds.). 2022. *Philosophie spéculative à l'Académie de Berlin. Mémoires 1745–1769*. Paris: Vrin.

Dyck, Corey and Falk Wunderlich (eds.). 2018. *Kant and His German Contemporaries*. Cambridge: Cambridge University Press.

Goldenbaum, Ursula. 2004. *Appel an das Publikum: Die Offentliche Debatte in der deutschen Aufklärung 1687–1796*. With contributions by Frank Grunert, Peter Weber, Gerda Heinrich, and Brigitte Erker and Winfried Siebers. Berlin: De Gruyter.

Goldenbaum, Ursula. 2013. "Understanding the Argument through Then-Current Public Debates or My Detective Method of History of Philosophy." In *Philosophy and Its History. Aims and Methods in the Study of Early Modern Philosophy*, edited by Mogens Laerke, Justin E. Smith, and Eric Schliesser, 71–90. Oxford: Oxford University Press.

Israel, Jonathan I. 2001. *Radical Enlightenment. Philosophy and the Making of Modernity (1650–1750)*. Oxford: Oxford University Press.

Israel, Jonathan I. 2006. *Enlightenment Contested. Philosophy, Modernity, and the Emancipation of Man (1670–1752)*. Oxford: Oxford University Press.

Kinzel, Till, Oliver Kock, and Anne Pollok. 2020. *Im Kontext des Spinozastreits: Lessing-Jacobi, Mendelssohn and Hamann*. Wolfenbüttel: Lessing Akademie.

Laerke, Mogens. 2008. "Apology for a Credo Maximum: On Three Basic Rules in Leibniz's Method of Religious Controversy." In *Leibniz: What Kind of Rationalist?*, edited by Marcelo Dascal, 397–407. Dordrecht: Springer.

Laerke, Mogens. 2013. "The Anthropological Analogy and the Constitution of Historical Perspectivism." In *Philosophy and Its History. Aims and Methods in the Study of Early Modern Philosophy*, edited by Mogens Laerke, Justin E. Smithy, and Eric Schliesser, 7–29. Oxford: Oxford University Press.

Laerke, Mogens. 2021. *Spinoza and the Freedom of Philosophizing*. Oxford: Oxford University Press.

Lifschitz, Avi. 2012. *Language and Enlightenment: The Berlin Debates of the Eighteenth Century*. Oxford: Oxford University Press.

Lyssy, Ansgar. 2022. "Maupertuis, Euler and the Leibnizian Metaphysics behind the Principle of Least Action." In *The Berlin Academy in the Reign of Frederick the Great: Philosophy and Science*, edited by Tinca Prunea-Bretonnet and Peter R. Anstey, Oxford University Studies in the Enlightenment, 123–52. Liverpool: Liverpool University Press.

Piché, David. 1999. *La condamnation parisienne de 1277*. Paris: Vrin.

Prunea-Bretonnet, Tinca and Peter R. Anstey (eds.). 2022. *The Berlin Academy in the Reign of Frederick the Great: Philosophy and Science*, Oxford University Studies in the Enlightenment. Liverpool: Liverpool University Press.

Prunea-Bretonnet, Tinca. 2022. "Eclectic Philosophy and 'Academic Spirit': The Berlin Academy and the Thomasian Legacy." In *The Berlin Academy in the Reign of Frederick the Great: Philosophy and Science*, edited by Tinca Prunea-Bretonnet and Peter R. Anstey, Oxford University Studies in the Enlightenment, 71–101. Liverpool: Liverpool University Press.

Rey, Anne-Lise and Alexis Tadié (eds.). 2016. "Disputes et territoires épistémiques." *Revue de synthèse*, 137, 3–4, 223–477.

Verbeek, Theo. 1992. *Descartes and the Dutch: Early Reactions to Cartesian Philosophy, 1637–1650*. Carbondale: Southern Illinois University Press.

Winegar, Reed. 2021. "Elise Reimarus: Reason, Religion, and Enlightenment." In *Women and Philosophy in Eighteenth-Century Germany*, edited by Corey Dyck, 110–33. Oxford: Oxford University Press.

Part One

Natural Law and History

1

The Presumption of Goodness and the Controversy over Christian Wolff's Cosmopolitanism

Andreas Blank

1. Introduction

Christian Wolff's cosmopolitanism did not share the fate of Immanuel Kant's. While Kant's political thought has turned out to be a major source of inspiration for late twentieth- and early twenty-first-century forms of cosmopolitanism, nothing comparable can be said of Wolff's concept of an all-encompassing political community called the *civitas maxima* (greatest citizenry). In contrast to Kant, who proposed an exceedingly short list of cosmopolitan rights and obligations, Wolff proposed an exceedingly long list of such rights and obligations. His list derives from the requirement that every people must contribute as much as is possible and necessary to the perfection of other peoples because doing so contributes to their own perfection.[1] If we suppose that the world would become infinitely better if the rights and obligations proposed by Kant were respected, would this not be much more the case if the rights and obligations proposed by Wolff were heeded? One of the reasons why the cosmopolitanism of Wolff did not gain traction can be found in the not-very-extensive controversy that his notion of *civitas maxima* stirred over the few years that followed the 1749 publication of his *Jus gentium methodo scientifica pertractatum* (JG) (The Law of Nations Treated According to a Scientific Method). It is a controversy for which the outright rejection of the notion of *civitas maxima* was coupled with attempts to adopt it while rejecting Wolff's suggestion that the *civitas maxima* should be regarded as a fiction.

Let me clarify from the outset that I am not using the concept of controversy in the narrow sense of a theoretical debate with a particular structure (for instance, that something counts as a controversy when a proponent makes a claim, an opponent objects, the proponent replies to the objection, and the opponent offers a rejoinder to the reply). No such structure can be found in the case of the reactions to Wolff's concept of *civitas maxima* for the simple reason that Wolff passed away shortly after the publication of the JG. Hence, certain questions cannot be asked here, such as the question of how the dynamics of the controversy led both proponents and opponents to modify their positions. Rather, I use the concept of controversy in the looser sense of a field of diverging responses to a theoretical claim. These responses articulate a field of diverging theoretical possibilities, and thinking about how Wolff's work relates to these possibilities may clarify aspects of his argumentative strategy that otherwise may go unnoticed.

Francis Cheneval has used such an approach in his attempt to rehabilitate Wolff's cosmopolitanism, an approach I will take up in the present chapter. I will not go over the entire range of the relevant controversy because I find much of Cheneval's discussion illuminating and persuasive. Cheneval focuses less on the more familiar and dismissive attitude toward Wolff's cosmopolitanism that is found in Emer de Vattel (1714–64)[2] than he does on the work of two less well-known contemporaries, Michael Christoph Hanov (1695–1773), the rector of the Academic Gymnasium in Danzig, and Hermann Friedrich Kahrel (1719–87), who had studied with Wolff and became a professor of philosophy at the University of Marburg. Hanov combined the notion of the *civitas maxima* with two elements that are foreign to Wolff's thought: a voluntarist theology and an adoption of the Augustinian conception of a *civitas Dei* (city of God) (Hanov 1756–1759, I, iii, §232). I will not go into these matters because I agree with Cheneval that Hanov did cosmopolitanism a bad service by burdening it with assumptions about the metaphysical status of the *civitas maxima* (supreme state) and with the well-known problems that voluntarism brings with it for the question of divine justice (Cheneval 2001, 137–8). I am less convinced by Cheneval's treatment of Kahrel's response to Wolff. Kahrel took up many of Wolff's cosmopolitan ideas but, contrary to Wolff's intention, eliminated the concept of fiction by assigning a central role to an idea that was prominent in the early modern legal tradition and that can also be found in Wolff: the idea that some legally binding obligations can, in the absence of either explicit or tacit consent, be derived from the *praesumptio bonitatis* (presumption of goodness). This presumption was understood to concern the willingness to accept obligations that derive from natural law.

Cheneval has tried to rehabilitate Wolff's cosmopolitanism by placing the notion of legal fiction at the center of his interpretation. According to Cheneval, what does the crucial work in Wolff's theory of a *civitas maxima* is "a normative fiction of a presumed rational consensus" of individuals and states around the globe (Cheneval 2001, 125). As Cheneval puts it, Wolff's basic methodological intention consists in forming a "fictive, normative hypothesis" (Cheneval 2001, 126).[3] Wolff regarded the consensus underlying the *civitas maxima* to fall under the Roman law category of quasi-contracts (such as tutelage), which he unambiguously described as fictions. And, as Wolff notes, quasi-contracts were grounded on the presumption that an individual A would consent to those actions of an individual B, which B performed for the sake of protecting the interests of A, even in situations where A has no knowledge of these actions or where A is not capable of offering reasoned consent. Taking up this line of thought, Cheneval understands the presumed consent to the decisions of the majority of peoples that protect the interest of the peoples who do not give explicit or tacit consent as a fiction of the law of peoples. As Cheneval argues, Kahrel's adoption of Wolffian ideas cannot be on the right track because he regarded the *civitas maxima* to be something actual, and he thereby overlooked that Wolff understood fictions in the law of peoples as normative prescriptions that articulate what reason demands (Cheneval 2001, 139).

The early modern controversy over the *civitas maxima* thus raises the question of how facts, fictions, and presumptions relate to each other in Wolff's cosmopolitanism. This is an interesting question because Wolff's position may be more confused than is evident at first sight. While the strand of thought concerning fictions is certainly present both in *Jus naturae methodo scientifica pertractatum* (JN) (The Law of Nature Treated According to a Scientific Method) and *Jus gentium*, there is also a strand of thought that does not seem to be adequately integrated with the former. According to the latter strand of thought, the *civitas maxima* is grounded on real obligations of natural law, on the presumption that rational beings will be ready to fulfill their natural obligations, and on the view that it is, therefore, legitimate to transform imperfect duties of natural law into the perfect duties of the voluntary law of peoples. Wolff thus uses both the concept of fiction and the concept of presumption to characterize the *civitas maxima*.

These notions were clearly distinguished in legal humanism. For instance, Andrea Alciato (1492-1550) maintains that a legal fiction is "a disposition of the law that goes against the truth in a possible situation and is introduced for a just cause" (Alciato 1551, 8).[4] For instance, Roman law introduces the fiction that an infant has consented to the acceptance of a heritage despite the fact that an infant cannot form the intention to do so. The justification of this law is that it thereby prevents situations where infants lose their inheritance rights (Alciato 1551, 11). By contrast, in his view, all presumptions are "based on the truth" (*fundantur in veritate*), in the sense that the presumption takes something to be true while one does not know whether it is true (Alciato 1551, 8). For instance, presumptions about the mental states of others are assumptions that could be the case, even though we cannot be certain (Alciato 1551, 53). This is why it makes a difference whether the *civitas maxima* is understood as fiction or as something that is grounded in assumptions concerning the mental states of others. The puzzles concerning Wolff's use of fictions and presumption result from the fact that Wolff does not seem to have drawn such a sharp distinction. This will be the topic of the second section.

Kahrel's treatment of the presumption of goodness may draw attention to how the non-fictionalist aspects of Wolff's cosmopolitanism were meant to function. This is so because Kahrel bundles together ideas that occur in much more scattered form in Wolff's work. Using Kahrel's cosmopolitanism as a point of comparison will clarify that the normative aspects of Wolff's cosmopolitanism derive from this treatment of the presumption of goodness, not from his treatment of legal fictions. Kahrel makes use of a conception of the presumption of goodness that includes both legal and ethical aspects. Such an understanding of the presumption of goodness can be found in the work of the legal humanists, whose writings continued to be consulted and cited throughout the seventeenth and eighteenth centuries. In the third section, I will draw from some of their work to elucidate some aspects of Kahrel's treatment of the presumption of goodness. In the fourth, finally, I will use this background to draw attention to the presence of closely analogous elements in Wolff's thought that provide a foundation for the normative aspects of his conception of a *civitas maxima* that does not invoke fictions.

2. Some Puzzles about Wolff's Use of Fictions and Presumptions

It may be helpful to start by considering why an investigation of the non-fictionalist strands in Wolff's cosmopolitanism is worthwhile. There seem to be tensions inherent in Wolff's use of fictions, and these tensions may indicate that fictions are not integrated as well into his natural law theory as Cheneval assumes. One tension derives from an evident, but inconsequential, blunder on Wolff's part; the other tension derives from a deep layer of Wolff's conception of the connection between obligation and presumption.

As to the former tension, Wolff advises us to form the fiction of a regent (*rector*) of the *civitas maxima* (JG, §21). To persuade us, he draws an analogy with the usefulness of fictions in astronomy, such as the fiction of circular movements of heavenly bodies. As Wolff explains, astronomic fictions work using the "equivalence of cases." The basic idea is that some imaginary situations are easier to understand. These situations help us analyze aspects of reality that are more difficult to understand because they allow us to explore similarities between imaginary and real situations (Wolff 1737, §193). The analogy with astronomic fictions indicates that the fiction of the regent of the *civitas maxima* is a heuristic device, not a suggestion concerning the constitutional structure of the *civitas maxima*.[5] But is the fictional regent of the *civitas maxima* a useful heuristic device that allows us to approximate the future institutional structure of the global order? The answer must be negative because the "equivalence of cases" is missing here. Wolff argues that the constitution of the *civitas maxima* is essentially democratic because different peoples stand in a relation of natural equality with each other (JG, §19). Yet if this is the case, then the idea of armchair legislation based on thought experiments will not lead to any significant insight. The concrete contents of the voluntary law of peoples cannot be anticipated by using the fiction of a regent of the *civitas maxima* precisely because these contents have to be the outcome of a democratic process of deliberation. Furthermore, Wolff never comes back to this thought experiment (in contrast to many of his other ideas that make countless appearances in JG). Quite possibly, the fiction of the regent of the *civitas maxima* does not do any useful work here and could have been eliminated without loss.

To the latter tension, Wolff compares the presumed consent to forming a universal human society with the presumed consent that is constitutive of "quasi-contracts" (such as tutelage) (JG, §9).[6] As he explains:

> A pupil is rightly presumed to consent to tutelage in so far as he should consent, and in fact, would have consented had he understood his advantage; in the same way, peoples that, due to a defect of acuity, do not understand how useful being a member of this greatest society would be, are nevertheless presumed to consent to this association.
>
> (JG, §9)[7]

Wolff holds that the effect of obligations that are constitutive of the *civitas maxima* could be compared with the effect of civil obligation in quasi-contracts. What motivates the comparison is the idea that in both cases "the consent is understood to have been wrought even, as it were, from the one who is unwilling" (JG, §9).⁸ He also unambiguously characterizes quasi-contracts as legal fictions (JN V, §538). More generally, he holds that all moral persons, including the *civitas maxima*, "have something fictitious" (JG, §21).⁹ Following his explanation in the *Philosophia moralis sive ethica* (PM) (Moral or Ethical Philosophy), moral persons are fictions in the exclusive sense that a multitude of real persons "is conceived as a unity that possesses separate existence and that possesses no other qualities than those that are ascribed to it" (PM V, §294).¹⁰ By contrast, Wolff regards the rights and obligations that are ascribed to a moral person to be something that does not deviate from the truth—that is, they are not fictional (PM V, §294).

Wolff takes a people to not only be a moral person but also a multitude of individuals who are bearers of emotions and acts of the will (JG, §35).¹¹ This dual character of his notion of a people explains why there are non-fictitious elements in his conception of the *civitas maxima*. He maintains "that peoples are driven toward this society [*civitas maxima*] by some natural impulse, is evident from their actions, for instance when they form confederations for the sake of commerce and war, or also for the sake of friendship" (JG, §9).¹² He is not blind to the fact that political leaders cause conflicts because they let themselves be carried away by emotions (JG, §12). Still, Wolff grounds the presumed consent of the members of the *civitas maxima* on the concept of obligation when he writes that "because they are obliged to consent, they are presumed to have consented" (JG, §12).¹³ These obligations are described as non-fictional: "Humans should not be made up to be what they are not when they are maximally obliged to be such and such" (ibid.).¹⁴ The non-fictional nature of obligations also comes to the fore when Wolff discusses an analogy that is made between the voluntary law of peoples and civil law. As he puts it, the voluntary law of peoples "cannot be said to be a gratuitously made up fable" (JG, §887),¹⁵ and he compares the status of the voluntary law of peoples with civil laws that "insofar as they recede from the rigor of natural law, need not be taken to be figments" (JG, §887).¹⁶ What does Wolff have in mind here: the contrast between fables without a purpose and fictions with a purpose or the contrast between fictions and what is not fictional? I think it is the latter because he goes on to explain that "the consent of peoples that is demanded by natural law cannot be taken to be fictitious, for when it is in the highest degree absent it is supplemented by natural law" (ibid.).¹⁷ Presumed consent here is characterized as non-fictional.

Of course, the sense in which consent can be understood to be "supplemented by natural law" still needs to be explained. However, given that the *civitas maxima* is constituted by the obligations of the voluntary law of peoples in Wolff's view, several passages imply that there is something non-fictional about the *civitas maxima*. It is thus hard to avoid the conclusion that there is a disconcerting confusion in Wolff's treatment of fictions. He seems to be affirming that the *civitas maxima* is a fiction while simultaneously denying that it is a fiction. This is reason enough to ask whether Wolff's practical philosophy offers resources to support a conception of the *civitas maxima* that does not depend on the concept of fiction. Having Kahrel's version of cosmopolitanism in mind, it will be easier to see that Wolff's treatment of the presumption of goodness could fulfill this task.

3. The Presumption of Goodness in Kahrel's Cosmopolitanism

3.1. Presumptions and the Causal Structure of Reality

What makes Kahrel's considerations interesting is that they draw attention to some connections between assumptions concerning human nature and forming presumptions in the early modern legal tradition. This reading seems to be in tension with Cheneval's interpretation. According to Cheneval, Kahrel came to the view that peoples and their regents have actually established a *civitas maxima* because he identified the presumed consent of peoples and their regent with tacit consent (Cheneval 2001, 130–1)—which, according to a standard view shared by Wolff in the *Philosophia practica universalis* (PPU) (Universal Practical Philosophy), is a form of actual consent (PPU I, §660). If so, then Kahrel's view that the *civitas maxima* exists actually would seem to rest on an obvious conceptual confusion. However, that Kahrel distinguished tacit from presumed consent becomes clear in his *Recht der Natur* (RN) (Right of Nature) of 1747, an eight hundred-page overview of the central themes in natural law. There, he describes the differences between *voluntas expressa*, *voluntas tacita*, and *voluntas praesumta* as follows:

> The free will of someone else can only be known through words or other equivalent signs and external actions or omissions. This is why one calls the will an explicit will when it is signaled with sufficient words; one calls a tacit will a will that, based on actions or omissions, one knows with certainty ... ; the latter is a true will, too. However, when one must infer based on signs or other reasons only with probability, it is a presumed will. Accordingly, the same difference shows itself in consent and dissent.
>
> (RN I, iii, §58)[18]

What distinguishes tacit will from presumed will is that in the former case, the will is known with certainty, while in the latter, knowledge about the will remains uncertain. This, however, is exactly the purpose of presumptions: presumptions are assumptions that are taken to be true unless and until contrary evidence becomes available. Such assumptions were understood to be cognitive tools that help us deal with uncertainty in a rational manner.[19] Rationality demands that presumptions are based on reasons, even if these reasons cannot confer certainty on the assumptions that we make. Kahrel describes the reasons underlying presumptions concerning the will as follows: "One always presumes that one who remains silent when he can and must speak consents with what the other or others want ... For in this case, there is no obstacle for revealing the opinion of his heart if he did not want the same as the other or others" (RN I, v, §14).[20] Drawing from the view that a reason is what enables us to understand why something is the case (RN I, ii, §16), Kahrel explains:

> A reason is sufficient when we can perfectly grasp the truth through it. But the particular reasons that constitute the sufficient reason, if they are taken separately, are of such a quality that one cannot yet grasp the truth perfectly but only probably.

Hence, probability consists essentially in the knowledge of some of the particular reasons that, taken together, constitute the sufficient reason.

(RN I, v, §16)[21]

Certainly, there are situations where the expectation that someone who disagrees will articulate dissent is so strong that their unanticipated silence is taken with certainty to be a sign of consent. In such situations, all particular reasons that together form a sufficient reason for knowing the tacit will are given. In other situations, we cannot be certain that all particular reasons are given that, together, form a sufficient reason for knowing a tacit will. This is why these are cases of presumed will.

The act of grounding presumptions in particular reasons implies that presumptions can be stronger or weaker depending on how many particular reasons are known: "The presumption is called stronger where there is a greater probability; weaker, where one finds a smaller probability. The more particular reasons enter the realm of our knowledge, and the more of them one knows with certainty, the stronger is the presumption" (RN I, v, §17).[22] Weighing presumptions also implies that there can be competing presumptions: "When some of the reasons are given that belong to the sufficient reason for knowing the truth of some proposition, but also other reasons for knowing the truth of its contrary …, it is said that the presumptions are contrary to each other" (RN I, v, §19).[23] The question, of course, is how a decision between competing presumptions can be reached. Kahrel holds that relative frequencies of events are relevant for forming presumptions. At the same time, he takes relative frequencies to be indicative of the causal structure of reality:

What happens most frequently, has more cases in the world where the reasons can be found that give birth to actuality than what happens more rarely. For the reason that nothing is known of these reasons, one has to direct presumptions toward what has the most instances and reasons for actuality in the world, rather than toward what has fewer.

(RN I, v, §7)[24]

Thus, higher relative frequencies are a sign of the more frequent occurrence of reasons for certain types of events. Using *Gründe* (reasons) instead of *Ursachen* (causes) indicates that Kahrel has both epistemological and ontological aspects in mind. Reasons in the world are the causes that contribute to actualizing an event, whereas reasons in the mind are what we know about the reasons in the world. On this basis, Kahrel formulates this rule for deciding between competing presumptions:

The presumption that agrees more with the essence and nature of a thing is stronger than the one that agrees less with the essence and nature of this thing … For one sees even with dim attention that the presumption that agrees more with the essence and nature of a thing carries with it more of the particular reasons that belong to the sufficient reason, through which the entire truth can be known.

(RN I, v, §22)[25]

Presumptions based on what belongs to human nature are ubiquitous in early modern legal discourse. One rule discussed by Alciato states that "the quality that naturally is in human beings is presumed to be always present" (Alciato 1551, 34).[26] This rule is based on an understanding of what the natural qualities of humans are—for instance, an understanding of emotional states—as well as an understanding of qualities that are essential to human beings, such as sensation and natural reason (Alciato 1551, 108).[27] To mention some of the examples that Alciato gives: fathers are presumed to love their sons and vice versa (Alciato 1551, 34); fathers are presumed to have more fear about their sons than about themselves (ibid.); brothers are not presumed to hate each other but "it rather has verisimilitude that brothers like each other" (ibid., 69);[28] and "sense and natural reason are presumed in each human being unless the contrary is proven" (ibid., 108).[29] Presumptions of this kind were understood as grounded in the distinction between essential and accidental qualities. Alciato notes that, concerning the thematic realm to which such revisable legal presumptions could be applied, two seemingly contradictory rules were often quoted. The first rule maintains that "a presumption relates only to the realm of the factual since only in this realm do conjectures have their place" (Alciato 1551, 30). The second rule maintains that "regularly, facts are not presumed but have to be proven" (ibid.). As Alciato explains, the second rule holds especially for accidental facts—those that do not derive from the essence of things—because "extrinsic accidents are not presumed" (Alciato 1551, 32).

3.2. The Presumption of Goodness and the Causal Structure of Action

The idea that there should be a presumption that is not only in favor of juridical goodness, but also of ethical goodness, was understood to be a special case of this argumentative pattern. It is a special case that makes clear that there was a concept of probability that did not coincide with the notion of relative frequency in the juridical tradition. Both aspects are taken into consideration by Aimone de Cravetta (1504–69), who discusses a case where the captain of an old vessel refused to transport some heavy goods through stormy weather, a discussion which starts with a presumption based on an assumption concerning a natural quality: "The desire for money, without which we cannot live, is natural to all humans; therefore, absence of bad faith should be presumed in someone whose act does not result in any pleasurable result for the agent" (Cravetta 1605, 1:64). This is why it should be presumed that the captain's refusal is motivated by the intention to avoid shipwreck. Cravetta uses the concept of verisimilitude to express this thought: "Because this cause possesses verisimilitude, it should be presumed. [...] When something possesses verisimilitude, it is said to be in accordance with natural law, because verisimilitude is said to be cognate with nature" (ibid.). Here, "being cognate with nature" is characterized as what is in accordance with natural law. Moreover, accordance with natural law is understood as a criterion for the rationality of a presumption.[30] The presumption of ethical goodness can be understood as an instance of arguing from verisimilitude: persons should be presumed to recognize what is naturally good for them. This sense of verisimilitude, understood as what is in agreement with the demands of natural law, is found in Jacopo Menochio (1532–1607):

> It has to be presumed that each person and each thing and each action is according to its nature and as nature requires ... A presumption is derived from nature itself, as when each person is presumed to be good, and hence not ungrateful unless it is argued for and proved.
>
> (Menochio 1608, 1:23)[31]

Kahrel borrows some of the basic ideas articulated by legal humanists. His understanding of the presumption of goodness includes the presumption of non-delinquency but goes beyond it. As to the presumption of conformity to laws, he states that "everyone is presumed to be good in the *forum externum* until the contrary is proven" (RN I, v, §13). Since this kind of presumption relates to court cases, it would not be of much help for understanding the sense in which the *civitas maxima* could be grounded on presumed consent. This is because, before the *civitas maxima* has come into being, the idea of a court in international relations does not make sense. This raises the question of what the causes for consent to the *civitas maxima* could be before the voluntary law of peoples had been formed.

In Kahrel's view, what matters for the presumption of ethical goodness are not relative frequencies (about which we know nothing), but our knowledge concerning the reasons that would support the presumption:

> In a doubtful case, one presumes that someone has lived according to his duty, ... as long as no particular reasons for the contrary overrule this presumption ... For presumption relates to what is probable. But what has more reasons for being possible is more probable. What obligation demands is not only naturally possible but also ethically possible; what is contrary to obligation, is naturally possible but not ethically possible. This is why in the former case there is more reason for possibility, and hence more probability.
>
> (RN I, v, §12)[32]

As Kahrel explains, "ethically possible is called what can exist together with the rightness of an action; but what cannot exist together with an unviolated rightness of an action, is used to be called ethically impossible" (RN I, ii, §3).[33] As he defines it, "that is ethically necessary whose contrary is ethically impossible" (RN I, ii, §4),[34] which is crucial for his definition of one kind of obligation: "passive obligation consists in the ethical or moral necessity to do or to omit something" (RN I, ii, §6). Ultimately, however, he holds that passive obligation is grounded in active obligation:

> The essence and nature of ourselves and the things and humans we encounter oblige us to do what is good and to omit what is bad ... For the representation of what is good ... is a motivation for the will ... This is why the essence and nature of ourselves and the things and humans we encounter have connected motivations with the actions that are good and bad in themselves.
>
> (RN I, ii, §10)[35]

Because thinking about what is good for beings of our kind is a motivation for wanting it, and thinking about what is bad for beings of our kind is a motivation for avoiding it, the obligations that arise from human nature are reasons for acting. This chain of reasoning underlies Kahrel's claim that ethical goodness should be presumed because this presumption has more reasons than the presumption of badness—reasons that correspond to the causal structure of reality.

3.3. Cosmopolitanism and the Presumption of Goodness

Kahrel's account of the presumption of goodness provides grounds for forming the presumption of consent to the *civitas maxima*. The actuality of the *civitas maxima* thus does not derive from the actuality of tacit consent but, rather, from a basic feature of presumptions: they concern matters of fact, even if these facts are not known with certainty. This is exactly how Kahrel makes use of presumptions in his *Völcker-Recht* (VR) (Law of Peoples) (1750), a comprehensive academic treatise on the various aspects of the law of peoples. What matters is the presumption that individuals will be ready to fulfill a particular kind of natural obligation. These obligations derive directly from the purpose of political communities: the attempt to foster general wellbeing, tranquility, and security. Given the global interconnectedness of peoples, this purpose cannot be achieved by any single people without cooperating with other peoples. Rather, the attempt to realize these goals independently from all other peoples would be a destabilizing factor in the international order. Thus, Kahrel argues, regents and peoples "are obliged to limit the condition of their natural freedom to strive for general well-being, tranquility, and security with conjoined forces" (VR, §497).[36] He regards customs and laws introduced with this purpose to form the *willkürliches Völcker-Recht* (voluntary law of peoples) (ibid.). As he claims, the voluntary law of peoples belongs not only to the realm of possible things but also to the realm of actual things (VR, §500). Accordingly, he holds that "all regents and free peoples of the earth have actually built up together a big world-state" (VR, §498).[37] This is so because "one always presumes that someone wants and has wanted what is in accordance with his obligation and most useful for him" (ibid.).[38]

This is why Kahrel holds that if the voluntary law of peoples "has a reason in the essence and nature of all regents who constitute the big world-state, then all regents are obliged to the voluntary law of peoples" (VR, §503).[39] The presumption of consent to the *civitas maxima*, in turn, gives rise to further presumptions, which includes the presumption that no one would like to be excluded from the world-state and that the regent of the world-state would not want a member to be excluded from the world-state (VR, §499). Despite his seemingly royalist terminology, Kahrel does not regard the regent of the world-state to be any single individual. Rather, he characterizes "all regents and people or their majority" as the regent of the world-state (VR, §496). In this sense, the regent of the world-state is always a multiplicity of individuals that comprises the majority of mankind. But once the voluntary law of peoples has been established through decisions of the majority, these decisions create obligations even for those who disagree. As Kahrel argues, it is possible to presume that all members of the world-state want to adhere to the voluntary law of peoples because everyone is presumed to want what is in accordance with his obligation (VR, §505).

The presumption of ethical goodness also plays a crucial role in Kahrel's account of the customary right of peoples (*Gewohnheits-Völcker-Recht*). As he defines it, "the customary right of peoples is the law that deals with the obligations and rights that belong to the regents and peoples on the earth as members of the big world-state on the basis of customs" (VR, §519).[40] And he holds that "a customary law is nothing but a voluntary law that is given through mere custom" (VR, §522).[41] In this sense, he takes the customary law of peoples to be a part of the voluntary law of peoples (VR, §523). Because the customary law of peoples, in Kahrel's view, is part of the voluntary law of peoples, the role of presumptions for the customary law of peoples is instructive for the role of presumptions in the constitution of the *civitas maxima*. As Kahrel puts it: "if a custom is to acquire the force of a customary law of peoples, one must have a reason to presume the actual will of all or at least the largest parts of regents of the earth" (VR, §529).[42] Thus, what Kahrel has in mind are presumptions concerning the actual motivational situation of political decision-makers. But one can presume consent to a custom only if there is a connection between the custom in question and the goal of political communities: "Customary law of peoples can arise from a custom only if it has a sufficient reason in general well-being, tranquility and security of the great world-state" (VR, §525).[43] Only from such a perspective is it possible to form presumptions concerning those who accept a particular custom. For instance, one can presume that an individual would want customs that help avoid wars, bring ongoing wars to an end, and protect civilians to become part of the customary law of peoples (VR, §537). And it is this presumption that, in Kahrel's view, indicates the sense in which the customary law of peoples should be taken to be something actual:

> One rightly presumes that those who constitute the regent of the great world-state want that a custom that promises a quick end to negotiations should be part of the customary law of peoples, and because the actuality of the customary law of peoples depends only on this will, the custom thereby becomes the actual customary law of peoples.
>
> (VR, §538)[44]

As Kahrel notes, this sense of the actuality of the customary law of peoples directly derives from the view that one always presumes that someone wants what corresponds to his obligation (VR, §537). Specifically, "in so far as it corresponds to the obligation of the regent of the great world-state that such customary laws of peoples be introduced, one rightly presumes that the regent wants such a custom to become the customary law of peoples" (VR, §539).[45]

4. Wolff's Cosmopolitanism and the Presumption of Goodness

In their versions of cosmopolitanism, Wolff and Kahrel use commonplaces that derive from the early modern legal tradition. This is why it is not surprising that there be substantial parallels between their treatments of the presumption of goodness. Having the argumentative function of the presumption of goodness in Kahrel's version of cosmopolitanism in mind will make it easier for us to see the presence of a similar argumentative pattern in Wolff's natural law theory. Considerations concerning relative frequencies do play a role in Wolff's account of presumptions—he regards the presumption that the possessor is also the owner as a presumption in favor of what happens more frequently—but so do considerations about natural obligations (JN III, §1033). For instance, Wolff holds that "in a doubtful case, someone ... is presumed to have said something that is morally true when he is obliged to say something that is morally true, for the sake of the certainty of human interactions" (JN III, §1018).[46] The case is the same for the presumption of truthfulness in situations where there is an obligation to be truthful (JN III, §1018). Again, Wolff argues that since there is a duty not to act without careful deliberation, one should presume that the actions of others follow careful deliberation (JN V, §563).

Something analogous holds for the figure of *restitutio indebiti*—the duty of restituting goods received by someone who erroneously believed them to be owed. Wolff holds that we should presume that everyone has the intention of restituting these goods as soon as the error becomes evident (JN V, §585). Since this is a case of quasi-contracts, Wolff's considerations show that the presumptions underlying quasi-contracts should be regarded as non-fictional, even if the quasi-contract should be regarded as fiction. Wolff's argument is not only based on considerations concerning natural obligations, such as the duty not to want to become wealthier to the detriment of others, but also the self-related obligation to uphold a good reputation (JN V, §585). The presumption that someone is ready to restitute a good that was not owed is thus grounded in an assumption about human nature: everyone will be motivated to avert consequences that are naturally bad for our social lives. This is a presumption about an actual state of mind. One can never be certain about this state of mind and, therefore, one could always be wrong. But we do not invoke any fictions while making such a presumption—we do not suppose something to be the case while knowing it not to be the case.

Like the legal humanists and Kahrel, Wolff thus makes use of the maxim that presumptions should be based on human nature and the nature of certain actions. Consequently, he includes ethical aspects in his understanding of the presumption of goodness:

> Humans most often judge the virtues of others only based on external actions, which they ascribe to virtue if they agree with natural law; and in a doubtful case, when dissimulation cannot be discovered, the correspondence between external and internal action is rightly presumed, following the commonplace: Everyone is presumed to be good until the contrary is proven.
>
> (PM V, §608)[47]

Forming assumptions not only about external conformity with positive law but also about internal states of mind that closely correspond to how legal humanists understood the presumption of goodness.

In Wolff's view, such an understanding of the presumption of goodness is grounded in Roman law. As he interprets it, the concept of justice articulated by the Roman jurist

Domitius Ulpianus (c. 170–223/228) involves not only certain qualities of external actions but also certain qualities of states of mind:

> When Ulpianus defines justice as a kind of will, he does so to indicate that someone who concedes to someone else his right when a legal title is presented is not yet just; rather, what is required is that he wants to do this even in the absence of all external reasons, with no other motivations than those deriving from the action itself, because it is just.
> (Wolff 1730, 232)[48]

As Wolff argues, this understanding of justice has the consequence that the presumption of goodness, too, is not restricted to the presumption of lawful external action but also includes a presumption concerning a state of mind:

> Even if in court only the conformity between the external deed and the law has to be taken into account, someone is not just in the juridical sense because his action has those external requisites that are characteristic of just action but because from this conformity a consensus between action and the internal law is also presumed, because everyone is presumed to be good until the contrary is proven.
> (Wolff 1730, 232–3)[49]

Wolff accepts such an inclusive understanding of the presumption of goodness despite that he was by no means unaware of the widespread occurrence of stupidity. For instance, he notes that "stupidity governs more persons than wisdom" (PM IV, §116),[50] that "the most stupid persons are those who do not want to recognize their stupidity" (PM IV, §263),[51] that "no one is wise in all matters" (RP, §692),[52] and that "we see daily that men of good will act imprudently and less than rightly, and not rarely stupidly" (PM II, §119).[53] Still, he did not suppose stupidity to be an obstacle to the presumption of goodness. The reasons for this can be sought in his insight that "*stupidity makes humans unhappy*" (PM I, §459).[54] Thereby, he identified an experience that could motivate us to overcome the problem arising from stupidity. Wolff argues as follows:

> For a stupid person sometimes acts for the sake of an illicit goal, sometimes uses illicit means, and sometimes means through which the goal cannot be pursued. When he uses means through which the goal cannot be pursued, he will regret his action because the outcome will not correspond to his wishes. When he acts for the sake of an illicit goal or uses illicit means, he does what is prohibited by the law of nature, hence he transgresses it. Because regret makes the mind troubled and sad, in such a way that discontent predominates in it, this most unpleasurable effect contributes much to unhappiness. And because the transgression of natural law makes humans unhappy, it is evident that stupidity makes humans unhappy.
> (PM I, §459)[55]

This argument draws on background assumptions that are central to Wolff's practical philosophy: the assumption that the obligations of natural law derive from considerations concerning what makes the condition of beings of our kind more perfect (PPU I, §125–9); the assumption that perfection consists in the congruence between acts of our will and our natural needs (JN I, §201; JN I, §§335–6); and the assumption that, therefore, the violation of the obligations of natural law leads to a less perfect condition in which our natural needs are not satisfied (PPU I, §405). This, Wolff points out, is a state of persisting discontent, which is nothing other than unhappiness (ibid.). Wolff does not deny that humans often act stupidly; he rather maintains that, insofar as they act stupidly, they are made unhappy. And unhappiness is a state that humans have a strong motivation to avoid. As Wolff puts it in his *Psychologica empirica* (PE) (Empirical Psychology), "from discontent arises aversion" (PE, §519).[56]

This is why it is not surprising that Wolff connects presumptions of consent with obligations deriving from natural law in a way that is akin to the connection established by Kahrel. As Wolff argues, "because someone is obliged to consent to something to which he is already obliged naturally, and everyone is presumed to consent to what he is already obliged naturally; the consent of someone else is presumed in what he is obliged naturally concerning ourselves" (JN V, §507).[57] This pattern of thought can also be particularly applied to the presumption that peoples and their rulers have consented or will consent to the voluntary law of peoples because this law contributes to the fulfillment of the natural goals of political communities. Understanding the presumption of consent to the *civitas maxima* as a particular case of the presumption of goodness substantiates Wolff's view that "the consent of peoples that is demanded by natural law cannot be taken to be fictitious, too, for when it is in the highest degree absent it is supplemented by natural law" (JG, §887).[58] And it could explain why Wolff describes the obligations that give rise to the presumption of consent to the *civitas maxima* as something non-fictional: "Humans should not be made up to be what they are not when they are maximally obliged to be such and such" (JG, §12).[59]

Thereby, the presumption of consent to the *civitas maxima* is characterized as a special case of the presumption that humans will be inclined toward fulfilling their natural obligations. In this sense, the consent to the *civitas maxima* can be subsumed under Wolff's concept of intrinsically good actions. Wolff defines intrinsically good actions as actions that are caused by the same final causes as natural actions (PPU I, §125). Intrinsically good actions, therefore, are actions that contribute to our perfection (PE, §554). Intrinsic goodness leads to natural obligations. As Wolff explains, "the essence and nature of humans and things has connected a motivation with the intrinsically good and bad actions" (PPU I, §127).[60] This is why there is an obligation to perform actions that contribute to our perfection (PPU I, §128). This is the obligation that Wolff describes as a natural obligation, that is, an obligation that has a sufficient reason in human nature (PPU I, §129). Recall Wolff's view that each people has the obligation to contribute as much as possible and necessary to the perfection of other peoples because doing so contributes to their own perfection.[61] Since the fulfillment of these cosmopolitan obligations is a necessary condition for the self-perfection of peoples, cosmopolitan obligations belong to natural obligations. This is why the presumption of consent to the *civitas maxima* does not pretend that individuals are other than what they actually are. Rather, this presumption is based on the assumption that the motivation for intrinsically good actions derives from human nature, together with the assumption that consent to the *civitas maxima* belongs to these intrinsically good actions.

5. Conclusion

This chapter has explored a specific aspect of the controversy over Wolff's cosmopolitanism. Kahrel adopted Wolff's theory of the *civitas maxima* without taking up Wolff's scattered remarks about fiction. I trust that pointing out the parallels between Kahrel's and Wolff's argumentative strategies has made the importance of non-fictionalist strands of thought in Wolff more visible than they would be otherwise. Wolff's use of fictions was not only an obstacle to the reception of his cosmopolitanism by his contemporaries. Of course, their reluctance could be explained by their failure to capture the subtlety of Wolff's views. Wolff's use of fictions was also fraught with internal tensions. To be sure, there is nothing wrong with ascribing a normative conception of fictions to Wolff—that is, a conception that uses fictions to articulate what would be reasonable for political agents to do. But does his use of fictions contribute much to how Wolff establishes the existence of cosmopolitan obligations? Wolff's remarks concerning the non-fictional nature of the obligations that provide grounds for the presumption of consent to the voluntary law of peoples seem to point in a different direction. For both Kahrel and Wolff, presumptions concerning the will of political agents are based on an account of what natural obligations consist in.

Because both Wolff and Kahrel believe that natural obligations are grounded in the actual motivational structure of humans, the presumption in favor of consent to the voluntary law of peoples follows a rule prominent in early modern legal thought: the rule that one should always form presumptions in favor of what lies in the nature of agents and their acts. For Wolff, the *civitas maxima* is not yet fully realized, but it is also not fictional. This is so because presumptions concerning human nature concern something factual about which there can be no certainty. This approach fits uneasily with the fictionalist strand of thought because uncertainty is not fictionality. But, as we have seen, this corresponds to a basic insight of early modern legal thought. If this line of interpretation is on the right track, then it turns out that the normative dimension of Wolff's cosmopolitanism does not derive from his use of fictions but rather from his use of a conception of the presumption of goodness that includes both juridical and ethical aspects.

Abbreviations

JG   Wolff, Christian. 1749. *Jus gentium methodo scientifica pertractatum*. Halle: Renger.

JN   Wolff, Christian. 1740–48. *Jus naturae methodo scientifica pertractatum*. Halle: Renger.

PM	Wolff, Christian. 1750-53. *Philosophia moralis sive ethica*. Halle: Renger.
PPU	Wolff, Christian. 1744. *Philosophia practica universalis*. Halle: Renger.
RN	Kahrel, Hermann F. 1747. *Das Recht der Natur*. Frankfurt: Andraeische Buchhandlung.
VR	Kahrel, Hermann F. 1750. *Völcker-Recht*. Herborn: Hegelein.

Notes

1 See JG, §166.
2 On Vattel's response to Wolff, see Greenwood Onuf 1994.
3 For a detailed discussion, see Cheneval 1999; Cheneval 2002, 132-202. Nokkala 2021, 13-14, follows this interpretation.
4 "Fictio est legis adversus veritatem in re possibili ex iusta causa dispositio." On early modern theories of legal fictions, see Maclean 1992, 101-3; König 1998, 144-55.
5 Contrary to Ben Holland's interpretation, which takes this passage to indicate a commitment to enlightened absolutism on the level of the *civitas maxima*. See Holland 2017, 120.
6 See JN V, §504.
7 "Quemadmodo vero in tutela recte praesumitur consentire pupillus, quatenus consentire deberet, immo consensurus esset, siquidem commoda sua intelligeret; ita non minus Gentes, quae defectu acuminis non perspiciunt, quantae utilitatis sit esse membrum civitatis illius maximae consentire in hanc consociationem praesumuntur."
8 "consensum extorquere intelligatur etiam quasi ab invito."
9 "aliquid fictitii habet."
10 "fictio tantummodo in eo est, quod id concipiatur per modum entis separatam existentiam habentis, & quod eidem non alia insint, quam quae eidem tribuimus."
11 See also JN VIII, §§4-5.
12 "Quod enim in istam societatem Gentes naturali quodam impetu ferantur, ex earum factis apparet, veluti dum foedera ineunt commerciorum & belli causa vel etiam amicitiae gratia."
13 "quia consentire debent, in eandem consensisse praesumantur."
14 "Neque enim fingendi sunt homines, quales non sunt, si vel maxime tales esse deberent."
15 "dici non potest, esse fabulam gratis conficta."
16 "dici nequit leges civiles, quatenus a rigore Juris naturae recedant necesse est, pro figmentis habendas esse."
17 "Gentium quoque consensus, quam Jus naturae imperat, pro ficto haberi nequit, quippe quem, si is vel maxime deficiat, ipsum jus naturae supplet."
18 "Der freye Wille eines andern aber kan unmöglich anders erkannt werden, als durch Worte, oder andere denenselben gleichgültigen Zeichen und äusserliche Handlungen, oder deren Unterlassungen. Daher kommt es, daß man den Willen einen ausdrücklichen Willen nennt, wann er mit zureichenden Worten angedeutet wird; einen schweigenden Willen aber, den man aus den Handlungen und deren Unterlassung … gewiß erkennen kan; und ist derselben also auch ein wahrer Wille. Allein wann man

denselbigen aus einigen Anzeigungen oder Gründen nur wahrscheinlich schliessen muß, so ist es muthmaßlicher Wille. Ein gleicher Unterscheid thut sich demnach auch unter der Inwilligung und Widriggesinnetheit herfür."

19   On presumptions in early modern argumentation theory, see Blank 2019.
20   "Man muthmasset allzeit, daß derjenige, welcher schweiget, wann er reden kan und muß, in das was der andere will oder die andern wollen, willige … Dann in diesem Fall hindert nichts, warum er nicht seines Hertzens Meynung an den Tag legte, wann er nicht eben dasselbe wollte, was der andere will oder die andern wollen."
21   "und zwar ist dieser Grund zureichend, daß man dadurch die Wahrheit vollkommen begreifen kan. Die besondern Gründe aber, woraus dieser zureichende Grund besteht, sind demnach einzeln so beschaffen, daß man daraus die Wahrheit noch nicht vollkommen verstehen kan, sondern nur wahrscheinlich. Die Wahrscheinlichkeit besteht also eigentlich in der Erkänntniß einiger von den besonderen Gründen, welche zusammen genommen den zureichenden Grund ausmachen."
22   "Die Muthmassung wird stärcker genant, wo eine grössere Wahrscheinlichkeit vorhanden ist; schwächer aber, wo man eine kleinere Wahrscheinlichkeit antrifft. Je mehr also von den besondern Gründen in den Bezirck unserer Erkänntniß treten, und je mehr man mit Gewißheit davon erkennt, je mehr stärcker ist die Muthmassung."
23   "Wann einige von den Gründen, die zu dem zureichenden Grunde, wodurch die Wahrheit einer Sache erkannt werden muß, gehören, vohanden sind; es sind aber auch andere von den Gründen da, wodurch die Wahrheit des Gegentheils, and also auch die Unwahrheit des erstern erkannt werden muß, so sagt man, die Muthmassungen lauffen gegen einander."
24   "Was aber am öfftern geschieht, das hat mehr Fälle in der Welt, in welchen die Gründe anzutreffen sind, die die Würcklichkeit gebähren als das, was seltner sich eräugnet. Derowegen, da von diesen Gründen nichts bekannt ist, so muß man die Muthmassung vielmehr auf das gehen lassen, was die meisten Fälle und Gründe der Würcklichkeit in der Welt hat, als auf das, wo weniger sind."
25   "Diejenige Muthmassung, die dem Wesen und der Natur eines Dinges gemässer ist, ist stärcker, als die, welche dem Wesen und der Natur desselben nicht so gemäß ist. Beweis: Dann man sieht mit halbstumpffer Aufmercksamkeit, daß die Muthmassung die dem Wesen und der Natur eines Dings gemässer ist, mehr von den besonderen Gründen mit sich führe, die zu dem zureichenden Grunde, wodurch die völlige Wahrheit erkannt werden muß, gehören."
26   "qualitas quae naturaliter inest homini, semper adesse praesumitur."
27   "Sensus & ratio naturalis praesumuntur in quolibet homine, nisi probetur contrarium … Probatur autem quis furiosus per signa extrinseca, puta quia loquitur verba more furiosorum."
28   "imo est verisimile quod alter alterum diligat."
29   "Sensus & ratio naturalis praesumuntur in quolibet homine, nisi probetur contrarium."
30   On this sense of verisimilitude in sixteenth-century legal theory, see Blank 2017.
31   "Praesumendum est, quod quaelibet persona & quaelibet res, & quilibet actus sit secundum suam naturam sicut eius requirit natura … Sumitur praesumptio ex ipsa natura, ut quilibet bonus esse praesumatur, atque ita non ingratus nisi arguatur & probetur."
32   "Man muthmasset in einem zweiffelhafften Fall, es habe einer seiner Pflicht nachgelebt, … wofern keine besondere Gründe vor das Gegentheil diese Muthmassung zu Schanden machen … Dann die Muthmassung geht auf das,

was wahrscheinlich ist. Es ist aber das wahrscheinlicher, was mehr Grund zur Möglichkeit. Das, was die Verbindlichkeit will, ist nicht allein natürlich, sondern auch sittlich-möglich; was aber wider dieselbe ist, das ist zwar natürlich, aber nicht sittlich-möglich. Derowegen ist in dem ersten Fall mehr Grund vor die Möglichkeit, und also mehr Wahrscheinlichkeit."

33 "Sittlich- oder moralisch-möglich heißt dasjenige, mit welchem die Richtigkeit einer Handlung bestehen kann; das aber, womit solche nicht bestehen oder unverletzt bleiben kan, pflegt man sittlich-unmöglich zu nennen."

34 "Sittlich-notwendig ist das, dessen Entgegengesetztes sittlich-unmöglich ist."

35 "Das Wesen und die Natur unserer selbst und anderer Dinge und Menschen verbindet uns, das Gute zu thun und das Böse zu lassen ... Dann die Vorstellung des Guten ... ist ein Beweg-Grund des Willens ... Derowegen so hat selbst das Wesen und die Natur unserer selbst und anderer Dinge und Menschen, mit denen an sich guten und bösen Handlungen, Beweg-Gründe verknüpft."

36 "sie sind verpflichtet dergestalt den Stand ihrer natürlichen Freyheit einzuschränken, daß sie eine Gesellschafft ausmachen, in welcher sich ein jeder von ihnen denen übrigen zusammen genommen, zulänglich verbindet, mit vereinigten Kräfften sich zu ihrer allgemeinen Wohlfahrt, Ruhe und Sicherheit hindurch zu arbeiten."

37 "Alle Regenten und freye Völcker der Erden haben würcklich mit einander einen grossen Welt-Staat errichtet."

38 "Man muthmasset aber allemal, daß einer das wolle und gewollt habe, was seiner Verbindlichkeit gemäß und ihm am nützlichsten ist."

39 "einen Grund in dem Wesen und in der Natur aller Regenten hat, aus welchem der grosse Welt-Staat besteht, so sind alle Regenten auf dem Creyß der Erden zu demselbigen verbunden."

40 "Das Gewohnheits-Völcker-Recht ist, welches die Verbindlichkeiten und Rechte, welche denen Regenten und Völckern der Erden, als Mitgliedern des grossen Welt-Staats, aus denen Gewohnheiten erwachsen, zum Vorwurff hat."

41 "Ein Gewohnheits-Gesetz ist nichts anders, als ein willkührliches Gesetz, welches durch die blosse Gewohnheit gegeben ist."

42 "Solchergestalt muß man ..., wann eine Gewohnheit die Krafft eines Gewohnheits-Völcker-Gesetzes erlangen soll, einen Grund haben, den wircklichen Willen aller oder doch der mehresten Regenten der Erden zu muthmassen."

43 "Es kan aus keiner Gewohnheit ein Gewohnheits-Völcker-Gesetz erwachsen, es muß dann einen zureichenden Grund in der allgemeinen Wohlfahrt, Ruhe und Sicherheit des grossen Welt-Staats haben."

44 "So muthmasset man auch mit Recht, daß diejenigen, welche den Regenten des grossen Welt-Staats ausmachen, wollen, daß eine solche Gewohnheit die denen Händeln einen baldigen Ausgang verheißt, ein Gewohnheits-Völcker-Gesetz seye; und weil von dieser Willen die Würcklichkeit der Gewohnheits-Völcker-Gesetzen allein abhängt; so wird sie dadurch zum würcklichen Gewohnheits-Völcker-Gesetze."

45 "in so weit es der Verbindlichkeit des Regenten des grossen Welt-Staats gemäß ist, daß dergleichen Gewohnheits-Völker-Gesetze eingeführet werden; So steht richtig zu muthmassen, daß derselbe wolle, daß eine solche Gewohnheit zum Gewohnheits-Völcker-Gesetze werde."

46 "praesumitur, quando in casu dubio certitudo haberi nequit, in gratiam certitudinis negotiorum humanorum, eum verum moraliter loqui, quando ad moraliter verum loquendum obligatur."

47 "Homines plerumque de virtute aliena saltem judicant ex actionibus externis, quae si legi naturae conformes sunt, ad virtutem adscribuntur, & in casu dubio, quando simulatio detegi nequit, convenientia actionis externae cum interna recte praesumitur, juxta illud pervulgatum: quilibet praesumitur bonus, donec probetur contrarium."

48 "Justitia … ab *Ulpiano* definitur per voluntatem, ut significatur, nondum justum esse, qui alia quacunque de causa adductus alteri tribuit jus suum; sed id potissimum requiri, ut quis id facere velit, absentibus licet omnibus rationibus extrinsecis, non aliunde desumptis motivis nisi ab ipsa actione, quatenus justa est."

49 "Etsi enim in foro non attendenda sit nisi actionis externae cum lege conformitas, non tamen ideo quis justus est in sensu juridico, quia actio ejus externa ea habet requisita, quae actioni justae conveniunt, sed quia ex hac conformitate actionis externae cum lege praesumitur consensus ejusdem cum interna, propterea quod tamdiu aliquis praesumatur bonus, donec probetur contrarium."

50 "Plures stultitia regit, quam sapientia."

51 "stultissimi vel hoc nomine, quod stultitiam suam agnoscere nolint."

52 *Psychologia rationalis* (Rational Psychology). "Hominum nullus in omnibus est sapiens."

53 "Indies quoque videmus, homines bonae voluntatis imprudenter & minus recte, immo haud raro stulte agere."

54 "*Stultitia homines reddit infelices.*" (Wolff's italics.)

55 "Stultus enim nunc agit propter finem illicitum, nunc utitur mediis illicitis, nunc mediis, quibus finem consequi nequit. Quodsi utatur mediis, quibus finem consequi nequit, cum eventus non respondeat votis, eum facti poenitet. Si vero agit propter finem illicitum, aut mediis utitur illicitis, quod lege naturali prohibitum facit, consequenter eandem transgreditur. Quamobrem cum poenitentia animum inquietum reddat, ac tristitia impleat, ut taedium in eo praedominetur; effectus hic molestissimus plurimum ad infelicitatem confert. Cumque transgressione legis naturalis homo fiat infelix, stultitiam homines reddere infelices manifestum est."

56 "ex taedio ortum tandem trahit aversatio."

57 "Quamobrem cum in id consentire debeat alter, ad quod tibi iam naturaliter obligatus est, quilibet autem consentire praesumatur in id, in quod consentire debet; consensus alterius recte praesumitur in eo, ad quod alter nobis jam obligatus est naturaliter sine ulla restrictione."

58 Quoted above; see endnote 30.

59 Quoted above; see endnote 27.

60 "nos obligat ad actiones committendas, qui motivum volitionis cum iisdem connectit."

61 See endnote 1.

Bibliography

Alciato, Andrea. 1551. *De praesumptionibus*. Lyon: Iunta.

Blank, Andreas. 2017. "Common Usage, Presumption, and Verisimilitude in Sixteenth-Century Theories of Juridical Interpretation." *History of European Ideas*, 43, 5, 401–15.

Blank, Andreas. 2019. *Arguing from Presumptions. Essays on Early Modern Ethics and Politics*. Munich: Philosophia.

Cheneval, Francis. 1999. "Der präsumptiv vernünftige Konsens der Menschen und Völker: Christian Wolffs Theorie der 'civitas maxima.'" *Archiv für Rechts- und Sozialphilosophie*, 85, 563–80.

Cheneval, Francis. 2001. "Auseinandersetzungen um die *civitas maxima* in der Nachfolge Christian Wolffs." *Studia Leibnitiana*, 33, 2, 125–44.

Cheneval, Francis. 2002. *Philosophie in weltbürgerlicher Bedeutung: über die Entstehung und die philosophischen Grundlagen des supranationalen und kosmopolitischen Denkens der Moderne*. Basel: Schwabe.

Cravetta, Aimone de. 1605. *Consiliorum sive responsionum ... primus & secundus tomus*. Frankfurt: Saurius.

Greenwood Onuf, Nicholas. 1994. "Civitas maxima: Wolff, Vattel and the Fate of Republicanism." *American Journal of International Law*, 88, 2, 280–303.

Hanov, Michael Christoph. 1756–1759. *Philosophia civilis sive politica*, 4 vols. Halle: Renger.

Holland, Ben. 2017. *The Moral Person of the State. Pufendorf, Sovereignty and Composite Polities*. Cambridge: Cambridge University Press.

Kahrel, Hermann Friedrich. 1747. *Das Recht der Natur*. Frankfurt: Andraeische Buchhandlung.

Kahrel, Hermann Friedrich. 1750. *Völcker-Recht*. Herborn: Hegelein.

König, Peter. 1998. "Das System des Rechts und die Lehre von den Fiktionen bei Leibniz. In Jan Schröder (Hg.)." *Entwicklung der Methodenlehre in Rechtswissenschaft und Philosophie vom 16. bis zum 18. Jahrhundert*, 137–61. Stuttgart: Steiner.

Maclean, Ian. 1992. *Interpretation and Meaning in the Renaissance*. Cambridge: Cambridge University Press.

Menochio, Jacopo. 1608. *De praesumptionibus, coniecturis, signis, et indiciis*, 3 vols. Lyon: Apud Viduam Antonii de Harsy.

Nokkala, Ere. 2021. "The Development of the Law of Nations. Wolff and Vattel." In *Concepts and Contexts of Vattel's Political and Legal Thought*, edited by Peter Schröder, 64–83. Cambridge: Cambridge University Press.

Wolff, Christian. 1730. *Horae subsecivae Marburgenses anni MDCCXXIX ... Trimestre Brumale*. Frankfurt and Leipzig: Renger.

Wolff, Christian. 1737. *Cosmologia generalis*. Frankfurt and Leipzig: Renger.

Wolff, Christian. 1738. *Psychologia empirica*. Frankfurt and Leipzig: Renger.

Wolff, Christian. 1740. *Psychologia rationalis*. Frankfurt and Leipzig: Renger.

Wolff, Christian. 1740–1748. *Jus naturae methodo scientifica pertractatum*. 8 Bde. Halle: Renger.

Wolff, Christian. 1749. *Jus gentium methodo scientifica pertractatum*. Halle: Renger.

Wolff, Christian. 1744. *Philosophia practica universalis*. 2 Bde. Halle: Renger.

Wolff, Christian. 1750–1753. *Philosophia moralis sive ethica*. 5 Bde. Halle: Renger.

2

The Duties of the Historian—Raynal's Failed Prize Question

Gesa Wellmann

1. Introduction

On April 8, 1783, the Berlin Academy of Sciences announced a prize question that read: "Quels sont les devoirs d'un Historien?"[1] (What are the duties of a historian?). The donor of the prize was Guillaume Raynal, who had been officially celebrated as the author of the best-selling work, *Histoire philosophique et politique des établissements et du commerce des Européens dans les deux Indes* (HTI).[2] In fact, he was the skillful editor of the contributions to the volume that were submitted anonymously at the time.[3] As it later turned out, Denis Diderot, Paul-Henry Thiry D'Holbach, and Jacques-André Naigeon were among the anonymous contributors.[4] The ten-volume encyclopedia, published between 1770 and 1789, covers the trade relations between Europe and the Far East, Africa, and the Americas and attempts to trace the impact of colonial commerce on European civilization. It was, along with Voltaire's *Candide* and Rousseau's *La nouvelle Héloïse*, the most successful book in late eighteenth-century France.[5] When the book was banned in France in 1781, Raynal, after moving between several different cities, fled to Berlin in 1782, where he had been a foreign member of the Academy since 1750.[6]

With the prize question, Raynal intended to popularize his work in Germany. But, despite his enormous fame and the generally celebrated reception of his main work, the prize was never awarded.[7] It is clear from the minutes of the Academy meeting of June 23, 1785, that the donated money was simply returned to its donor. Various historians attribute this to sparse and unsatisfactory submissions to the Academy.[8] In fact, today, no submissions can be found in the archives of the *Berlin-Brandenburgische Akademie der Wissenschaften*. It can therefore be assumed that either they have been lost or there were in fact no submissions at all.[9]

Despite the failure of Raynal's proposed prize question to reach an audience, there is evidence that it did nevertheless generate some debate. In 1791, Carlo Giovanni Maria Denina, an Italian historian who had been living in Berlin since 1782 and was a full member of the Prussian Academy of Sciences, published the first volume of his treatise *La Prusse littéraire sous Frédéric II*. This work provided a brief history of the authors, academics, and artists who had lived in Prussia between 1740 and 1786.[10] It is one of the first sources to mention Raynal's prize announcement. Denina describes the organizational details around the prize question—namely, that entries could be submitted in French, Latin, English, German, Latin, Italian, or Spanish; that the deadline would be December 31, 1784; and that the announcement of the award would be made at the public meeting of the Academy on May 31, 1785—while also reporting on the lack of satisfactory entries and the return of the prize donation to Raynal. Denina further refers to what can be considered a late response to the prize question by Ewald Friedrich von Hertzberg (1725–95), second Minister of State and Cabinet under Frederick II, Curator of the Prussian Academy since 1786 and Head of Foreign Policy under William II.[11] According to Denina, Hertzberg "read and published a dissertation on this subject [the historian's duty] in 1788"—the *Treatise on the True Ideal of a Good History and on the Second Year of the Reign of Frederick William II*.[12]

Denina concludes his report by contrasting Hertzberg's treatise with Raynal's understanding of history as presented in the *HTI*: "One would be curious to know if the abbé Raynal finds the ideal of the academic minister in conformity with the one he would have liked to see crowned. Judging by the way in which the philosophical history of the trade in the two Indies is written," Denina states, it is clear that Raynal would disagree with Hertzberg (Denina 1786, 201–2).

In his treatise, Denina was not interested in conducting a philosophical-historical contrast between Hertzberg and Raynal, but rather in advancing a historical-anecdotal account. He does not address in which respects the donor of the prize question would have distanced himself from Hertzberg's belated answer.[13] It also remains questionable to what extent Hertzberg's treatise was elaborated, if ever, as a direct answer to Raynal's prize question—in any case, Hertzberg does not mention Raynal at all.

Nonetheless, Denina's comparison between the *HTI* and Hertzberg's work did not arise unexpectedly. Denina mentions that Hertzberg's treatise on the ideal approach to history was a festive speech delivered in 1788 while he was the curator of the Prussian Academy (i.e., the potential prize-giver). The prize question would still have been on the audience's mind at the time. Moreover, Hertzberg had used his access to the secret state archives as minister of state to write a history of the Brandenburg-African Company, entitled *Histoire de la marine et de la compagnie africaine de Prusse* (1755). This treatise was the first-ever study of the Brandenburg colonial enterprise that was based on intensive source research and, along with his treatise on the duty of the historian, provides an excellent comparative foil for Raynal and his co-authors' large-scale encyclopedia on colonial history.[14]

The aim of this chapter is to spell out Hertzberg's opposition to the *HTI*, as indicated by Denina, and thus, to reconstruct certain parts of the controversy over the philosophy of history that Raynal presumably hoped to see addressed when he announced his prize question. Through such an analysis, on the one hand, I hope to contribute to the development of the still rather limited research on the reception of the *HTI* in Germany.[15] On the other, I intend to investigate Ewald Friedrich von Hertzberg's historical-philosophical contribution, an examination that, to my knowledge, has yet to be undertaken. From a systematic point of view, this chapter is a case study intending to provide a micro-view into the complex web of reflections of history in the late eighteenth century. The controversy between Hertzberg and Raynal reconstructed here can thus be broadly understood as part of a longstanding controversy about the meaning of history and historiography in general, its best-known offshoot probably being the debate between Kant and Herder.[16]

More specifically, I will contrast Hertzberg's essay to the *HTI* in three respects: In Section 2, I contrast Hertzberg's documentary method with what I will refer to as "the speculative method" of the *HTI*. Section 3 then contrasts Hertzberg's ideal of an instructive historiography with the idea of a formative historiography in the *HTI*. Finally, Section 4 contrasts a "local history" with the claim of a universal history.

2. Methods of Historiography

The speech that Hertzberg delivered at the Prussian Academy in 1788 consisted of a thirty-page treatise. As indicated in the title, it deals with the "true ideal" of good historiography. He presents this ideal in a general theoretical reflection of about fifteen pages and a practical sample of the same length.

According to Hertzberg, the fundamental duty of the historian is to "instruct and enlighten" the reader (*Treatise*, 3). This enlightenment, however, occurs only if the historiography adheres to certain essential principles: "the truth and certainty of the facts which it narrates and about which judgment is due both to the reader and the historian."[17] Lengthy passages from the theoretical part of the treatise analyze how one can establish "certainty of the facts."

Drawing on countless examples of ancient and modern historians, Hertzberg explains that the quality of the historian depends on his ability to process and indicate his sources (*Treatise*, 6–8). The sources must be "certain, irrefutable and credible." Hertzberg provides two strategies for ensuring this certainty. First, the sources should not consist of "newspapers and public rumors," but rather, they should follow from meticulous work in the archives, where the closest examination of testimonies, public hearings, deeds, letters, lectures, edicts, state writings, dispatches, and reports can be guaranteed (*Treatise*, 4–12). We find an impressive application of this idea in Hertzberg's *Histoire de la marine et de la compagnie africaine de Prusse* (History of the Prussian Navy and African Company). In this work, Hertzberg accurately compiles an exhaustive history of the Brandenburg African Company by examining and processing previously unstudied archival material. Reflecting on Hertzberg's *Histoire*, a contemporary author states:

> This trading company [Brandenburg African Company] has finally ceased, and the true circumstances of how it came into being, was continued, and reached its end, would perhaps have remained unknown forever, if the greatest connoisseur and promoter of Prussian history had not taken the infinite trouble to free from their dust all the papers, news, reports, and documents which Berlin, Emden, and Großfriedrichsburg retained, and from them to draw up this history in French from the most reliable sources.[18]

Second, the credibility of the sources should be ensured by the fact that the history either is composed by an archivist enlisted by the king, who not only has access to the secret archives but also acts as a contemporary witness, or is written down "by the noblest acting persons themselves," that is, the regent (*Treatise*, 5). Hertzberg's model of this ideal was Frederick II, who not only explained the same idea in his *Histoire de mon temps* (History of My Time), but also put it into practice. Hertzberg is convinced that "any history written long after the demise of the acting persons can never be sufficiently put into perspective because of the lack of contemporaneous witnesses and evidence" (*Treatise*, 5). Thus, testimony based on direct experience is the most reliable, particularly when accompanied by some guarantor of its truthful documentation. However, as Hertzberg points out in his history of the Brandenburg African Company, which is based on travel reports, the information from and credibility of eyewitnesses are equally decisive.[19]

Finally, once the data are established, it is possible to show how "cause and effect are related according to a proper combination of well-established observations" (Hertzberg 1780, 25). Hertzberg provided an example of a historiographical use of the relation between cause and effect eight years prior in yet another speech, in which he decidedly proposes a *philosophy* of history: *Abhandlung, worin man die Ursachen der Überlegenheit der Teutschen über die Römer zu entwickeln sucht* (Treatise, in which One Tries to Develop the Causes of the Superiority of the Germans over the Romans). In this work, Hertzberg sets out to prove his thesis of the superiority of the Germans, and to do so, he refers to factors such as climatic conditions or linguistic kinship between different peoples.[20] Thus, for Hertzberg, the true interrelationships of historical events (i.e., their cause and effect) can only be grasped if sufficient and verified empirical data are available.

Having illuminated Hertzberg's criteria of an ideal historical-philosophical method, let us now examine the criteria for such a method as presented in the *HTI*. Since the *HTI* is a very heterogeneous work—written by many authors in different styles—it is difficult to make generalizing statements about its approach. Despite its diversity, however, the work does seem to employ a coherent method. As we will see in what follows, this method is diametrically opposed to Hertzberg's ideal and has been devastatingly criticized in many places.

The *HTI* is characterized, first of all, by a remarkable collection of material. Raynal, as a skillful editor, was able to compile an entire collection of knowledge about the colonial world, which he assembled by processing archival sources, travel reports, registers, and newspaper articles, all with the help of numerous correspondents, informants, and collaborators.[21] The preface of the *HTI* admits as follows:

> I have called to my support the men of all nations who have been informed of it. I have consulted the living and the dead: the living whose voice can be heard in my regions; the dead who have left us their opinions and their knowledge, in whatever language they have written. I have weighed their credibility, contrasted their testimonies, clarified the facts. If one had mentioned to me under the equator or under the pole a man who could have enlightened me about an important point, I would have gone under the pole or under the line and asked him to discover

himself to me. The sublime image of truth has always been present to me. O holy truth, you alone have I worshipped!

(HTI, 2)

However, apart from this statement of affirmation, the reader hardly receives any concrete information about the sources. One of the biggest criticisms in the German-language reception from that period makes this same point.[22] Christoph Wilhelm Dohm, "one of the greatest statisticians of his time," and archivist in Berlin since 1779, praised the *HTI* for its political and statistical depth; however, he pointed out that it handled its sources according to a deeply unhistorical method.[23] He criticized both the sheer lack of sources and the criteria for how the material was selected. Furthermore, Dohm states that from the outset, the *HTI* pursues a method that differs from the ideal he and his colleagues tried to realize: historical data (i.e., data from the past) are used for the purpose of establishing connections in a merely speculative way. He argues:

> [A]part from the most current statistical data, he [Raynal] does not bring back any historical information, but only presumes it and uses history as a direct thread to articulate his philosophical and political reflections and it is very probable to me that Mr. Raynal has not made any critical investigations of the historical material of his work, but has only read some, mostly very well-known, and not always the best books on older history and then, with his rich imagination, has put together a general picture of the context of the events.[24]

Instead of a representation *of* history (Darstellung *der* Geschichte), Raynal provides only a "general *raisonnement* and beautiful declamation *about* [*über*] history."[25] For Dohm, such a method does not belong to the realm of historiography: "Raynal is an excellent, outspoken, articulate philosophical politician and statistician—but a historian he is not."[26]

It is indeed true that the *HTI* largely follows a method concerned neither with the historical source evidence, as Hertzberg had demanded, with the search for credible witnesses, nor with showing a cause-effect relationship of the events that could be drawn from these sources.[27] Instead, it attempts to speculatively deduce a purposeful course of history from a limited number of contingent historical facts and understands this deduction as an activity of reason that rises above historical knowledge to the knowledge of higher objects.[28]

The secondary literature has already pointed out that Raynal followed the method of De Pauw, who, in the much-noted Berlin debate of the 1760s as well as in the supplementary volume (vol. 18) of the *Encyclopédie* of 1776, sweepingly dismissed the old chronicles, documents, and reports from his considerations. He believed these matters to be completely implausible, thus leading him to advance a purely speculative thesis about the new world instead.[29] De Pauw based his influential method above all on an "enlightenment" devaluation of all experiences according to the testimony of authorities or doubtful "conquerors." Rather, he promoted a valorization of the individual's discursive power of reason, which is supposed to establish the connections between events. This valorization of the subject is clear especially in the preface to the *HTI* (cf. *HTI*, 42–53).

As we can see, instead of an archivist adhering to a royal obligation, the *HTI* relied on the international cooperation of all those who felt united under the banner of the "sacred truth," a truth that has little to do with the historically empirically secured "certainty" of Hertzberg. The result was an encyclopedia whose main achievement was not the preservation of its sources, but rather their recreation—or at least their reinterpretation. For example, Rigobert Bonne created an atlas especially for the *HTI* and Antoine-Laurent de Jussieu provided contributions on botany. It is no coincidence then that the *HTI* was seen as a reference for helping merchants and administrators in their respective dealings in the colonies.[30]

The great methodological difference between Hertzberg's empirically committed certainty and Raynal's encyclopedic speculation points to a serious difference in the objectives of these methods, which will be dealt with in the next section.

3. The Historian and the Court

In addition to these methodological considerations, Hertzberg also presented some general thoughts on the objectives of historiography as a whole in his speech on the ideal of historiography. In the spirit of his method of establishing sources based on direct testimony, Hertzberg pleads above all for an "institution of an official history" (*Treatise*, 13). He suggests that every state should have an official, impartial historian who carefully keeps a diary of the current events of government. After the death of the regent, this historian should compile all data and add it to a history that serves as a "venerable court" (*Treatise*, 13). By pronouncing honor and dishonor on the respective regent, this court would serve as a lesson to future "princes and the generals and ministers participating in their government" to make an example of praiseworthy deeds and to avoid reprehensible ones (*Treatise*, 12). Hertzberg foregoes a precise elaboration of the preconditions of such a "perfect [*vollkommene*] history" and refers to the roughly sketched idea of an evaluative historiography as an "ideal"—that is, the ideal from which he derives the title of the work (*Treatise*, 13-14). It was to this aim that Hertzberg then recorded the events of the second year of Wilhelm II's reign in the second part of his speech, as a practical rehearsal of his general remarks and as material to be assembled into a "court" in the future.[31]

Thus, for Hertzberg, the first task of historiography is to judge the actions of a regent or great man. Historiography is a "judgmental and contiguous collection of strange revolutions and incidents that have affected nations and state government, [intended to give] a brief outline of the strange actions of statesmen and private individuals" (*Treatise*, 3). Such judgments are designed to provide lessons for future regents. History is thus understood as a collection of examples to be made useful for future generations. This applies, on the one hand, to statecraft since it provides examples of "successful" governments and, on the other hand, to a moral purpose, insofar as it is meant to reveal "virtues and vices" in general in the actions of the powerful (*Treatise*, 3). In this sense, history is the "best school for princes, for statesmen, and for all men in general."[32]

Hertzberg refers to such a historiography as "pragmatic" (*Treatise*, 1). Although he does not define this term, he clearly understands it to mean a historiography that draws from empirical facts (*Treatise*, 13). In this sense, the task of the historian is to conscientiously select the right examples and to present them in an appealing way.[33] Individual events of the past are to be understood for the sake of the future.

Hertzberg confirms this view of history even though he does not directly address governmental events. For example, in his *Histoire de la marine et de la compagnie africaine de Prusse*, his sparse reflections on specific colonial events are included solely for the purpose of praising Prussian statesmanship or depicting its patriotic wisdom in the face of adverse circumstances (Hertzberg 1864, 80; 86). It serves as a source of instruction and a warning for future regents. But even the instruction "with the intention of morality" is subject to this purpose: the description of a slave revolt merely serves to illustrate its "happy" outcome in a trade—to model future diplomatic skill (Hertzberg 1864, 76).

Thus, the two steps that Hertzberg proposes in his treatise on ideal historiography— an empirical-historical method that guarantees the certainty of the facts and a "venerable court" of those facts—intertwine. The pragmatic use of history presupposes that the available data reliably correspond to the events. Only then can a clear lesson actually be learned from history. Now, it is striking that the *HTI* also situates the purpose of historiography in a court. And, in this context, only the historian can make an informed judgment:

> When dealing with important matters for the welfare of mankind, the first concern, the first duty must be to purify one's soul of all fear, all hope. When elevated above [*élevé au-dessus*] all human considerations, only then one flies up above the haze, only then one sees the globe below. Only then does one let tears fall over the persecuted genius, the forgotten talent, the unfortunate virtue. From there, one pours out curses and shame on those who deceive people and those who oppress them. From there one sees the haughty head of the tyrant bowed and covered with excrement, while the modest forehead of the righteous touches the vault of heaven. From here I have been able to truthfully exclaim, I am free and at the level of my subject [*au niveau de mon sujet*].
>
> (*HTI*, 3)

Although this quote also takes the task of historiography to be that of judging, it highlights two important differences between Hertzberg and the *HTI*. First, unlike in Hertzberg, the *HTI* maintains that the obligation of the historian is not to a future regent, but to humanity as a whole. The court of historiography is not interested in what constitutes a good regent, as with Hertzberg, but in what constitutes the good of humanity in general.

Second, the last line of the quote suggests that historiography is not simply a matter of the *historian* judging history, but of understanding *history* itself as a judgment. Indeed, the historian speaks the curse, but the tyrant bows his head to the course of history itself. Now, how is the judgment of history related to the judgment perpetrated by the historian?

Numerous passages of the *HTI*, traced primarily to Diderot, first identify history as earthly judgment. The most famous passage that makes this claim can be found in the eleventh book, which evokes retribution for atrocities committed against slaves: "Where is he, this great man, whom nature owes to her offended, oppressed, and tormented children? Where is he?" Diderot argues here, as elsewhere, in favor of a nature [*la nature*] characterized, in Locke's sense, by a natural freedom of all (*HTI*, 193; 204). If the freedom provided by nature is impaired (e.g., by slavery), nature retaliates. The course of history is thus a balancing act of this entitled freedom, an act of justice that gives back to those who have been deprived of what they were originally entitled to (*HTI*, 193; 204). It thus acquires a teleological dimension and individual actions receive their moral reference only against such a framework.

The historian no longer judges history pragmatically (i.e., by drawing benefit from the empirical). He can cast out the curse by judging the guilty and the innocent, but he can do so only by having penetrated the regularities of the "natural judgment" of history, which cannot be read directly in an empirical manner. Strictly speaking, then, the historian does not judge, but rather allows history to pronounce its own verdict.[34]

In order to understand this verdict, the historian needs a position in which he literally elevates himself above history as a mere sequence of events ("*élevé au-dessus*"). The historian is only able to delve into his subject, namely, history ("*au niveau de mon sujet*"), when he detaches himself from the way in which he is historically empirically interwoven with the world. Thus, from the outset, the *HTI* is not concerned with an empirical-historical account of colonialism in the way, for instance, Hertzberg presented it in his *Histoire de la marine et de la compagnie africaine de Prusse*.[35] Rather, the *HTI* argues that the world can only be correctly interpreted from the perspective of the historian's elevated (i.e., moral) point of view. This standpoint alone allows one to understand events as what they actually are.[36] The representation *of* history is precisely the reflection *on* [*über—au-dessus—from above*] history.

Since the historian can identify these inner (i.e., generally valid) regularities of history, which cannot be seen directly through experience, he can also use them to predict the course of history.[37] Moreover, the historian bears the task of predicting the condemnation of the immoral being and to bring moral postulates to their fulfillment.[38] The historian is therefore "in league" with history.[39] Raynal is celebrated in Europe and overseas in this sense as an "apostle of freedom," as a clear-sighted "*machine de guerre.*" (Without question, however, this fame should have been given to the author of almost every passage that asserts this claim, namely, Diderot).[40] As such, the *HTI* can respond to the question of where the "great man," who restores those unjustly denied their freedom, is:

> He will appear, we have no doubt, he will show himself, he will raise the sacred banner of freedom. This venerable signal will gather around him the companions of his misfortune. They will be more torrential than the rivers and will leave everywhere the indelible marks of their righteous resentment. Spaniards, Portuguese, English, French, Dutch, all their tyrants will become a prey to iron and flame. The American fields will become intoxicated with the blood for which they have waited so long, and the bones of so many unhappy people, heaped up for three centuries, will twitch with joy. The old world will join in the new acclaim. Everywhere the name of the hero who restored the rights of mankind will be

blessed, and everywhere trophies will be erected to his glory. Then the *code noir* will disappear; and how terrible will be the *code blanc*, if the victor consults only the right of retribution!"[41]

Thus, while the historian in Hertzberg's treatise has *to look back* on history as a pragmatic collection of examples in order to laboriously extract individual lessons from it for one's own actions that are rooted in empiricism, the historian in the *HTI* opens up the way to *the future*. He creates the overall framework in which individual action is to be understood as inscribed in the service of universal historical development.

4. The Scope of History

Finally, we have to relate the difference between a past- and a future-oriented historiography to the concept of history itself. Let us first consider the Hertzbergian notion of history. We have already noted that Hertzberg's historical ambitions were solely aimed at instructing the Prussian regent, or at best, the Prussian citizen. The lessons that can be drawn from history hardly have a specific temporal or spatial dimension. Whether Hertzberg refers to ancient models or to the exotic world of colonial enterprise, by stiffening the descriptions into examples, they always lead back (in time and space) to the Prussian ideal state, which he saw as already realized under Frederick II. History thus becomes motionless because it is ultimately tied to the court in Berlin.

By contrast, the history considered in the *HTI* is obviously a universal history (Sommer 2006, 54). It claims, both spatially and temporally, to encompass all of history. Spatially, it is to be understood as global history in that it encompasses the entire globe. The "two Indies" of the title stand for East Indies, Africa, South and North America. More importantly, however, it argues that the whole world is linked by destiny through colonialism, or "trade" (*HTI*, 2). Thus, there is no such thing as an "outside" of history. History *is* world history.

The history of the *HTI* is universal also in a temporal sense. What made the *HTI* such a successful book (i.e., one that appealed to the taste of a European bourgeoisie on the verge of revolution) is, as Lüsebrink clearly points out, the symbolic power it evokes regarding the history of colonialism.[42] We have already noted that from the external standpoint of the historian, the empirically given appears as a reference to the underlying regularity of history. The representations of the colonial world are a parable, or more precisely, a utopia. Numerous authors have already argued that the eighteenth century stylizes an "exotic" world and a *"bon sauvage."*[43] This stylization draws an ideal, original world or a utopia, which realizes the universal morality, against whose innocence injustices stand out in all their reprehensibility. In this sense, the *HTI* portrays the peoples of the non-European world as "meek, humane, fearful." It claims, furthermore, that "nothing has been able to accustom him [the 'Indian'] to the sight of blood, nor to give him the courage and the desire for outrage. He has only the vices of weakness about him."[44] Non-European people thus stand for the childhood of humankind (a childhood understood in terms of natural law).[45] The innocence of the human being (the "savage") of its childhood must now be defended against its own abuses in the mature age of humankind (the "European"). With the tracing of colonial history and its protagonists—the noble, weak savage, and the corrupted European—the entire history of humankind is thus understood, from its childhood to its coming of age. Treated in this way, it is perpetually under threat of collapsing into degeneration.

Ironically, however, the utopian undertone of the *HTI*, by which it was supposed to be an all-encompassing history of mankind, leads straight back to late eighteenth-century France. Indeed, at the time, the overwhelming majority of readers regarded the colonies mentioned in the *HTI* as a metaphor for the course of European history (Lüsebrink 2013, 341). The innocence of the "savage" stands here for the innocence of the citizen, the immorality of the conquerors for the injustice of the absolutist state. In this light, the statistics and figures documenting colonial events appear only as a "detour across the globe" to illustrate the crisis of the *ancien régime*.[46] In this sense, then, both Hertzberg's understanding of history and the *HTI* are anything but world histories. They are both histories of Europe only with different political intents.

5. Conclusion

The abbé Denina has been proven right: Hertzberg's festive speech was certainly not what Raynal had imagined as a satisfactory contribution to his prize question. The duty of the historian as understood in the *HTI*—namely, to convey the inner regularity of history—should be implemented according to a speculative method and a utopian universal history. The duty of the historian as understood in Hertzberg's treatise, to instruct pragmatically by example, is to be realized via a locally situated, empirical-historical method.

These two positions mark the intricacies of a debate that was only just beginning to appear at the time, a debate in which the traditional example-history, as portrayed by Hertzberg, stands apart both from the emerging speculative-universalist philosophies of history, as presented by Anne Robert Jacques Turgot, Isaak Iselin, the *HTI*, and Immanuel Kant, and from the academic study of history, which was also just emerging.[47] At the same time, we can perceive the change of course being chartered by the Prussian Academy under Hertzberg: the focus was shifting toward a national self-confidence in the form of praise for the Prussian monarchy and an "empirical" approach to study that was imbued with national character. The duty of the historian became that of patriotism. Guillaume Raynal left Prussia in 1783, never to return.

Abbreviations

HTI   Raynal, Guillaume. 1780. *Histoire philosophique et politique des établissements et du commerce des Européens dans les deux Indes*. Genève: Pellet.

TREATISE   Hertzberg, Ewald F. v. 1789. *Abhandlung über das wahre Ideal einer guten Geschichte und über das zweite Regierungsjahr Friedrich Wilhelms II*. Berlin.

Notes

1. See the minutes of meetings of the BBAW, especially 10.04.1783 (I IV 32/BI 349v); 25.11.1784 (I IV 32/BI 384v); 23.06.1785 (I IV 32/BI 397r).
2. I use the 1780 French edition unless otherwise noted (*Histoire philosophique et politique des établissements et du commerce des Européens dans les deux Indes*, 1780, Genève: Pellet). All translations of the *HTI* are my own.
3. For more details on the discovery of Diderot as a significant co-author, see Duchet 1978; Lüsebrink 1984; Lüsebrink 2013.
4. On the reception of Raynal himself in Germany, see Denina 1788, 365–72; Denina 1791, 197–201.
5. For more details on the success of the Colonial Encyclopedia, see Gilles Bancarel, "Le succès inattendu d'un Rouergat au XVIIIe siècle," in *Procès Verbaux des Sciences de la Société des Lettres, Sciences et Arts de l'Aveyron* (Rodez) XLV, 2°.
6. For a detailed account of the history of the edition of the *HTI*, see Bancarel 2004. Jakob Mauvillon (1778), as well as Johann Martin Abele (1782-8), translated the various print versions of the *HTI* that appeared in French (1770, 1774, 1780—a later version appeared posthumously in Paris in 1820 with corrections and additions that Raynal had made some time before his death).
7. See the minutes of meetings of the *BBAW*, 23.06. 1785, I IV/BI 397r. The *BBAW* has no documented submissions and the prize money was definitely returned to Raynal. However, from Denina's somewhat vague description, it is at least possible to infer that there had been some (albeit, unsatisfactory) submissions. See Denina 1791, 201–2; Bancarel 1991.
8. See Denina 1791, 201–2.
9. However, Bancarel points out that among the other possible competitors, there might have been Brissot de Warville who published in 1783, the year of the competition, in his *Correspondance sur ce qui intéresse le bonheur de l'homme et de la société*, a text titled *Mémoire relatif au Prix sur l'Histoire proposé par M. l'abbé Raynal* (Bancarel 2004, 137).
10. Denina had already published the *Essai sur la vie de Frédéric II* in 1788.
11. Raynal and Hertzberg knew each other and appeared together, for example, at the public meeting of the Academy in 1783. Cf. AAB Registre de l'Académie, "Best. PAW (1700–1811) I-IV-32, f° 344."
12. Denina 1791, 201–2. All translations of Hertzberg's writings are my own.
13. That Denina was quite ideologically opposed to Hertzberg can be found in Köpke 1844, 2. For Denina's anecdotal report, see also: Denina 1791, vol. 1, 320–6. In his comparison between Raynal and Hertzberg, Denina refers to Gabriel Bonnot Mably, who published the treatise *De la manière d'écrire l'histoire* in 1783. Denina draws a parallel between Raynal's and Mably's conceptions of history. On Mably's philosophy of history, see Pujol 2011, 125–50.
14. Hertzberg's treatise can be found in German translation in the "Allgemeinen preußischen Staatsgeschichte" by the jurist, philosopher, and historian Carl Friedrich Pauli (1723–78), as the first of several appendices to the seventh volume from 1767. There, Pauli 1767, 2 mentions the brevity and inaccuracy of Pufendorf's history of Prussian naval subjugation, which had already been mentioned by Hertzberg. Another improved translation can be found in Borcke, Heinrich Adrian Graf: *The Brandenburg Prussian Navy and the African Company. According to a Manuscript Written in French and Dated 1755*, Cologne 1864; see Leschke 2021.

15 For more on the reception in Germany, see Fontius 1991, 155–88; Mondot 1991, 189–204; and Bancarel 2004. The present chapter owes a great deal to these mainly historical studies. It sets itself apart from them on the one hand, through a historical-philosophical analysis of the reception, and on the other hand, as a philosophical investigation of Hertzberg's writing that has not yet been undertaken. For more on the *HTI* in general, see Wolpe 1956. Israel describes the *HTI* as the "ultimate climax of publishing events in all history" (Israel 2011, 420). See Israel 2011.

16 Kant and Herder engage in a debate that is reflected in several writings, especially during the 1780s. The debate was primarily about the nature of history (for example, whether it runs in a linear fashion) and the nature of the philosophy of history (for example, what role the intellect plays in grasping the meaning of history).

17 *Treatise*, 3. However, Hertzberg was not always faithful to this principle in his own treatises as already indicated by Köpke (Köpke 1844, 13–14).

18 Pauli 1767, 2. Christian Weidlich expresses a similar opinion on Ewald Friedrich Hertzberg. See Christoph Weidlich, 1781, *Rechts-Consulentens zu Halle Biographische Nachrichten von den jetztlebenden Rechts-Gelehrten in Teutschland*. With a preface titled *Von dem gegenwärtigen Zustande der Juristischen Litteratur in Teutschland*. First part. Halle: Hemmerdeische Buchhandlung, 281–304.

19 Cf. Hertzberg 1864, 81–2. The question of historical certainty was discussed at length at the Academy. See, for example, the treatises by Wegelin (1783) *Sur les notions claires et obscures, distinctes et confuses en fait d'Histoire*, and (1787) *Sur la probabilité historique*, *Nouveaux Mémoires de l'Académie Royale des Sciences et Belles-Lettres*, Berlin: Decker.

20 Hertzberg 1780, 24; 19. For the philosophical conception, see page 3. The fact that a national feeling developed in Germany in the eighteenth century has been highlighted by a wide range of authors. See Nipperdey, Th., 1983, *Deutsche Geschichte 1800–1866*, München: Beck, 300ff; Dann, O., 1993, *Nation und Nationalismus in Deutschland. 1770–1990*. München: Beck'sche Reihe, 494; Schulze, H. 1985, *Der Weg zum Nationalstaat. Die deutsche Nationalbewegung vom 18. Jahrhundert bis zur Reichsgründung*. München: dtv; and Vazsonyi, N., 1999, *Montesquieu, Friedrich Carl von Moser, and the "National Spirit Debate" in Germany, 1765–1767*. German Studies Review, 22, 2, 225–46. Friedrich Carl von Moser's treatise "Von dem deutschen Nationalgeist", published in 1765, can be cited here, as well as Johann Elias Schlegel's "Herrmann, ein Trauerspiel" (1766) or Justus Möser's "Arminius" (1762). The thesis that this national feeling only turned into militant and xenophobic nationalism after 1789 has been convincingly challenged. See, for example, Jeismann, M., 1992, *Das Vaterland der Feinde. Studien zum nationalen Feindbegriff und Selbstverständnis in Deutschland und Frankreich 1792–1918*, Stuttgart: Klett-Cotta; Hermann, H.P., 1999, "»Wer Rom nicht hassen kann, kann nicht die Deutschen lieben«. Deutscher Nationalismus im 18. Jahrhundert", in *Korrespondenzen. Festschrift für Joachim W. Storck aus Anlaß seines 75. Geburtstages*, 109–32, St. Ingbert: Röhrig (= Mannheimer Studien zur Literatur—und Kunstwissenschaft 20).

21 As Duchet points out in her influential monograph, it was above all thanks to the meticulous reports by administrators of the colonial trade that writers on the European mainland had material (Duchet 1971, 65–136).

22 Albrecht Haller, a respected physician and naturalist, expresses similar views in his review of the *HTI* for the *Göttingische Anzeigen für gelehrte Sachen* in 1772, Encore, 31st issue, August 15, CCLVII-VIII. As an important natural scientist, Haller not

only wrote about 900 reviews of learned works for the *Göttingische Anzeigen*, but also led an expedition to America in 1752. For a discussion of Haller's review, see also Fontius 1991, 158-61.

23   Dohm 1786, viii–xii. *The History of the Revolution of North America*, originally part of the 9th volume of the *HTI*, was published separately, translated into English (and in the process, reviewed by Payne), and then finally translated into German in 1786. Wernitz, the translator of the *History of the Revolution of North America* by Abbot Raynal, rates Dohm as the greatest statistician of his time. Wernitz's translation includes not only Dohm's review, but also Thomas Payne's notes on the *HTI*. For a discussion of Dohm's critique of Raynal, see also Fontius 1991, 161-6. Dohm was familiar with Hertzberg and reported on Hertzberg's political decisions in, among other places, Dohm, Christian Conrad Wilhelm von, *Denkwürdigkeiten meiner Zeit oder Beiträge zur Geschichte vom letzten Viertel des achtzehnten und vom Anfang des neunzehnten Jahrhunderts*, vol.1, 447.

24   Dohm 1786, viii–xii. Similarly, on 11. 5. 1772, Voltaire wrote to Condorcet—who had advised him to read the *HTI*—that he expected no more from Raynal's work than "du réchauffé avec de la déclamation." Condorcet, 1847, *Œuvres de Condorcet*, vol. 1, Paris: Didot, 8.

25   Dohm 1786, xii. My italics.

26   Dohm 1786, 8.

27   Pernety refers to De Pauw's method pejoratively as a "méthode philosophique"—a term that he applies equally to the *HTI*. Pernety, Antoine-Joseph, *Dissertation sur l'Amérique et les Naturels de cette partie du Monde*, 51. The famous dispute between De Pauw and Pernety, which sparked the Berlin debate over the nature of the Americans as well as the question of whether the conquest of the New World had been beneficial, had just dissipated—Pernety had left Berlin in 1783. For a detailed discussion of this debate, also with regard to Raynal, see Ette 2021, 432, and the classic work by Gerbi, Antonello, 1973, *The Dispute of the New World. The History of a Polemic, 1750-1900*, Pittsburgh: University Press.

28   Here, I adopt Sommer's definition of a speculative philosophy of history. Sommer characterizes this kind of philosophy of history by virtue of the way it creates meaning—that is, it assumes that history, instead of "only" *having* a meaning, is itself capable of *creating* meaning (Sommer 2006).

29   For more on the Berlin debate on the New World, see Bernaschina, Vicente, Tobias Kraft, and Anne Kraume, 2015, *Globalisierung in Zeiten der Aufklärung. Texte und Kontexte zur "Berliner Debatte" um die Neue Welt (17./18. Jh.)*. 2 vols., Frankfurt am Main—Bern—New York: Peter Lang Edition, 27-55. Ette (Ette 2021, 443-58) points out that this was a matter of eradicating not only textual sources, but also accounts of experience—for example, by rejecting the reports of the Spanish conquistadors. For more on the methodological disputes between Raynal and Diderot, see Brot 2015.

30   For a detailed discussion of this, see Lüsebrink 2013, 350.

31   Biographically, this view must be seen in the context of Hertzberg's being an official of the king. Here, Hertzberg proves his affiliation with the enlightened ruling class of the Prussian bureaucracy. From a theoretical point of view, his closeness to Frederick II, who in his own historical writings emphasized the study primarily of recent history as the basis for major institutional decisions by the monarch, should be mentioned. In practical terms, Hertzberg had been active (and quite unsuccessful) in helping to shape Prussian foreign policy, especially since 1786—his interest in a "pattern of excellent government" is, as an extremely educated minister, thus also of

a pragmatic nature. On the relationship between Hertzberg and Frederick II, see also Schui 2013, 79.

32 Hertzberg, *Treatise*, 3. Here, Hertzberg follows Tacitus, whom he repeatedly cites, and who in his *Annals* sees the purpose of historiography as "to prevent virtues from being silenced and so that the fear of infamy and posterity's judgment should accompany crooked words and deeds." Tacitus, 1983, *Annals*, 3.65.1, Teubner: Heubner. One should make reference to Bolingbroke's *Letters on the Study and Use of History* (1751), in which Bolingbroke not only discusses historiography in its function as a tribunal with recourse to Tacitus, but also gives the example of the Egyptian court of the dead used by Hertzberg (1780, 13). See Bolingbroke, *Letter II*, 24. In contrast to Hertzberg, however, Bolingbroke here also highlights the aspect of transience (also present in Tacitus): historiography as judgment also prevents a man's virtue from being forgotten. As the following quotation from the *HTI* shows, we also find this element in Raynal-Diderot.

33 *Treatise*, 6–8. Köpke emphasizes that, given Hertzberg's great concern for neutrality, it is "a strange suggestion" to have this judgment written by men officially instructed to do so and employed by the king (Köpke 1844, 14). On the "exempla history," see Sommer 2006, 370–83; 250.

34 The prize question posed by Raynal shortly thereafter in Lyon must be understood in precisely this sense. The answer to the question "if the discovery of America has done more good or harm?" is given by history; history, however, is grasped through the categories of moral criticism. Cf. Koselleck 1973, 149. For more on the prize question in Lyon: Denina 1791, 201–2.

35 An empirical history is presented, for example, by Mathias Christian Sprengel, a geographer and professor of history and statistics in Halle, who in the 1770s and 1780s produced and publicized a whole series of writings on the history of colonialism and the "new world." It is striking how Sprengel, whom Dohm reveres as a shining example of a thorough historian, takes a completely different view than Raynal (or Diderot). For example, in his treatise *Vom Ursprung des Negerhandels* (1779), Sprengel argues that the allegedly barbaric behavior of Guinea's inhabitants was a major driving force behind the slave trade. Cf. Sprengel, Mathias, 1779, *Vom Ursprung des Negerhandels*, Halle: Hendel, 12–13.

36 From this point of view, it turns out that the driving force of history is trade. Cf. *HTI*, 2. On the relationship of universal history to *histoire sainte* (sacred history) and to *histoire profane* (profane history), see Sommer 2006, 99.

37 This "generality," of course, is itself a prime example of what Stuart Hall called the "white eye," that is, a deeply Eurocentrist-colored gaze that claims objectivity. For more on the metaphor of the gaze, which is omnipresent in the introduction of the *HTI*, see Habermann 2008, 195–8. A concrete methodological example of this Eurocentric gaze is discussed by Ette (Ette 2021, 445–58). Not only does the rejection of empirical sources challenge the neutrality of the conquistadors' experiences, but it also avoids drawing on indigenous sources. In the *HTI*, Ette makes it clear that indigenous sources are simply non-existent. They appear only as the symbol of a lost innocence, as an object of mourning.

38 Cf. Koselleck 1973, 55–6.

39 Koselleck 1973, 147. Cf. Koselleck 1973, 148; 7–9.

40 M. Isnard, 1790, *Discours*, Marseille, 8. I take this citation from Koselleck 1973. On the dialectic between "recognizing" and "accomplishing", see Koselleck 1973, 156. Koselleck's thesis, however, is more complex, especially if we take into account the concept of crisis, which has not been considered in this essay. Of course, Raynal was

also ridiculed as a "clairvoyant," for example, by Johann Georg Hamann in his *Lettre perdue d'un sauvage du Nord à un financier de Pe-Kin* in 1773 or by Johann Gottfried Herder in his letter of June 1, 1782 to Johannes von Müller. Both were concerned with dismissing Raynal as an "enthusiast" and "homme à conjectures."

41 Edition 1780, 186–204 (Book 11, Chapter 24). For more details on the relation between the contributions of Raynal and Diderot, see Duchet 1971. On the project of an "enlightened colonialism," see Michaud 2014, Anthony Strugnell 2005, and Carey and Festa 2009.

42 The symbolic power of the colony, however, should not obscure the fact that the *HTI* is also, as Michaud says, "an experiment in early anthropological methodology that draws upon descriptive and analytical portraits of non-European Peoples in order to elaborate a plan for a more humane colonization" (Michaud 2014, 18). In this sense, it should not be forgotten that the *HTI* makes a very clear distinction between the symbolic level and "reality." See *HTI*, 200.

43 Cf. for instance Ette 2021, 427, with reference to Rousseau. In this context, Koselleck uses the concept of "transoceanicity" (Koselleck 1973, 153). The world "outside" Europe, as an ideal image, justifies the discharge of the tension between innocence (the non-European world) and guilt (Europe) in a revolution, while this discharge is necessary and remains transcendent to the citizen. Cf. also Saage 2001, 177. Although the dualism between innocence and guilt is most strongly attached to the New World, this is also true for the other continents discussed by the *HTI*, such as the East Indies (*HTI* 34–6).

44 Of course, as throughout the *HTI*, it is important to carefully distinguish between the authors: one of the reasons why the book has been so controversially received is that its message is often particularly confusing. For example, while in one place Diderot argues for a slave revolt, in others the work claims that a reform or a more humanistic treatment of slaves would be more appropriate (cf. *HTI* 181–6 and *HTI* 186–204). It is noteworthy, however, that even the most radical passages, such as Diderot's call for slave revolt (*HTI* 204), refer to the transatlantic slave as a "child."

45 In this sense, Locke wrote in his *Two Treatises of Government* of 1690 (Chapter V, Sec. 49): "Thus in the beginning all the world was America." On the movement of return and on the role of a utopia shifted to the exotic, see Jimack and Manders 2008, Saage 2001. It is in this sense that Diderot's lines about Tahiti, written in 1772, are to be understood: "The Tahitian is so close to the beginning of the world, the European to her old age!"

46 Here, Lüsebrink refers to Koselleck (Koselleck 1973, 149), although Koselleck's thesis is far more complex: not only "the globe" is a detour, but also the philosophy of history itself.

47 See Summer 2006.

Selected Bibliography

Bancarel, Gilles. 2004. *Raynal ou le devoir de vérité*. Genève: Champion.

Bodingbroke, Henry St. John. [1751] 1788. *Letters on the Study and Use of History*. Basil: Tourneisen.

Brot, Muriel. 2015. "Écrire et éditer une histoire philosophique et politique: l'histoire des deux Indes de l'abbé Raynal (1770–1780)." In *Société Française d'Histoire des Outre-Mers*, 1 (N° 386-7), 9–28.

Carey, Daniel and Lynn Festa. 2009. *The Post Colonial Enlightenment: Eighteenth-Century Colonialism and Postcolonial Theory*. Oxford: Oxford University Press.
Denina, Carlo. 1788. *Essai sur la vie et le règne de Frédéric II, Roi de Prusse, pour servir de préliminaire à l'édition de ses oeuvres posthumes*. Berlin: Rottmann.
Denina, Carlo. [1786] 1791. *La Prusse littéraire sous Frédéric II, ou histoire abrégée de la plupart des auteurs, des académiciens, et des artistes qui sont nés ou qui ont vécu dans les États Prussiens depuis 1740 jusqu'à 1786*, vol. 1–3. Berlin: Rottmann.
Dohm, Christoph. 1786. *Vorerinnerung zu der Schrift des Herrn Payne*. In *Geschichte der Revolution von Nord-America vom Abt Raynal, nebst Anmerkungen über diese Geschichte von Thomas Payne, übersetzt aus dem Französischen*. Berlin: Wernitz.
Duchet, Michèle. 1971. *Anthropologie et histoire au siècle des Lumières*. Paris: Albin Michel.
Duchet, Michèle. 1978. *Diderot et l'histoire des deux Indes. Ou l'écriture fragmentaire*. Paris: Edition Nizet.
Ette, Ottmar. 2021. *Aufklärung zwischen zwei Welten: Potsdamer Vorlesungen zu den Hauptwerken der romanischen Literaturen des 18. Jahrhunderts*. Berlin: De Gruyter.
Fontius, Martin. 1991. "L'histoire des deux Indes de Raynal vue par les Allemands." In *Lectures de Raynal. L'Histoire des deux Indes en Europe et en Amérique au XVIIIe siècle. Actes du Colloque de Wolfenbüttel*, edited by Hans-Jürgen Lüsebrink and Manfred Tietz, 155–88. Oxford: Alden Press.
Habermann, Friederieke. 2008. *Der homo oeconomicus und das Andere: Hegemonie, Identität und Emanzipation*. Baden-Baden: Nomos.
Hertzberg, Ewald Friedrich von. 1767. "Geschichte der preußischen Seemacht und der afrikanischen Handelsgesellschaft und Friedrich Wilhelm dem Großen und Friedrich dem I." In *Der Weltweisheit und Geschichtkunde öffentlichen ordentlichen Lehrers und der königl. deutschen Gesellschaft zu Königsberg Mitgliedes allgemeine preußische Staats—Geschichte des dazu gehörigen Königsreichs, Churfürstenthums und aller Herzogthümer, Fürstenthümer, Graf—und Herrschaften aus bewährten Schriftstellern und Urkunden bis auf gegenwärtige Regierung*, vol. 7, edited by Carl Friedrich Pauli, 483–528. Halle: Christoph Peter Franckens.
Hertzberg, Ewald Friedrich von. 1780. *Abhandlung, worin man die Ursachen der Ueberlegenheit der Teutschen über die Römer zu entwickeln, und zu beweisen sucht, daß der Norden des alten Teutschlands zwischen dem Rhein und der Weichsel und vorzüglich die gegenwärtige Preussische Monarchie das Stammland der heroischen Nationen gewesen sey, welche in der berühmten Völker-Wanderung das Römische Reich zerstöret und die Haupt-Staaten des heutigen Europa gegründet und bevölkert haben*. Berlin: Decker.
Hertzberg, Ewald Friedrich von. 1789. *Abhandlung über das wahre Ideal einer guten Geschichte und über das zweite Regierungsjahr Friedrich Wilhelms II*. Berlin.
Hertzberg, Ewald Friedrich von. 1864. *Die brandenburgisch-preußische Marine und die Africanische Compagnie: nach einem vom Jahr 1755 datierten, in französischer Sprache geschriebenen Manuskripte*, translated by Heinrich Graf von Borcke. Köln: Du Mont-Schauburgsche Buchhandlung.
Israel, Jonathan. 2011. *Democratic Enlightenment: Philosophy, Revolution, and Human Rights 1750–1790*. Oxford: Oxford University Press.
Jimack, Peter and Jenny Manders. 2008. "Rewriting the World: The Pacific in Raynal's Histoire des deux Indes." In *Eighteenth Century Studies*, vol. 41. no. 2 (Winter 2008). 189–202. Baltimore: Johns Hopkins University Press.

Köpke, Rudolf. 1844. "Über des Grafen Hertzberg Abriss seiner diplomatischen Laufbahn." In *Zeitschrift für Geschichtswissenschaft*, vol. 1. Berlin: von Veit.

Koselleck, Reinhart. 1973. *Kritik und Krise*. Freiburg/München: Suhrkamp.

Leschke, Gabriele. 2021. *Otto Friedrich von der Gröben und der koloniale Diskurs*. Freie Universität Berlin. https://refubium.fu-berlin.de/handle/fub188/30407http://dx.doi.org/10.17169/refubium-30148urn:nbn:de:kobv:188-refubium-30407-5.

Lüsebrink, Hans-Jürgen. 1984. "Le Livre qui fait naître des Brutus ... Zur Verhüllung und sukzessiven Aufdeckung der Autorschaft Diderots an der Histoire des deux Indes." In *Denis Diderot, 1713 bis 1748. Zeit—Werk—Wirkung. Zehn Beiträge*, edited by Titus Heydenreich, Hinrich Hudde, and Franz Josef Hausmann, 107–26. Erlangen: Universitätsbund Erlangen-Nürnberg (Erlangen Forschungen).

Lüsebrink, Hans-Jürgen. 2013. *Appendix to Die Geschichte beider Indien*. Berlin: Die Andere Bibliothek.

McDonald, Christie and Susan Rubin Suleiman. 2010. *French Global. A New Approach to Literary History*. New York: Columbia University Press.

Michaud, Monica. 2014. "Culture as Colonizer: Raynal's 'colonialisme éclairé' in the Histoire des deux Indes'". In *French Forum*, 39:2/3, 17–32. Pennsylvania: University of Pennsylvania Press.

Mondot, Jean. 1991. "La réception de Raynal en Allemagne: l'exemple de Wekhrlin." In *Lectures de Raynal. L'Histoire des deux Indes en Europe et en Amérique au XVIIIe siècle. Actes du Colloque de Wolfenbüttel*, edited by Hans-Jürgen Lüsebrink and Manfred Tietz, 189–204. Oxford: Alden Press.

Pauli, Carl Friedrich. 1767. *Der Weltweisheit und Geschichtkunde öffentlichen ordentlichen Lehrers und der königl. deutschen Gesellschaft zu Königsberg Mitgliedes allgemeine preußische Staats—Geschichte des dazu gehörigen Königsreichs, Churfürstenthums und aller Herzogthümer, Fürstenthümer, Graf—und Herrschaften aus bewährten Schriftstellern und Urkunden bis auf gegenwärtige Regierung*, vol. 7, 483–528. Halle: Christoph Peter Franckens.

Pujol, Stéphane. 2011. "Histoire, morale et politique chez Mably." In *Les philosophes et l'histoire au XVIIIe siècle*, edited by Muriel Brot, 125–50. Paris: Hermann.

Raynal, Guillaume. 1780. *Histoire philosophique et politique des établissements et du commerce des Européens dans les deux Indes*. Genève: Pellet.

Saage, Richard. 2001. "Zwischen Natur und Zivilisation. Zu Denis Diderots »Nachtrag zu ›Bougainvilles Reise‹«." *Zeitschrift für Politik*, 48, 2, 168–88.

Schui, Florian. 2013. *Rebellious Prussians. Urban Political Culture under Frederick the Great and his Successors*. Oxford: Oxford University Press.

Sommer, Andreas Urs. 2006. *Sinnstiftung durch Geschichte? Zur Entstehung spekulativ-universalistischer Geschichtsphilosophie zwischen Bayle und Kant*. Basel: Schwabe.

Strugnell, Anthony. 2005. "Colonialism and Its Discourses." In *The Eighteenth Century Now. Boundaries and Perspectives*, vol. 10, edited by Jonathan Mallinson, 171–81. Oxford: Oxford University Press.

Wolpe, Hans. 1956. *Raynal et sa machine de guerre. L'histoire des deux Indes et ses perfectionnements*. Paris: Génin.

Part Two

Metaphysics

3

A Negative Monadology: Condillac's Answer to the Berlin Academy Prize Competition

Christian Leduc

1. Introduction

The prize competition on monads was the first that the Berlin Academy organized following the renewal of the institution by Frederick the Great during the 1740s. It immediately followed the creation of a class of speculative philosophy from which competitions on metaphysical matters emanate.¹ From this renewal onward, the Berlin Academy announced questions on several topics, including optimism, the comparison between mathematical and metaphysical methods, and the nature of substantial forces.² Some competitions fostered occasions to discuss or confront the Leibnizian and Wolffian philosophies that still dominated the German intellectual and academic world. However, the 1746 question on monads was particularly significant since it provided the first official opportunity in Berlin for Leibnizian and anti-Leibnizian figures to oppose each other, sometimes in a particularly virulent way. Many members of the Academy, including Christian Wolff of course, were favorable to Leibniz's doctrines, whereas some tended to reject Leibnizianism either in part or totally. The most hostile figure to Leibniz throughout the competition was certainly Leonhard Euler, who was recruited in 1741 and played a central role during the competition. Additionally, the prize winner, Johann Heinrich Gottlob von Justi, clearly offers arguments that dismiss Leibniz and Wolff. While the prize competition was taking place, Euler himself published his *Gedanken von den Elementen der Körper* (Thoughts on the Elements of Bodies), which contains a general critique of the thoughts of both Leibniz and Wolff.³ In sum, for some academicians, the prize competition was perceived as an opportunity to try to end the Leibnizian-Wolffian intellectual domination.⁴

However, the committee's decision greatly displeased the followers of Leibniz and Wolff (Samuel Formey, for instance),⁵ and it was agreed that it would be preferable to publish Justi's text accompanied by other answers.⁶ Some of these answers argued for the system of monads, such as Plouquet's *Primaria Monadologiae capita* (First Chapters of the Monadology). Among the published texts, a work by Condillac, entitled *Les Monades* (The Monads), was featured. Up until the end of the twentieth century, his contribution remained anonymous, despite the fact that Condillac mentions this work in his *Traité des animaux* (Treatise on Animals).[7] It has since been convincingly shown that Condillac is the genuine author of *Les Monades*, considering the numerous theoretical overlaps with later works, particularly the *Traité des systèmes* (Treatise on Systems) of 1749.[8] Indeed, the *Traité* repeats many of the criticisms against the Leibnizian system that are first expressed in the prize essay. At first sight, the essay could simply be viewed as a preparatory work to *Traité des systèmes* and would thus certainly have some historiographical and contextual values, albeit in a limited way. Condillac's interpretation of Leibniz was crucial for his reception in France, but also for the rest of Europe. His prize essay would thus be an additional proof of a leading interpretation during the Enlightenment according to which Leibnizianism is an abstract and hypothetical system that is at odds with empirical knowledge.

A closer reading should, however, convince us to mitigate this first impression since Condillac does not only raise criticisms but also adopt, in the second half of the essay, a new form of monadology that is inspired by Leibniz. Despite his rejection of many aspects of Leibnizianism, especially its general conception of substance, Condillac surprisingly shows himself to be one of his followers. Nevertheless, we should not be mistaken: Condillac has not completely changed his mind with respect to what he said in his 1746 *Essai sur l'origine de la connaissance humaine* (Essay on the Origin of Human Knowledge). In the introduction, Condillac claims that the ambitious and more classical form of metaphysics, which inquires into the nature of beings, their essences, and hidden causes—a project with which Leibniz's philosophy is undoubtedly associated—must be dismissed in order to give way to a more specific kind of metaphysics, whose object corresponds to the scope of the human mind (*Essai sur l'origine de la connaissance humaine*, OP I, 3). The version of the monadology that can be found in the prize essay certainly goes beyond this limitation, but Condillac does not renounce the principles of his empiricism, according to which all knowledge originates from sensation. It seems that this contribution must be read as the extension of a specific metaphysical perspective, the content of which regards the sensations and ideas of the mind, while occasionally venturing into the realm of classical metaphysics.

In his commentary, Laurence Bongie defends an interpretation of Condillac's new monadology that ties in with considerations found elsewhere in his work, with a specific focus on the *Traité des sensations*. According to his view, Condillac is particularly concerned with the spiritual nature of monads, and he essentially offers an idealist ontology. The main proof for this idealism would be that extension is not real and that it should instead be considered as a phenomenon in the same way as sensible qualities are (Bongie 1980, 69-71).[9] It is true that Leibniz's metaphysics was often characterized as idealist because of the phenomenal reality of extension and matter.[10] In the same spirit, but in his own way, Condillac would argue that the world is essentially composed of non-extended and simple substances. Without completely dismissing Bongie's reading, I believe that Condillac held another intention for the prize essay. Let us remember that it is certainly his most ontological work, but that the prize essay could not reasonably be at complete odds with the content of the *Essai* or with his later *Traité des sensations*. In my view, its most important feature is that it aimed to take part in debates about rational cosmology that were contemporary to him. In other words, the scope of *Les Monades* is primarily cosmological rather than psychological or ontological since Condillac defends positions that mainly relate to issues in the metaphysics of nature. What is specific about his monadology is that it could also be considered *negative* since it demonstrates the existence of monads while maintaining that they remain unknowable. To support this interpretation, I will examine three problems: the scope of the metaphysics of nature, the general order of things, and the reality of space. Although Condillac would probably give up answering such questions in his other writings, I argue that in the context of the prize essay, he believes that these positions are compatible with a restricted definition of metaphysics that derives its foundations from sensible perception.

2. The General Notion of Substance

Before examining Condillac's negative monadology and its cosmological consequences, it is worth recalling some of the criticisms contained in the first part of the essay. This initial part mainly concerns the notion of substance and its Leibnizian attributes, or more precisely, force and perception. For each of these attributes, Condillac elaborates specific arguments that serve to invalidate Leibniz's metaphysics in general. As previously mentioned, the *Traité des systèmes* is, in large part, based on these objections. Condillac refers not only to Leibniz but also to figures that are associated with him. Leibnizianism is thus here reconstructed from a plurality of sources, the main ones not being Leibniz's well-known texts at the time, such as the *Monadology* or the *Theodicy*, but rather those of Christian Wolff, particularly the *Philosophia prima sive Ontologia* (First Philosophy, or Ontology) of 1730.[11] Condillac's target is thus a certain form of Leibnizian-Wolffian philosophy. As a reminder, the *Ontologia* is a work that accounts for the fundamental concepts and principles of metaphysics in an abstract way, with specific parts reserved for special disciplines, namely: cosmology, psychology, and theology. This approach is specific to Wolff, who is the first to theorize such a division of metaphysics in the eighteenth century and to confer a preparatory and fundamental function to ontology. In the first part of the prize essay, Condillac employs this order of exposition, starting with the general notion of substance as defined in the *Ontologia*. This, of course, introduces a Wolffian interpretative bias, which is to say one that starts from abstract reflections on metaphysical concepts such as being, possibility, and necessity, and that subsequently elaborates a doctrine of substance. Condillac's intention is twofold. On the one hand, he aims to reconstruct a general concept of being, as it is adopted by Leibniz's followers, even though Leibniz himself never offers such a conceptualization.[12] This general statement is already present in the *Essai*, but it is applied for the first time to a specific doctrine in the prize essay. On the other hand, Condillac closely follows Locke's empiricism, to whom he was still indebted at the time. According to this Lockean empiricism, it would be a common error to maintain that one can cognize substance through abstract ideas, regardless of sensation. The case of Wolff is obviously exemplary and certainly explains why Condillac addresses it, since Wolff himself begins by providing an abstract definition of substance (*Ontologia*, §§768–78; GW II, 3, 574–86). Here is how Condillac summarizes his objection:

> Also, the philosophies believing to know the subject or essence of substance all held this behavior. M. Wolff is an example. He arrives at the notion of substance through that of being; and he arrived at this latter through that of possibility and impossibility, which are the most abstract notions. Regarding particular substances, he can say nothing that is not explainable from what he said of substance in general.
>
> (*Les Monades*, 267)

Condillac comes to the same conclusion as Locke: the knowledge of things begins with the sensation of individual qualities, which are subsequently abstracted for reasons of cognitive utility and use of signs and language. One must, therefore, never operate inversely from abstract entities or principles to more specific ones, as Wolff proposes, since this will certainly lead to unfounded propositions that remain imaginary suppositions rather than adequate ones that allow us to learn from concrete substances. In other words, Condillac applies a Lockean model to a later doctrine that commits a common fault among systematic thinkers.

Condillac proceeds in the same manner throughout the subsequent chapters that deal with force and perception. It should be noted that most of the references are once again taken from Wolff's *Ontologia*, but also from his *Cosmologia generalis* (General Cosmology) and the two treatises on psychology, empirical and rational. There are certainly a few quotations from Leibniz's writings, some of which are taken from the *Système nouveau de la nature* (New System of Nature) of 1695, but Condillac's reconstruction follows Wolff more than Leibniz.[13] This is notably the case in the treatment of force. As is well known, Leibniz and Wolff claim that force is an essential property of substance. There is a wide variety of arguments in Leibniz's work that attempt to demonstrate that substances are necessarily endowed with force, of which some particularly aim to articulate the numerous undesirable consequences of the doctrine of occasional causes, making God the only true causal agent in the world (*De Ipsa natura*, GP IV, 509). Condillac is aware of such demonstrations but prefers to examine the sections of Wolff's *Ontologia* that argue force to be an essential attribute due to the principle of sufficient reason (*Ontologia*, §§722–4; GW II, 3, 542–3). The summary reads as follows:

> Because substance is modifiable, it can have different successive determinations and change its state. Thus, the possibility of change finds its sufficient reason in the essence of being. But when a change is possible, it does not mean that it is actual. The essence that determines its possibility does not, therefore, suffice to determine its existence. It must, therefore, be admitted that there is another reason in each substance through which we can understand why and how a particular change becomes actual rather than any other. Now, this reason is what is called force.
>
> (*Les Monades*, 267–8)

This reconstruction concludes that force must exist in substances. The argument draws from the general concepts of possibility, change, existence, and sufficient reason in order to demonstrate the reality of substantial force. The same applies to the other subjects in this section, whether it be the simplicity of substances, the definition of force as a continual effort to act, or the continuity of change. Since this is the most critical part of the prize essay, Condillac consistently responds with an objection or with conceptual adjustments to account for the notion or thesis at stake. For example, he agrees with Leibniz and Wolff that we perceive force or action, but it is rather, first and foremost, the idea that is derived from what we feel while using our faculties. Like Locke, Condillac considers that it is from this empirical idea of the force of our faculties, or of the will in particular, that we can then analogically represent the action involved in the change of bodies to ourselves (*Les Monades*, 268–9). Condillac nevertheless adds a further point: sensation informs us that force is always known through a perceptual complex, namely, a faculty that acts on ideas (ibid., 270); therefore, attributing force to simple substances would have no cognitive basis. For these reasons, it is again necessary to proscribe any reasoning that proceeds with the help of abstract principles because it is precisely an abstract and demonstrative method that made Wolff believe that simple substances were endowed with force, whereas sensible experience shows us that force always involves several sensations, in which one acts on the other.

We could certainly provide other examples, but this one suffices for us to understand two points: first, it is above all Wolff's method that Condillac uses as a means to reconstruct Leibnizianism prior to criticizing it. The scarce references to Leibniz's writings are, therefore, inscribed in an argumentative structure that is extraneous to them. Second, the main characteristic of this Wolffian method is to proceed by general definitions and demonstrations, which is at odds with Condillac's approach to the metaphysics of mind that consists in the attempt to establish relations between the contents of knowledge and sensations. The question is how a new monadology is possible when we start from such an epistemological condition and then neglect the abstract synthetic method.

3. Negative Monadology

The second part of the prize essay is meant to offer an affirmative answer to the Berlin prize competition question by elaborating a new theory of monads. The fact that it is now a question of monads, and not only of substances in general, supports the idea that Condillac wishes to exchange with Leibniz here rather than Wolff, who distanced himself from the monadological metaphysics.[14] This section nevertheless begins with considerations about substance, through which Condillac summarizes what he maintained in the *Essai* and that he repeats in the *Traité des sensations*, namely, that the only notion of substance that we can represent to ourselves is the one that relates to our own self. This notion is obtained by abstraction when we separate all the qualities or modifications perceived in the self (*Les Monades*, 293). However, as Locke argued before, Condillac considers that the self remains unknowable in its individual essence, for we only know the modifications that are gathered under the same subject, but not the thinking substance in itself (ibid., 295). In the rest of this chapter, Condillac explains how the self is also a model for the recognition of other external substances. In other words, he argues that it is by comparison with our own nature that we identify other substances in nature. Relying again on Locke, Condillac concludes "that we cannot say anything else of the substance in general, except that a certain *je ne sais quoi* supports the qualities that come to our knowledge by way of sensation and reflection" (ibid., 297–8).

The role of these reflections in the general economy of the prize essay is not clear. Even though Condillac expresses ideas that were defended in the *Essai*, this conception of substance would seem like an obstacle to the elaboration of a theory of monads. If the notion of substance is unknowable, how are monadological considerations even possible? In my view, this is the only chapter that must be read in strict opposition to the first part of the prize essay, which mainly repeats the objection that the abstract method of reasoning is sterile. At the same time, we can reach some theoretical results by considering the self as a substance, for instance, and by recognizing corporeal substances in experience. This means that the empirical method of analysis provides a very limited kind of knowledge of metaphysical entities. It seems that Condillac is beginning to establish an explanatory model that he follows in the next chapters: metaphysical distinctions and reasoning are only conceivable when they pertain to sensible ideas and to arguments that exclusively rely on these contents.

Chapters 2 to 4 are devoted to the notions of unity, numbers, and infinity and serve distinct purposes. Condillac takes positions on issues regarding the conception of mathematical objects, and he mostly engages with French thinkers, including the logicians of Port-Royal, Antoine Arnauld, and Pierre Nicole, but mostly with Bernard Le Bouyer de Fontenelle. Several objections are formulated against Fontenelle's conception of the infinite, and they examine the cognitive processes that lead to the perception of numbers and figures.[15] However, such considerations are not essential to the present analysis and will, for this reason, be set aside. In Chapter 5, Condillac begins his examination of the concept of monads, during which we find the basic elements of his theory. Condillac initially wants to prove that monads exist and that the main argument for this purpose is the one found in the opening paragraphs of Leibniz's *Monadology*, according to which monads or simple substances are said to exist because they are at the foundations of compounds in nature. The status of these compounds could be explained in different ways, for Condillac, particularly by the means of geometrical operations that the preceding chapters have analyzed. More precisely, it is said that complex numbers are known when successive simple unities in objects are perceived through either arithmetical or geometrical calculations (*Les Monades*, 299–300).[16] Yet it is far from clear that Leibniz would accept such an explanation, since mathematical entities are ideal and must not be confused with real and metaphysical substances.[17] The main interest of this reasoning lies elsewhere. Condillac's aim is twofold: he wishes to prove the existence of monads and to explore a way to explain the foundation of corporeal beings, on the one hand, and to invalidate the thesis according to which matter and bodies are infinitely divisible, on the other. The argument unfolds as follows:

> But, either it must be supposed that in every body there are parts which subdivide to infinity, or they must be attributed, as the Leibnizians held, simple beings as elements—doubtless, this impression bears no contradiction. All that is, is one

or a collection of unities. So, what is one is not itself a collection, otherwise there would be collections of units, although there would be no units, which would obviously be contradictory. Now in the proper sense, the unity—which is to say, that which is not a collection—cannot be suitable for a compound being—which is to say, a collection. So, there are simple beings, which is to say, monads.

(*Les Monades*, 316)

The reasoning has a very Leibnizian tone.[18] Even though no reference is provided, the argument remains seemingly faithful to Leibniz's *Monadology*. Condillac nevertheless affirms a thesis that is unique in his work: monads are the reason or foundation of collections of beings, such as bodies. From this moment onward, a theory of monads is clearly in the making. At the same time, this theory also rules out a major metaphysical position with regard to matter, which consists in its infinite divisibility. For Condillac, if we do have the sensible idea of a monad or a simple substance, which makes the compound conceivable, the consequence is that we cannot infinitely divide substances, an operation which can only be a supposition of our imagination. A compound or body is, then, an aggregate that is made up of monads and not parts of matter that could be further divided into smaller parts. Once again, this theoretical position occurs in a context where the classical debate on the composition of matter has been revived. This is particularly the case at the Berlin Academy. For instance, in his *Gedanken von den Elementen der Körper*, Euler maintains the hypothesis of an infinite division of bodies—and this, against Leibnizians (*Gedanken*, II, 69, 18). On such a point, Euler is more or less correct given that Leibniz, likewise, considers matter to be infinitely divisible. Leibniz does go on to specify, however, that matter *per se* does not constitute a substantial being in the manner of monads and bodies (*Theodicy* GP VI, 232). Condillac's originality is that he relies on the empirical method of analysis: sensation yields the ideas of simplicity and composition, on which the demonstration of monads is based, whereas it cannot provide us with the idea of infinite divisibility.

This proof of the existence of monads and the composition of bodies is, however, undertaken with a crucial restriction. According to Condillac, the monad, as was the case with substance in general, remains a being whose intrinsic nature is unknown to us. The notion of a monad "does not suppose that it is the nature of simple beings, nor what the relations between monads are" (*Les Monades*, 318). This new monadology is, therefore, certainly affirmed, but it comes with important limitations since it does not allow us to discover the essential properties of simple substances. It only stipulates that bodies are composed of monads and that they cannot be divisible *ad infinitum*. If Condillac is thought to side with the Leibnizian position about the existence of monads, he would only be thought to do so while maintaining a strong skepticism that invalidates many other details of the Leibnizian account.

4. The Principle of Restriction

Despite these limitations, does this mean that Condillac wishes to elaborate what Wolff calls a general ontology that aims at the determination of the kinds of metaphysical entities that constitute the world? Does he imply that what exists fundamentally in the world are spiritual entities, called monads, which would make the soul the human constituent that is ontologically prior? It is undeniable that some passages might lead us to believe that the prize essay exposes an ontology of monadic and perceptive beings, wherein matter or extension does not belong to the primary and fundamental entities of reality. For instance, the following excerpt appears to take such a direction:

> We cannot know anything save through perceptions that we relate back to ourselves and outside of ourselves; and the consciousness that we have of ourselves makes us regard as outside of ourselves all the things that are distinguished from it, and as one outside the other, all those that are between them. It is therefore a necessary consequence of our way of knowing that the beings that we distinguish appear to us as one outside the other. This is (the origin of) the phenomenon of extension.
> (*Les Monades*, 317)

In a way that is very similar to Leibniz, Condillac analyzes the notion of extension with the help of our perceptive abilities and concludes that we conceive of the compound nature of extension when it is compared with other parts of bodies.[19] Bodies are not extended beings but aggregates of simple things or monads (*Les Monades*, 318). And if extension is not a real determination of bodies, the same should be said about properties that depend on it such as location, figure, situation, and motion. Condillac agrees that this position might frighten the imagination, but it corresponds to the knowledge that we have of ourselves and of things outside of ourselves.

This interpretation may seem plausible, but to suppose that Condillac's monadology mostly aims to establish a form of ontological idealism is partially incorrect.[20] This position is never clearly formulated, nor does it seem to be the common trend of his work. Establishing a general ontology of monads would also go against the way in which Condillac conceives metaphysics in the *Essai*. As it has already been noted, only the weaker form of metaphysics is acceptable, whereas the more ambitious one, which searches for the general essence and causes of things, must be forbidden. Here, I argue that the scope of Condillac's monadology lies elsewhere. It mainly concerns cosmological topics that were discussed at length during the same period among scientists and philosophers, especially at the Berlin Academy. In other words, the prize essay pertains to specific questions in metaphysics of nature rather than the attempt to establish a fundamental ontology, as was the case for Wolff and some of his disciples. Sensation remains the sole source of knowledge, but Condillac appears to be largely interested in using it to resolve cosmological questions that are useful to physics and other natural sciences. The problem of the divisibility of matter is a first, important, theoretical position, but there are other reflections regarding cosmology that ought to be considered as well.

In the same chapter on monads, the epistemological restriction that was previously mentioned is clearly formulated to guide anyone who wants to discuss metaphysical questions concerning the world, its constituents, and its general organization. The metaphysics of nature is conceivable if we bear in mind that it cannot venture beyond what experience teaches us. This was already applied in the analysis of monads: sensation tells us that monads exist and that they compose bodies, for we properly perceive simple elements in bodies; yet sensation alone cannot determine the internal essence of these entities. By generalizing this principle, no metaphysical principle could express the internal constitution of things, to borrow from Locke's expression (*Essay*, III.6.9, 444). This analysis of the notion of extension can be a good illustration: Condillac considers extension to be described in terms of perceptions, not necessarily because he intends to adopt an idealist approach in metaphysics, but because an ontologization of extension would violate the epistemological restriction according to which any truth must be based on experience. The criticism is clearly directed toward Descartes and the Cartesians who claim that the essence of bodies is extension:

> It is necessary to avoid two errors with respect to which Cartesians have fallen. The first is to imagine that the ideas we have of extension and motion correspond to the reality of things; the second is to judge that extension is what is first in matter, when we imagine nothing that is prior to it. What basis would we have for believing that there are no other qualities in substances than those of which we have ideas?
>
> (*Les Monades*, 321)

Both errors originate from the same mistaken belief that ideas of sensation provide knowledge of the internal structure of bodies. Nothing in our experience permits us to claim that extension and motion are real ontological properties of bodies nor that extension constitutes the very essence of matter. There could be other properties that remain inaccessible to our senses. On the other hand, to claim that extension, motion, figure, and other material properties are phenomena, as Condillac does, does not signify that we can explain how monads constitute extended bodies nor how phenomenal entities are the result of monadic activities. It simply implies that experience limits us to treat them as appearances that depend on perception, that their aggregative nature is the result of simple substances that remain unknown to us. For Condillac, this principle of restriction not only detects metaphysical theories that have no full empirical basis, like Cartesian ontology, but also adequately circumscribes the scope of physics and metaphysics. It tells us that we must consider corporeal properties as phenomena, that these phenomena presuppose monadological entities, yet that the relationship between monads and phenomena will nonetheless remain a mystery for us. This is the reason why Condillac's position should be considered as a *negative* monadology:

> We must therefore, once again, be firmly convinced that it is not possible for us to discover in simple beings the first principles of phenomena, and that consequently physics must consider things only according to the order and the dependency of phenomena, by explaining them one by the other, and by observing how the last originate from the first.
>
> (*Les Monades*, 321–2)

5. The Order of Things

In the last chapters, Condillac turns his attention to the cosmological problems of the general order of things in the world, including souls and bodies, and the reality of space and time.[21] Quite clearly, both sets of interrogations relate to lively debates in the metaphysics of nature. Let us first examine the question of the order of things, which became an unavoidable and topical question, at least in Germany, given that Wolffian philosophy dominated the question. As is well known, Wolff was the first, during the early modern period, to relate objects of metaphysics to specific domains. The world, as an important entity discussed in metaphysics since Antiquity, is conceived of as the object of rational cosmology (*Discursus praeliminaris*, §§77–8, GW II, 1.1, 36). His *Cosmologia generalis* is devoted to the world, and it approaches problems related to its order and constituents, the reality of space and time, the laws of motion, and its perfection. Wolff provides details about his theory of elements or simple substances, which is partly inspired by Leibniz's monadology, while also strongly distances itself from the latter. Wolff mainly argues that bodies are composed of simple and active elements, but he refuses to consider them, as Leibniz does, as possessing perceptions (*Cosmologia* §182; GW II, 4, 146).

In the *Cosmologia*, Wolff is primarily interested in the relationships between things that constitute the world. A world or universe is even defined as a series of finite entities that are simultaneously and successively connected (*Cosmologia* §48; GW II, 4, 44). It is from this definition that the rest of his cosmology follows, especially his account of the essential attributes of the universe. As mentioned earlier, Wolff's cosmology is one of the main sources from which Condillac derives his understanding of Leibnizianism. But he was aware that Wolff also attempted to differentiate himself from Leibniz regarding the order and relation of things in the world. When Wolff maintains that bodies are causally interconnected, Leibniz considers that these external causal relations are founded in the internal perceptive abilities of the monads (*Les Monades*, 286). Since such a conception is difficult to ground for Wolff, he is therefore led to deny the perceptive power of simple substances.

It is no surprise that Condillac comes back during the second part of the prize essay to the question of the order or harmony of things in the world. As would be expected, our mind can say very little about how monads and bodies are metaphysically related to one another. But Condillac insists on the fact that what sensation tells us should not be neglected (*Les Monades*, 322). And it seems that it teaches us more than what could have been anticipated. His reasoning can be reconstructed in three steps: the first consists of the claim that experience confirms that monads change according to an internal principle. If bodies change, then the monads that compose them must also change. Considering that they are endowed with an ability to act, which is already an additional result, it should also be possible to determine whether these modifications follow one another depending on external or internal causes. Yet Condillac repeats the argument that we know at least that our own soul, which is a kind of monad, passes from one perception or sensation to another according to an internal power. The ontological nature of such a force remains unknown, but force is undoubtedly internal to the soul. The conclusion that other substances act the same way is a mere conjecture that can only be weakly confirmed. If, however, it is necessary to identify a causal origin by which the modifications of the substance are produced, Condillac seems to favor an internal principle of change at this stage.

Secondly, Condillac dwells on the question of the interaction between things, which is obviously central to any cosmological doctrine. Although the possibility of external causation is still affirmed, it appears that things might metaphysically interact in an ideal way alone. The main argument pertains to the extraneous distinction between monads. If monads are truly external to each other, then they cannot act on one another:

> Now created monads could not act on each other; for a being cannot act where it is not. Yet we have seen that they are properly apart from each other. On the contrary, God can act on all of them because they are all in him. I will demonstrate this elsewhere. That a substance cannot act where it is not; this is to me evident. All action is a modification of the substance that acts; thus a modification cannot be separated from its subject.
>
> (*Les Monades*, 323)

Without knowing what the essence of monads is, nor how they compose bodies and thus form aggregates, Condillac clearly draws from a quite straightforward Leibnizian idea, which is that finite beings or monads do not act on one another. But when Leibniz insists on the internal closure of monads to explain that they have no windows through which their modes could come out and influence external substances (*Monadology* §7, GP VI, 607) Condillac rests on the same principle of restriction to claim that experience simply cannot account for the external interaction between two or several substances. The fact that things are external to perception is justified by Condillac's own definition of sensation, in which the act of perception is always distinguished from the object that it represents, whether the latter is a real entity outside the mind or not.[22] This does not mean that other kinds of interactions are impossible *per se*, but only that the sole causal relationship that is empirically conceivable rests on an internal principle of change.

In the same passage, Condillac asserts that God, the primary monad (*Les Monades*, 349),[23] is the only substance that can act on all finite beings. This leads to the reappropriation of another central Leibnizian idea, that of universal harmony, and more specifically of the pre-established harmony in the soul and the body. In fact, the very idea of universal harmony is an expansion of the more local correspondence between the soul and the body, both originating from God's action:

> My soul, for instance, experiences different successive successions [sic], and it will experience them equally in the same order, when it is not united to any body. My body also, without recourse to its influence, changes state continuously, and these changes are only the effects of its mechanism. In a word, everything occurs in the soul as if there were no body, and everything occurs in the bodies, as if there were no souls, and the harmony of these two substances consists in the sequence of changes in one that corresponds perfectly to the sequence of changes in the other, and not that they act on each other.
>
> (*Les Monades*, 323)

Later, Condillac goes on to state:

> To imagine the harmony of all the universe, at least as far as we can know, it suffices to represent it following what has been said about the harmony between the soul and the body.
>
> (*Les Monades*, 324)

The order of the world is thus based on the Leibnizian doctrine of pre-established harmony according to which there is no interaction between the soul and the body. By extension, there are also no such interactions between all finite beings in the universe, but only a harmony that takes its origin from God. Condillac carefully explains that his view does not lead to a kind of necessitarianism since the soul is not determined by corporeal actions. But most of Leibniz's doctrine remains, to the extent that Condillac even uses the clock analogy to illustrate how the soul and the body correspond to each other, although only in an ideal interaction (*Les Monades*, 325). The endorsement of universal harmony is certainly at odds with the rest of the prize essay because it contravenes the principle of restriction and implies many ideas that could not be grounded on experience. For instance, Condillac does not provide empirical evidence that the soul and the body are set like concordant clocks. The divine action on finite substances is also briefly elaborated, without there being any foundation in sensation. Despite these problems, it is evident that Condillac wishes to take part in the debates during his period that concern the soul-body relationship, but also those concerning Wolff's primary interrogation about the order and connection of things in the world. And Condillac's answers clearly rest on the elements of Leibniz's theory of universal harmony.

6. The Reality of Space

Another cosmological topic of the eighteenth century concerns the reality of space and time. Documented in ample detail, the period was dominated by the positions defended by Newton and Leibniz, the former claiming that space and time are real, absolute entities, and the latter arguing that they are relative and secondary properties. For Leibniz, space and time are respectively orders of coexistence and succession (Letter to Clarke of February 25, 1716, GP VII, 363). At the time, numerous thinkers attempted to expose conceptions that concurred either with Leibniz or Newton— among others, Wolff himself—but also Raphson, Hume, and Du Châtelet. The debate even resounded at the Berlin Academy, given that Euler wrote a paper on space and time that mostly aligned with the Newtonian doctrine (Euler 1751). For his part, Condillac provides reflections in the *Essai* to account for the origin of the idea of space. Contrary to the Lockean view, according to which space is a simple idea obtained with the help of sensation (*Essay*, II.xiii.11, 172), Condillac maintains that space is the result of an analytical reflexive procedure. More precisely, it requires a series of abstractions that begin with complex and particular ideas, the ideas of individual substances endowed with concrete qualities and end up with a simple and pure idea of space

(*Essai sur l'origine des connaissances*, OP I, 109). We find this explanation repeated in the prize essay (that space is perceived when the mind subtracts space from particular qualities), but also from other general ideas such as extension, motion, and divisibility (*Les Monades*, 329). Space is, thus, the notion of an empty being that is immobile and indivisible.

The originality of the prize essay rests elsewhere, however. It aims to prove that space is a phenomenon, so a secondary and relative being, which once again establishes him as a proponent of the thought of Leibniz rather than of Newton. Although space and time are both abundantly analyzed in the prize essay, let us emphasize the notion of space. The main argument is based on the monadic framework and the premise according to which monads are external to one another, which is why they are not actually connected causally:

> The perceptions that I experience, for instance, put relations between my thinking being and the rest of creatures, which distinguish it from them, as from so many things which are outside of it. By analogy, we can imagine such relations between all beings […] If simple beings cannot occupy real distinct locations, collections of such sorts of beings cannot as well. Therefore, bodies not being aggregates of simple beings, the connection of all, or the universe, does not occupy a more real space than a single being. In a word, space is only a phenomenon.
> (*Les Monades*, 325–6)

The fact that sensation should immediately enable us to make a distinction between the perceiving mind and external things is not obvious, and Condillac will revise this idea in the *Traité des sensations* to show how the mind, through the experience of the statue, manages to represent the external world essentially by means of tactile experiences. For now, Condillac presumes that the structure of sensation leads to the distinction between the inner experience and external things. In the chapter on monads, Condillac claims that "it is therefore a necessary consequence of our way of knowing that the beings we distinguish appear to us to be one outside the other" (*Les Monades*, 317). And because of this perceptual structure, the origin of the phenomenal notion of extension can be explained: extension, which is closely related to space, accompanies the sensation of a plurality of things that are external to one another. In fact, all the phenomenal properties of bodies, such as motion and figure, are accounted for through this fundamental characteristic of human sensation. For instance, motion results from the succession of external beings, namely, the perception of this linear passage from one to the other.

Space, which belongs to the same category, is therefore a phenomenon, not a real being, as Newtonians would argue. As we can read in the *Essai*, space is the representation of the order of things in an abstract way, that is to say, a generic idea that is mentally detached from concrete individuals. This conclusion authorizes us to invalidate unfounded positions: in the first place, it is metaphysically incorrect to say that beings, either monads or collections of monads, are located or situated in space. If space is a secondary and phenomenal being, and monads and their aggregates are primary metaphysical entities, the former cannot constitute a criterion of distinction or individuation for the latter. On the contrary, monads are non-extended, thus non-spatial beings, for space is the representation of their external and coexistent order (*Les Monades*, 326).

In the second place, Condillac wishes to defend a position concerning immensity, which could be associated with space as an empty and infinite being. Without offering any clear references, it seems that what Condillac has in mind is Newton's idea according to which space is a *sensorium Dei* (the sensorium of God), the infinite place through which God perceives all things in the world (Newton 1706, 315; Letter to Leibniz of January 10, 1716, GP VII, 361–2). On the basis of his quasi Leibnizian conception of space, Condillac appears to reject this position, or more precisely, he rejects the association between divine immensity and pure space:

> Indeed, since with several simple beings it cannot be measured or filled, however it is multiplied. Immensity is thus one, simple, unextended, like God. Therefore, it cannot contain beings that are really extended. Therefore, it cannot contain truly extended beings. Thus everything contributes to proving that there exist only simple beings, or aggregates of simple beings, and that the phenomenon of extension and space does not at all conform to the reality of things.
>
> (*Les Monades*, 328)

In sum, immensity has nothing to do with space or extension, which is an abstraction, and must rather be related to God's perfect and infinite essence. The reality of space as an absolute being is thus false because it pretends to locate simple substances and their aggregates and because it confuses the phenomenal order of things with divine immensity and perfection. Once again, Condillac cannot explain how monads could produce extension or space, nor how space, as well as time, is the result of the order of monads. He simply notes that our sensation makes this distinction and forbids reifying or divinizing space. This is, of course, another important result of Condillac's cosmology regarding a crucial discussion at the time. Space and time are phenomena, and we should never employ them to characterize the metaphysical structure of the world. Monads and aggregates are clearly fundamental elements of the universe, not the space and time in which they would be situated.

7. Conclusion

Condillac's essay response to the Berlin Academy prize competition displays certain unique aspects of his philosophy. Despite the empiricist principle of restriction, he offers a new monadology that prevents us from determining the first cause and essential nature of monads and aggregates, while providing solutions to certain cosmological problems that were crucial during his time. More precisely, his cosmology enables us to discern bad theories with the help of what has been called a negative monadology—a doctrine of monads that does not explain their true essence. Three of these theories have been analyzed here: the indivisibility of matter, the causal relationship between substances, and the absolute reality of space. These doctrines are considered to be erroneous because the existence of monads precludes such metaphysical views. At the same time, this revised monadology contains sufficient principles to provide answers for different cosmological solutions. Condillac's defense of universal and pre-established harmony is certainly the most astonishing of these solutions—it is needless for us to repeat why the doctrine of universal harmony appears to violate his principle of restriction.

The originality of such a cosmology becomes more evident when compared with his later works, notably the *Traité des systèmes* that was published one year after the essay. There, Condillac claims that "It is therefore necessary, in order to conceive the monads, not only to know what they are not; it is also necessary to know what they are" (*Traité des systèmes*, OP I, 160). He then argues that Leibniz does not offer a sufficiently rigorous demonstration that monads are perceptive substances endowed with force and that their order forms a general harmony of things. Hence, this system must be refuted since it exceeds the knowledge we derive from sensation. The prize essay exactly tries to do the contrary by deducing cosmological views from a theory of monads that does not pretend to account for their essence. This was perhaps a risky, if not impossible, task to achieve, though it illustrates Condillac's conviction that his empiricist metaphysics of the mind, on the one hand, and a sort of Leibnizian monadology, on the other, are compatible. As he later claims in a letter to Cramer: "Leibniz's definitions are very admissible, when they are separated, as you do, from this philosopher's hypotheses; but that is what the Leibnizians would not want to do" (*Lettres inédites*, 95). Perhaps he had his attempt at the prize essay in mind.

Notes

1 On speculative philosophy at the Berlin Academy, see Duchesneau et al. 2022.
2 For a complete list of these competitions, see Harnack 1970, II, 305–10.
3 On Euler's contribution, see Leduc 2013.
4 For details on this competition and its place in the intellectual debates, see Broman 2012.
5 For this text, see Rey 2013.
6 This selection of answers was published in 1748; see Justi et al. 1748.
7 Condillac affirms that his chapter on the knowledge of God is entirely derived from the prize essay: "Ce chapitre est presque tiré tout entier d'une Dissertation que j'ai faite, il y a quelques années, qui est imprimée dans un recueil de l'Académie de Berlin, et à laquelle je n'ai pas mis mon nom" (*Traité des animaux*, OP I, 365).
8 Laurence Bongie introduced and published Condillac's prize essay in 1980. See Condillac 1980.
9 For an interpretation of Condillac's idealism, see Baertschi 1988.
10 For instance, see Adams 1994.
11 To a lesser extent, Condillac also refers to Michael Hansch, who was the first Latin translator of the *Monadology* and had provided a systematic exposition of Leibniz's philosophy. See Hansch 1728.
12 This approach will also be the one that Condillac takes in the *Traité des systèmes*. See Leduc 2018.

13 Nevertheless, this is not a simple confusion of the two doctrines. Regarding a major theoretical element, Condillac was right: when Leibniz confers to any simple substance or monad a capacity of perception or representation, Wolff, for his part, restricts such a capacity to the souls endowed with consciousness. Taking the Wolffian expositional order as a guideline is thus clearly a choice, and not a blind spot or negligence. See Condillac's *Les Monades*, 286–7.
14 As is well documented, Wolff prefers the title "elements" for the simple substances composing bodies rather than monads (*Cosmologia*, §§181–2; GW II, 4, 145–6).
15 See Fontenelle 1727.
16 Similar analyses have been provided in the *Essai* (*Essai sur l'origine de la connaissance*, OP I, 108–9).
17 Letter to Clarke of August 1716, GP VII, 395–6.
18 Condillac knows the *Monadologie* through Hansch's translation (*Traité des systèmes*, OP I, 159).
19 This idea was already in the *Essai* (*Essai sur l'origine de la connaissance*, OP I, 109).
20 Condillac's later works focus on the question of idealism. See Baertschi 1988.
21 The final chapter pertains to God and has little to do with his monadology, and will thus be set aside.
22 Condillac, *Essai sur l'origine des connaissances*, OP I, 9.
23 Condillac offers a rather common interpretation of the Leibnizian doctrine here, according to which God is the first and supreme monad. Since monads can be created and annihilated for Leibniz, such a category is unsuitable for divine nature (*Monadologie*, §6, GP VI, 607).

Bibliography

Adams, Robert Merrihew. 1994. *Leibniz: Determinist, Theist, Idealist*. Oxford: Oxford University Press.

Baertschi, Bernard. 1988. "Le problème du réalisme chez Condillac." *Les Études philosophiques*, 3, 371–93.

Broman, Thomas. 2012. "Metaphysics for an Enlightened Public: The Controversy over Monads in Germany, 1746–1748." *Isis*, 103, 1, 1–23.

Condillac, Étienne Bonnot de. 1748. "Les Monades." In *Dissertation qui a remporté le prix proposé par l'Académie royale des sciences et belles lettres sur le système des monades avec les pièces qui ont concouru*, 259–362. Berlin: Haude and Spener.

Condillac, Étienne Bonnot de. 1947–51. *Œuvres philosophiques de Condillac*, 3 vols, edited by Georges Le Roy. Paris: Presses Universitaires de France.

Condillac, Étienne Bonnot de. 1953. *Lettres inédites à Gabriel Cramer*, edited by Georges Le Roy. Paris: Presses Universitaires de France.

Condillac, Étienne Bonnot de. 1980. *Les Monades*, edited by Laurence L. Bongie. Oxford: The Voltaire Foundation at the Taylor Institution.

Duchesneau, François, Daniel Dumouchel, Angela Ferraro, and Christian Leduc. 2022. *Philosophie spéculative à l'Académie de Berlin. Mémoires 1745–1769*. Paris: Vrin.

Euler, Leonhard. 1746. *Gedanken von den Elementen der Körper*. Berlin: Haude and Spener.

Euler, Leonhard. 1751. "Réflexions sur l'espace et le temps." In *Histoire de l'Académie Royale des Sciences et des Belles-Lettres*, 324–33. Berlin: Haude and Spener.

Fontenelle, Bernard le Bouyer de. 1727. *Éléments de la géométrie de l'infini*. Paris: Imprimerie Royale.

Justi, Johann Heinrich Gottlob von et al. 1748. *Dissertation qui a remporté le prix proposé par l'Académie royale des sciences et belles lettres sur le système des monades avec les pièces qui ont concouru*. Berlin: Haude and Spener.

Hansch, Michael. 1728. *Godefridi Guilielmi Leibnitii Principia philosophiae, more geometrico demonstrata*. Frankfurt/Leipzig: Monath.

Harnack, Adolf von. 1970. *Geschichte der Königlich Preußischen Akademie der Wissenschaften zu Berlin*, 2 vols. Hildesheim: Olms.

Leduc, Christian. 2013. "Euler et le monadisme." *Studia Leibnitiana*, 45, 2, 150–69.

Leduc, Christian. 2018. "Condillac et la critique d'un système. Le cas leibnizien." *Dialogue*, 57, 4, 767–89.

Leibniz, Gottfried Wilhelm. 1965. *Die philosophischen Schriften von G. W. Leibniz*, 7 vols, edited by C. I. Gerhardt. Hildesheim: Olms.

Locke, John. 1975. *An Essay Concerning Human Understanding*, edited by Peter Nidditch. Oxford: Clarendon Press.

Newton, Isaac. 1706. *Optice sive De reflexionibus, refractionibus, inflexionibus et coloribus lucis*. London: Smith and Walford.

Rey, Anne-Lise. 2013. "Les monades selon Samuel Formey." *Studia Leibnitiana*, 45, 2, 135–49.

Wolff, Christian. 1962–. *Gesammelte Werke*. Hildesheim: Olms.

4

Between Optimism and Anti-Optimism: Prémontval's "Middle Point"

Lloyd Strickland

1. Introduction

In 1753, the Berlin Academy decided that the focus of its prize essay contest of 1755 would be optimism. The official minutes of the Academy for June 7, 1753, record the decision:[1]

> The question proposed for the prize of 1755 was stated in these terms.
> We request an examination of Pope's system, contained in the proposition "All is good".
> It is a matter of: (1) determining the true meaning of that proposition according to the hypothesis of its author; (2) comparing it with the system of optimism, or the choice of the best, to indicate the connections and differences between them; (3) lastly, to put forward arguments that will be thought most fitting to confirm or destroy this system.[2]

In fact, the question had been decided more than three weeks earlier. The Academy's minutes for May 17, 1753, state: "The class of speculative philosophy determined, by a majority vote, the question to propose for the prize of 1755, and the choice fell on the Examination of Pope's System."[3] The minutes also identify the members of the class of speculative philosophy who collectively made that decision: Johann Philipp Heinius (1688–1775), Nicolas de Béguelin (1714–89), Jean-Bernard Merian (1723–1807), Johann Georg Sulzer (1720–79), André-Pierre Le Guay de Prémontval (1716–64), and the Academy's perpetual secretary, Jean Henri Samuel Formey (1711–97). Five of the six also served as judges when, two years later, the time came to select the winning essay—only Béguelin was absent for that.

In all, eighteen essays were submitted by the deadline of January 1, 1755,[4] and on June 5 it was announced that the winning entrant was Adolf Friedrich Reinhard (1726–83), chamber secretary to the Duke of Mecklenburg-Strelitz.[5] The title of Reinhard's essay, "Le système de Mr Pope sur la perfection de monde, comparé à celui de Mr de Leibnitz, avec un examen de l'optimisme" (The System of Mr. Pope Concerning the Perfection of the World, Compared with That of Leibniz, with an Examination of Optimism), gives no hint that the work is a strident attack on optimism. The crowning of Reinhard's essay, which is at times novel but ultimately second-rate, quickly attracted a great deal of criticism, from both inside and outside the Academy. As a result of this furor, there appeared a much more original contribution to the optimism debate. It was the work not of any of the entrants, but of one of the judges: Prémontval, who had joined the Academy in June 1752. Prémontval was disappointed that all of the essay submissions were either pro- or anti-optimism, despite this being in line with the Academy's original instructions "to confirm or destroy" the system of optimism. By his own admission, he had surreptitiously attempted to influence the entrants by sketching out in a series of books published between 1754 and 1755 a "middle point" between the polarized pro- and anti-optimist positions—in essence a novel form of meliorism. The aim of this chapter is to contextualize and elucidate Prémontval's highly original "middle point," as outlined implicitly in the aforementioned books and much more explicitly in a series of writings published after the 1755 essay contest had concluded. We shall begin with some context: in Section 2, we shall examine the machinations behind the 1755 essay contest and, in particular, the mystery of who cast the deciding vote, while in Section 3 we shall briefly consider Reinhard's essay, the furor that surrounded its selection as the winning entry, and Prémontval's response to Reinhard. The focus of Section 4 will be Prémontval's middle point between optimism and anti-optimism, and Section 5 will consider how Prémontval's meliorism anticipated later thinking.

2. The 1755 Prize Essay and the Mystery of the Deciding Vote

Let us start by detailing the circumstances under which the prize for the 1755 essay contest was awarded, or rather, the differing, indeed conflicting accounts of how Reinhard's essay came to be crowned. It is well known that the Academy, at the time, was split between factions that could be loosely described as Leibnizian-Wolffian and Newtonian. The division was embedded right at the top of the Academy's hierarchy— Pierre-Louis Moreau de Maupertuis (1698–1759), the Academy's president, was a fervent supporter of natural philosophy *à la* Newton, while Formey, the Academy's perpetual secretary, was a supporter and indeed renowned popularizer of Leibniz's and Wolff's rationalist philosophy. The members of the class of speculative philosophy, who had set the 1755 prize essay contest on optimism and would ultimately be its judges, were similarly divided. One of its pro-Leibnizian members, Johann Georg Sulzer, believed the numbers were on its side to ensure that a pro-Leibnizian (for which read: pro-optimism) entrant would win the contest. To that end, Sulzer approached one of his friends, Martin Künzli (1709–65), encouraging him to submit a pro-optimism essay. On August 10, 1754, Sulzer wrote to Künzli, urging him to get on with the task.[6] In a subsequent letter of September 22 the same year, Sulzer intimated that he would be able to guarantee victory for Künzli, writing:

> I am one of your judges and at least three quarters of your judges have the principles that you inevitably have too. I can tell you in confidence: [Johann Philipp] Heinius,

[Samuel] Formey, [Jean-Bertrand] Merian and myself actually make up the entire class of philosophers at the Academy. The first two are sworn Leibnizians, Merian on his own cannot do anything.

(Hirzel 1891, 110)

Sulzer's claim here is untrue: the Academy's class of speculative philosophy also included Prémontval and Béguelin. Sulzer may have thought it not worth mentioning Béguelin, who was sympathetic to the philosophies of Leibniz and Wolff, on the grounds that he was unlikely to be present for the vote, since at the time he rarely attended the Academy's meetings (in fact he attended only a single meeting of the Academy between May 1753, when the question on optimism had been agreed, and June 1755, when the winning essay was announced). But it is unclear why Sulzer failed to mention Prémontval, who was at the time a regular attendee of the Academy's meetings. In any case, buoyed by Sulzer's encouragement, Künzli duly submitted his essay. Even after learning how many other essays had been submitted, Sulzer remained confident that Künzli's would prevail. Writing on May 3, 1755, to Künzli, Sulzer declared that only three of the submissions were being seriously considered:

In four weeks, our prize is to be handed out. I don't want to give you any firm hope of that just yet. But chances are you'll get it, that is, by rights. There is only one point about which I'm not in agreement with Dr. Heinius, who finds another writing as excellent as yours. This much is certain, that only 3 came under consideration; among them is yours.

(Hirzel 1891, 111)

But Sulzer's confidence was misplaced and his machinations to no avail: on June 5, 1755, the Academy announced that it had awarded the prize to Reinhard.[7] What had happened? Here is where we are presented with two accounts that differ in a key detail.

The first comes from Sulzer, who provided a (now lost) confidential report to his friend, Christoph Martin Wieland (1733–1813), who claimed in a letter to another friend, Zimmermann,[8] that initially "the votes were divided between reason and unreason," but then the perpetual secretary of the Academy, Samuel Formey, who had initially been in favor of Künzli's essay, gave the casting vote to Reinhard's out of consideration for the Academy's president, Maupertuis, who as a vocal opponent of the "Leibnizian-Wolffian" philosophy was no supporter of optimism. Since Maupertuis abstained from voting,[9] it was left to the members of the class of speculative philosophy to decide which essay to crown. Sulzer pointed the finger of blame at three members in particular:

Merian and Prémontval are quite unhinged, and Formey is a most miserly and vile man; the first two deny the principle of sufficient reason in their publications, and Formey talks and writes for money. So what else can one expect from such men but, as you put it, to turn the rights of humanity upside down.

(Hirzel 1891, 115)

It doesn't take much reading between the lines here to interpret Sulzer as claiming that Formey, along with Merian and Prémontval, had voted for Reinhard's essay (with

Sulzer and Heinius voting for Künzli's essay). But the story Sulzer privately fed back to Künzli is not quite the same as the one that Prémontval told much more publicly after the result was announced.

Prémontval's account of the voting comes from a letter he wrote to Reinhard, the winning entrant, on July 18, 1755, a little over a month after the result had been announced. In this letter, Prémontval explicitly tells Reinhard that the casting vote had been his: "Know, then, that with the votes equal between your piece and another, I—as much a supporter of optimism as I am—twice tipped the scales on your side" (Prémontval 1757, II: 69). We shall see in Section 4 that Prémontval's claim to be a supporter of optimism is not as straightforward as he makes out here. In any case, Prémontval continues:

> The first time [Prémontval voted for Reinhard's essay], our very astonished Wolffians protested that I had not been able to read the other piece [i.e. Künzli's essay], which is in German.[10] I agreed, and asked that it be explained to me. This having been done the next day with great precision, I firmly persisted in the preference I had given to number VII, which is yours.
>
> (Prémontval 1757, II: 69–70)

Prémontval subsequently published this letter in 1757, in volume 2 of his *Vues philosophiques* (Philosophical Views).[11] His account was not publicly disputed, and only contradicted by claims made in the private correspondence between Sulzer and his friends that was published at the end of the nineteenth century.

On the matter of the voting in the 1755 contest, scholars have tended to give preference to Sulzer's account over Prémontval's. For example, Hirzel and Harnack both relate Sulzer's account in detail and relegate Prémontval's to a footnote, giving the impression that the former is more reliable than the latter.[12] Other scholars, for example, Hellwig and Calinger, present Sulzer's account and do not mention Prémontval's at all.[13] Sulzer's account certainly plays into the well-established narrative about competing factions within the Academy. Nevertheless, there are good reasons to treat Sulzer's account with caution. First of all, it must be remembered that Sulzer was writing privately for Künzli and his circle after having tried and failed to get the 1755 essay prize awarded to Künzli. He would have known that the recipients of his letters had no way to verify his claims. Following on from this, second, Sulzer's description of Prémontval's place in the internal politics of the Berlin Academy is at best inaccurate and at worst plainly false. He appears to have informed Künzli that Prémontval and Merian were the stooges of the Academy's president, Maupertuis, as Künzli reports on April 25, 1757:

> Mr. Sulzer writes: "This Prémontval and his comrade, Merian, serve under the whip of the Frenchman Maupertuis, who has set his mind to take revenge on Leibniz and Wolff for allowing these Germans to be greater philosophers and mathematicians than the French themselves".
>
> (Hirzel 1891, 117)

Sulzer is partly correct here, for it was no secret that Maupertuis was at the time hostile to both Leibniz and Wolff.[14] But the first part of Sulzer's claim, that Prémontval was under the thumb of Maupertuis, is ludicrous.[15] Prémontval was certainly hostile to Leibniz and Wolff, though this was hardly at Maupertuis' bidding because he was no less hostile to Maupertuis![16] On October 19, 1752, less than four months after he had been admitted to the Academy, Prémontval delivered a memoir attacking a proof of God's existence developed by Maupertuis—a rather brazen attack on the Academy's president and on his own home turf too.[17] Even a casual glance at Prémontval's work reveals that he was no respecter of reputation or status and that he was as far from Maupertuis philosophically as he was from Leibniz and Wolff. This in fact made it difficult for him to find publishers for his work, as he complained to a friend in February 1755: "It is known that those [i.e. booksellers] of Berlin are dissuaded from dealing with a man without reputation, equally unwelcome among Maupertuists and Wolffians, freethinkers and hypocrites."[18]

Unfortunately, we have no other accounts of how the votes were cast in the 1755 prize essay contest, so no way of checking whether the decisive vote was cast by Formey or by Prémontval. But there are, as we have seen, good reasons to doubt the reliability of at least some of the information Sulzer privately fed back to his friends.[19] Of course, the fact that Sulzer's account of the prize essay voting is sometimes doubtful does not mean that Prémontval's is reliable. Though here it should be noted that Prémontval did publish his account in 1757, thus opening himself up to public scrutiny and potential public correction from other eyewitnesses in a way that Sulzer did not—and it should be further noted that no such correction was ever made. Furthermore, it is difficult to see what ulterior motive Prémontval could have had for being untruthful about how the votes were cast. Certainly, in telling Reinhard that he had voted for his essay, Prémontval was not attempting to win Reinhard's favor or gain a supporter; in fact, as we shall see, in his letter to Reinhard, Prémontval went on to tell him just how bad his winning essay was!

3. Reinhard's Winning Essay and Prémontval's Response

In order to understand Prémontval's misgivings about Reinhard's essay, a brief overview of its contents is in order.[20] The first half of Reinhard's essay is concerned to show that Pope and Leibniz taught the same doctrine ("No difference; same mind, same ideas, same system"), though his methodology is somewhat questionable (Reinhard 1755, 8). Reinhard expounds Pope's ideas at length, supporting his detailed exposition with numerous quotations from the poet while occasionally interjecting that Leibniz held precisely the same ideas, though Reinhard does not offer any textual evidence to support these claims (while he cites Pope frequently, he does not cite Leibniz at all). In this part of the essay, Reinhard demonstrates an impressive knowledge of Pope's poem and an unfamiliarity with Leibniz that is equally noteworthy. In one of the more egregious examples, he states that on the principles of Leibniz's optimism "it necessarily follows that God has created all possible substances" (Reinhard 1755, 12).

The second half of Reinhard's essay contains a critique of optimism, which consists of two main points. The first objection charges that optimism strips God of free will, while the second is directed at the optimist's claim that there is a single best possible world, which Reinhard dubs "the dogma of the unique greatest perfection" (Reinhard 1755, 29). The first objection focuses on Leibniz's insistence that God's perfect nature is such that he would choose to create no other world than the best, to which Reinhard responds: "If God's perfections contain the determining reason of his volitions then there is no longer any freedom; all his actions are as necessary as mathematical truths" (Reinhard 1755, 38). The second objection, which is unique to Reinhard, seeks to establish that an intelligent being's primary end, or chief goal, is usually served by multiple secondary or tertiary ends, and that all of these ends can be attained in many different ways. This is true also for world-creation, he supposes, since in addition to the many different primary and secondary ends God could propose, there are likely many different ways of attaining each and every one of them and the optimist is in no position to deny that some of these will be just as good as others, leading to worlds of equal perfection.[21] Hence there is no single best world and thus no requirement for God to create one world in particular.

Reinhard's essay was a controversial choice as winner and it soon attracted widespread criticism. The Academy's perpetual secretary, Samuel Formey, found Reinhard's reasoning so weak that he was uncharacteristically moved to publish a critical review of the prize-winning essay in the *Nouvelle bibliothèque germanique*, a journal under his editorial control (Formey 1756, especially 29–32). Other criticisms were leveled by a pre-critical Immanuel Kant and Moses Mendelssohn.[22] Prémontval, as we know, opted for a more direct approach, writing to Reinhard to tell him that despite his misgivings about Reinhard's essay, he had voted for it anyway. And Prémontval was not shy about revealing his misgivings: in his letter to Reinhard, immediately after claiming that he had twice voted for Reinhard's essay, Prémontval states: "Not—in truth, sir, I tell you frankly—not that I am much edified by it. What ideas you have of God! And you live in peace!" (Prémontval 1757, II: 69–70)

Prémontval's concern was that Reinhard had insisted that God was entirely free in his choice of world, and indeed free to choose whether to create or not, it being a matter of complete indifference to him whether other beings existed or not (Reinhard 1755, 36). For Prémontval, this made God's actions entirely arbitrary. As he wrote in *On Chance under the Rule of Providence*: "a God who wills things without any reason for willing them, or who has no other reason for willing them except that he wills to will them" is "in a word, pure arbitrariness."[23] As abhorrent as such thinking was to Prémontval, he told Reinhard that the pro-optimism essay by Künzli had an even worse failing: "What made me give preference to your piece, Sir, in addition to the spirit of research I noticed in it, is largely its distance from Leibnizian fatalism, which is even worse than your arbitrariness" (Prémontval 1757, II: 72–3).[24] Although in his letter Prémontval objected only to the idea of an arbitrary God, this was not the only problem he had with Reinhard's essay. In fact, Prémontval found so much wrong with it that he compiled a lengthy point-by-point rebuttal, enclosing it with his letter to Reinhard. Two years later, he published both his letter and his rebuttal in volume 2 of his *Vues philosophiques*.[25]

In his letter, in addition to telling Reinhard what was wrong with his essay, Prémontval gave a brief and often elusive sketch of his own position vis-à-vis optimism:

> Surely what the greatest wisdom prefers is the wisest; what the greatest goodness does is the best, or else there is neither wisdom nor goodness if there is no object of wisdom and goodness, that is, a most perfect possible, the object of the greatest wisdom, and a best possible, the object of the greatest goodness. But sovereign wisdom, Sir, and sovereign goodness, do not do everything. We do something too, we others who make up this world; an infinite collection of stray and wicked beings, existing of themselves in a perpetual conflict of actions and interests. We do, and do only too much: here is the knot. Is there so much mystery there? This is what I intend to bring to the highest point of demonstration in my *Essay on Theocharis*.
>
> (Prémontval 1757, II: 71–2)

Prémontval never did write his projected *Essay on Theocharis*. Eight years later, in 1763, the year before his death, he stated that he was earnestly thinking about starting it![26] Nevertheless, he did develop many of the ideas raised in his letter to Reinhard, most notably in an essay entitled "General Misunderstanding on the Question of Optimism," which was written to serve as a sort of preface to his letter to Reinhard and the lengthy rebuttal of his essay when both were published.[27] Prémontval devotes much of this essay to sketching out his own views and presenting them as the "middle point" between the sharply pro- and anti-optimist positions he had encountered in the essays submitted to the Academy's prize contest. Let us turn, then, to Prémontval's "middle point."

4. Prémontval's "Middle Point" between Optimism and Anti-optimism

Prémontval creates the space for his "middle point" by drawing a sharp distinction between these two propositions:

1. God essentially chooses the best among all the possibles.
2. The world is the best of all possible worlds.[28]

He rightly notes that both partisans and detractors of optimism typically conflated the two, or at best construed (2) as the logical consequence of (1). Against this, however, Prémontval claims that while (1) is necessarily true, (2) is completely false. The first proposition is true because it is of the essence of an all-wise, all-powerful, and all-good being to always choose the greatest good or best course:

> God is as essentially all that he is as the triangle is angular, the circle is round, and two and two are four. God is as essentially good as intelligent. God loves and wills a greater good as essentially as he knows this greater good, and he knows

it essentially, indispensably, necessarily, logically, and metaphysically. What God wills, what God does, is therefore essentially, indispensably, necessarily, logically, and metaphysically the best.[29]

Needless to say, for Prémontval, affirming the first proposition thus amounts to accepting that God's actions are necessitated (albeit by his own nature rather than by something external to him).[30] While such a thought was generally anathema to optimists and anti-optimists alike,[31] Prémontval considers it an inevitable consequence of the traditional view that God is essentially perfectly good and perfectly wise. Hence the first proposition, that God essentially chooses the best among all the possibles, is necessarily true.

Yet Prémontval denies that accepting the first proposition automatically entails accepting the second proposition, that the world is the best of all possible worlds. Indeed, he insists that this proposition must be rejected on the grounds that our world could clearly be better. He states: "The smallest good action that we can perform but don't, would make it better. The most trivial crime, the slightest error into which we could avoiding falling but into which we do fall, makes it worse."[32] On the surface, such thinking appears overly simplistic, inasmuch as it seems to presuppose that actions and events occur in isolation, such that improving the world would be rather like correcting typos in a manuscript, each corrected error leaving everything else unchanged.[33] But Prémontval does not base his rejection of the second proposition on such sloppy reasoning. Instead, he points to the traditional idea that God commands certain actions, prohibits others, and even promises punishment for transgressors. Since God is perfectly wise and wants only the best, Prémontval reasons that God promotes good actions because they make the world better and he forbids bad ones because they make it worse; if this were not the case, if the world was in some way made better by certain transgressions, it would be perverse, indeed absurd for a perfectly wise God to forbid them, let alone punish them. By *reductio*, then, Prémontval concludes from the fact that some people do not always obey God's commands that this cannot be the best of all possible worlds.

Having teased apart two propositions that were usually conflated by the protagonists in the optimism debate, Prémontval seeks to harmonize his acceptance of (1) and rejection of (2) by offering a philosophical theology clearly indebted to Plato's *Timaeus* or Timaeus of Locri's *On the Nature of the World and the Soul*, in particular to their account of the formation of the cosmos by the divine craftsman, the demiurge. Both Plato and the author writing as Timaeus of Locri suppose that the demiurge acts on pre-existing matter that is by nature disorderly, chaotic, and unpredictable.[34] In conferring order upon this material, the demiurge seeks to bring about the best arrangement, though as the material has natural properties that are in opposition to the order imposed on it, the effects of these properties can only be partially subjugated by the demiurge, never wholly eradicated. In a similar vein, Prémontval envisages God as being faced with a world of beings he had not created and over which he does not have direct control, though in his account this is because some or all of these beings are naturally endowed with free will, which God cannot override or remove even if he wanted to.[35]

To this Platonic-Timaean vision, Prémontval adds an important twist: he proclaims that God's principal (and indeed overriding) aim is to make all beings holy and happy, and this on the grounds that no other aim is consistent with supreme goodness.[36] But since not all beings are happy and holy (as experience attests), we may surmise that it is not possible for God to make all happy and holy by fiat. Instead, he is restricted to interventions designed to guide these beings to his goal of universal happiness and holiness:

> At each moment his infinite wisdom, animated by boundless affection, intervenes with all the weight of his power and all the efficacy of his grace, to increase goods, reduce evils, cure, put right, relieve, and heal; to right wrongs, to heal the wounds that blind or wicked beings constantly cause by mutual blows. If all is not better; if all is not holy and happy (confirmed by the facts, it is my turn to say this openly) it is because the thing is not yet possible: it is because it is possible only by development and by degrees and that it is a matter of leading beings to make themselves such rather than to make them such, which is absurd. If it were only a matter of willing them to be such for them to be all *holy, happy, identified with God himself*, infinite goodness would not hesitate, would not defer for a moment.[37]

As the world is still a long way from being as good as it could be, Prémontval rejects the optimist's claim that it is the best possible, opting instead for a more nuanced position. While he accepts that the world is the best with regard to that which depends upon God, who ensures that the world contains as much perfection at each moment as is possible, Prémontval holds that it is not best with regard to that which depends upon free beings—though he envisages these beings improving continuously under the guidance of God.[38] Although Prémontval described himself as an optimist when writing to Reinhard, it should be clear from the above that the label is ill-fitting,[39] and he is more accurately described as a meliorist, albeit *avant la lettre*, since the term "meliorism" and its derivatives appeared in English only in 1877, while "méliorisme" first appeared in French in 1915 and the derivative "mélioriste" in 1931.

Prémontval believed that the idea of God found in his melioristic philosophy was more plausible and attractive than that possessed either by optimists or by anti-optimists. The optimist, he complained, tended to place excessive emphasis on God's wisdom, while the anti-optimist did likewise with God's independence. It is worth examining Prémontval's thinking here. Optimists such as Leibniz insinuated that God's desire to make all beings holy and happy was not an overriding one, as Prémontval insisted, but rather subordinated to another, more important aim. Hence in his *Theodicy* of 1710, Leibniz had claimed that while the happiness of intelligent beings "is the principal part of God's design," it should not be thought that this was his sole aim.[40] Leibniz stressed that God would also prize simplicity of means and the observation of general laws, intimating that this would result in a certain amount of evil: "God can follow a simple, productive, regular plan; but I do not believe that the best and the most regular is always opportune for all creatures simultaneously."[41] Nicolas Malebranche, from whom Leibniz appropriated these ideas, argued that God opts for simple means and general laws, despite the drawbacks these have for creatures, because these are what wisdom demands. Just as skilled artisans and craftsmen complete their work via the simplest means at their disposal, so God, as an artisan or craftsman par excellence, would make use of the simplest possible means to bring about his intended effect, as anything else would not be in keeping with supreme wisdom.[42] By contrast, Prémontval found it bizarre to suppose that God would prize his own wisdom above the happiness and holiness of his creatures, the only aim worthy of God's supreme goodness.[43] In Prémontval's eyes, then, Leibniz and his ilk had erred by supposing that God had identified more important considerations than the happiness and holiness of other beings.

On the other extreme, opponents of optimism erred by overemphasizing God's *independence* to the point of denying that God essentially chooses the best. Such a denial typically stemmed from the concern that if God essentially chooses the best, then he must do so necessarily, which destroys divine freedom at a stroke. To counter this, some opponents of optimism, Reinhard among them, stressed God's *independence*, insisting that God was entirely free in his choice of world, and indeed free to choose whether to create, it being a matter of complete indifference to him whether other beings existed or not.[44] Prémontval offers a twofold response to this. First, he notes that as goodness is a propensity to do good, God's essential goodness *presupposes* the existence of things outside of him to which he can do good, implying that it was not up to God whether these things existed or not.[45] Second, Prémontval insists that an infinite goodness that was in any way indifferent toward the good of other beings would not be worthy of the name of infinite goodness, or indeed worthy of our love.[46]

In "General Misunderstanding on the Question of Optimism," Prémontval expresses his dismay that none of the entrants of the 1755 prize essay contest had hit upon his preferred "middle point," instead being clearly polarized, either fervently in favor of optimism or against it. Prémontval's dismay was compounded by the fact that he had—he said—tacitly outlined his "middle point" in three of the books he had published between 1754 and 1755, namely *Thoughts on Freedom*, *The Diogenes of d'Alembert*, and *On Chance under the Rule of Providence*, doing so in the hope that it would lead some of the competition's entrants to arrive at the same "middle point" he favored:

> Nothing has contributed more to convince me of the need to open new paths, or to reopen old, neglected, long-lost paths, than the question proposed by the Academy on optimism. I do not speak of the serious application, of which the examination of this multitude of pieces submitted to us made me a duty; I mean of the character and the very opposition of the pieces. It cannot be denied that there were many estimable by their subtlety or by the depth of research, and the winning one was like this. But good God! In all of them, what opinions! In all of them, towards what extremities are we carried, determinedly, without looking behind us! Not the slightest attempt; not the slightest attempt at a mean between the opposing sides. Whichever side is chosen is endorsed entirely and with no turning back. I had suspected as much. It suited no one, least of all me, to claim as guide to those who entered this fray. However, I could try to inspire views, especially by doing it in such an indirect manner that no one spotted my intention. To this end I hastened to produce my *Thoughts on Freedom*, many of my *Thoughts on Man*,[47] and my

Treatise on Chance under the Rule of Providence, which even appeared in time, at the end of 1754. There, without making an express mention of the subject of optimism, as proposed by the Academy, I nonetheless present with some ingenuity all the light and all the shadows necessary to bring out the idea I wanted to see developed.[48]

Of the three books mentioned here, *On Chance under the Rule of Providence* is the richest source of arguments and doctrines that would be subsequently fleshed out in "General Misunderstanding on the Question of Optimism." However, Prémontval's claim that this book appeared at the end of 1754 is incorrect. In a letter to a friend written on February 21, 1755, Prémontval explained that the book was still "15 days or 3 weeks" away from being printed.[49] Therefore, by the time that book was published, in mid-March 1755, the deadline for submissions to the 1755 essay contest—January 1—had passed, and with it any chance of the book influencing the entrants.

The two other books that Prémontval claimed were written in the hope of influencing the entrants of the prize essay contest contain only traces of the ideas later outlined in more detail in "General Misunderstanding on the Question of Optimism." For example, in an appendix to *Thoughts on Freedom*, having argued that it is of God's essence not to do a lesser good, and thus that God is necessitated by his own perfect nature always to take the best course, Prémontval rails against "those who, on the pretext of preserving a freedom which is monstrous or chimerical, make him act arbitrarily."[50] And in *De Dieu et de la Religion: Suite du Diogène décent* (*On God and Religion: Follow-up to Decent Diogenes*), Prémontval states that "Goodness has an essential and necessary relation to beings capable of being made happy; it cannot subsist without this relation. Consequently, God could not be God if there were no beings capable of feeling that he is good" (Prémontval 1754a, 49). While such passages certainly gesture toward the ideas Prémontval would later sketch out more explicitly in *On Chance under the Rule of Providence* and "General Misunderstanding on the Question of Optimism," it would be difficult to reconstruct the later position from the scattered hints of it found in those earlier works.

Not surprisingly, Prémontval's oblique attempt to influence the entrants of the 1755 essay contest was not successful. On the one hand, the writings he published prior to January 1, 1755, did not contain sufficient seeds of the doctrine he wanted to see blossom in the minds of others to enable them to cultivate it, and, on the other, Prémontval's melioristic philosophy, sketched out in "General Misunderstanding" and more obliquely in the books he published in 1754, was too heterodox to win widespread support. His rejection of the doctrine of creation as an unhelpful theological prejudice would have been seen as abhorrent in an age that still prized orthodoxy. And his claim that God's principal aim was the happiness and holiness of his creatures was at odds with the mainstream Christian confessions, which typically saw God's sole aim as the glorification of himself, something that was widely seen as quite compatible with the misery and even damnation of many creatures. Prémontval's insistence that God's principal aim was (and could only be) the happiness and holiness of his creatures would no doubt have been seen as the error of a philosopher working out the logic of God's goodness and love independently of any other theological or scriptural concerns, which may well have been precisely how he arrived at it. As Prémontval relates in his memoirs, when he began studying philosophy at the age of sixteen or seventeen, he underwent a crisis of faith that led him to endorse atheistic Pyrrhonism before turning to deism and eventually converting to an unspecified branch of Protestantism at the age of thirty.[51] Nevertheless, his writings suggest that he continued to entertain a philosophical notion of God over one that was recognizably Lutheran or Calvinist, a point that was not lost on his critics who castigated him for it.[52]

5. Meliorism in and after Prémontval

Although Prémontval declared himself a partisan of optimism, I have suggested that he is better described as a meliorist, in that he believed the world (in fact, its inhabitants) improves ceaselessly over time. While ideas of human progress and perfectibility have a long history and were hardly uncommon during the Enlightenment,[53] it is worth noting the distinctive features of Prémontval's form of meliorism:

> 1) Progress and improvement are universal; that is, all creatures, human and non-human alike, will experience them. Prémontval often claims that God will make "all" or "every being" happy and holy, suggesting that human beings are not God's only concern.[54] Moreover, Prémontval states that God is not indifferent toward the plight of nonhuman creatures, which he claims suffer as much as, if not more than, human beings and thereby have a right to the favors of divine goodness.[55]
>
> 2) Progress and improvement take place both in this life and in the afterlife, though mostly in the latter. That this is Prémontval's position can be inferred from his repeated claims that God will ultimately make all happy and holy and the acknowledged fact that this has not yet been achieved.
>
> 3) Progress and improvement are God-driven rather than human-driven, and in this life, they occur more in spite of human activity than because of it. Indeed, Prémontval insisted that so far from free will being a divine gift, as was traditionally thought, it was more of an imperfection or curse since it enables those who have it to go wrong as well as right. Because this conflicts with God's principal aim of bringing about a harmonious whole in which all creatures are holy and happy, Prémontval supposed that if it had been possible for God to remove or override the free wills of human beings, then he would have done so; the fact that he hadn't suggested it wasn't possible.[56]

Unfortunately, Prémontval leaves no clues as to how he came to endorse such a set of ideas. One could speculate that his influences were various, and that he drew upon ideas such as universalism (i.e., the doctrine of universal salvation), Christian utopian ideas such as those of Joachim of Fiore (c. 1135–1202),[57] Calvin's belief that in the perfecting of human beings, God's manner of action leads to gradual rather than instantaneous improvement,[58] and perhaps—though this is a stretch—even Wolff's doctrine of perfectibility, which taught that it was within human power (and indeed the supreme human good) to make unimpeded progress toward ever greater perfections.[59]

We may presume that Prémontval was familiar with all these ideas, or cognate ones at least, and conjecture that he fused and reworked some or all of them into a novel position of his own, though it should be stressed that there is no direct evidence for this. And we ought not rule out the possibility that Prémontval arrived at the component ideas of his meliorism philosophically, which indeed is the impression he gives.

We have already seen that, in spite of (or probably because of) its novelty, Prémontval's melioristic philosophy failed to find adherents in his own age. This would not have surprised him in the slightest, as he fully expected that his ideas would receive a warmer reception in the decades and centuries to come. And in a sense, he was correct because his forthright endorsement of meliorism anticipated an important twist in the optimism debate that occurred in the nineteenth century, especially in France, where optimism experienced a renaissance, albeit not in quite the same form as it had been entertained in previous centuries. This renaissance was sparked in 1847 by Louis Auguste Javary (1820-52), who insisted that God placed the very idea of good in the world so as to be "an inexhaustible principle of love and moral force" and thus serve as "a germ of improvement, which can fertilize, develop, and lead this world from an inferior state to a greater perfection" (Javary 1847, 525). Insisting that there was no limit as to how perfect the world could become, Javary offered a vision of an ever-improving universe:

> The divine will can work only for the best, says optimism: we agree; but as a determinate best is never absolutely realizable, are not the two principles in agreement when we conceive that the state of the world—necessarily always imperfect—is nevertheless constantly improving, and approaching an absolute perfection, which it will doubtless never attain, but which ultimately it conceives and towards which it tends ever more?
>
> (Javary 1847, 525)

Inspired by Javary's suggestion, a series of philosophers endorsed and elaborated upon it. Hence in 1854, Francisque Bouillier (1813-99) claimed that as there could be no upper limit for the perfection of a universe, the optimist's belief that our universe is the best one possible had to be reworked into a form of meliorism, which recognized that the universe was not (and could not be) statically the best at every moment but was instead ceaselessly increasing in perfection. Therefore, according to Bouillier, the best world of the optimist "is not the world such as it is, the world in actuality, it is the world in potentiality, such as it is becoming and ceaselessly will become in the endless progression of its developments" (Bouillier 1854, 455).

Later meliorists drew a distinction between true and false optimism, that is, between the idea of a world always exemplifying maximal perfection (false optimism) and the idea of a world continually increasing in perfection (true optimism). Émile Boirac, for example, supposed that the best world was infinitely perfectible, acquiring its perfections by the free efforts of creatures.[60] Boirac stressed that whereas false optimism, with its claim of absolute perfection, inevitably leads to resignation and inaction, true optimism, on the other hand, concludes in favor of action, stimulating us to contribute to the ongoing development and improvement of the world.

As close as some of these ideas are to those developed by Prémontval, it would be a stretch to suppose that he influenced or inspired them. None of the aforementioned thinkers mention him in their discussions of optimism or meliorism, and indeed Bouillier, one of the earliest proponents of nineteenth-century French meliorism, identifies the seeds of his melioristic ideas in the work of Leibniz, Descartes, and Malebranche.[61] A number of other doctrines in Prémontval's work likewise anticipated later developments, such as open theism, process theology, and animal theodicy, without him having any claim to have shaped or inspired them.[62] And so it was for Prémontval: ever the anticipator, never—in modern parlance—the influencer.[63]

Notes

1 From the register for June 7, 1753, held by the Archiv der Berlin-Brandenburgischen Akademie der Wissenschaften under the shelfmark I IV 31/06, Bl. 48. All translations in this paper are my own. Where an English translation is available, I cite the original language source first followed by the English translation.
2 The question was publicly announced in the June 1753 issue of *Nouvelle Bibliothèque Germanique ou Histoire Littéraire de l'Allemagne, de la Suisse et des Pays du Nord* (1753, 457–8), edited by Samuel Formey. The question was subsequently publicized in the twice-weekly Hamburg journal *Freye Urtheile und Nachrichten zum Aufnehmen der Wissenschaften und Historie überhaupt* (1753, 461–2) on July 27, 1753 (not August 27, 1753 as is sometimes claimed; there was in fact no issue of the journal published on that date), and then in the Paris journal *Suite de la Clef, ou Journal historique sur les matières du tems* (1753, 149) in August 1753.
3 From the register for May 14, 1753, held by the Archiv der Berlin-Brandenburgischen Akademie der Wissenschaften under the shelfmark I IV 31/06, Bl. 46.
4 See Buschmann 1989, 199n63. For an overview of these entries, see Hellwig 2008, 276–97.
5 See the register for June 5, 1755, held by the Archiv der Berlin-Brandenburgischen Akademie der Wissenschaften under the shelfmark I IV 31/08, Bl. 35: "The perpetual secretary opened the session by declaring that the piece which had won the prize proposed for this year by the Class of Speculative Philosophy was No. 7 ... Whereupon, having opened the sealed letter, the name of Mr. Adolf Friedrich Reinhard was found therein."
6 See Hirzel 1891, 110.
7 See the register for June 5, 1755, held by the Archiv der Berlin-Brandenburgischen Akademie der Wissenschaften under the shelfmark I IV 31/08, Bl. 35.
8 Probably Johann Georg Ritter von Zimmermann (1728–95).
9 As reported in Hirzel 1891, 115. It is possible that Maupertuis was not even in Berlin at the time the Academy members were reading, weighing, and voting on the submissions: according to the Academy's records, the first meeting he attended in 1755 was that of June 5, the day Reinhard was crowned winner of the essay contest.
10 Prémontval's inability to read German meant that he could have read fewer than half of the eighteen entries, of which eleven were in German, four in French, and three in Latin (see Buschmann 1989, 199n63).
11 In a separate text, addressed to Johann Christoph Gottsched (1700–66), Prémontval wrote: "Nothing has been more straightforward and more free from intrigue and

bickering than the affair of the prize of 1755" (Prémontval 1757, II: 137). While it is tempting to take this as a reference to the voting, this should be resisted, as Gottsched had raised no concerns about that. He had, however, complained about the prize essay question itself when it was announced in 1753. Indeed, upon learning of the topic, Gottsched (Gottsched 1753) published a short tract against what he perceived to be the negative and trivializing tone of the Academy's question, his concern even extending to the use of the term "optimism," which he correctly noted had been invented as a pejorative term (though he mistakenly thought it had been invented by Jean Pierre de Crousaz, whereas it had in fact been coined by Louis Bertrand Castel in a review of Leibniz's *Theodicy*; see Castel 1737, 207). Gottsched was not the only one to complain about the choice of question for 1755; another attack came from Lessing and Mendelssohn, who ridiculed the juxtaposition of Pope and Leibniz in the Academy's question, noting that the aims and approaches of the poet and philosopher were too different to warrant the sort of comparison the Academy proposed (see Lessing and Mendelssohn 1755). Prémontval later defended the Academy's prize essay question, even stating that he had voted for it: "Certainly, although critiques of it [the question] have been made, the question is fine and very well presented. I took pleasure in contributing my voice to the preference it obtained" (Prémontval 1757, II: 9).

12 See Hirzel 1891, 114 and Harnack 1900, 405.
13 See Hellwig 2008, 276 and Calinger 2016, 403.
14 There has been some debate about Maupertuis' attitude toward Leibniz. For example, while Cassirer (1951, 86) saw an "objective kinship" between Maupertuis' ideas and Leibniz's, Beeson (1992) portrayed Maupertuis as straightforwardly anti-Leibniz, and Terrall (2002) depicted Maupertuis as more ambivalent toward Leibniz, albeit punctuated by periods of hostility. It is beyond the scope of this paper to enter into this debate, and it will suffice here to note that in the mid-1750s Maupertuis was certainly hostile to Leibniz, no doubt in part because of the controversy over his principle of least action, which a number of detractors claimed to be an original invention of Leibniz's. This sparked a pamphlet war between supporters of Maupertuis and Leibniz that lasted for several years. See Terrall 2002, 286–309.
15 Interestingly, in a history of the Berlin Academy, written in the mid-nineteenth century, Bartholmèss claimed that Sulzer was a follower of Béguelin and Merian (Bartholmèss 1851, II: 111).
16 In his biographical novel of Lessing, Hermann Klencke has Lessing tell Mendelssohn that Prémontval "is bitterly hostile to Maupertuis" because he didn't want to serve him as a tool (Klencke 1850, III: 285).
17 See Prémontval 1757, II: 243–68 (2018, 1–10).
18 Prémontval to François Thomas Marie de Baculard d'Arnauld, February 21, 1755. Berlin Staatsbibliothek, Preußischer Kulturbesitz, Darmstädter Collection.
19 Sulzer's claim that Prémontval denied the principle of sufficient reason in his publications is also inaccurate. In fact, Prémontval did not reject the principle of sufficient reason outright; he merely denied that it applied universally, as the Leibnizians and Wolffians claimed. While Prémontval accepted that there was always a sufficient reason for God's (necessary) choice, he denied that this was always the case for the choices of other beings that stemmed from their free will. See Prémontval 1754c (2018, 11–56) and 1755 (2018, 75–129).
20 For a more in-depth examination of Reinhard's essay, see Caro 2020, 146–71.
21 See Reinhard 1755, 41.

22 See Kant 1759 and Mendelssohn 1844, IV, 1, 508–10; the latter was written in 1759.
23 Prémontval 1755, 19 (2018, 86).
24 Although Prémontval offered no further detail of this charge, his concern was probably that Künzli (1755, 42–3), following Leibniz, supposed that God had the idea or pattern for this world in his mind prior to creation, such that any question about why such-and-such an event happens or why things are thus rather than otherwise must be referred back to this idea or pattern, the upshot of which is that all events are determined. Because of this, and in spite of Leibniz's protestations to the contrary, some opponents of optimism supposed that Leibniz's system was fatalistic (e.g., Warburton 1740, 18). In his essay, Künzli actually addressed this objection, but did no more than quote Leibniz's own words denying fatalism (Künzli 1755, 28–33). Since it was Leibniz's own words that had caused opponents to bring the charge of fatalism in the first place, Künzli's approach did little to assuage those who, like Prémontval, were inclined to see Leibniz's optimism as fatalistic.
25 For the letter and the rebuttal, see Prémontval 1757, II: 67–74 and 75–136. The two pieces were subsequently republished in German translation along with a number of other pieces prompted by Reinhard's winning essay; see Ziegra 1759.
26 See Prémontval 2018, 320.
27 Prémontval 1757, II: 33–66 (Strickland 2020, 324–8).
28 Prémontval 1757, II: 34 (Strickland 2020, 325).
29 Prémontval 1757, II: 49–50 (Strickland 2020, 326).
30 This point is made more explicitly in Prémontval (1755, 137–8/2018, 120): "with regard to the Supreme Being which is infinitely wise and infinitely good, we can only conceive that, placed again in the same set of circumstances an infinity of times, it would take the same course of action an infinity of times, namely the *best*. Why? In short, because it is as *essential* to him—inasmuch as he has infinite wisdom and infinite goodness—to take nothing but the best course as it is for the circle to be a round figure, and the roundest of all figures. Thus God is *subject to necessity*, but to the necessity of his nature. In other words, God is no more free not to be infinitely good in name and in effect than he is free not to be God. He is no more free not to be what is *essential to God* than he is free not to be God."
31 With the occasional exception, such as the Scottish philosopher William Dudgeon (1705/1706–1743), who cheerfully accepted that God had created the best world out of necessity; see Dudgeon 1739, 7; cf. 12.
32 Prémontval 1757, II: 37–8 (Strickland 2020, 325).
33 Some anti-optimists do appear to have thought of the matter this way. See for example Du Phanjas 1767, 149.
34 See Plato 1997, 1236 and Timaeus of Locri 1985.
35 See Prémontval 1757, II: 50 (Strickland 2020, 326–7).
36 Prémontval 1757, II: 50; Strickland 2020, 326. Additionally, see Prémontval 1754c, 38–49 (2018, 25–8) and 1755, 45–7 (2018, 94–5).
37 Prémontval 1757, II: 53–4 (Strickland 2020, 327).
38 See Prémontval 1757, II: 51 (Strickland 2020, 327).
39 Despite Prémontval's vocal opposition to Leibniz and his rejection of the central claim of Leibnizian optimism—that our world is best—he has sometimes been incorrectly pegged as endorsing an optimism not dissimilar to Leibniz's own. For example, see Barber 1955, 168.
40 GP VI, 168 (Leibniz 1985, 188).
41 GP VI, 244 (Leibniz 1985, 260)

42 See Malebranche 1992, 116.
43 See Prémontval 1757, II: 58 (Strickland 2020, 327).
44 Although Prémontval does not mention it, similar claims were also sometimes made by optimists. For example, in a work in which he argued that ours is the best of all possible worlds, Christian Wolff (Wolff 1736, 401–2, §430) also claimed that God is sufficient unto himself and so indifferent as to whether to create or not.
45 See Prémontval 1757, II: 61 (Strickland 2020, 328). The same argument would later be used by twentieth-century process or neoclassical theists to reject the doctrine of *creatio ex nihilo*. See for example Dombrowski 2016, 56–7.
46 See Prémontval 1757, II: 64 (Strickland 2020, 328).
47 This is part of the subtitle of Prémontval 1754b.
48 Prémontval 1757, II: 47–9 (Strickland 2020, 326).
49 See Prémontval to Francois Thomas Marie de Baculard d'Arnauld, February 21, 1755, unpublished letter held by the Berlin Staatsbibliothek, Preußischer Kulturbesitz, Darmstädter Collection.
50 Prémontval 1754c, 148 (2018, 60).
51 See Prémontval 1749, 227.
52 For example, one reviewer of Prémontval's *Vues philosophiques* (namely, Anon 1757, 36–7) complained that "The Christianity the author professes is very different from the Christianity Jesus Christ established. His writings offer us only a mangled Christianity, less suited to feature in the School of Jesus Christ than in an Academy of philosophers; in wanting to ease our faith, he continually upsets it."
53 See, for example, the discussion in Passmore 2000 and the texts in Hourcade, Morel, and Yuva 2022.
54 For example, Prémontval 1757, II: 398/2018, 184: "he is the creator of the world only in the sense that he is the creator of the order, the perfection, and the good, of an infinite good, toward which he leads every being by the fastest progress possible."
55 See Prémontval 1757, II: 209 (2018, 236).
56 See Prémontval 1754c, 14 (2018, 18); 1754c, 31–2 (2018, 23).
57 For Christian utopianism, see Manuel and Manuel 1979, 205–410; for Joachim, see Passmore 2000, 332–6.
58 Calvin 2006, I, 601 (III.iii.9): "this restoration does not take place in one moment or one day or one year; but through continual and sometimes even slow advances God wipes out in his elect the corruptions of the flesh."
59 See Wolff 1738, 293–4, §374.
60 See Boirac 1892, 391–2.
61 See Bouiller 1854, 457.
62 See Prémontval 2018, xxvi–xxvii.
63 I would like to thank Christian Leduc and Tinca Prunea for their helpful comments on an earlier version of this paper, and Julia Weckend for her kind assistance with some of the translated passages.

Bibliography

Anon. 1757. "Vues philosophiques ou Protestations & Declarations sur les principaux objets des connoissances humaines, par Mr. de Prémontval." In *Journal Encyclopédique*, *par une société de gens de lettres. Pour le 15. mai 1757. Tome IV. Première partie*. 28–40. Liège: Everard Kints.

Barber, W. H. 1955. *Leibniz in France, from Arnauld to Voltaire: A Study in French Reactions to Leibnizianism, 1670–1760*. Oxford: Clarendon Press.

Beeson, David. 1992. *Maupertuis: An Intellectual Biography*. Oxford: Voltaire Foundation.

Boirac, Emile. 1892. *La dissertation philosophique*, 2nd edition. Paris: Felix Alcan.

Bouillier, Francisque. 1854. *Histoire de la philosophie Cartésienne. Tome second*. Paris: Durand.

Buschmann, Cornelia. 1989. "Die Philosophischen Preisfragen und Preisschriften der Berliner Akademie der Wissenschaften im 18. Jahrhundert." In *Aufklärung in Berlin*, edited by Wolfgang Förster, 165–228. Berlin: Akademie-Verlag.

Calinger, Ronald S. 2016. *Leonhard Euler: Mathematical Genius in the Enlightenment*. Princeton: Princeton University Press.

Calvin, John. 2006. *Institutes of the Christian Religion*, edited by John T. McNeill, translated by Ford Lewis Battles. Louisville: Westminster John Knox Press.

Caro, Hernán D. 2020. *The Best of All Possible Worlds? Leibniz's Philosophical Optimism and Its Critics 1710–1755*. Leiden: Brill.

Cassirer, Ernst. 1951. *The Philosophy of the Enlightenment*, translated by Fritz C. A. Koelln and James P. Pettegrove. Princeton: Princeton University Press.

Castel, Louis-Bertrand. 1737. "Essais de Théodicée." *Mémoires pour l'histoire des sciences & des beaux-arts*, 5–36, 197–241, and 444–71.

Dombrowski, Daniel A. 2016. *A History of the Concept of God: A Process Approach*. New York: State University of New York Press.

Dudgeon, William. 1739. *A View of the Necessitarian or Best Scheme: Freed from the Objections of M. Crousaz, in His Examination of Mr. Pope's Essay on Man*. London: T. Cooper.

Formey, Samuel. 1756. "Dissertation qui a remporté le prix proposé par l'Académie Royale des Sciences & Belles-Lettres de Prusse, sur L'OPTIMISME." *Nouvelle bibliothèque germanique*, 18, 22–32.

Freye Urtheile und Nachrichten zum Aufnehmen der Wissenschaften und Historie überhaupt. 1753. Hamburg: Georg Christian Grund.

Gottsched, Johann Christoph. 1753. *De optimismi macula diserte nuper Alexandro Popio anglo, tacite autem G. G. Leibnitio, perperam licet, inusta*. Leipzig: Breitkopf.

Harnack, Adolf. 1900. *Geschichte der Königlich Preussischen Akademie der Wissenschaften zu Berlin*, 2 vols. Berlin: Reichsdruckerei.

Hellwig, Marion. 2008. *Alles ist gut: Untersuchungen zur Geschichte einer Theodizee-Formel im 18 Jahrhundert in Deutschland, England und Frankreich*. Würzburg: Verlag Königshausen & Neumann.

Hirzel, Ludwig. 1891. *Wieland und Martin und Regula Künzli*. Leipzig: S. Hirzel.

Hourcade, Emmanuel, Charlotte Morel, and Ayse Yuva (eds.). 2022. *La perfectibilité de l'homme*. Paris: Garnier.

Javary, Louis Auguste. 1847. *De la certitude*. Paris: Librairie philosophique de Ladrange.

Kant, Immanuel. 1759. "An Attempt at Some Reflections on Optimism by M. Immanuel Kant, also Containing an Announcement of His Lecture for the Coming Semester 7 October 1759." In *Theoretical Philosophy, 1755–1770*, edited and translated by David Walford and Ralf Meerbote, 67–76. Cambridge: Cambridge University Press.

Klencke, Hermann. 1850. *Lessing: Roman*, 5 vols. Leipzig: Christian Ernst Kollmann.

Künzli, Martin. 1755. "Abhandlung über den Satz des Herrn Pope: Alles was ist, das ist gut." In *Dissertation qui a remporté le prix proposé par l'Académie Royale des Sciences et*

Belles Lettres de Prusse, sur l'optimsme, avec les pièces qui ont concouru, 1–46 [separate pagination]. Berlin: Haude and Spener.
Leibniz, Gottfried Wilhelm. 1885. *Die philosophischen Schriften von Gottfried Wilhelm Leibniz. Sechster Band*, edited by C. I. Gerhardt. Berlin: Weidmann. (Cited as GP).
Leibniz, Gottfried Wilhelm. 1985. *Theodicy*, translated by E. M. Huggard. Chicago: Open Court.
Lessing, Gotthold Ephraim and Moses Mendelssohn. 1755. *Pope—ein Metaphysiker!*. Danzig: Johann Christian Schuster.
Malebranche, Nicolas. 1992. *Treatise on Nature and Grace*, edited and translated by Patrick Riley. Oxford: Clarendon Press.
Manuel, Frank E. and Fritzie P. Manuel. 1979. *Utopian Thought in the Western World*. Cambridge, MA: The Belknap Press.
Mendelssohn, Moses. 1844. *Moses Mendelssohns gesammelte Schriften*, edited by G. B. Mendelssohn, 7 vols. Leipzig: Brockhaus.
Nouvelle Bibliothèque Germanique ou Histoire Littéraire de l'Allemagne, de la Suisse et des Pays du Nord. 1753. Amsterdam: Pierre Mortier.
Passmore, John. 2000. *The Perfectibility of Man*, 3rd edition. Indianapolis: Liberty Fund.
Phanjas, François Para Du. 1767. *Éléments de métaphysique sacrée et profane, ou Théorie des êtres insensibles*. Paris: Jombert.
Plato. 1997. *Complete Works*, edited by John M. Cooper, Indianapolis: Hackett.
Prémontval, André-Pierre Leguay de. 1749. *Mémoires d'André Pierre Leguai de Prémontval, Professeur en Mathématiques et Belles-Lettres*. The Hague.
Prémontval, André-Pierre Leguay de. 1754a. *De Dieu et de la Religion: Suite du Diogene décent*. Frankfurt.
Prémontval, André-Pierre Leguay de. 1754b. *Le Diogene de d'Alembert; ou Diogene décent: pensées libres sur l'home & sur les principaux objets des conoissances de l'home*. Berlin.
Prémontval, André-Pierre Leguay de. 1754c. *Pensées sur la Liberté, tirées d'un ouvrage qui a pour titre: protestations et déclarations philosophiques sur les principaux objets des conoissances humaines*. Berlin and Potsdam: Chrétien Frédéric Voss.
Prémontval, André-Pierre Leguay de. 1755. *Du hazard sous l'empire de la providence*. Berlin: J. C. Kluter.
Prémontval, André-Pierre Leguay de. 1757. *Vues philosophiques; ou protestations et déclarations sur les principaux objets des connoissances humaines*, 2 vols. Berlin: Joachim Pauli.
Prémontval, André-Pierre Leguay de. 2018. *The Philosophical Writings of Prémontval*, edited and translated by Lloyd Strickland, Lanham, MD: Lexington.
Reinhard, Adolph Friedrich. 1755. *Le système de Mr Pope sur la perfection du monde, comparé à celui de Mr de Leibnitz, avec un examen de l'optimisme*. Berlin: Haude and Spener.
Strickland, Lloyd. 2020. "Prémontval's 'General Misunderstanding on the Question of Optimism.'" *Philosophical Readings*, 12, 2, 321–30.
Suite de la Clef, ou Journal historique sur les matières du tems. 1753. Paris: Ganeau.
Terrall, Mary. 2002. *The Man Who Flattened the Earth: Maupertuis and the Sciences in the Enlightenment*. Chicago: University of Chicago Press.
Timaeus of Locri. 1985. *On the Nature of the World and the Soul*, translated by Thomas H. Tobin. Chico, CA: Scholars Press.
Warburton, William. 1740. *A Vindication of Mr. Pope's Essay on Man, from the Misrepresentations of Mr de Crousaz*. London: J. Robinson.

Wolff, Christian. 1736. *Theologia naturalis, methodo scientifica pertractata. Pars prior, integrum systema complectens, qua existentia et attributa Dei a posteriori demonstrantur.* Frankfurt and Leipzig: Renger.

Wolff, Christian. 1738. *Philosophia practica universalis, methodo scientifica pertractata, pars prior, theoriam complectens, qua omnis actionum humanarum differentia, omnisque juris ac obligationum omnium, principia, a priori demonstantur.* Frankfurt and Leipzig: Renger.

Ziegra, Christian. 1759. *Sammlung der Streitschriften über die Lehre von der besten Welt, und verschiedene damit verknüpfte wichtige Wahrheiten, welche zwischen dem Verfasser der im Jahr 1755. von der Akademie zu Berlin gekrönten Schrift vom Optimismo, und einigen berühmten Gelehrten gewechselt worden.* Rostock and Wismar: Berger and Boedner.

5

The *Public Debate* about the Abuse of Power by the Berlin Academy against Samuel König

Ursula Goldenbaum

> *That, however, the entire Academy declared Mr. Maupertuis' assumption to be true with certainty, presenting Mr. König as a deliberate lyer, that is—in the free republic of scholars—an unprecedented incident.*
>
> (Freye Urtheile, August 15, 1752)[1]

The public debate about the *Jugement de l'Académie royale des sciences et belles lettres sur une lettre prétendue de M. de Leibnitz* (Judgment of the Royal Academy of Sciences and Belles Lettres about a Pretended Letter of Mr. Leibniz)—beginning in the summer of 1752 and lasting until the fall of 1753—directly calls into question the long-standing prejudice about an allegedly a-political German Enlightenment that shied away from any resistance against authorities. While the history of the *Jugement* has been recounted many times, the *public debate* about the *Jugement* has rarely been the focus of attention.[2] The latter must be distinguished (1) from the related scientific controversy about Maupertuis' principle of least action, and (2) from the scholarly controversy about the authenticity of a Leibniz letter. Namely, the subject of the *public debate* of the *Jugement* was freedom of speech, an eminent political subject. The common presentations of the history of the *Jugement* do not distinguish these different aspects. They usually present it from the perspective of the most famous participants: Maupertuis, Leonhard Euler, Frederick II, and, above all, Voltaire. It has been written mostly by historians of science and mathematics,[3] of French literature (Mervaud 1985; Magnan 1986), or of Prussia (Korff 1918, 592-4), and—using them all—by the historian of the Berlin Academy, Adolph von Harnack (Harnack 1900, 245-345). Accordingly, they all defend their respective heroes.

Meanwhile, there is general agreement in the scholarship that the *Jugement* was a blunt abuse of power by the Berlin Academy against a respectable scientist. But scholars sharply disagree about the question of who should be held responsible for such a violation of academic rules. They all try to excuse their own heroes and blame the others. Thus, Voltaire scholars praise Voltaire for his fearless defense of freedom of thought (allegedly in contrast to the docile German enlightened thinkers). Historians of science, conversely, blame him for meddling in a scientific controversy without adequate competence (Beeson 1992, 243-5) and they try to excuse the actions of

Maupertuis and Euler.[4] Likewise, historians of Prussia defend Frederick II despite his embarrassing intervention, the 1752 *Lettre d'un académicien de Berlin à un académicien de Paris* (Letter of a Member of the Berlin Academy to a Member of the Academy of Paris). Although Frederick's letter consists of nothing but slander against Samuel König, exaggerated appraisals of Maupertuis, and falsehoods when accounting for the cause of the controversy, they excuse him because he had only tried to stop the actual wrongdoer, the jealous Voltaire, from damaging Maupertuis (Diels 1898; Harnack 1900, 339–45). This line-up within scholarship nicely mirrors the historical alliances between Maupertuis and Euler, who were supported by the king, and Voltaire's aligning with Samuel König, who had dared to criticize the president of the Berlin Academy, Maupertuis.

Focusing here on the *public debate*, I will first present the *Jugement* of the Royal Academy against Samuel König, then explore its pre-history, namely, Maupertuis' discovery of the principle of least action and König's criticism of it, which motivated Euler and Maupertuis to launch the *Jugement*. I will then turn to the emerging public reaction in German and Dutch learned newspapers and journals in Section 3. In Section 4, I will show that the responses of Maupertuis and Euler in their *Lettres concernant le Jugement* (Letters Concerning the Judgment) presented mere slander of their opponents—the letters were evaluated as such in the public sphere. In Section 5, Samuel König's *Appel au public* (Appeal to the Public) presents his extended invitation for the public to play the role of the judge of his case, an appeal that displayed all the pertinent documents that were available to him. Section 6 is dedicated to Voltaire's rehabilitation from the common but wrong accusation that he had meddled in a controversy he did not understand. I would also like to show that while Voltaire was the most famous, and thus most influential, participant in the controversy, the controversy was already an ongoing German public debate about the abuse of power and free speech, before he joined it.

1. What Was the *Jugement?*

At a meeting of the Royal Academy in Berlin on April 13, 1752, Leonhard Euler presented the *Jugement* as a court verdict by the Academy against the Swiss mathematician and lawyer Samuel König, who held a position at the Dutch court (Jugement 1753). Euler claimed that Maupertuis had been accused by Samuel König of having plagiarized Leibniz as if Maupertuis had taken his famous principle of least action from the German philosopher. Since Maupertuis was the president of the Academy, such an accusation would concern the institution as well which thus had to defend its president. It is very likely that Euler had the infamous case of the Royal Society against Leibniz in mind, where Leibniz was accused of plagiarizing Newton (*Commercium epistolicum* 1722). On that occasion, the *Society* simultaneously played the role of judge and prosecutor, publishing the verdict without hearing Leibniz's defense as the other party. With regards to the alleged accusation of plagiarism, Euler focused on a passage cited by Samuel König from a Leibniz letter (*Nova acta eruditorum* 1751, 125–35; 162–76; see especially 176) and concluded that this passage was forged, presumably due to König's

Wolffian eagerness to ascribe all discoveries to Leibniz and none to Maupertuis: "Mr. le Professeur Koenig a fait ses efforts en plusieurs manières pour détruire cette grande découverte" (Jugement 1752, 5; see also 9).

The most significant mathematician of the eighteenth century, Euler provided five reasons aiming to prove that the cited passage could not have been written by Leibniz. Only one is still under discussion today because it depends on the interpretation of what the incriminating passage of the Leibniz letter *actually* says.[5] Four of his arguments are, to say the least, weak. The fifth objection, for instance, claimed that the Leibniz letter could not be authentic because König had received a copy from a man who had later been beheaded by the authorities of the city of Bern for political reasons. Today, we would certainly not consider such an objection to be valid since this man, Samuel Henzi, defended the constitution of the city of Bern.

Euler's objections that the cited letter was unknown and that the cited formulation could not be found in any published Leibniz letter (second argument) or work (third argument) did not make much sense either because, during the 1750s, many of Leibniz's writings had not yet been published. Euler's fourth argument addresses an obvious misprint, one so obvious that it was publicly pointed out early on. We might rather ask why, if Euler was truly concerned with the truth, he reprinted the mistaken version of the passage time and again, despite the fact that the correction was known to him even before the very first publication of the *Jugement* (Costabel 1979, 31–2). The first argument is the only mathematical argument that still deserves to be discussed. It simply denies that Leibniz had the mathematical knowledge to write this passage, due to the huge progress made in mathematics following Leibniz' death, progress that would have been available to Maupertuis and Euler. I discussed this argument elsewhere (Goldenbaum 2016, 30–2, 52–65). Here, I will focus on the *public* debate.

According to the proceedings of the Academy, *all* its members voted in favor of the *Jugement* (Jugement 1953, 23). That is, they *voted about the truth* of the claim that the cited passage must have been forged, insinuating that Samuel König had performed the forgery. It would soon become public knowledge that only half of the members, instead of them all, had attended the meeting and that nobody at the meeting was sufficiently competent to judge Euler's arguments apart from Euler himself.[6] One of the members had even dared to protest the *procedure* as such, Johann Georg Sulzer.[7] Nonetheless, he is still listed as one of the members who voted in favor of the *Jugement* against König. Likewise, the Perpetual Secretary of the Academy, Samuel Formey, who had not attended the meeting, had been urged to sign the vote days after the meeting. He obviously signed under the threat of losing his position (Best.D, 5195) and indeed, Johann Bernhard Merian, an unknown young man from Switzerland, had already been appointed as a second Perpetual Secretary during these months in honor of his services to Maupertuis and Euler.[8]

The allegedly unanimous *Jugement* of the Academy was not only published in the proceedings of the Academy. In June 1752, it was splendidly printed as an independent book, furnished with a Moroccan leather cover and gilt edging to be sent to European academies, famous scholars, to a few princes,[9] and—in a less grand presentation— to all important European newspapers and journals. Last but not least, it was also published in the European *Journal de sçavans* (Journal 162, June 1752, 286–331). The

Nova acta eruditorum, however, the well-known German scholarly journal, refused to publish the text because it already had been sufficiently published. When Maupertuis expressed his obvious anger about this, Kästner tried to calm him down by pointing to the less important status of this Latin-speaking journal (Kästner 1912, 23). What made Maupertuis so angry about the refusal of this journal of German science, with a limited influence in Europe, was the refusal itself. He understood it as a sign of resistance to the Academy's *Jugement* against König, and rightly so.

If we look for Maupertuis' and Euler's intentions for the launch of the *Jugement*, we see that it was supposed *to stop* the controversy about the Maupertuisian principle of least action. The *formal* character of the tribunal of the Academy members who voted on it, the title of a *Jugement*, its splendid presentation, and its distribution to all scientists, academies, journals, and even to princes in the name of the Royal Academy of Berlin were supposed to give it some ultimate official character, pre-empting all further discussion. Given this purpose—trying to control the opinion of the scientific community, it was certainly important to gain the support of each and every European scientific journal. This can also be seen by the campaign-like shipping of the *Jugement* in various designs according to the rank of the addressees during the summer, all of which was undertaken at the Academy's expense (Goldenbaum 2004b, 519–22). Only from this perspective does Maupertuis' anger about the refusal of the *Nova acta eruditorum* to publish the *Jugement* begin to make sense. My interpretation of the *Jugement* as an attempt to stop any further discussion is confirmed by Maupertuis' attempts to suppress a possible response by Samuel König to the *Jugement*. When Maupertuis sent the *Jugement* to the Princess of Orange (whom Samuel König served as a librarian), he asked her to forbid König any response to the *Jugement* (Magnan 1986, 307–8).[10] He could not have dared to address a princess in such a way without the support of the Prussian king.

It was the *Jugement*'s character as an ultimate court verdict against a scientist and the *authoritarian* attitude of the leaders of the Academy that provoked the public debate. This debate began right after the *Jugement*'s publication in the leading German so-called learned newspapers. But before I turn to them, part of the historical background of the public debate should be presented.

2. Pre-history of the Public Debate

In the proceedings of the Berlin Academy for the year 1746, published in 1748 (Maupertuis 1748), its president Maupertuis had presented his new great discovery to the world: the principle of least action from which all changes in the world could be explained.[11] Above all, this principle was meant to serve as a new demonstration of the existence of God. Presenting his new principle, Maupertuis extensively mocked all former demonstrations of God, especially physico-teleological demonstrations. He ridiculed Descartes and Fermat for their failure, but Leibniz even further. They all had missed the principle of least action that he finally discovered. Thus, it did not come as a surprise that Leibnizians felt challenged (Kästner 1912, 23). In March 1751, Samuel König published his criticism of Maupertuis' principle in the *Nova acta eruditorum* as a mere mathematical-mechanical argument.[12]

König was born in Switzerland but grew up in German exile, because his father had been expelled by the city of Bern. The son had nonetheless been admitted to the University of Bern, and due to his brilliant performance, his father's ban was lifted. After finishing his law studies in 1731, König went to Basel and studied the most recent mathematics with the Bernoullis—Johann Bernoulli I, Daniel Bernoulli, Nicolaus Bernoulli, and Jacob Hermann, who is also considered to be a part of the Bernoulli school. He stayed there until the summer of 1733 and made great progress in the calculus, as we know from a letter from Daniel Bernoulli to his friend Euler in Petersburg.[13]

König also continued to study law with Nicolaus Bernoulli, who was a lawyer. In 1733, he went to Halle to pursue his studies of law and mathematics with Christian Wolff. Four years later in 1737, he applied (in vain) for a position at the University of Bern, and then settled there as a lawyer. By 1738, he was invited by Johann Bernoulli II to join him on a trip to Paris where they met Maupertuis, and through him Émilie du Châtelet, Voltaire, and René Antoine Réaumur. For Réaumur König solved the problem of whether bees would build their honeycombs in the most geometrically perfect way by producing the most space possible with the least amount of material. He summarizes his positive mathematical results with near Leibnizian expressions: "Nature took the path that one can demonstrate to be the best, the shortest, or the most advantageous."[14] In consequence, König became a member of the French Academy, and also served as Madame du Châtelet's teacher of Leibniz's calculus and metaphysics for about a year while she was working on her *Institutions de Physique* (Foundations of Physics). In 1740, he returned to Bern as a lawyer, where he wrote some mathematical essays and translated Maupertuis' *De observationibus pro figura telluris determinanda in Gallia habitis disquisitio* (Investigation about the Observations Concerning the Figure of the Earth) into German (Upsala 1738).[15] He dedicated the work to Frederick II, in the obvious hope to be considered for the recently reorganized Berlin Academy. In the meantime, he worked with Gabriel Cramer on the edition of Johann Bernoulli's correspondence with Leibniz.

Samuel König was, however, also engaged in the ongoing battle of the citizens of his home city of Bern. In 1743, he signed the so-called *Memorandum*, a petition of the citizens of Bern asking the High Council of the city to return to the written constitution and to reinstall their citizen rights. As a result, the High Council banned the leading participants, among them Samuel König. He asked his famous compatriot Albrecht von Haller at the University of Göttingen for help and indeed received a position at the University of Groningen in the Netherlands, in September 1744. On April 26, 1746, he held his inaugural lecture on how to unify the best methods of Wolff and Newton, *De optimis Wolfianae et Newtonianae philosophiae methodis earumque consensus* (On the Best Methods of Wolffian and Newtonian Philosophy and their Agreement) (Franeker 1749). In 1748, he was appointed by Prince William Charles Friso of Orange as a professor of philosophy and natural law at the Knight Academy at The Hague. He was also assigned the position of court librarian and the title of court council. During the same year, he became a corresponding member of the Berlin Academy thanks to the suggestion of Maupertuis. In 1749, the so-called Henzi conspiracy took place in his home town of Bern, and, after its discovery, was cruelly persecuted by the High Council. Samuel Henzi, an erudite man and collector of Leibniz's manuscripts, was beheaded after a "process" of less than two weeks. All his private papers were burned. This event not only firmly blocked König's return to his home town, but also caused problems for our understanding of the history of the disputed Leibniz letter. This letter was one of four that König had received from Henzi, on his request.

König had already drafted his criticism of Maupertuis' principle of least action and sent it to the *Nova acta eruditorum* for publication by 1748, immediately after reading Maupertuis' publication in the proceedings of the Berlin Academy. But he soon withdrew it due to his respect for Maupertuis and the latter's high position at the Berlin Academy. He also knew about Maupertuis' sensitivity to criticism. Thus, he waited for an opportunity to personally present his article to Maupertuis, which occurred in 1750. When, during their meeting, König discovered that Maupertuis still held on to the opinion that Leibniz had plagiarized Newton in respect of the differential calculus, the Bernoulli student, familiar with both Leibniz and Newton, vehemently contradicted the accusation, which resulted in a heated discussion. The following day, Maupertuis sent König the manuscript back, asking him to publish it anyway and promising that he would respond.

In his article, König used the Leibnizian calculus while raising some fundamental objections against Maupertuis' principle, with due respect. His clear intention was to show, against Maupertuis' criticism of Leibniz' concept of "living force" (*vis viva*), that Leibniz' principle of the conservation of living forces was more fundamental than Maupertuis' principle of least action because the latter principle could be reduced to the former. König's paper concluded with a quotation from the disputed Leibniz letter. He cited the passage to show that, in contrast to the then-published writings, Leibniz had already dwelled on a theory of action that was based on the concept of living forces. König's article appeared in two parts in March 1751 in the *Nova acta eruditorum* under the title "De universali principio aequilibrii & motus, in Vi viva reperto, deque nexu inter Vim vivam & Actionem, utriusque minimo, Dissertatio" ("Treatise on the Universal Principle of the Aequilibrium and of Motion, Found in the Living Force, and about the Connection between Living Force and Action, and the Minimum of Both").[16]

As soon as the paper was published, Maupertuis sent a letter to König asking whether he had the original Leibniz letter available. However, König explained that he only had received the Leibniz letter as a copy. He sent a copy of the entire letter to Maupertuis who did not answer. Instead, the Perpetual Secretary sent an official request to König to provide the original letter. At the same time, Euler and Maupertuis, with the support of the Prussian king, initiated a search for the original Leibniz letter in Switzerland. König also tried to search for the original (Appel 1753, 157–9). Alas, the letter was not found.[17] On April 13, 1752, the meeting of the Berlin Academy took place, during which Leonhard Euler presented a report and provided the above-mentioned five arguments.[18] The *Jugement de l'Académie royale des sciences et belles-lettres sur une prétendue lettre de M. de Leibnitz* appeared in June 1752 in the *Mémoires* of the Berlin Academy, in the *Journal des sçavans* and also in various separate prints, as mentioned above.

Since the *Jugement* had been authored by the famous Leonhard Euler, historians of science still take his views for granted. Other scholars who avoid mathematical texts simply rely on his judgment. I cannot otherwise explain how any serious scholar can hold on to the claim that König's article accused Maupertuis of plagiarizing.[19] Nobody who truly reads it can find such an accusation. Neither did König claim that Leibniz had already found the principle of least action. Instead, König promoted that an *alternative* principle was more fundamental than that of least action: Leibniz' principle of *vis viva*.

With the *Jugement*, both Maupertuis and Euler made the Academy complain about Samuel König, who allegedly accused its president of plagiarizing—although König had never done so. It was their intention to use the Academy as an institution that had to defend its president.[20] If the *Jugement* had been merely about the truth of the principle, or the authenticity of the Leibniz letter, Euler as well as Maupertuis could have simply responded in any European journal. Maupertuis and Euler tacitly accepted the possible damage to König's reputation, if not his entire career as a scientist—as well as his position at the court of the Princess of Orange. Moreover, they did this to a respected and morally flawless scientist.[21] And, although the *Jugement* was meant to be a court verdict, the roles of plaintiff and judge were played by the same actor: the Berlin Academy (under Euler and Maupertuis). It was *this procedure* of the Academy that became the subject of the *public debate*, one that began very soon after the publication of the *Jugement*.

3. The Public Debate

The strategy of Maupertuis and Euler to stop *any* further discussion about the *Jugement* did work quite successfully within Prussia. There, the censorship of the "enlightened" Frederick worked absolutely in favor of the king's Academy president. Not a single critical publication could ever be printed in Prussia.[22] That does not mean that it was not discussed in public. As Sulzer reported to Albrecht von Haller: "Tout Berlin en parle, et d'une manière assez honorable pour Mr. König" (The entire city of Berlin is talking about this, and in a rather honorable way for König) (Consentius 1903, 543).

The situation was, however, quite different outside Prussia, where Frederick's censorship did not reach. It seems that neither the French scholar Maupertuis nor the Swiss mathematician Euler had been aware of the degree of independence of the most important German learned newspapers (*Gelehrte Zeitungen*) in Leipzig, Hamburg, and Göttingen. Such learned newspapers were written in German and had, as their audience, educated but not necessarily erudite people who lived in the cities, serving at courts, in schools and churches, and moreover in businesses. These papers contained reviews of recent literature, provided reports about scholarly appointments at universities, and controversies among scholars.

After the publication of the *Jugement* in June 1752, it was reviewed in these newspapers throughout the summer. While all the reviews were written politely and respectfully, they unanimously criticized the unheard-of *procedure* of the Academy against one of its members. If the Academy pretended to act as a court, why did they not listen to the defendant, and how could the plaintiff also be the judge? While the procedure was the major objection in all reviews, Euler's five reasons for the *Jugement* were considered as insufficient to ultimately *prove* the inauthenticity of the Leibniz letter. Reviews appeared in the *Neue Zeitungen von gelehrten Sachen* from Leipzig on

June 22, in *Die Göttingischen Zeitungen von gelehrten Sachen* in July, in *Das Neueste aus der anmuthigen Gelehrsamkeit* in August (N. 50), and in the *Freye Urtheile und Nachrichten zum Aufnehmen der Wissenschaften und der Historie überhaupt* from Hamburg on August 15 (Freye Urtheile 63, 498). The *Neue Zeitungen* stated with great self-confidence:

> To publicly declare an erudite, famous, and always flawless man a *Falsario*, is something which can neither be measured with a circle nor calculated by algebra; much less can it be decided by a onesided certificate of a self-appointed judge; but, since every *Falsum*, be it produced in scholarly or other things, is a shameful and punishable crime, one has to follow through according to the laws, the defendant has to be heard sufficiently, a judge has to be appointed who is not biased by either love or hatred, and the reason for a judgment of damnation must not be based on hectically gathered instances of mediocre probability but on certainty and conviction.
>
> (ibid., 444–5)

The review even asked Samuel König to appeal to a regular court in response to such calumnious accusations (Freye Urtheile 63, 445). A revocation of the *Jugement* by the Academy could be expected. The journal from Göttingen also expressed curiosity for König's response (*Göttingen Zeitungen*, July, 703–5) and all reviewers agreed that Samuel König had the right to respond. To sum it up: it is clear that the *Jugement* had not been accepted as the ultimate verdict as it had been intended by its authors.

Given their outraged reaction, we can conclude that neither the president Maupertuis nor the de facto vice-president of the Berlin Academy, Euler, had expected any such criticism. In spite of their great efforts to spread the *Jugement* as the *official* verdict of the Royal Academy and to silence Samuel König by asking his rulers[23] to forbid him to respond, their *Jugement* nonetheless faced criticism and their procedure was questioned in its entirety. As a result, the attention turned from König's criticism of Maupertuis and the authenticity of the Leibniz letter, as discussed among academics, to a public debate about the rules of discourse, about the rights and obligations of the contenders, and more generally, about freedom of speech.

The reviewer of the *Freye Urtheile* from Hamburg went beyond such a sober and objective discussion of the *Jugement* when he published internal information about the idiosyncratic Academy meeting where the *Jugement* had been presented. It is from this report that the public audience came to know of Sulzer's protest against the procedure, thereby questioning the alleged unanimity of the Academy (Freye Urtheile 63, 498). Moreover, the author—obviously being an insider—explicitly raised general questions about the authoritarian constitution of the Academy.[24]

On August 18, Maupertuis' above-mentioned letter to the princess of Orange was reported in a newspaper (Magnan 1986, 307–8), causing another flurry of commentaries in the learned newspapers. The fact that Maupertuis had relied on political means in a scientific discussion was considered a clear offense to the rules of the dispute. The Dutch author who had sent the letter from Utrecht to the German newspaper asked why the president of the Academy was so afraid of Samuel König's reponse, concluding: "Les gens éclairés sont extrêmement surpris de ce procédé inouï de M." (Magnan 1986,

308). Thus, Maupertuis and Euler had to face the fact that these learned newspapers challenged them to justify their procedure, against their expectation of silence about König's criticism and about the *Jugement*.

4. Maupertuis and Euler's Reaction to the Public Criticism: Changing the Point of Question and Slander

Maupertuis and Euler were certainly not happy about this unexpected reaction. Despite the authority of the Berlin Academy and in spite of Maupertuis' close relationship with the Prussian king, German and later Dutch newspapers dared to criticize their *Jugement*. Maupertuis raved and raged, as we know from a report about his first reaction to the reviews. The author of this anonymous report, Christlob Mylius, was an insider. A scientist himself, he worked for the Academy, and especially for Maupertuis and Euler. In the summer of 1748, he had been invited by the Academy for the observation of a solar eclipse (Trillmich 1914, 75-6) and he joined Euler at the observation of the lunar eclipse on August 8-9 of the same year. Mylius had also translated the works of Maupertuis and Clairaut into German, and regularly wrote articles and reviewed books for the Hamburgian learned newspapers. In a letter of August 22 to Albrecht von Haller, the president of the Academy at Göttingen, he vividly described Maupertuis' anger:

> My review of the *Jugement* is now printed in the Hamburgian Newspaper, and you may already have read it. Maupertuis read it too and he is almost raging about it. He makes every effort to figure out the author, but I hope indeed that nobody will denounce me to him. Meanwhile he is completely of the opinion that König himself sent this review to the newspaper, and I for myself do not contradict him. He is asking every day in the bookshops for news from König and other journals about the *Jugement*.
>
> (Consentius 1903, 541-2)

Maupertuis was clearly not interested in answering König's critique,[25] but was rather eager to find the authors of the critical reviews. Euler though aimed to find the author of the Hamburg review. In an anonymous letter to the *Berlinische Relationen*, which was published or at least initiated by him (according to the well-informed Mylius), he wrote: "I asked around and can tell that none of the Academy members has the honor to be acquainted with the author of the review from Hamburg. Also, none of them could be persuaded to have judged unjustly [by the *Jugement*]. Finally, none of them does complain about being rushed [into the vote on the *Jugement*]."[26] From his interrogation of the members of the Academy, the anonymous author concludes that the journalist from Hamburg must have faked his report. Mylius, being this journalist and being very familiar with the Berlin Academy and its members, cited and already mocked this letter by the following week in the *Freye Urtheile*.[27]

During the first half of September, the *Lettres concernant le Jugement de l'Académie* were published in Berlin, written by Johann Bernhard Merian, Euler, and Maupertuis.

Merian was still an unknown young man from Switzerland who had just become a member of the Academy, on the recommendation of Johann II Bernoulli to Maupertuis. His eager support for Maupertuis and Euler during the years of this public debate would lay the ground for his successful career at the Academy, far beyond the death of the two leaders. The publication of these *Letters* shows that Euler and Maupertuis felt the need to react to the unexpected public resistance to the *Jugement*; but it reveals their fury even more. These *Letters* are replete with invectives against the "miserable band of journalists," referring to the authors of the reviews in the learned newspapers, especially the ignorant "compilators" from Hamburg and Leipzig (Lettres 1752, 4). They were addressed as malicious, brazen, and iniquitous, and blamed for their (alleged) complete ignorance of science. They are further described as have-nots and as starving, a slander supposed to belittle their social ranking in the eyes of the public. Merian was the most eager in slandering the journalists and even addressed the journalists as the "slaves of König" by whom they may be paid (Lettres 1752, 34–56). This being said, Euler as well as Maupertuis had authorized and co-authored all three letters with all the invectives.

Obviously, the authors of the *Lettres* were disappointed. By attacking the objective criticism of the *Jugement* in the journals instead of responding through arguments, they made it quite clear that they would not tolerate any criticism of the *Jugement*. They considered such criticism as a lack of respect for the authority of the Royal Academy. But the thus-maligned "journalists" were by no means such unlearned, starving, or malicious people. The only one who may have starved at times was Mylius, who did not yet hold a permanent position. But this young scientist and journalist, a close friend of the young Lessing, and author of the Hamburgian *Freye Urtheile*, had already acquired some reputation as an astronomer and physicist. Even Euler had recommended him to the Academy at Petersburg twice, on December 18/29, 1749, and again on February 10/21, 1750 (Juškevič/Winter, 185 and 189–90).[28] And Albrecht von Haller appointed him to lead a scientific expedition to East-India by the Academy at Göttingen. The other three targeted "journalists," however, were themselves members of the Berlin Academy: Abraham Gotthelf Kästner, Albrecht von Haller, and Christoph Gottsched. Therefore, the rumor launched by Euler and Merian that the authors of the critical reviews of the *Jugement* were starving and incompetent journalists who had just published for money (and were perhaps paid by König) did not fit with the profile of any of these authors.

There is nothing interesting in these *Lettres concernant le Jugement*, except one point, which is rarely noticed: Euler *changed* his argument. He no longer accused Samuel König of forgery nor of consciously quoting a forgery. To justify the Academy's *procedure* against the criticism in the learned newspapers, he *now* claimed that the *Jugement* had not been a court verdict against König at all, but a mere demonstration of the insufficient evidence of the authenticity of the Leibniz letter (Lettres 1752, 5–7). Therefore, all the public excitement about an offense to König would lack any reason. Unfortunately, Euler's blunt argumentative *change* concerning the *Jugement* is still used today by historians of science to excuse Euler or at least to mitigate his responsibility in the abuse of power that the *Jugement* is still recognized to be today.[29] That this is simply false, however, can be shown by a simple comparison of this last statement of Euler's with that of the actual *Jugement*.

5. Samuel König's Synopsis

König, who had been in correspondence about the cited Leibniz letter first with Maupertuis, then with the Perpetual Secretary of the Academy, Samuel Formey, learned about the content of the *Jugement* while it was still in print. He received a separate print of it on June 18, 1752. On the very same day, he protested it by returning the certificate of his membership to the Berlin Academy. Then, in early September, his *Appel au public* came out, written and published shortly before the three *Lettres* would appear.[30] As the title of the book indicates, König thereby presented his entire case to the public sphere, asking it to be his judge. He offers evidence for everything he reports in the first parts of the book.

In the first section, König presents the origin of the dispute, beginning with his criticism of Maupertuis' principle of least action in the *Nova acta eruditorum* of March 1751, which contained the Leibniz citation. He reports that Maupertuis had promised him a response to his critique before asking for the original version of the Leibniz letter. However, after learning that König only owned a copy received from Samuel Henzi in Bern, he ended the correspondence. Instead, the Academy officially asked König to provide the original on October 8. König concluded that the accusation against him was no more than a strategy to prevent a critical discussion of Maupertuis' principle. He saw this confirmed by Maupertuis' remark in the introduction to a recent re-edition of his *Works* (Appel 1753, 16) that, contrary to his promise, he did not intend to answer König's criticism. In his introduction, Maupertuis indeed stated, after presenting his view of his controversy with König about his principle, that he will not respond to König's objections—against his promise—because "geometricians and philosophers would judge according to their own values."[31] He thereby suggested that König was a mere Wolffian metaphysician while he, Maupertuis, aimed for mere science. This statement was inappropriate since König's critical essay shows him as an advanced mathematician and mechanical theorist, who hardly discusses metaphysics. But the distinction between good scientists and bad metaphysicians would be widely used by Euler against the Wolffians, and it became—due to his authority—a standard judgment of history of science about the eighteenth century and, particularly, about the controversies within the Berlin Academy.[32]

In the second section, König vehemently dismisses the accusation expressed by the *Jugement*, that—by quoting the Leibniz letter—he had intended to accuse Maupertuis of plagiarizing Leibniz. This is crucial, since without this alleged accusation, the Academy as an institution would not have retained any excuse to intervene at all. If the *Jugement* had indeed been a mere discussion of the authenticity of the Leibniz letter—as Euler pretended in the *Lettres*—why should the Academy as an institution have been concerned with it at all? König then explains his earlier argument, that Maupertuis' principle of least action can be reduced to Leibniz' *vis viva* principle, which is thus more fundamental. Since Leibniz and Maupertuis held two different although related principles, König asks: "how could the latter come up with the idea that the fragment [of the cited Leibniz letter] indicated his theory?" (Appel 1753, 27) He had cited the Leibniz passage alone to emphasize that Leibniz very likely already had an alternative foundation of dynamics in the making.

In the third section, König raises the question that would dominate the public debate throughout: whether the Academy had a right to decide the controversy among scholars by vote. Being a lawyer by profession, he provides a systematic juridical argument about the rights of the Academy and the competences of its members. He concludes that neither its installment by the king nor any of the paragraphs of its constitution gave them any right to ultimately decide cases of honor or truth. Instead, the freedom and equality of all scholars in and outside of the Academy remained completely unaffected by the *Jugement* (Appel 1753, 43–4).

The fourth section contains all the letters that provide evidence in support of König's presentation of the case: (1) his correspondence with Maupertuis about their controversy and about the Leibniz letter, alongside his official correspondence with the Academy (with Samuel Formey as its Perpetual Secretary), and (2) the four Leibniz letters received from Samuel Henzi, including the disputed one. The *Appel au public* appeared in French at the Dutch publishing house Luzac in Leiden. It was immediately translated into German, promoted by Christoph Gottsched, and published by Breitkopf in Leipzig. Since French had been the *lingua franca* of academics in Germany as well, educated Germans were able to read the French version (Mahlmann-Maurer 2017, 5–14). The enormous public interest in this debate can be inferred from the fact that both editions had to be reprinted, already, by the spring and early summer of 1753.

6. Voltaire's Entry into the Public Debate

Voltaire entered this public debate rather late. His short and sober *Réponse d'un académicien de Berlin à un académicien de Paris* (*Response of a member of the Berlin Academy to a member of the Academy of Paris*) appeared on September 18, 1752, in the *Journal de sçavans* (Journal 163, 559–61), after he had read König's *Appel au public*.[33] Of course, as a member of the Academy, he had taken notice of the *Jugement* right after its publication in June and had mocked it in a letter to Formey (Best.D, 4934; Formey 1789, 276–7). But only after reading the *Appel* did he decide to support König's cause against the Academy, despite his notable opposition to the Leibniz-Wolffian philosophy.

At this point, he entered an ongoing public debate in Germany about freedom of speech. I am emphasizing this against the common prejudice that Voltaire was the only hero who dared to speak up for Samuel König. Rather, he participated in the existing German public debate on freedom of speech, including König's *Appel*. Likewise, when historians of science complain with Euler about Voltaire for meddling into a scientific controversy that he did not understand, they completely ignore that Voltaire did not enter any scientific or metaphysical controversy here. He took sides in the *public debate* on freedom of speech. And this was, as nobody will deny, his particular competence.

It was soon known that Voltaire was the author whose anonymous *Response* caused the king to enter the public sphere. The "enlightened" Frederick, however, was not interested in a free discussion. Instead, he worried about the reputation of his Royal Academy and its president. His *Lettre d'un académicien de Berlin à un académicien de Paris* from mid-November 1752 (Friedrich II 1753, 53–74)[34] did not contain any serious argument. It is rather a long, mere slander of Samuel König and the "incompetent journalists," as well as a highly exaggerated, and thereby embarrassing, appraisal of Maupertuis. The king clearly demonstrated his incompetence by directly accusing König of having forged the Leibniz letter, which was not even claimed by either Euler or Maupertuis. He urges the members of his Academy to write in support of their "father," Maupertuis.

A review of this *Lettre* in the *Freye Urtheile* in Hamburg on November 24, 1752, calls it the worst among all bad contributions to the public debate so far, stating: "It is a bastard of a pamphlet" (Freye Urtheile 91, 735), meaning that it is mere slander. The reviewer summarizes that the author did not understand the least bit of the discussion. The second edition of Frederick's *Lettre* had the Royal seal on its cover to avoid a further similar critique of the royal author! Voltaire was pleased, however, and praised the courage of the German journalists (Best.D, 5067).

Voltaire responded to Frederick's *Lettre*. In the same month, he circulated a handwritten letter (formally addressed to König but directed at Frederick and the court) in Berlin and at the court wherein he explained the admittedly confusing controversies (on the principle of least action, the authenticity of the Leibniz letter, and the public debate about the Academy's procedure) to a lay audience, including the king (*Maupertuisiana* 1753).[35] He admits that he had shared his "colleague's" (Frederick's) opinion, but that he changed his mind after reading the *Appel*, urging the "colleague" to read it as well. In addition, Voltaire began his more satirical writings, which still objectively presented the events: *Lettre d'un savant au Marquis de L* N** and *Extrait d'une lettre d'un académicien de Berlin à un membre de la Société Royale de Londres*. If we compare Voltaire's writings with the king's pamphlet, the French author favorably distinguishes himself: while remaining slightly ironic toward Maupertuis, he provides the facts objectively and almost correctly. Keeping regular contact with the king and seeing that his attempts were to no avail, he drafted his merciless *Diatribe du Dr. Akakia, médecin du Pape* and tried to get it printed in Potsdam with a Royal privilege for another writing.

Voltaire's surprising familiarity with the subjects of the above-mentioned scientific controversies between König and Maupertuis seems at least partially due to his new acquaintance in Berlin, the German journalist and scientist Christlob Mylius. Together with the duchess Bentinck, they constituted an "Anti-Triumvirat," as they ironically named themselves (Consentius 1903, 548). It was an allusion to the "Triumvirat" formed by Maupertuis, Euler, and Merian (Goldenbaum 2004b, 592–609). The latter title had been frequently used by German newspapers to address these "académiciens" after their publication of the three *Lettres concernant le Jugement*.

As mentioned above, Mylius was a scientist. As a former student of Abraham Kästner, he was as familiar with Leibniz-Wolffian philosophy as he was with mechanics and mathematics. This is confirmed by Euler's judgment, which recommended him to the Academy of Petersburg.[36] Thus, Mylius understood the mechanical-dynamical arguments advanced by both Maupertuis and König. In addition, he knew the internal situation of the Academy very well and was also acquainted with the authors of the German critical reviews. Last but not least, throughout the course of the public debate, he began a correspondence with König. After all, he had been involved himself in the public debate since mid-August of 1752. This should be emphasized against the common prejudice of Voltaire scholarship that Mylius was a mere aide of Voltaire (Fontius 1966, 50; Magnan 1986, 399–421). He could offer scientific as well as an insider's knowledge about the Academy to the reputed Voltaire.

The most famous text of Voltaire, the *Dr. Akakia*, displays quite some familiarity of the author with the scientific and metaphysical arguments of both opponents and moreover, with the internal conditions of the Berlin Academy, and it provides many details about the authoritarian style of its leaders, Maupertuis and Euler. The satire is additionally laden with allusions to Maupertuis' works, particularly his *Essay on Cosmology*, which Voltaire especially mocked. It seems that Voltaire could make great use of Mylius' scientific knowledge and his insights about the Academy. After all, Mylius was the translator of Maupertuis' *Essay on Cosmology*.

The cooperation between the famous French enlightener and the rather unknown German scientist and journalist continued until they both left Berlin for Leipzig in March 1753. They did not meet in Leipzig as planned because Voltaire could not receive his farewell from Frederick before Mylius' departure from Leipzig for his expedition to East-India on behalf of the Academy of Göttingen. But during their respective stays in Leipzig, they both continued to work on their shared project—fueling the *public debate* about the *Jugement*. They both worked together with Christoph Gottsched and his publisher Breitkopf. They produced an entire collection of all the writings in German and French and did not only include Voltaire's satirical pieces, but all of the previously mentioned German articles and more. Both versions of the collection appeared in the spring of 1753, in German at Breitkopf in Leipzig, and in French at Luzac the Younger in Leiden. The two publishers even cooperated about the illustrations. These collections further fueled the public debate since both were, of course, widely reviewed and commented.

Jonathan Israel dismisses Voltaire as only a moderate enlightener who even served the king.[37] But Voltaire's engagement in this public debate was a tough and risky challenge to the king. Frederick had already been furious about Voltaire's *Dr. Akakia* and admonished him to not publish it (Goldenbaum 2004b, 579–81).[38] The king was even more angry when the publication nevertheless arrived in Berlin. The book was burned by the hangman on the order of Frederick, on December 23, 1752, on the central squares of Berlin. To be sure, this book-burning was not just an expression of royal anger but an official punishment, and a further warning to Voltaire! Notwithstanding such Prussian censorship, a German translation of *Dr. Akakia* with additional mocking verses was distributed in the streets of Berlin, very likely by Mylius. This distribution was, of course, only completed in handwriting, since no printer in Prussia would have taken up the printing (Magnan 1986, 321).

Only after some difficult negotiations could Voltaire get his farewell from Prussia in late March 1753. When Voltaire and Mylius dared, notwithstanding, to continue to publish in order to continue fueling the public debate, Frederick gave the order to imprison Voltaire as soon as he reached the territory of Frankfurt on the Main on May 31, 1753, where he remained detained until July 7 (Haupt 1909). It was also rumored that Mylius had been detained at the citadel of Spandau, but he safely arrived in Göttingen, well on his way to London (Goldenbaum 2004b, 638). That Voltaire expressed his serious concerns about the fate of his friend shows,[39] however, that he was aware of the danger they both faced.

7. The Public Debate

The entire public debate, with all the mutual responses and satires, cannot be exhaustively recounted here (see Goldenbaum 2004b, 509-651). König's *Appel au public* was certainly discussed in all German learned newspapers, as were all the major writings that came out until 1753. Since the famous Voltaire entered the debate and constantly produced new satires, he further fueled the public debate and stirred up curiosity, even in France (Goldenbaum 2004b, 633-5).[40] All his statements and satires were widely reviewed. In addition, the *Bibliothèque impartiale* in Leiden started an extended and impartial presentation of all contributions of this case from July 1752 up to the end of the year by chiefly focusing on the scientific controversies.

In February 1753, *Das Neueste aus der anmuthigen Gelehrsamkeit* filled eight pages with reviews of further contributions to this public debate (Windmonath [november] 1753, n. 8, pp. 850-57). The extension of this public debate about freedom of speech is most obvious given the fact that it was crowned by the publication of a double collection of all the contributions, promoted by Voltaire and Mylius. On March 16, it had already been reviewed in the *Hamburgische Unpartheyische Correspondent*, a general newspaper with an audience reaching well beyond the German Empire, and then of course by all the above-mentioned learned newspapers. That the *Vollständige Sammlung*, the German collection, had its second edition as early as May 1753 indicates the great interest of German readers in the subject. The French second edition of the collection, appearing at Luzac in Leiden under the title *Maupertuisiana*, appeared early in the summer of 1753 with a second edition of the *Appel au public*.

In contrast, Maupertuis and Euler, the powerful opponents of König, withdrew behind the walls of the Academy to remain in their own circles. In April 1753, Maupertuis traveled to Paris trying to save his reputation there against Voltaire's satirical critiques. *Dr. Akakia* sold very well in Paris and gained great popularity within the city (Best.D, 5163).[41] Besides, the French Academy had already applauded a critique of the principle of least action, presented by Patrice Marquis d'Arcy on February 7, 1753 (Magnan, 334-6).[42] Maupertuis returned to Berlin for a short period of time, and he ultimately escaped damage to his reputation by visiting his old friend, Johann II Bernoulli, in Switzerland in 1756, where he died in 1759.

Euler, however, published his criticism of König's views almost exclusively in the proceedings of the Academy, pretending to focus on scientific arguments alone but still slandering König. He could never provide a conclusive argument that would prove a mistake was committed on the latter's part. At least, he took up the task that Maupertuis had not fulfilled: to respond to König's original criticism of the principle of least action. Under the pressure of the public debate, he tried to show that König's critical discussion of the principle of least action had no basis at all.[43]

But besides *this* remarkable success of the public debate, which at least forced Euler to finally respond to König, its greatest and most astonishing result was the open public debate that questioned the abuse of power by the Royal Academy not only against Maupertuis and Euler, but the Prussian king himself. Obviously, this public debate saved Samuel König's moral and scientific reputation from the harsh accusations of forgery that were not brought forward by just any two famous colleagues, but by the representatives of the powerful Berlin Academy and the Prussian king.

This achievement of the public debate is even more obvious if we compare it with Leibniz's fate half a century earlier, when he had been accused by the Royal Society of plagiarizing Newton. While he received some support from individual scholars, he had to defend himself on his own, without any public support. The prejudice against him would shape the English-speaking academic world's view of Leibniz at least until the First World War. Leibniz did not yet have a public sphere that was available.

Finally, for more than two years of this public debate, the *rules of a fair discourse* and the right for freedom of speech were extensively and constantly explained and discussed in the entire public sphere, especially in the Protestant area of the German Empire, but well beyond its borders, in the Netherlands and in France (Goldenbaum 2004a, 111–5). Moreover, Samuel König explicitly addressed the public sphere with his *Appel au public*. In its "Avertissement" (Announcement), he called the *public* the only judge capable of deciding the case in a knowable way. Therefore, he makes all the documents available to this public sphere, enabling it to make an informed decision. He concludes: "We hope that the public, enlightened [by the documents], will do due justice to [König] and—by its judgment—render ineffective the one made by the Academy, without hearing both parties and without a careful deliberation" (Appel 1753, 6). It is within these years that the neologism "*Publikum*" emerged in the German language. This is very likely due to the frequent use of the French term "publique" during this public debate. Against this neologism, Gottsched's German translation of the term as "*gemeines Wesen*" had no chance. It had not been mentioned in any review except to refer to the complete German book title of the *Appel au public*: *Beruffung auf das gemeine Wesen*.

Abbreviations

Best.D	Voltaire. 1968–77. *Correspondence and related documents. Definitive edition by Theodore Besterman. In The complete works of Voltaire*, Genève: Institut et Musée Voltaire, vols. I-LI (resp. vols. 85–135).
Correspondance	Bernoulli, Daniel. 1843. *Correspondance mathématique et physique de quelques célèbres géomètres du XVIIIe siècle*, 2 vols., edited by P.-H. Fuss. St. Petersbourg [Reprint: New York 1968].
Berlinische Relationen	*Wöchentliche Relationen der merkwürdigsten Sachen aus dem Reiche der Natur, der Staaten und der Wissenschaften*, Berlin: Verlag der Buchhandlung der Realschule.

Notes

1. All English translations of historical sources in this chapter are my own.
2. To the best of my knowledge, my own extended investigation of this public debate in the framework of public debates in German Enlightenment is the first attempt. See Goldenbaum 2004b.
3. See Mayer 1877; Helmholtz 1887; Kneser 1928; Brunet 1938; Szabó 1976, 86–107; and Pulte 1989.
4. See Brunet 1929, 130–58; Szabo 1976, 89, 99; and Pulte 1989, 200–4, 216–25.
5. "Mais l'Action n'est point ce que vous pensez: la considération du tems y entre; elle est comme le produit de la masse par l'espace & la vitesse, ou du tems par la force vive. J'ai remarqué que, dans les modifications des mouvemens, elle devient ordinairement un *Maximum* ou un *Minimum*: on en peut déduire plusieurs propositions de grande conséquence elle pourroit servir à déterminer les courbes que décrivent les Corps attirés à un ou plusieurs Centres. Je voulois traiter de ces choses entre autres dans la seconde partie de ma Dynamique, que j'ai supprimée, le mauvais accueil, que le préjugé a fait à la première, m'aïant dégouté." (Appel 1752, 171–2). I am quoting this passage without the obvious misprint in the original publication, i.e., according to the version cited in König's *Appel au public*. Although Euler knew this correct version even before he authored the *Jugement* (from a letter König had written to the Academy), he would continue to use the misprinted formulation when citing the letter.
6. The minutes ("Protokolle") of the meeting mention the following members as "voting":

    Keith and Redern as trustees, Marschall and Cagnony as honoraries, Eller, Heinius, and Euler as directors of the classes, Formey as the Perpetual Secretary, and Pelloutier, Sproegel, M.M. Ludolff, Gleditsch, Beausobre, Meckel, Sulzer, Lalande, Pott, Küster, Beemann, C.L. Ludolff, Kies, and Merian. The only one who would *become* a great mathematician was Lalande, who was nineteen years old at that time. He had used the Berlin planetary in 1750 on behalf of the French Academy, and had been hosted by Euler, who was paid for it by the Academy (Knobloch 1984, 111, II N. 403). In December 1751, he became a "corresponding member" of the Berlin Academy. In April 1752, he was, however, not yet capable to judge Euler's arguments against Leibniz' authorship of the letter. Neither was the astronomer Kies who is also listed. When he entered the Academy, it was his intention to make himself more familiar "with higher geometry" and with "Newton's philosophy" (Knobloch 1984, 435, III N. 3). Besides, he viewed the procedure of the Academy rather critically and left Berlin in the aftermath of the *Jugement*. See Goldenbaum 2004b, 532–3.
7. He would later publicly deny that he had protested (Goldenbaum 2004b, 529–30). That this was only due to the pressure by the Academy leaders is obvious from his private letter to a Swiss friend, wherein he again confirmed his actual protest at the meeting (Consentius 1903, 543, Anm. 3).
8. While this is explicitly reported by Voltaire alone, it makes perfect sense. Already by August 1, 1752, Mylius wrote to Haller about the situation at the Academy after the *Jugement*: "M. de Maupertuis made himself much hated by it and the Academy mightily suffers from it. The world, however, does not know how few of the members of the Academy gave their Yes [to the *Jugement*] from their heart, and that M. de

Maupertuis treats the regular members of the Academy in no other way than a colonel his soldiers since here everything is despotic" (Consentius, 538–9). Formey—to escape the constant demand to engage in the defense of Maupertuis and of the Academy against the public critics—even declared himself sick from November 1752 until the summer of 1753, when Maupertuis departed for Paris (Formey 1789, 185). See Wolff's ironic letter about Formey while under pressure by Maupertuis and Euler, cited in Goldenbaum 2004b, 534.

9   See the list of mail messages sent out by the Berlin Academy throughout June and July 1752 (AABAW: PAW (1700–1811), I-XVI-224, 221–2) and the receipts about the various bindings of the *Jugement* (ibid., 149).

10 Obviously, the princess shared Maupertuis' letter with König, who distributed it to his friends. We know that he copied it to Albrecht von Haller on September 5, 1752 (*Mittheilungen* 1845, 69–72, ftn. 34).

11 Maupertuis, 1746, "Les Lois du mouvement et du repos déduites d'un principe de métaphysique." He had already presented his discovery at the Paris Academy in 1744. It was published in its proceedings "for the year 1744," which came out much later, however. See Maupertuis, 1744, "Accord de différentes loix de la nature qui avoient jusqu'ici paru incompatibles."

12 König 1751, March, 125–35 and 162–76; König 2016, 101–42. He had sent the manuscript to the *Nova acta eruditorum* in 1748. In his *Appel*, he explains why he then withdrew his manuscript and went forward again with this publication in 1751, after his personal meeting with Maupertuis in Berlin in 1750 (Appel 1753, 9–12).

13 Daniel Bernoulli to Euler on June 4, 1735 (*Correspondance*, 426).

14 Cited after Graf 1889, 28. For Leibniz, see his *Discours de métaphysique*, §5.

15 *Figur der Erden bestimmt durch die Beobachtungen der Herren von Maupertuis, Clairaut, Camus, le Monnier, von der Academie der Wissenschaften, und des Hrn Abts Outhiers, Correspondents der gleichen Academie, in Begleitung des Herrn Celsius, Professor in der Academie zu Upsal, auf Ordre des Königs, beym Polar-Zirkel angestellet durch Hrn. Maupertuis. Aus dem Französischen übersetzt, und mit Hrn. Celsius Untersuchung der Cassinischen Messungen vermehret* (Zürich 1741).

16 *Nova acta eruditorum*, I, 125–35; II, 162–76. Reprinted in Euler's *Opera omnia* II, 5, 303–24.

17 Jugement 1752, 18–22; Appel, 95–102.

18 Knobloch 1984, III, N. 282, 375.

19 The only exception is Szabo, who clearly states that this accusation of König is simply wrong (Szabo 1976, 97).

20 I have shown elsewhere that the entire project of the *Jugement*—with its alleged accusation that König accused Maupertuis of plagiarizing Leibniz—had indeed been invented by Euler, who then persuaded Maupertuis to proceed in this way. The latter was, however, certainly relieved that he did not have to respond to König. See Goldenbaum 2008, 103–21.

21 The *Neue Zeitungen von gelehrten Sachen* wrote, on June 22, 1752, in a very critical manner: "To declare an erudite, famous, and always righteous scholar a public forger, is something that cannot be measured by a compass nor calculated by algebra" (ibid., 444–5). König was in good standing with Jacob Bodmer, Haller, Réaumur, and Wolff, who all saw him as gifted *and* integral. Daniel Bernoulli recommended him warmly to his friend Euler.

22 Voltaire had tried to get his *Dr. Akakia* printed in Prussia but was denounced by somebody who randomly discovered the manuscript in the printery (Fleischauer 1964, 76–9). The king burned the manuscript in his fireplace, in Voltaire's presence, and warned the poet not to dare publishing it again. When the book, notwithstanding, arrived in Prussia, having been printed in the Netherlands, Frederick had it burned in public on the central squares of Berlin by the hangman. This was the end of Frederick's famous "Roundtable of Sanssouci," which lasted less than three years.
23 This was, on the one hand, the princess Anna of Orange, and on the other, Louis Ernest Duke of Brunswick-Wolfenbüttel. The Prince of Orange had appointed the latter as field marshal of the Netherlands in 1747 and shortly before his death in 1751, as one of the regents for his heir (together with Anna).
24 The constitution of the Academy already conferred all the power to its president (Harnack 1900, 228–9). Pensions, publications, purchases of scientific instruments, even traveling were all left to the decision of Maupertuis. But due to Maupertuis' vanity and imperiousness, which were strengthened by Euler's support, the Academy was indeed ruled in a despotic way. See Goldenbaum 2004b, 529–35.
25 See the next endnote.
26 *Berlinische Relationen* 36, Week, 2nd piece, 595–6. Reprinted in *Maupertuisiana* 1753, 39–41; see especially 41.
27 Freye 73, 577; September 15, 1752.
28 The double dates are due to the use of different calendars used in different states within the [German] Empire and in Europe–the Gregorian and the Julian Calendar.
29 Szabo 1976, 98; Pulte 1989, 200–4.
30 That is the reason why Euler will add an appendix to his letter where he comments on the *Appel* (Lettres 1752, 17–26).
31 "Ceux qui connoissent le culte que M. K. rend au nom de M. de Leybnitz, trouveront qu'il ne pouvoit pas nous faire plus d'honneur que lui attribuer une partie de notre ouvrage: Quant aux objections qu'il a faites contre le reste, les Philosophes & les Géomètres jugeront de leur Valeur. Mon intention n'est pas d'y répondre" (Maupertuis' *Oeuvres* 1752, unpaginated; the quote is from the last page of the introduction).
32 Euler 1753a, 211–13; Euler 1753b, 230, 238–9. Since the papers of the Academy dissertations were usually published two years after their presentation at the Academy, the volumes have the (later) year of printing on the cover but add the earlier year of presentations, covered by the volume. In the case of the currently mentioned papers by Euler, they were all printed in the very same year as they were presented due to the public debate. This often misleads historians of science to assume that Euler had written them by 1751, that is, before the controversy had even started.
33 While he would prefer Pascal's style of the *Lettres provinciales* over that of König's *Appel*, Voltaire approves of the latter by this pointed statement: "L'ouvrage est convaincant, c'est tout ce qu'il faut." (Best.D, 5021)
34 The book re-published two *Éloges* that were authored by Frederick and that dealt with Jordan and La Mettrie, two members of the Berlin Academy. It also contained Frederick's anonymously published *Lettre d'un académicien de Berlin*. While one aim of the anonymous editors of this odd combination was to demonstrate the "elogious" character of Frederick's *Lettre*, treating Maupertuis as if he had already died, this

pointed edition directly aimed at the king's uncritical position toward Maupertuis and La Mettrie. For more context about this edition, see Goldenbaum 2004, 573–5.
35   The *Maupertuisiana*, the French collection of the papers of this public debate, keep the page numbers of the original prints of the larger writings. Voltaire's letter to Samuel König, which he circulated at the court in Berlin, is listed in the table of contents as "Extrait d'une Lettre de Berlin, du 12. Novembre 1752."
36   Juškevič/Winter 1959, II, 185 and 189–90.
37   Israel's attacks against Voltaire are spread throughout his books, but chapter 6 ("Voltaire versus Spinoza") in his *Revolution of the Mind* is especially aggressive, and biased—making Voltaire even fight his fellow enlighteners and side with the nobility: "As Voltaire envisaged it, the unrelenting *war between Moderate and Radical Enlightenment* after 1770 was philosophical in the first place but far from being only philosophical. Voltaire's life-long fight for more toleration and to discredit the Church among the higher echelons of society was an attempt to change the world *in alliance with Europe's nobility and courts*, weakening only ecclesiastical power and theology while leaving the faith of the common people intact." (Israel 2010, 217; emphasis added).
38   See endnote 22 above.
39   "Monsieur Milius n'est point en Hollande. On dit que Maupertuis l'a fait arrêter en chemin sur une accusation d'affaires d'État. La chose n'est que trop vraisemblable." (Voltaire to Gottsched on April 19, 1753, in UB Leipzig, Ms 0342, vol. 18, Bl. 336r)
40   At the end of June 1753, Melchior Grimm (a former student of Gottsched) asked his teacher to send him the *Maupertuisiana* to Paris since he felt pressed by the "entire city" to come up with information about the controversy (Grimm to Gottsched on June 29, 1753, in UB Leipzig, vol. 17, Bl. 327r). On July 22, he urges Gottsched to immediately send it by express mail. He would pay any amount to quickly receive it in Paris (ibid., vol. 18, Bl. 403r). That was during Maupertuis' stay at Paris!
41   That 6,000 copies of *Dr. Akakia* were sold in Paris per day was perhaps an exaggeration of Voltaire, but the satire was highly in demand. See Fleischauer 1964, 94–9.
42   Maupertuis felt under pressure to react to the critical wave against him (Maupertuis 1754, 293–8). For more detailed information, see Goldenbaum 2004b, 635.
43   These publications, completely taken out of the context of the public debate, are still the exclusive basis of historians of science when they write about the history of the *Jugement*. This has even led to mistakes in the dating of Euler's writings (for instance, see Pulte 1989, 278). As a *de facto* vice-president, Euler could certainly get his works published without the common delay of two years, and even more so when writing in the president's favor! Compare with endnote 32.

Bibliography

Journals and Newspapers

1752. *Bibliothèque impartiale*. Leiden: Luzac, fils.
1752–1753. *Das Neueste aus der anmuthigen Gelehrsamkeit*. Leipzig: Breitkopf.
1752–1753. *Freye Urtheile und Nachrichten zum Aufnehmen der Wissenschaften und der Historie überhaupt*. Hamburg: Grund.
1752–1753. *Göttingische Zeitungen von gelehrten Sachen*. Göttingen: Universitätsbuchhandlung.

1752–1753. *Neue Zeitungen von gelehrten Sachen*. Leipzig: Zeitungs-Expedition.
1751–1753. *Nova acta eruditorum*, ed. by Friedrich Otto Mencke. Leipzig.
1752–1753. *Wöchentliche Relationen der merkwürdigsten Sachen aus dem Reiche der Natur, der Staaten und der Wissenschaften*. Berlin: Verlag der Buchhandlung der Realschule.
1753. *Hamburgische Unpartheyische Correspondent*. Hamburg: Grund.
1845. *Mittheilungen der naturforschenden Gesellschaft in Bern*. Nr. 46–49. Bern.

Other Sources

Beeson, David. 1992. *Maupertuis: An Intellectual Biography*. Oxford: Voltaire Foundation at the Taylor Institution.
Brunet, Pierre. 1938. *Étude historique sur le principe de la moindre action* Paris: Hermann.
Commercium epistolicum D. Johannis Collins et aliorum de analysi promota. Jussu societatis Regiae in lucem editum. 1722. London: Ex officina J. Tonson & J. Watts.
Consentius, Ernst. 1903. "Briefe eines Berliner Journalisten aus dem 18. Jahrhundert." *Euphorion. Zeitschrift für Literaturgeschichte*, 10, 518–49 and 776–87.
Costabel, Pierre. 1979. "L'Affaire Maupertuis—Koenig et « les questions de fait »." In *Arithmos-Arrythmos. Skizzen aus der Wissenschaftsgeschichte. Eine Festschrift für J. O. Fleckenstein*, edited by Karin Figala and Ernst H. Berninger, 29–48. München: Minerva-Publ.
Diels, Hermann. 1898. "Maupertuis und Friedrich der Große. Festrede." In *Sitzungsberichte der Preuss. Akademie der Wissenschaften*. 51–76. Berlin: Verlag der kgl.-pr. Akademie der Wissenschaften in Kommission bei Reimer.
Euler, Leonhard. 1751. (1753). "Harmonie entre les Principes généraux de repos & de mouvement par Mr. Maupertuis." In *Histoire de l'Académie Royale des Sciences et Belles Lettres, pour l'année 1751*. 169–98. Berlin: Haude & Spener.
Euler, Leonhard. 1753a. (1751). "Sur le Principe de la moindre action." In *Histoire de l'Académie Royale des Sciences et Belles Lettres, pour l'année 1751*. [presented in 1753], 199–218. Berlin: Haude & Spener.
Euler, Leonhard. 1753b. (1751). "Examen de la Dissertation de M. le Professeur Koenig, inserée dans les Actes de Leipsig pour le mois de mars 1751." In *Histoire de l'Académie Royale des Sciences et Belles Lettres, pour l'année 1751*. [presented in 1753], 219–39. Berlin: Haude & Spener.
Fleischauer, Charles. 1964. "Introduction." In *L'Akakia de Voltaire. Éd. critique*, 7–99. Studies on Voltaire and the Eighteenth Century, 30.
Fontius, Martin. 1966. *Voltaire in Berlin. Zur Geschichte der bei G.C. Walther veröffentlichten Werke Voltaires*. Berlin: Rütten & Loening.
Formey, Jean-Henri-Samuel. 1789. *Souvenir d'un citoyen*. Berlin: La Garde.
Frederick II. 1752. *Lettre d'un académicien de Berlin à un académicien de Paris. 1752*. Berlin: Bourdeaux.
Frederick II. 1752. *Lettre d'un académicien de Berlin à un académicien de Paris*. Berlin. (Cited after the reprint in: *Eloges de Trois Philosophes*, 53–74). Leiden: Luzac.
Frederick II. 1753. *Éloges de Trois Philosophes*. London.
Goldenbaum, Ursula. 2004a. *Appell an das Publikum. Die öffentliche Debatte in der deutschen Aufklärung 1687–1796. Mit Beiträgen von Frank Grunert, Peter Weber, Gerda Heinrich, Brigitte Erker und Winfried Siebers*. Berlin: Akademie Verlag.
Goldenbaum, Ursula. 2004b. "Das Publikum als Garant der Freiheit der Gelehrtenrepublik. Die öffentliche Debatte über den *Jugement de l'Académie Royale des Sciences et Belles Lettres sur une Lettre prétendue de M. De Leibnitz* 1752-1753." In *Appell an das Publikum. Die öffentliche Debatte in der deutschen Aufklärung 1687–*

1796. Mit Beiträgen von Frank Grunert, Peter Weber, Gerda Heinrich, Brigitte Erker und Winfried Siebers. 509–651. Berlin: Akademie-Verlag.

Goldenbaum, Ursula. 2008. "Leonhard Eulers Schwierigkeiten mit der Freiheit der Gelehrtenrepublik." In *Kosmos und Zahl. Beiträge zur Mathematik und Astronomiegeschichte, zu Alexander von Humboldt und Leibniz*, edited by Hartmut Hecht, Regina Mikosch, Ingo Schwarz, Harald Siebert, and Romy Werther, in collaboration with Katharina Zeitz, 103–21. Stuttgart: Steiner.

Goldenbaum, Ursula. 2016. *Ein gefälschter Leibnizbrief? Plädoyer für die Echtheit des angeblich gefälschten Leibnizbriefes*. Reihe der Leibniz-Stiftungsprofessur Prof. Dr. Wenchao Li, 6. Hannover: Wehrhahn.

Graf, J. H. 1889. *Geschichte der Mathematik und Naturwissenschaften in bernischen Landen*, 3. H. (1. Abt.): *Die erste Hälfte des 18. Jahrhunderts*, Bern/Basel: Wyss.

Harnack, Adolph von. 1900. *Geschichte der Königlich Preussischen Akademie der Wissenschaften zu Berlin*, 3 vols. Berlin: Reichsverlag.

Hartkopf, Werner. 1992. *Die Berliner Akademie der Wissenschaften. Ihre Mitglieder und Preisträger 1700–1990*. Berlin: Akademie-Verlag.

Haupt, Herman. 1909. *Voltaire in Frankfurt 1753. Mit Benutzung von ungedruckten Akten und Briefen des Dichters*. Zeitschrift für französische Sprache und Litteratur. Chemnitz/Leipzig: Gronau.

Helmholtz, Hermann von. 1887. "Rede über die Entdeckungsgeschichte des Prinzips der kleinsten Aktion." In *Sitzungsberichte der Preussischen Akademie der Wissenschaften*. 282–96. Berlin: Verlag der kgl.-pr. Akademie der Wissenschaften in Kommission bei Reimer.

Israel, Jonathan. 2010. *A Revolution of the Mind: Radical Enlightenment and the Intellectual Origins of Modern Democracy*. Princeton/Oxford: Oxford University Press.

Journal de sçavans. 1752. Vol. CLXIII. Paris.

Jugement de l'Académie royale des sciences et belles lettres sur une prétendue lettre de M. de Leibniz. 1752. Berlin: Bourdeaux.

Juškevič, A. P., Eduard Winter eds. 1959. *Die Berliner und die Petersburger Akademie der Wissenschaften im Briefwechsel Leonhard Eulers*, 2 parts. Berlin: Akademie-Verlag.

Kästner, Abraham Gotthelf. 1912. *Briefe aus sechs Jahrzehnten 1745–1800*. Berlin: Behr.

Kneser, Adolf. 1928. *Das Prinzip der kleinsten Wirkung von Leibniz bis zur Gegenwart*. Leipzig: Teubner.

Knobloch, Wolfgang. 1984. *Leonhard Eulers Wirken an der Berliner Akademie der Wissenschaften 1741–1766. Spezialinventar*. Berlin: Akademie-Verlag.

König, Samuel. 1749. *De optimis Wolfianae et Newtonianae philosophiae methodis earumque consensus*. Coulon: Franeker.

König, Samuel. 1751. "De universali Principi Aequilibri & motus, in Vi viva reperto. Deque nexu inter Vim vivam & Actionem, utriusque Minimo, Dissertatio." In *Nova acta eruditorum*, March, 125–35; 162–76. Leipzig: Gleditsch.

König, Samuel. 1753. *Appel au public, du Jugement de l'Académie Royale de Berlin sur un Fragment de Lettre de Mr. De Leibnitz, cité par Mr. Koenig*. 2nd ed. Leiden: Luzac.

König, Samuel. 2016. "Abhandlung über das universale Prinzip des Gleichgewichts und der Bewegung, das in der lebendigen Kraft gefunden wurde, sowie über die Verbindung von lebendiger Kraft und Aktion und beider Minimum." In Goldenbaum, Ursula, *Ein gefälschter Leibnizbrief? Plädoyer für seine Authentizität*, 101–42. Reihe der Leibniz-Stiftungsprofessur Prof. Dr. Wenchao Li, 6. Hannover: Wehrhahn.

Korff, Hermann August. 1918. *Voltaire im literarischen Urteil Deutschlands des 18. Jahrhunderts*. Heidelberg: Winter.

Lettres concernant le Jugement de l'Académie. [Johann Bernhard Merian, Leonhard Euler, and Pierre-Louis Moreau de Maupertuis]. 1752. Berlin.

Magnan, André. 1986. *Dossier Voltaire en Prusse (1750-1753)*. Studies on Voltaire, 244, Oxford: The Voltaire Foundation at the Taylor Institution.

Mahlmann-Maurer, Barbara. 2017. "Gallotropismus und Kulturvergleich aus der Perspektive der Eidgenossen. Einleitung." In *Gallotropismus aus helvetischer Sicht/Le gallotropisme dans une perspective helvétique*, edited by Barbara Mahlmann-Maurer and Michèle Crogiez Labarthe, 1–43. Heidelberg: Universitätsverlag Winter.

Maupertuis, Pierre-Louis Moreau de. 1748. "Les Loix du Mouvement & du repos, déduites d'un Principe Métaphysique." In *Histoire de l'Académie Royale des Sciences et Belles Lettres, pour l'année 1746*. 267–94. Berlin: Haude und Spener.

Maupertuis, Pierre-Louis Moreau de. 1754. "Réponse à un Mémoire de M. d'Arcy inseré dans le volume de l'Académie Royale des Sciences de Paris pour l'année 1749." In *Histoire de l'Académie Royale des Sciences et Belles Lettres, pour l'année 1752*. 267–98. Berlin: Haude und Spener.

Maupertuisiana. 1752. Leiden: Luzac. (The pieces contained in this collection of contributions to the public debate are each left with their original page numbers). [2nd ed. 1753]

Mayer, Adolph. 1877. *Geschichte des Princips der kleinsten Action*. Leipzig: Veit & Comp.

Mervaud, Christiane. 1985. *Voltaire et Frédéric II: une dramaturgie des Lumières 1736-1778*. Studies on Voltaire and the Eighteenth Century, 234. Oxford: The Voltaire Foundation at the Taylor Institution.

Pulte, Helmut. 1989. *Das Prinzip der kleinsten Wirkung und die Kraftkonzeptionen der rationalen Mechanik. Eine Untersuchung zur Grundlagenproblematik bei Leonhard Euler, Pierre Louis Moreau de Maupertuis und Joseph Louis Lagrange*. Studia Leibnitiana, Sonderheft 19. Stuttgart: Franz Steiner Verlag.

Szabó, István. 1976. *Geschichte der mechanischen Prinzipien und ihrer wichtigsten Anwendungen*. 86-107. Basel/Stuttgart: Birkhäuser.

Trillmich, Rudolf. 1914. *Christlob Mylius. Ein Beitrag zum Verständnis seines Lebens und seiner Schriften*. PhD Dissertation. Leipzig: H. John.

Vollständige Sammlung aller Streitschriften, die neulich über das vorgebliche Gesetz der Natur, von der kleinsten Kraft, in den Wirkungen der Körper, zwischen dem Herrn Präsidenten von Maupertuis zu Berlin, Herrn Professor König in Holland, und andern mehr, gewechselt worden, unpartheyisch ins Deutsche übersetzet. 1753. 2nd ed. Leipzig: Breitkopf.

Voltaire. 1752. *Diatribe du Dr. Akakia, médecin du Pape; Decret de l'Inquisition; et Rapport des professeurs de Rome, Au sujet d'un prétendu président*. Rome.

Voltaire. 1752. *Lettre de Berlin du 12 Novembre 1752*. (Cited after its reprint in: Maupertuisiana).

Voltaire. 1752. *Extrait d'une lettre d'un académicien de Berlin à un membre de la Société Royale de Londres*. Maupertuisiana. (Cited after its reprint in: Maupertuisiana).

Voltaire. 1752. *Lettre d'un savant au Marquis de L* N**. (Cited after its reprint in: Maupertuisiana).

Voltaire. 1752. "Réponse d'un académicien de Berlin à un académicien de Paris. À Berlin le 18 September 1752". In *Journal des sçavans*, 163, 559–61.

Voltaire. 1752. *Réponse d'un académicien de Berlin à un académicien de Paris*. 18. Sep. Berlin. In: Maupertuisiana.

Voltaire. 1753. *Réponse d'un académicien de Paris à un académicien de Berlin*. London: [Leiden: Luzac].

Voltaire. 1968–77. *Correspondence and related documents*. Definitive edition by Theodore Besterman. In *The complete works of Voltaire*, Genève: Institut et Musée Voltaire. vols. I-LI (resp. vols. 85–135) (referred to as Best.D with the Roman number of the volume and the Arabic number of the letter).

6

On Progress in Metaphysics: Responses to the Berlin Academy's 1792/1795 Prize Essay Question

Stephen Howard and Pavel Reichl

1. Introduction

In 1790, the Prussian Royal Academy of the Sciences publicly announced a prize essay competition on the question: "What real progress has metaphysics made in Germany since the time of Leibniz and Wolff?"[1] In late eighteenth-century Prussia, metaphysics was a discipline that still enjoyed a broad popular interest, and its status had been a subject of intense debate among members of the Academy since the latter's reform in 1744/1746.[2] Interest in the concept of progress, a buzzword of the Enlightenment, had only increased after the recent events in neighboring France. From this perspective, it was natural that the Berlin Academy would inquire about the progress that metaphysics had made in recent years. From another perspective, though, the question was less innocent than it may have seemed.

Between 1781 and 1790, Kant had published, alongside other works, his three *Critiques*. Kant made bold claims about the achievements of his critical philosophy: the prefaces to the first *Critique* assert that the work solves all the problems of metaphysics (Axiii) and represents a "transformation in our way of thinking" regarding metaphysics that is comparable to what Copernicus accomplished in cosmology (Bxxii n). Although the critical philosophy did not immediately gain a large readership, its impact was such that, by 1790, the philosophical landscape in Germany had largely split into self-appointed Kantians and opponents of Kant's philosophy.[3] One focal point of this early reception was the theoretical part of the critical philosophy, as set out in the first *Critique* and the *Prolegomena*, and the question of whether a securely grounded metaphysics was possible.

The Berlin Academy's 1792/1795 question targeted this theoretical side of the debate that was opened by Kant's critical philosophy. A Wolffian could answer the prize question by arguing that no progress had been made since Wolff. But the question was a thornier one for Kantians. A common view among Kant's early supporters was that the critical philosophy does not itself advance metaphysics but suspends progress in order to ask whether metaphysics is possible at all. Salomon Maimon, for example, wrote in his response to the Academy's question that the critical philosophy renders metaphysics "impossible" and "unable to make any progress" (Maimon 1793, 3). Maimon therefore claimed that an orthodox Kantian could provide an answer to the Academy's question "in one pen stroke" (Maimon 1793, 3). By posing the question of the philosophical developments since the time of Wolff in terms of the progress in *metaphysics* in particular the Academy might be thought to have biased the contest against the Kantians from the outset.

This was how Maimon saw the matter. Believing that the Academy would not favor an essay by a Kantian critic of metaphysics, he published his contribution independently instead of submitting it for the prize.[4] Maimon had reason to worry about bias in the Academy. The Halle professor Johann August Eberhard had been a member of the Berlin Academy since 1786. From 1789 on, Eberhard and his associates began publishing vicious attacks against Kant's critical philosophy, from a Leibniz-Wolffian perspective, in their *Philosophisches Magazin*. One of Eberhard's central claims was that everything worthwhile in the Kantian philosophy had already been said by Leibniz.[5] The Academy's question thus invited scholars to respond on precisely the terrain of Eberhard's attack: does Kant's critical philosophy contribute anything new to the history of metaphysics?

Ultimately, Maimon's fears were confirmed when the first prize was awarded to the anti-Kantian Johann Christoph Schwab, who worked with Eberhard on the *Philosophisches Magazin*. However, second- and third-place prizes went to the self-appointed Kantians, Johann Heinrich Abicht and Karl Leonhard Reinhold. These three essays, which were published together in a volume in 1796, thus provide an instructive cross-section of the philosophical debate in Germany during the period that immediately followed the publication of Kant's major critical works. The winning essays have rarely received careful attention: it is common for Kant scholars to note only that Schwab was a Wolffian and that Abicht and Reinhold defended broadly Kantian positions.[6]

In the first half of this chapter, we examine the responses to the Academy's question in the three winning essays. We show how each author characterizes the movements through which metaphysics has progressed—or failed to progress—since Wolff's great systematic contributions to German metaphysics. Schwab's essay does indeed defend an orthodox Wolffian position, although aspects of his depiction of the recent history of metaphysics surprisingly echo Kant's account of the battlefield of metaphysics. But closer attention is due to the allegedly "Kantian" essays by Abicht and Reinhold. Both assume that there can be no properly Kantian account of progress in metaphysics because the critical philosophy is only destructive, so even a Kantian response to the Academy's question must take a perspective that goes beyond Kant's philosophy. This leads Abicht to return to a broadly Leibnizian metaphysics and Reinhold to present a curiously indifferent survey of the post-Kantian "war" between philosophical positions.

There is a further interesting aspect of the debate that was provoked by the Academy's question: Kant himself wrote a series of drafts toward a response. He did not work them up into an essay that was suitable for submission and they remained in a fragmentary form when, during his final years, he passed them to his friend Friedrich Theodor Rink, who published them in their unfinished state immediately after Kant's death. In the second half of the chapter, we turn to Kant's drafts. Our guiding concern will be the extent to which the position defended in the drafts can be considered "Kantian." That is, how close does Kant's sketched response come to the views that his supporters, such as Abicht and Reinhold, would ascribe to him? By examining, firstly, Kant's conception of metaphysics, and, secondly, his account of the history of metaphysics, we show that Kant foregrounds elements that are very different from those that his self-appointed Kantian contemporaries considered central to the critical philosophy. Kant's conception of a "critical" metaphysics in his drafts was far from evident to his earliest readers, and it retains the capacity to surprise his readers today.

2. Schwab

Johann Christoph Schwab (1743–1821) spent a large part of his academic career as professor of logic and metaphysics at the Karlsschule in Stuttgart. As well as collaborating with Eberhard on the Wolffian, anti-Kantian *Philosophisches Magazin*, he was a prolific and remarkably successful essay writer. He won the Berlin Academy prize competitions of 1784 and 1788 with contributions on the French language and on the imitation of foreign literature, respectively, as well as two prize competitions from the Russian Academy of Sciences (Klemme and Kuehn 2010, 713).

Schwab begins his essay by distinguishing between two ways of completing a science: materially, by adding new content, or formally, by ordering the elements of the science in a more perfect manner (PF, 6).[7] An example of material progress is map-making: recent voyages of discovery generated much new information and thereby expanded the scope of the science of cartography. Socrates is Schwab's example of formal progress: although he did not provide any new ideas or content to metaphysics, Socrates re-formulated some basic proofs in a clearer and more compelling manner. Due to the nature of metaphysics, Schwab claims, progress is usually formal (PF, 7). He then adds a third kind of progress, which he calls "negative" (PF, 8–9). This type of progress has an affinity with the general category of formal progress because it does not aim to add new content. Nevertheless, its import is wholly negative in that it consists of eliminating errors and misconceptions from a given system of knowledge. With this third category, Schwab clearly has Kant in mind. He notes that a critical philosopher who succeeded in determining the limits of metaphysics in this negative manner would count as "a true benefactor" of metaphysics (PF, 9). Using the above "three-fold criterion," Schwab proposes to determine the progress made in metaphysics in four 20-year periods, beginning in 1720 (PF, 9).

The first period (1720–40) is dominated by Leibniz and Wolff. Schwab argues that Leibniz made very little material progress in metaphysics because his key ideas, such as the principle of sufficient reason and pre-established harmony, had a long history and had been well known for centuries (PF, 9–11). Leibniz nevertheless provided metaphysical concepts and principles with a clearer, more precise, and more compelling formulation than any predecessor. He thus achieved significant formal progress, since "everything that passed through his hands took on a better form" (PF, 12). But because Leibniz's "free spirit did not like the fetters" of systematicity, Wolff's subsequent systematization of the Leibnizian doctrine represented further progress at the formal level (PF, 14–15). Not only did Wolff bring formal order to Leibniz's ideas, but he also achieved negative progress by eliminating several confusions from the Leibnizian doctrine of monads, for example (PF, 17). Wolff's progress in metaphysics was such that, according to Schwab, his system can be used as a touchstone to assess all subsequent metaphysical systems (although, as Schwab points out several times, only by those who have studied Wolff in depth).[8]

After the Leibniz-Wolffian period, Schwab identifies a second period that runs from 1740 to 1760. It is said to be characterized by criticisms of Wolff's geometrical method and attempts to make it more readable (PF, 22ff.). Significant figures included Meier and Crusius. The former attempted to rewrite aspects of Wolff's philosophy in a more readable manner, while the latter gained prominence as a critic of Wolff's rationalism more generally (PF, 23, 27ff.). Against Meier, Schwab argues that philosophy need not be readable in order to be true. The value of Crusius' criticisms, for Schwab, is only to alert Wolff's followers to some potential limitations of his doctrine (PF, 26). Consequently, the overall progress metaphysics could achieve in this period is minimal: "not a single important truth was discovered," and no system more "solid" or "coherent" than the Wolffian one was produced (PF, 35–6).

The third period (1760–80) is characterized, on the one hand, by a new generation of talented metaphysicians headed by Mendelssohn and Lambert and, on the other, by the rise of skeptics, especially Hume and Tetens (PF, 38ff.).[9] Mendelssohn managed to achieve some measure of progress by applying Wolffian doctrine in previously unexplored areas, such as aesthetics. Lambert's system was an attempt to forge a slightly different path to that of Wolff, especially in empirical psychology. At the same time, the skepticism of Hume and Tetens challenged metaphysics. Schwab draws various conclusions about the progress of metaphysics in this more philosophically rich period, but his general assessment is that while some new ideas appear in the writings from this period, systematic metaphysics did not progress (PF, 103). Moreover, a rejection of the systematic form by the above-mentioned metaphysicians engendered skepticism. This skepticism, in turn, generated a certain anarchy among philosophically minded individuals, which in turn seemed to demand a new "dictator" (PF, 104).[10] This dictator in fact appeared, and with him the fourth age of metaphysics begins.

Regarding this final period of metaphysics, Schwab deals exclusively with the new dictator, Kant (PF, 104ff.). However, because he claims to lack the space to provide a detailed assessment of all of Kant's central claims, Schwab focusses solely on the general approach and "spirit" of Kant's philosophy (PF, 114). Schwab first provides lengthy quotations to document Kant's main arguments. Curiously, however, most of these quotations come not from Kant's text but from Schultz's explication of Kant in *Erläuterungen über des Herrn Professor Kant Critik der reinen Vernunft* (Explanations of Professor Kant's Critique of Pure Reason) (1784/1791). Schwab excuses this by claiming that Kant endorses Schultz's interpretation of the critical philosophy (PF, 106 fn.). Schwab proceeds to raise a variety of critical points. While acknowledging that one of Kant's primary aims is to establish a new theory of cognition, Schwab nevertheless claims that the Kantian forms of understanding and sensibility are "entirely subjective": it is impossible to know whether other individuals have the same forms as I do, so objective knowledge is impossible (PF, 120–1). For example, because the judgment 2 × 2 = 4 has a subjective ground, Schwab claims, it will not be true in the same way for every particular subject and hence will lack "objectivity" and "truth" (PF, 121). Consequently, Kant is said to ultimately arrive at a skeptical position no different to Hume's, because both deny the possibility of objective knowledge due to the subjective status of our cognitions.

In a seemingly confessional manner, Schwab regularly states that the Kantian philosophy is too difficult to understand (PF, 131–2, for instance). Rather than considering this to be a potential caveat to his criticisms, however, he takes it to confirm the lack of formal perfection in Kant's philosophy. He complains that in the first *Critique* Kant does not include a single citation, does not use paragraphs, and fails to define his key concepts. Thus, in formal terms, the Leibniz-Wolffian philosophy is said to be superior, especially in the form of Wolff's geometrical system (PF, 144). In material terms, Schwab claims that Kant himself renounces any possibility of progress because his aims are wholly negative. But, even in a negative sense, Kant fails to achieve any progress because it is paradoxical to try to prove apodictically that no apodictic knowledge is possible (PF, 131). Therefore, the final assessment of the critical philosophy is that "the new theory of the faculty of representation … does not stand up to scrutiny, and that the metaphysical system based on it does not equal the Leibniz-Wolffian one in terms of rigor, order, and consistency" (PF, 144). Consequently, again, "we have in this new period made no progress in metaphysics" (PF, 144).

In sum, Schwab's answer to the prize question is that there has been no progress in metaphysics since the period of Leibniz and Wolff. His underlying conception of metaphysics, nowhere explicitly stated but evident from his individual comments and overall approach, is similar to Kant's conception of logic: the science is basically complete, with minor supplementations to be made here and there. Schwab's judgment on the progress of metaphysics since Leibniz and Wolff thus echoes Kant's judgment on the progress of logic since Aristotle, namely that it "has been unable to take a single step forward" (Bviii).

3. Abicht

Johann Heinrich Abicht (1762–1816) was a professor of logic and metaphysics in Erlangen and later in Vilnius. In contrast to Schwab, Abicht was a self-professed Kantian and lectured not only on Kant's theoretical philosophy but also on his ethics and aesthetics. He begins his prize essay by pointing out that for a Kantian, the question concerning the progress made by metaphysics must be preceded by the question of whether metaphysics is possible. Abicht's own answer to this question is affirmative: the Kantian quake shook but did not destroy metaphysics, so a new, more solid metaphysics can soon be constructed on its basis (PF, 258). On his interpretation, the prize question should be understood as asking whether such a new, post-Kantian approach to metaphysics really represents progress with respect to Leibniz and Wolff (PF, 260).

For Abicht, the "spirit of the Kantian system" is the claim that sensible representations of conditioned objects have objective validity while rational representations of the unconditioned must renounce any claims to objective validity (PF, 301–2). The consequence of this claim is that the whole of metaphysics, since it deals with the unconditioned, is merely "an empty figment of the brain [*Hirngespinst*]" (PF, 302). Abicht praises the "brilliance" of this argument, "worthy of a great man" such as Kant, which puts an end to various metaphysical excesses. Nevertheless, the "shine wears off" when one realizes that the striving to cognize metaphysical objects is a function not of reason but of our understanding. In this manner, the distinction breaks down between the understanding and its objectively valid sensible representations, on the one hand, and reason and its inaccessible unconditioned objects, on the other. Stated otherwise, the understanding is capable of producing objectively valid representations of both sensible and metaphysical objects (PF, 304).

Abicht's conception of the relation between the understanding, reason, and objects in this new framework is somewhat obscure—indeed, his frequent failure to clearly state what he was trying to prove earned him the moniker "the German Heraclitus" (Klemme and Kuehn 2010, 6). Nevertheless, by rejecting the Kantian "conclusion" that metaphysics is impossible, Abicht is clear that he wishes to open the space for a "new dogmatism" in the post-Kantian landscape (PF, 305). According to this new dogmatism, metaphysical objects are no longer unknowable things-in-themselves located beyond the boundary of experience. Instead, for Abicht, metaphysics should provide knowledge of that which "cannot be represented," that which is "hidden," "unperceivable," and "internal to a thing" (PF, 268). That which is perceivable, on the other hand, is the "outer shell of a thing" (PF, 268). Although the "unperceivable" is not available to the senses, it is nonetheless "provable [*erweislich*]" and can be reached by means of reasoning [*vermittelst eines Schlusses*]" (PF, 268). Despite the fact that such unperceivables are not objects of experience, our reasoning about them is in some manner confirmed through experience. Thus, Abicht writes that it is impossible to deny the "fact" that we "have representations of substances" and that these representations are "co-effected by things" (PF, 299). Consequently, the "central truth" (*Hauptwahrheit*) of the new dogmatism is that "our metaphysical cognitions a priori attain objective-real truth through experience, and provide us with true certitude of the metaphysical" (PF, 305).

Abicht associates this new dogmatism with Reinhold's *Elementarphilosophie* and, above all, with his own philosophy, which he had articulated in works such as *Versuch einer krittischen Untersuchung über das Willensgeschäfte* (Attempt at a Critical Investigation of the Activity of the Will) (1788) and *Hermias, oder Auflösung der die gültige Elementarphilosophie betreffenden Aenesidemischen Zweifel* (Hermias, or Resolution of the Valid Aenesidemian Doubts Concerning Elementary Philosophy) (1794). In apparent agreement with Reinhold that a first principle is required in order to provide a solid basis for a "new" metaphysics, in these works, Abicht sought to articulate what he called the soul's certainty of itself (*die unabänderliche Gewißheit von der Beseelung in mir*) (see Di Giovanni 2005, 55–6). The extent to which his metaphysics attempts to bypass Kantian restrictions on knowledge becomes apparent when he argues in the prize essay that the "I" is a "substance, an essence, something self-standing (*Selbständiges*)," and that it is a "power (*Kraft*) that is knowable through its effects" (PF, 310). Metaphysics can then be divided into three primary parts, each corresponding to a basic power of the soul: a theory of the power of cognition, of the power of feeling, and a doctrine of the will (PF, 318-9). These claims undoubtedly loosely draw on passages from the *Critiques*: the reference to the "standing and lasting I (of pure apperception)" in the A Deduction (A123), the threefold division in the third *Critique* of the critical philosophy according to the faculties of cognition, pleasure and displeasure, and will (KU, 5:198). But Abicht boldly affirms knowledge of a *substantial* I, which Kant rejects in the first Paralogism, and projects Kant's division between the three *Critiques* onto a newly re-grounded metaphysics.

Abicht assesses the progress made in each of these parts of metaphysics before moving onto other categories of metaphysical objects, such as God and the world as a whole. In the case of the power of cognition, Abicht focuses on our pure representations, and he compares Leibniz's innate ideas with Kant's categories. Echoing Kant's claims about Aristotle's list of categories, Abicht criticizes Leibniz's stock of innate concepts for being incomplete, composed in a merely "rhapsodic manner" (PF, 341), and for containing a mixture of pure and experiential elements. Kant's primary merit, then, was to clarify and systematize our stock of a priori concepts through the table of categories. At bottom, however, Abicht views Kant's categories as more precise versions of Leibnizian innate ideas. For example, Abicht asserts that Kant's proof of the origin of the categories "agrees almost completely" in content with Leibniz's proof of the innate ideas, though it may differ "in words" (PF, 315). Kant's main service to metaphysics was thus to provide more "life and expansion [*Leben und Wachsthum*]" to Leibniz's doctrine of innate ideas. Not only does Abicht ignore Kant's clear denial that the categories should not be understood as Leibnizian innate ideas, but he seems to miss the novel nature of the critical conception of the a priori.[11]

This Leibnizian reading of Kant allows Abicht not only to reduce Kant's progress in metaphysics to an updating or a systematization of Leibniz but also to develop his own broadly Leibnizian metaphysics in a way that bypasses Kantian restrictions on knowledge. In a section of his essay dedicated to cosmology, for example, Abicht rejects Kant's refutation of the possibility of cognition of the world as a whole, claiming that Kant misconstrues the concepts of space and limitation (PF, 454). In the theology section, Abicht briefly remarks that Kant's objections to the speculative proof of God are confused (PF, 466). He goes on to present a threefold proof of God, said to improve on the Leibnizian proof, with no more references to Kant's general restrictions on the use of speculative reason in theology.

Overall, Abicht's response to the Academy question points to the progress made predominantly in his own works, where he develops further arguments for the substantiality of the soul and the existence of God. Because, unlike Schwab, Abicht is influenced by Kant and has a positive view of the latter's contribution to philosophy, he considers himself to argue for the possibility of progress in Kantian metaphysics. As Di Giovanni states, "there should be no doubt that Abicht thought of himself as a Kantian."[12] Nevertheless, in order to defend his "Kantian" metaphysics, Abicht unwittingly undoes the main tenets of the critical philosophy and defends elements of a pre-critical metaphysics. With respect to his practical philosophy, Abicht has been cited as an example of a "typical dogmatic development of Kant's thought," and this is equally accurate with regard to the theoretical philosophy he defends in the prize essay.[13] Thus, while Schwab explicitly denies that there could be progress in a Kantian metaphysics, Abicht suggests that for metaphysics to progress, the orthodox Kantian philosophy, especially its wholesale rejection of metaphysics, needs to be bypassed and its limits to cognition transcended (PF, 302).

4. Reinhold

In stark contrast to Kant's description of metaphysics as a battlefield, Karl Leonhard Reinhold (1757–1823) refers to the period between the waning of the Leibniz-Wolffian philosophy and the publication of the first *Critique* as one of "peace" (PF, 176). Nevertheless, according to Reinhold, this was not a peace built on the overcoming of old disagreements or on a consensus regarding the truth of one particular metaphysical system. Instead, this peace resulted from a confusion of metaphysical principles, which meant that fundamental disagreements were not overcome but instead covered over and lost from view (176). Although he does not specify when precisely this period began, he associates Lambert's *Architektonik* (1765/1771) and its popularity with the end of the dominance of the Leibniz-Wolffian school. Presumably because critics like Lambert had weakened its rational basis, the "heterogenous material" that fell under the name of "metaphysics" came to take on "every possible dress" (PF, 175). This eclectic metaphysics, Reinhold continues, was spread across German universities by Feder's and Plattner's "rhapsodic" and "aphoristic" lectures (PF, 175). Differences between schools were treated merely "historically rather than philosophically" and were thus "suppressed rather than illuminated" (PF, 175), leading to all sorts of "coalitions" between ostensibly opposed camps, such as empiricists and rationalists, or dogmatists and skeptics (PF, 174). Hence, Reinhold calls this the "eclectic" or "syncretic" period (PF, 174).[14] This period, according to Reinhold, closes with the publication of the *Critique of Pure Reason* in 1781. The innocent "peace" that characterized the proceeding period came to an abrupt end because Kant "declared war" against all existing parties (PF, 176). In order to defend themselves against Kant's bellicose intervention, these parties had to wake from the "slumber" (*Schlummer*) into which they had fallen. Kant's new "mode of attack" necessitated a "new mode of defense," so they attempted to strengthen their existing systems, turning to examine "the true" (*das Wahre*) (PF, 176). But the more "astute, well-judged, and thorough" their defenses of their systems were, the more the residual differences and contradictions between these various systems became apparent (PF, 176–7).

Not only did the differences between competing metaphysical positions become clearer after Kant, but the old "cantankerousness" (*Unverträglichkeit*) toward one another also resurfaced. Consequently, Reinhold characterizes the period between 1781 and the publication of the prize question as one in which the diversity in the conceptions within metaphysics and about metaphysics was more pronounced than at any previous point in history. This, in turn, makes the prize academy question about the progress of metaphysics both timely and difficult to answer (PF, 173). The diversity of conceptions and lack of consensus mean that every party to the conflict would frame the question differently, making it difficult to find a common standard against which any progress can be measured (PF, 177). Consequently, the strategy Reinhold adopts is to allow each party to speak in their own voice and give an account of what they have accomplished in metaphysics. Reinhold himself assumes the role of an unbiased observer, who, in the final section of his essay, comments on the alleged progress achieved in these attempts.

Reinhold divides the different parties into the critical and non-critical philosophers. The latter are then divided into skeptics and dogmatists, with the latter of these further divided into dualists, pantheists, materialists, and idealists. Reinhold summarizes each party's conception of metaphysics on the basis of their own accounts, which mainly turn on the concept of substance. The idealists, for example, acknowledge no other substance apart from the representing subject (PF, 178). This category breaks down into further sub-groups. For example, those who conceive of the representing substance as equipped with will and thought are "spiritualists," and those who conceive of a variety of essentially distinct representing substances are "monadologists" or "Leibnizian idealists" (PF, 179). The idealists in general are contrasted with the materialists, who insist on the "substantiality of bodies," the "reality of extension," and thus, in short, on "healthy common sense" (PF, 199–200). The dualists and the pantheists are also defined in terms of their respective conceptions of substance, while the skeptics deny that substance, as something independent of representation, can be known.[15]

The rationale behind Reinhold's classificatory scheme can be gleaned from his discussion of the critical philosophy's conception of the possible permutations of metaphysics, which Reinhold presents in terms of the criterion of truth. Namely, those who locate truth in the simple, immediate product of experience are termed empiricists, while those who locate it in the innate, immediate product of the intellect are rationalists (PF, 214). Pure rationalism then leads to idealism while pure empiricism leads to materialism. A mixture of the two generates the two remaining dogmatic (i.e., non-critical and non-skeptical) schools, depending on which element predominates: "rational empiricism" leads to pantheism, while "empirical rationalism" leads to dualism (PF, 216).

The critical philosopher, Reinhold claims, rejects an assumption common to all of the above dogmatic schools as well as to skepticism, namely that truth is the result of a correspondence between the representation and a thing in itself that is independent of representation (PF, 243). Among the most important results of the critical enterprise is thus the refutation of dogmatism and skepticism based on the conception of truth that it introduces (PF, 244–5). Although the critical philosophy has not yet managed to construct a metaphysics, it lays out a clear plan for a future metaphysics. The "future metaphysics," according to Reinhold, should be not a science of the thing in itself but a "science of the real object of representation in respect of the necessary and universal predicates, in so far as these are grounded in the capacity for representation (*Vorstellungsvermögen*)" (PF, 249). The mention of *Vorstellungsvermögen* may recall Reinhold's own innovative approach to critical philosophy, but his subsequent account of the division of metaphysics, the main parts of which are a "metaphysics of physical nature" and a "metaphysics of moral nature," with the *Critique of Pure Reason* as a "propaedeutic" (PF, 249–50), largely mirrors Kant's division of metaphysics in the first *Critique* (A845-7/B873-5).

In the final section, Reinhold adopts the voice of an impartial observer to assess the progress achieved in metaphysics in the defined period. Because all of the metaphysical positions described above, including the critical one, lack "general recognition and validity," they must renounce their claim to scientificity and be viewed as mere "attempts" (PF, 250). Consequently, Reinhold, as an impartial observer, merely lists the most important attempts that "philosophical reason" has undertaken since the period of Leibniz and Wolff. Although he complains that metaphysical systems are often presented more "historically" than philosophically and "descriptively rather than probingly" (*mehr erzählend als untersuchend*) in textbooks (PF, 174), he does not attempt to rectify this situation in the present essay.[16]

Revealingly, Reinhold later rewrote his prize essay for publication in his *Auswahl vermischter Schriften* in 1797. It has been argued that it was precisely when preparing this new version that Reinhold came to question his own allegiance to the Kantian philosophy (see Zöller 2004 and Imhoff 2020). One of the "essential additions" that Reinhold inserts is an explication of his own conception of metaphysics (1797, 3). This addition allows him to provide a more critical and philosophically ambitious account of the development of metaphysics, but it also highlights what is missing in the draft submitted for the prize competition. In the first version of the essay, Reinhold's detached approach contrasts not only with his other writings, but also with the approach of Abicht, who uses the conception of metaphysics presented in his own works as a standard against which to measure others. Thus, in terms of Kant's image of the battlefield of metaphysics, Reinhold's account of the progress in metaphysics in the submitted version of his prize essay is surprisingly indifferentist. This is conceivably because Reinhold was already primarily interested in the next step beyond these previous philosophies, Kant included. But unlike Abicht, who explicitly affirms that followers of Kant like himself should build a new metaphysics on the ruins of the old, Reinhold, in his indifferent survey, only implicitly indicates his interest in the post-Kantian metaphysics that he sought to develop.

5. Kant

Kant's response to the prize question differs most obviously from the three winning essays in that he did not finish it. In 1804, a few months after Kant's death, his dinner companion Friedrich Theodor Rink published three manuscripts containing Kant's drafts toward an essay. The problems that stem from the haphazard way that Rink edited Kant's manuscripts are well documented.[17] The drafts nevertheless provide a fascinating contribution to the debates over the implications of the critical philosophy for the history of metaphysics—in this case, from the pen of Kant himself.

5.1. Kant's Conception of Metaphysics in the Drafts

Unlike the winning essays, Kant's response does not assume that the meaning of "metaphysics" is self-evident. An exchange of letters between Kant and his former student Kiesewetter about the prize competition illustrates how Kant's conception of metaphysics differs from the one that his "Kantian" followers might have expected him to hold. In a letter dated the 15th of October 1795, Kant asks Kiesewetter whether he has any inside information from Berlin about the outcome of the prize essay competition. Noting that he "would love to be informed about the remarkable procedure with the prize competition of the Academy of Sciences," Kant asks "how it could come about that Schwab, Abicht, and Reinhold are assembled in a colorful arrangement [*in bunter Ordnung*] and something harmonious brought forth out of so much dissonance" (Br, 12:45). The winning essays were not published until 1796, so Kant's reference to their "colorful arrangement" cannot be to anything more specific than the order in which the prizes were awarded. Kant is no doubt sardonically referring to the fact that Eberhard's Wolffian associate Schwab was awarded the first prize.

In his reply, Kiesewetter complains that the Academy posed the question about the progress of metaphysics "without allowing the *question prealable* [sic, preliminary question] of whether there would even be metaphysics at all [*ob es überhaupt nur Metaphysik gäbe*] to precede it, so it was also no surprise that they ranked Schwab, Abicht, Reinhold in that way" (Br, 12:48). Kiesewetter dismisses the contest because the Academy failed to ask the preliminary, "critical" question of whether metaphysics is possible at all. He seems to assume that Kant, his former teacher, will share this view. As we have seen, Abicht began his avowedly Kantian essay in just the same way.[18] And in order to discuss the positive recent progress of metaphysics, Abicht felt he must go beyond Kant's destructive intervention, his questioning of the very possibility of metaphysics, and independently construct a new, solid metaphysics on the critical foundations.

Kiesewetter was more familiar than most with the critical philosophy, having authored a number of textbooks that popularized Kantian thought.[19] The "Kantian" position he assumes in his letter seems justified by passages such as the opening of the *Prolegomena*, where Kant recommends that metaphysicians suspend their work, disregard everything done in metaphysics to date, and "before everything else first pose the question: whether such a thing as metaphysics is even possible at all" (*ob auch so etwas als Metaphysik überall nur möglich sei*) (P, 4:255). This question, which Kiesewetter echoes in his letter, is the basis of Kant's often repeated and provocative claim that, prior to the *Critique of Pure Reason*, there has been no metaphysics, or even no philosophy at all.[20]

Strikingly, and unbeknownst to Kiesewetter or the winning essayists, Kant does not take this approach in his prize essay drafts. He does not dismiss the Academy's question by insisting that a critical investigation into the very possibility of metaphysics must precede any discussion of its progress. He does ask a *question préalable*, but not the one his "Kantian" followers would apparently expect; instead, he asks: what is metaphysics? In the draft introductions in the first and third manuscripts, Kant answers by defining metaphysics as "the science of progressing [*fortzuschreiten*], through reason, from cognition of the sensible to that of the supersensible."[21] As has often been noted, this definition plays on the notion of *Fortschritte*, the German term for the *progrès* in the Academy's question. Kant discusses the three steps (*Schritte*) that have recently been made in metaphysics (FM, 20:265–6) and considers how reason can "risk a transition [or, literally, an 'overstep': *Überschritt*]" from objects of possible experience to those that lie beyond possible experience.[22] In sharp contrast with the three winning essays, Kant's first move in his evaluation of the progress recently made in metaphysics is to *define* metaphysics *as* progress. This provides the focus for the rest of drafts: how to legitimately progress beyond the bounds of possible experience to the supersensible.

Just as Kiesewetter's reaction to the Academy's question is supported by passages in his teacher's critical works, so Kant's contrasting position in the drafts is rooted in these same earlier works. In order to appreciate this, it is helpful to distinguish two conceptions of metaphysics in the first *Critique*. According to the first, metaphysics is the activity of thinking *beyond* the boundaries of possible experience. Metaphysics thus results from a natural tendency of reason to incessantly ask questions that it is incapable of answering. This is reason's "peculiar fate," as the opening of the A Preface famously puts it (Avii). Due to this tendency, Kant insists that there will always be metaphysics, in this sense of the transgression of cognitive boundaries.[23]

The second conception of metaphysics appears on first glance to be very different: it is the unified system of all a priori cognitions, which encompasses all "true as well as apparent" cognitions (A841/B869). Such systematic unity is possible because pure reason is the "seat" or source of a priori cognition (A845/B873). Metaphysics in this second sense is subdivided into the metaphysics of morals and the metaphysics of nature, with the latter divided in turn into modified versions of traditional general and special metaphysics, that is, ontology and rational psychology, physics, cosmology, and theology (A845–6/B873–4).[24]

The first *Critique* therefore contains two conceptions of metaphysics, and the critical philosophy should serve as a propaedeutic for metaphysics in both senses. Kant's preliminary investigation aims to provide the conceptual foundations for, on the one hand, a determination of the boundaries of possible experience and an account of how they can be legitimately exceeded, and, on the other, a system of all a priori cognition. These two tasks of the critical philosophy, keyed to Kant's two conceptions of metaphysics, have been noted in the literature, but the precise relation between them arguably remains obscure.[25]

Kant's definition of metaphysics at the beginning of both draft introductions to the prize essay is closest to the first of the *Critique*'s two characterizations of the discipline. The version in the first manuscript begins by alluding to the natural tendency of reason to pose metaphysical questions. Everyone "participates more or less in metaphysics" because it stems from the "innermost interest" of reason (FM, 20:259–60). This leads to Kant's definition of metaphysics as the progression to the supersensible and the question of how to legitimately make this transition. Kant goes on, however, to allude to metaphysics in his second sense, and he even suggests a way to understand the connection between the two senses of the term. The opening definition of metaphysics, he states, "merely indicates what one *wants with* metaphysics, not what is to be done *in it*" (FM, 20:261). Kant clarifies what is to be done in metaphysics as follows: "the explanation of metaphysics according to the concept of the schools will be that it is the system of all principles of pure theoretical rational knowledge through concepts; or in brief: it is the system of pure theoretical philosophy" (FM, 20:261). Metaphysics should produce the system of all a priori cognitions, which is what we have called Kant's second conception of metaphysics.

By designating this system as the scholastic concept of metaphysics, Kant alludes to his distinction in the first *Critique*'s Transcendental Doctrine of Method between the "school concept" and the "world concept" of philosophy (A838–9/B866–7).[26] The school concept seeks a system of cognitions for no other sake than systematic unity and logical perfection. Here in the prize essay drafts, Kant adds that the school concept, the system of pure theoretical philosophy, is what metaphysics produces in order to attain its aim: progress to the supersensible. The third manuscript's version of the introduction explicitly claims that the scholastic system is a "means [*Mitteln*]" to the "end [*Zweck*]" of cognition of the supersensible. In order to extend "cognition *beyond* the boundaries of the sensible," we require "complete knowledge [*Kenntnis*] of all a priori principles, which can also be applied to the sensible" (FM, 20:317). Producing the system of a priori principles that is valid for sensible cognition is apparently a necessary step in the direction of the supersensible.

So far, we have seen that Kant's position in the drafts is far from Abicht's view of the critical philosophy as nothing but a destructive "quake" that shook metaphysics. Kant is instead concerned with how to make a legitimate transition to the supersensible. He does not explicitly explain, either in the introductions or elsewhere in the drafts, why metaphysics in his second sense (as a scholastic system) is required for there to be metaphysics in the first sense (as progression to the supersensible). But the main body of the essay shows that the answer he has reached in the early 1790s revolves around his account of the three stages of metaphysics. Our next section turns to this account. There, Kant will introduce something comparable to what the *Critique* calls the "world concept" of philosophy, namely, a conception of metaphysics that is attuned to the practical as well as the theoretical ends of reason.

5.2. The Three Stages of Metaphysics and the Practical-Dogmatic Transition to the Supersensible

The three manuscripts all indicate that Kant intended to structure his essay by dividing the history of metaphysics into three stages (*Stadien*). In a key paragraph, which many commentators have argued is misplaced in Rink's edition, Kant describes the "stages of pure reason" as follows:

> doctrine of science, as a sure progress; doctrine of doubt, as a standstill; and doctrine of wisdom, as a transition to the final end of metaphysics: so that the first will contain a theoretical-dogmatic doctrine, the second a skeptical discipline, and the third a practical-dogmatic doctrine.
>
> (FM, 20:273)[27]

In a later section, where Rink should probably have situated this passage, Kant adds that the first stage proceeds within ontology, the second within cosmology, and the third within theology (FM, 20:281). Each of the three stages thus receives multiple designations:

1. doctrine of science—theoretical-dogmatic doctrine—ontology—making (or believing itself to make) sure progress;

2. doctrine of doubt—skeptical discipline—cosmology—a standstill;
3. doctrine of wisdom—practical-dogmatic doctrine—theology—a transition to the final end of metaphysics.

By depicting these three stages as branches of metaphysics (ontology, cosmology, and theology),[28] Kant depicts them as a systematic, logical development of thought. As he puts it, the "temporal order" of the stages of metaphysics "is grounded in the nature of the human cognitive faculty" (FM, 20:264). But at the same time, he clearly intends his account to provide a genuinely historical account of the development of metaphysics through different temporal periods.[29]

The historical character of the threefold development in the drafts is admittedly vague. Kant suggests that the first, theoretical-dogmatic stage includes philosophers "from an older time than that of Plato and Aristotle" but also Leibniz and Wolff (FM, 20:262). When fleshing out his account of the first stage, Kant only discusses Leibniz (FM, 20:281–6). The second stage, similarly, is at once ancient—"almost as old" as the first (FM, 20:262)—and recent, since it "continues to persist in good minds everywhere" (FM, 20:263). This skeptical stage thus includes both Pyrrhonic and, we would assume, Humean skepticism; Kant's elaboration, however, only refers to his own critique of cosmology in the Antinomy chapter of the first *Critique*.[30] In the drafts as they stand, Kant cannot be said to have resolved the issue of how to reconcile his conception of metaphysics as an ahistorical "natural tendency" of reason with a genuinely historical periodization of the stages of its development.

How does Kant's history of metaphysics compare to those in the three winning essays? As we have seen, Schwab identified four precise temporal periods between 1720 and the early 1790s. Abicht's main temporal distinction is between the Kantian "quake" and the period of the reconstruction of a properly grounded metaphysics (where the architect-builders are Reinhold and, particularly, Abicht himself). In addition, he alludes to a third, pre-Kantian era. Reinhold makes a twofold periodization: the eclectic, pre-Kantian period of peace, and the post-Kantian era of war. The tumultuous post-Kantian era is subdivided by Reinhold on a conceptual basis through his complex classificatory schemes.

Kant's threefold history of metaphysics therefore differs from the periodizations of all three winning essayists. One could suppose that the reason for this divergence is that none of the three winning authors follow Kant's account of the history of metaphysics in the first *Critique*. In the Transcendental Doctrine of Method—a chapter situated late in the book that Kant's contemporaries may not have adequately studied—Kant distinguishes three steps "in matters of pure reason." These are dogmatism, skepticism (here explicitly aligned with Hume), and critique (A761/B789). Kant uses the imagery of the organic development of reason: from a childlike dogmatism to a "mature and adult" critical stage. The final page of the *Critique* recaps this development and names Wolff, Hume, and Kant's own "critical path" as the three steps (A856/B884). The opening pages of the first edition present a slightly more complex history: the despotic rule of the dogmatists, the anarchy of the skeptics, a Lockean "physiology of the human understanding," and a more dangerous "indifferentism"; these are finally succeeded by the arrival of (Kantian) critique (Aix–xii). Ironically, of the three winning essayists, the anti-Kantian Schwab is closest to Kant's history of metaphysics, particularly in his worries about skepticism. However, he parodically presents Kant not as the figure who pacifies and completes metaphysics, but as a late skeptic whose dictatorial ascension threatens what Schwab sees as the true Leibniz-Wolffian metaphysics.

It is not only the winning essayists who diverge from the history of metaphysics outlined in the *Critique*, though; in his drafts, Kant does too. While the first stage is straightforwardly identified with Leibniz-Wolffian dogmatism in the *Critique*, Kant suggests at various points in the prize essay that the first stage should also contain a positive part, which would contain the doctrines of the Transcendental Aesthetic and Analytic.[31] The extant draft of the first stage only contains the critical assessment of Leibniz, not the positive "ontology."[32] However, if he had further elaborated the first stage, Kant could have used some of the material from his summaries of the progress made by the first *Critique*.[33] With regard to the second stage, as noted above, Kant's discussion in the prize essay drafts refers only to the Antinomy chapter and, unlike the history in the *Critique*, makes no reference to Hume.

The most interesting and complex issue is how the third stage in the drafts relates to the critical philosophy. On first glance, there is a great difference between the third stage in the *Critique* (the "critical path") and the equivalent stage in the drafts (the practical-dogmatic transition to the supersensible). Kant does write, however, at the end of the introduction in the first manuscript of the drafts:

> The third and most recent step that metaphysics has taken, and by which its fate must be decided, is the critique of pure reason itself with regard to its capacity to extend human cognition [*Erkenntnis*] in general a priori, whether it concerns the sensible or the supersensible.
>
> (FM, 20:263–4)

The third step is here designated as "the critique of pure reason." Importantly, Kant immediately adds the caveat that this is such a critique insofar as it extends (*erweitert*) our cognition a priori. This extension can be directed toward the sensible or the supersensible. Kant therefore conceives of the critical philosophy in terms of his guiding definition of metaphysics here: it extends cognition toward the supersensible. He adds: "If this critique has accomplished what it promises, namely to determine the scope, the content, and the boundaries of such cognition," within the geographical and temporal space in the Academy's question, "then the task of the Royal Academy of Sciences will have been resolved" (FM, 20:264).

On this view, the critical philosophy as a whole is not a mere propaedeutic to a future metaphysics, as influential presentations in the first *Critique* and the *Prolegomena* imply, and as Kant's first "Kantian" followers thought. The propaedeutic, Kant now suggests, is provided by the Transcendental Analytic. This part of the *Critique* provides "a system of all concepts of the understanding and principles, but only insofar as they refer to objects that can be given to the senses." Kant calls this system of categories and principles "ontology," "transcendental philosophy," or the "hall or forecourt [*die Halle, oder der Vorhof*] of metaphysics proper" (FM, 20:260). The system in the Analytic is a limited, preliminary contribution to metaphysics. The critical philosophy's main contribution, as Kant presents it in the passage above, is rather the threefold task of determining the scope, content, and boundaries of a priori cognition.[34] Of this triad of aims, the determination of the boundaries of our cognition is of particular importance. By this, Kant does not mean a mere limitation of our knowledge, but rather an investigation into how human cognition can be legitimately extended to the supersensible, a theoretical endeavor that is warranted only from a practical perspective.[35] The primary place in which Kant pursues this investigation is the Dialectic of the second *Critique*, but there are also important references to it in the B Preface to the first *Critique* and at the conclusion of the third *Critique*.[36]

In the prize essay drafts, Kant presents the positive, critical metaphysics, which is both the critique of pure reason and the legitimate extension of reason beyond the boundary of possible experience, when discussing the "third stage" of metaphysics in the second manuscript (FM, 20:293–310). The third stage is famously designated by Kant as the "practical-dogmatic overstep to the supersensible" (FM, 20:293). Kant's discussion of this practical-dogmatic third stage is dense and convoluted. It brings together various aspects of his previous works and provides a fascinating insight into how he conceived of the positive results of the critical philosophy in the early to mid-1790s. The elements of the major critical works that Kant synthesizes here include the following. From the first *Critique*: the A and B edition Prefaces and the chapters on the Ideal, the Canon, and the History of Pure Reason. From the *Prolegomena*: §§57–60 entitled "On Pure Reason's Boundary-Determination." From the second *Critique*: the discussion in the Antinomy of the highest good and the doctrine of the Postulates of Pure Practical Reason. From the third *Critique*: the account of purposiveness in general and the Appendix on the Methodology of the Teleological Power of Judgement, particularly §§85–6 on physicotheology and ethicotheology. Kant additionally draws on his various discussions of propositional attitudes such as assent, opinion, belief, and knowledge, alongside material from his lectures on religion. In the systematic terms of the drafts, the transition to the supersensible proceeds by way of a progression from the skeptical "standstill" in cosmology to the "practical-dogmatic transition" in theology. Many aspects of Kant's account remain underdeveloped, not least the questions of the character, status, and role of psychology in this critical system.[37]

We cannot here evaluate the virtues and shortcomings of Kant's unfinished attempt to synthesize all these elements of his previous works.[38] Instead, we shall restrict our analysis to a general overview and note that if, as he suggests, Kant considered his critical philosophy to contribute to the history of metaphysics through this synthesis, then this is a very different and significantly more complicated account than that which prevailed among his "Kantian" contemporaries. Both Abicht and Reinhold took the critical philosophy's impact on metaphysics to be negative. For Abicht, Kant's philosophy is an earthquake that toppled previous systems; for Reinhold, it instigated an unruly war between discordant philosophies. Both authors saw it as a task for Kant's successors to rebuild what Reinhold called a "future metaphysics."

Contrary to what Kant, on the evidence of his letters, would have wished, Abicht and Reinhold take this task to require substantive developments of Kant's critical philosophy. Abicht's post-Kantian metaphysics goes beyond the critical limitations of knowledge of the supersensible and makes constitutive claims about the substantial

I, the world as a whole, and God. Reinhold's indifferent survey of the post-Kantian battlefield opens the space for his own attempt to make peace by securely grounding "Kantian" philosophy on a single first principle. In line with their conception of Kant's philosophy, Abicht and Reinhold both consider it necessary to go beyond the results of the three *Critiques* to answer the Academy's question about progress in metaphysics since the time of Leibniz and Wolff.

By contrast, Kant's draft response to the prize question argues that the critical philosophy *itself* represents progress in metaphysics. The conception of metaphysics in Kant's drafts is consistent with the *Critiques*, but only if the *Critiques* are read in a way that prioritizes certain elements, such as the Postulates of Pure Practical Reason, the critique of teleology, propositional attitudes, and the determination of the boundary of reason, over the results of the Transcendental Aesthetic and Analytic. That is, in the drafts, Kant foregrounds aspects of his previous philosophy that his immediate followers overlooked—as have many readers since.

6. Conclusion

The 1792/1795 Berlin Academy prize question touched a neuralgic point in the early reception of Kant's philosophy. It forced respondents to take a position on the issue of whether the critical philosophy positively contributed to metaphysics or whether it was simply a negative suspension of the progress of metaphysics. This is a complex issue facing interpreters of Kant's philosophy, one that remains hotly debated today, so it is no surprise that early self-appointed Kantians like Abicht and Reinhold were almost as far from Kant's own views on the matter as an anti-Kantian like Schwab. In different ways, Abicht and Reinhold considered it necessary to go beyond Kant's own writings to make progress in metaphysics in the wake of the critical philosophy. They assume that the prize question cannot be answered if one strictly remains within the perspective of Kant's philosophy, because in their view the latter only suspends the progress of metaphysics.

The fact that Schwab's explicitly anti-Kantian essay was awarded first prize by the Academy was a clear blow to the Kantian cause. But Kant may have been equally displeased by Abicht's speculative post-critical metaphysics and Reinhold's indifferent survey of the post-Kantian "war." The 1792/1795 essay contest may have seemed to Kant to well exemplify the "Italian proverb" that he liked to quote (Br, 12:371; ÜE, 8:247, 250–1): we need more protection from our friends than from our enemies.

Kant's drafts toward a response to the prize question show his distance from his "Kantian" followers. He defines metaphysics *as* progress, namely progress toward the supersensible, and draws together various doctrines from his critical works to sketch a picture of how this progress is achieved *by* the critical philosophy. This particular synthesis has been rarely viewed as Kant's primary philosophical contribution, either by Kant's first readers or by the majority of interpreters over the two subsequent centuries. The prize essay contest ultimately illuminated a threefold split in the philosophical landscape in the 1790s: firstly, anti-Kantians; secondly, supposed "Kantians" who, Kant would think, inadequately understood the relation of the critical philosophy to the history of metaphysics; and thirdly, those who had a complete understanding of the critical philosophy's contribution to metaphysics. Among the essayists, Kant appears to be a lonely member of the latter group.

Abbreviations

Schwab, Reinhold, and Abicht

PF *Preisschriften über die Frage: welche Fortschritte hat die Metaphysik seit Leibnitzens und Wolffs Zeiten in Deutschland gemacht?*: Schwab, Reinhold, and Abicht 1796.

Kant

A/B The A (1781) and B (1787) editions of the *Critique of Pure Reason* (AA 3–4).

AA The Academy Edition of Kant's Writings: Kant 1902–.

BR *Briefe/Letters* (AA 10–13).

FM *Welches sind die wirklichen Fortschritte, die die Metaphysik seit Leibnitzens und Wolf's Zeiten in Deutschland gemacht hat?/What Real Progress Has Metaphysics Made in Germany since the Time of Leibniz and Wolff?* (AA 20): Kant 1983, 2002.

KPV *Kritik der praktischen Vernunft/Critique of Practical Reason* (AA 05).

KU *Kritik der Urteilskraft/Critique of the Power of Judgment* (AA 05).

LOG *Logik Jäsche/Jäsche Logic* (AA 09).

MS *Die Metaphysik der Sitten/The Metaphysics of Morals* (AA 06).

P *Prolegomena zu einer jeden künftigen Metaphysik, die als Wissenschaft wird auftreten können/Prolegomena to Any Future Metaphysics That Will Be Able to Come Forward as Science* (AA 04).

ÜE *Über eine Entdeckung, nach der alle neue Kritik der reinen Vernunft durch eine ältere entbehrlich gemacht werden soll/On a Discovery Whereby Any New Critique of Pure Reason Is to Be Made Superfluous by an Older One* (AA 08).

Notes

1   The Academy, under the auspices of the Francophile Frederick the Great and taking the Paris Academy as its model, posed the question in French: *Quels sont les progrès réels de la Métaphysique en Allemagne depuis le temps de Leibniz et de Wolf?* We refer

to the 1792/1795 question with these dates because 1792 was the original deadline; having received only one submission (Schwab's), the Academy extended the deadline to 1795 and doubled the prize money. For more information about the 1792/1795 contest, see de Vleeschauwer 1974, 299–300 and the introductions in Kant 1983, 11–12 and Kant 2002, 339.
2   Particularly important figures in this debate were Nicolas Béguelin and Jean Bernard Merian. See Grosse 2022 and Prunea-Bretonnet 2022.
3   For example, writing in 1790, one early reviewer of Maimon's work states that after the Kantian Revolution, "the educated world was divided into two great parties … Kantian and anti-Kantian," and one must "openly profess to belong to the one or the other" (cited in Look 2018, 95).
4   For more on Maimon's contribution, see Reichl 2020.
5   Kant would directly respond to Eberhard's attack on this front in the polemical "On a Discovery" written in 1790 (ÜE, 8:187–251). With regard to the bias in the Academy, de Vleeschauwer estimates that the Wolffian side had a slight majority over the Kantians at the time when the 1792/1795 question was published (1974, 300).
6   De Vleeschauwer notes that the Academy "couronna le wolffien Schwab et les deux semi-kantiens, Abicht et Reinhold" (1974, 301). Allison writes that both Abicht and Reinhold "advocated a basically Kantian position, though they were primarily concerned to defend their own ideas" (Kant 2002, 339). Frank provides a discussion of the general positions of both Schwab and Abicht that briefly touches on their contributions to the prize question (1997, 328ff.). Reinhold's contribution has received more scholarly attention, especially regarding his re-writing of his original essay, in Zöller 2004 and Imhof 2020.
7   All references to the three prize essays are to the Academy's 1796 publication (PF).
8   He adds that this is not because Wolff's system constitutes the "measure of all truth" or the "outer boundary of all human speculation," but because his rigorous geometrical method can be used (by an unbiased "investigator of truth") to uncover any errors and sophistries concealed in a given system (PF, 19).
9   There are some difficulties with the inclusion of Hume here. Hume's works were published before Schwab's "third period." Furthermore, throughout his discussion, Schwab cites Jacob's German translation of the *Treatise* from 1790, which postdates the dating of the period. Presumably, Hume is inserted into this period because of the influence he had on the state of metaphysics in Germany at this time (PF, 76). For more on the reception of Hume in this period, see Brandt and Klemme 1989 and Kuehn 2005.
10   It is striking that Schwab here repeats Kant's description, in the Preface to the first edition of the *Critique*, of the "anarchy" engendered by skepticism (Aix). His claim that this leads to the reign of a dictator seems to be an ironic alternative conclusion, replacing Kant's account of how the *Critique* brings peace to the battlefield of metaphysics. We shall see that Reinhold also takes up the battlefield imagery from the A Preface in his contribution.
11   See, for example, how Kant distinguishes his categories from innate ideas in the *Discovery* essay, published several years before the prize competition (ÜE, 8:223ff.). For accounts defending the novelty of Kant's understanding of the a priori, see De Pierris 1987, Zöller 1989, and Yuichiro 2008. For an opposed view of the parallels between the Kantian and Leibnizian understanding of the a priori, see Vanzo 2018.
12   Di Giovanni 2005, 59.
13   Ameriks 2000, 231 fn. 81.

14 Reinhold may not have this in mind but it is interesting to note that in the period he is discussing, leading figures in the Berlin Academy were explicitly adopting an eclectic approach to metaphysics. See Prunea-Bretonnet 2022, 78–87, 92–101.
15 On this, see PF, 210–11, 224–5, 233–4.
16 In other works from the period, Reinhold attempts to articulate such a new philosophical conception of the history of metaphysics, particularly in *Ueber den Begriff der Geschichte der Philosophie* (1791). On this issue, see Ameriks 2006, 193ff.; Breazeale 2010; and Reichl 2021.
17 See AA 20:479–80; de Vleeschauwer 1974, 307–8; Kant 1983, 13–14; and Kant 2002, 340–1. The original manuscripts are now lost, but Rink's Preface does provide sufficient information to enable us to reconstruct what was contained in each. Roughly speaking, there are two drafts of an introduction (in manuscripts 1 and 3), one summary of the *Critique*'s transcendental philosophy (manuscript 1) plus a few additional paragraphs on the topic (manuscript 3), one account of the "first stage" of metaphysics (manuscript 1), two "second stages" (manuscripts 1 and 2), and a long "third stage" (manuscript 2). Additionally, Rink's edition contained various marginal notes, separated from their context in the manuscripts. The Academy edition collects further passages from loose sheets that Gerhard Lehmann considered relevant. See the editors' overviews of the drafts in Kant 1983, 14–15; and Kant 2002, 340.
18 As did Maimon: see the Introduction above.
19 Kiesewetter's major popular presentation appeared the year before this exchange of letters: *Versuch einer fasslichen Darstellung der wichtigsten Wahrheiten der neuern Philosophie* (1795). For more details, see Naragon's entry on Kiesewetter in Klemme and Kuehn 2010, 415–17.
20 See Grandjean 2017, 222–3, and the passages he quotes: KU, 4:256–7; P, 4:368; Bxiv; B21; A852/B880; and MS, 6:206–7.
21 FM, 20:260; cf. 20:316.
22 FM, 20:260; cf. 20:272–3, 287–8, 293.
23 On this conception of reason, see Ferrarin 2015, 25–34; and Willaschek 2018, 21–36. Alongside Avii-viii, some of the key passages for this conception of metaphysics are: A407/B433–4; P, 4: 339, 353–4, 367; Bxiv; and KU, 5: 473. For further discussion of Kant's conception of the (positive) boundary of reason, see Howard 2022.
24 For a discussion of the system that Kant envisages here, see De Boer 2020, 212–54.
25 While each more or less explicitly acknowledges both senses of metaphysics, three recent contributions each foreground only one of them. Ferrarin 2015 focuses on the first sense of metaphysics in its positive sense: how ideas result from the needs and strivings of reason and guide reason in its teleological orientation toward the highest good. Ferrarin considers the analogy of an organism to best capture Kant's conception of reason, but he does not explain why this leads to a transformed system of traditional metaphysics (Ferrarin 2015, 34–57). Willaschek 2018 also focuses on the first sense of metaphysics, but negatively (compared to Ferrarin): he reconstructs Kant's explanation of how reason moves from a logical maxim to a regulative, and then a constitutive, "Supreme Principle" and thereby strays into illusion. The system of pure reason is, on Willaschek's account, constituted to a large extent by merely pretended sciences (Willaschek 2018, 36–44). De Boer 2020 emphasizes the second sense of metaphysics: how Kant planned to flesh out the system of metaphysics sketched in the Architectonic chapter of the *Critique*. Reason's practical interests and ends play only a minor role in her account (De Boer 2020, 248–9).

26 For discussion, see De Boer 2020, 248; Ferrarin 2015, 82–90; Fugate 2019; and Hinske 2013.
27 We follow Humphreys (Kant 1983, 79) and Thisted 2017, 208, in adding "doctrine" after "practical-dogmatic" (in Kant 2002, Heath adds "creed"). On the misplacement of the passage, see Kant 1983, 79n; Thisted 2017, 207n30, quoting Caimi; and Brandt 2017, 190.
28 The fourth branch, rational psychology, is contained in the second stage, Kant suggests (20:281); we return to this below. Some further complexities in Kant's systematic-historical periodization, notably with regard to ontology, will also be discussed below.
29 In our opinion, Grandjean 2017 and Thisted 2017 overemphasize the systematic and ahistorical side of Kant's account. For a discussion that emphasizes the historical side of Kant's drafts, see Reichl 2021. Brandt 2017 shows the tension in Kant's (unfinished) attempt to unify historical "epochs" with systematic "stages" of metaphysics.
30 FM, 20:286–92, 326–9.
31 Thisted 2017, 209n36, points to the following passages for hints of the positive part of the first stage: FM, 20:286, 337–8, 338–9.
32 See Thisted 2017, 209n36, on the uneven development of the stages in the manuscripts: "The greatest problem lies in the first stage: Kant was only able to write a critique of Leibniz-Wolffian ontology but failed to introduce the positive part of this theoretico-dogmatic stage in that critique."
33 FM, 20:265–80; cf. 20:322–6. Brandt 2017, 189, summarizes the first manuscript's extended discussion of the Transcendental Aesthetic and Analytic of the first *Critique*.
34 See KpV, 5:134–41; Bxx–xxi; Bxxiv–xxv; KU, 5:473–4. This is a version of a threefold depiction of critique that regularly appears in Kant's writings and lecture notes. Kant replaces "sources," which usually appears in the triad of aims, with "content": cf., for example, Axii, KpV, 5:10, Log, 9:25, AA 28:533, 29:750, 29:767–8, 29:955–6. This could be a slip of the pen, if "content" is considered a synonym for "extent." Alternatively, Kant's substitution could be taken to indicate his greater interest in the *content* of pure rational cognition in the prize essay drafts when compared to earlier works.
35 The determination of the boundary of pure reason is not a mere limitation; instead, it constitutes an investigation into reason's capacity for extending beyond this boundary. This is because, on Kant's conception, a boundary, unlike a limit, is not a mere negation but indicates a space "beyond." On this, see Howard 2022.
36 For an argument that this aspect of Kant's project shifts as he works on it, with reference to the Orientation essay and the issue of moral motivation, see Chance and Pasternack 2018.
37 Kant makes brief references to psychology, both positive and negative. Positively, when he (somewhat unconvincingly) subsumes psychology under cosmology, reconceiving the latter as "*physica et psychologia rationalis*": this is how rational *physiology* is glossed in the *Critique* (FM, 20:281; cf. A846–7/B874–5). Negatively, when he criticizes the alleged theoretical-dogmatic progress of Leibniz and Wolff in the field of psychology (FM, 20:308–9). Mario Caimi (2017) attempts to reconstruct the systematic structure of the metaphysics in the prize essay drafts according to the traditional divisions of metaphysics. In our opinion, Caimi's attempt is overly interpretative and not well supported by the text.
38 For an extended discussion of the third stage, see Langthaler 2017.

Bibliography

Primary sources

Abicht, Johann Heinrich. 1788. *Versuch einer krittischen Untersuchung über das Willensgeschäfte*. Frankfurt am Main: Jäger.
Abicht, Johann Heinrich. 1794. *Hermias, oder Auflösung der die gültige Elementarphilosophie betreffenden Aenesidemischen Zweifel*. Erlangen: Walther.
Kant, Immanuel. 1902. *Kants gesammelte Schriften: herausgegeben von der Deutschen Akademie der Wissenschaften*. Berlin: De Gruyter.
Kant, Immanuel. 1983. *What Real Progress Has Metaphysics Made in Germany since the Time of Leibniz and Wolff?*, translated by Ted Humphrey. New York: Abaris.
Kant, Immanuel. 2002. "What Real Progress Has Metaphysics Made in Germany since the Time of Leibniz and Wolff?." translated by Peter Heath. In *Theoretical Philosophy after 1781*, edited by Henry Allison and Peter Heath, 337–423. Cambridge: Cambridge University Press.
Maimon, Salomon. 1793. *Über die Progressen der Philosophie*. Berlin: Wilhelm Vieweg.
Reinhold, Karl Leonhard. 1791. "Ueber den Begriff der Geschichte der Philosophie." In *Beyträge zur Geschichte der Philosophie*, edited by Georg Gustav Fülleborn, 5–35. Jena: Friedrich Fromman.
Reinhold, Karl Leonhard. 1797. *Auswahl vermischter Schriften*, vol. 2. Jena: Mauke.
Schultz, Johann. (1784) 1791. *Erläuterungen über des Herrn Professor Kant Critik der reinen Vernunft*. Königsberg: Hartungsche Buchhandlung.
Schwab, Johann Christoph, Karl Leonhard Reinhold, and Johann Heinrich Abicht. 1796. *Preisschriften über die Frage: welche Fortschritte hat die Metaphysik seit Leibnitzens und Wolffs Zeiten in Deutschland gemacht?*. Berlin: Maurer.

Secondary sources

Ameriks, Karl. 2000. *Kant's Theory of Mind: An Analysis of the Paralogisms of Pure Reason*. Oxford: Oxford University Press.
Ameriks, Karl. 2006. *Kant and the Historical Turn: Philosophy as Critical Interpretation*. Oxford: Oxford University Press.
Ameriks, Karl. 2012. "Reinhold, History, and the Foundation of Philosophy." In *Karl Leonhard Reinhold and the Enlightenment*, edited by George di Giovanni, 89–111. Dordrecht: Springer.
Ameriks, Karl. 2017. "The Historical Turn in Late Modernity." In *Hegel on Philosophy in History*, edited by James Kreines and Rachel Zuckert, 139–56. Cambridge: Cambridge University Press.
Beiser, Frederick. 1987. *The Fate of Reason: German Philosophy from Kant to Fichte*. Cambridge: Harvard University Press.
Brandt, Andreas. 2017. "Epochen und Stadien der Metaphysik: Der Doppelte Fortschrittsbegriff in Kants Entwürfen der Späten Preisschrift." In *Über die Fortschritte der kritischen Metaphysik: Beiträge zu System und Architektonik der kantischen Philosophie*, edited by Andree Hahmann and Bernd Ludwig, 183–98. Hamburg: Felix Meiner Verlag.
Brandt, Reinhard and Heiner Klemme, (eds.). 1989. *David Hume in Deutschland. Literatur zur Hume-Rezeption in Marburger Bibliotheken*. Marburg: Universitätsbibliothek.

Breazeale, Daniel. 2010. "Reason's Changing Needs: From Kant to Reinhold." In *Karl Leonhard Reinhold and the Enlightenment*, edited by George di Giovanni, 89–111. Dordrecht: Springer.

Caimi, Mario. 2017. "Der Begriff der praktisch-dogmatischen Metaphysik." In *Über die Fortschritte der kritischen Metaphysik: Beiträge zu System und Architektonik der kantischen Philosophie*, edited by Andree Hahmann and Bernd Ludwig, 157–70. Hamburg: Felix Meiner Verlag.

Chance, Brian A. and Lawrence Pasternack. 2018. "Rational Faith and the Pantheism Controversy." In *Kant and His German Contemporaries: Volume 2, Aesthetics, History, Politics, and Religion*, edited by Daniel Dahlstrom, 195–214. Cambridge: Cambridge University Press.

De Boer, Karin. 2020. *Kant's Reform of Metaphysics: The Critique of Pure Reason Reconsidered*. Cambridge: Cambridge University Press.

De Pierris, Graciela. 1987. "Kant and Innatism," *Pacific Philosophical Quarterly*, 68, 3–4, 285–305.

De Vleeschauwer, Herman Jean. 1974. "La Cinderella dans l'œuvre Kantienne." In *Akten des 4. Internationalen Kant-Kongresses: Mainz, 6.–10. April 1974*, vol. 1, edited by Gerhard Funke, 6–10. Berlin: De Gruyter.

Di Giovanni, George. 2005. *Freedom and Religion in Kant and His Immediate Successors: The Vocation of Humankind, 1774–1800*. Cambridge: Cambridge University Press.

Ferrarin, Alfredo. 2015. *The Powers of Pure Reason: Kant and the Idea of Cosmic Philosophy*. Chicago: University of Chicago Press.

Frank, Manfred. 1997. "*Unendliche Annäherung*": *Die Anfänge der philosophischen Frühromantik*. Frankfurt am Main: Suhrkamp.

Fugate, Courtney. 2019. "Kant's World Concept of Philosophy and Cosmopolitanism," *Archiv für Geschichte der Philosophie*, 101, 4, 535–83.

Grandjean, Antoine. 2017. "Kant als Historiker der Metaphysik: ein Fortschritt ohne Geschichte." In *Über die Fortschritte der kritischen Metaphysik: Beiträge zu System und Architektonik der kantischen Philosophie*, edited by Andree Hahmann and Bernd Ludwig, 217–26. Hamburg: Felix Meiner Verlag.

Grosse, Annelie. 2022. "'Mother of All Sciences' or Mere Speculation? The Justification of Metaphysics at the Berlin Academy between 1746 and 1765." In *The Berlin Academy in the Reign of Frederick the Great: Philosophy and Science*, edited by Tinca Prunea-Bretonnet and Peter R. Anstey, 39–69. Liverpool: Liverpool University Press.

Hahmann, Andree and Bernd Ludwig, (eds.) 2017. *Über die Fortschritte der kritischen Metaphysik: Beiträge zu System und Architektonik der Kantischen Philosophie*. Hamburg: Felix Meiner Verlag.

Hinske, Norbert. 2013. "Kants Verankerung der Kritik im Weltbegriff. Einige Anmerkungen zu KrV B 866 ff." In *Kant und die Philosophie in weltbürgerlicher Absicht: Akten des XI. Kant-Kongresses 2010*, vol. 1, edited by Stefano Bacin, Alfredo Ferrarin, Claudio La Rocca, and Margit Ruffing, 263–75. Berlin: De Gruyter.

Howard, Stephen. 2022. "Kant on Limits, Boundaries, and the Positive Function of Ideas," *European Journal of Philosophy*, 30, 64–78.

Imhof, Silvan. 2020. "The 'Weak Side of Critical Philosophy' or Why Reinhold Abandoned His Elementarphilosophie." In *Reinhold and Fichte in Confrontation: A Tale of Mutual Appreciation and Criticism*, edited by Martin Bondeli and Silvan Imhof, 151–78. Berlin: De Gruyter.

Israel, Jonathan. 2011. *Democratic Enlightenment: Philosophy, Revolution, and Human Rights 1750–1790*. Oxford: Oxford University Press.

Klemme, Heiner and Manfred Kuehn, (eds.) 2010. *The Dictionary of Eighteenth-Century German Philosophers*. London: Continuum.

Kuehn, Manfred. 2005. "The Reception of Hume in Germany." In *The Reception of David Hume in Europe*, edited by Peter Jones, 98–138. London: Continuum.

Langthaler, Rudolf. 2017. "Die Kennzeichnung des 'dritten Stadiums' der neueren Metaphysik als 'Theologie' in Kants später Preisschrift und damit verbundene systematische Perspektiven." In *Über die Fortschritte der kritischen Metaphysik: Beiträge zu System und Architektonik der kantischen Philosophie*, edited by Andree Hahmann and Bernd Ludwig, 119–56. Hamburg: Felix Meiner Verlag.

Look, Brandon C. 2018. "Maimon and Kant on the Nature of the Mind." In *Kant and His German Contemporaries: Volume 1, Logic, Mind, Epistemology, Science and Ethics*, edited by Corey W. Dyck and Falk Wunderlich, 94–110. Cambridge: Cambridge University Press.

Prunea-Bretonnet, Tinca. 2022. "Eclectic Philosophy and 'Academic Spirit': The Berlin Academy and the Thomasian Legacy." In *The Berlin Academy in the Reign of Frederick the Great: Philosophy and Science*, edited by Tinca Prunea-Bretonnet and Peter R. Anstey, 71–101. Liverpool: Liverpool University Press.

Prunea-Bretonnet, Tinca and Peter R. Anstey, (eds.) 2022. *The Berlin Academy in the Reign of Frederick the Great: Philosophy and Science*. Liverpool: Liverpool University Press.

Reichl, Pavel. 2020. "Making History Philosophical: Kant, Maimon, and the Evolution of the Historiography of Philosophy in the Critical Period," *British Journal for the History of Philosophy*, 28, 3, 463–82.

Reichl, Pavel. 2021. "Kant's A Priori History of Metaphysics: Systematicity, Progress, and the Ends of Reason," *European Journal of Philosophy*, 29, 4, 811–26.

Thisted, Marcos A. 2017. "Kant's Late Metaphysics: On 'Metaphysics Proper' in the Fortschritte der Metaphysik." In *Über die Fortschritte der kritischen Metaphysik: Beiträge zu System und Architektonik der kantischen Philosophie*, edited by Andree Hahmann and Bernd Ludwig, 199–216. Hamburg: Felix Meiner Verlag.

Vanzo, Alberto. 2018. "Leibniz on Innate Ideas and Kant on the Origin of the Categories," *Archiv für Geschichte der Philosophie*, 100, 1, 19–45.

Willaschek, Marcus. 2018. *Kant on the Sources of Metaphysics: The Dialectic of Pure Reason*. Cambridge: Cambridge University Press.

Yamane, Yuichiro. 2008. "Zur kritischen Verwandlung des Begriffs 'angeboren' bei Kant." In *Recht und Frieden in der Philosophie Kants*, edited by Valerio Rohden and Ricardo R. Terra, 831–44. Berlin: De Gruyter.

Zöller, Günter. 1989. "From Innate to 'A Priori': Kant's Radical Transformation of a Cartesian-Leibnizian Legacy," *The Monist*, 72, 2, 222–35.

Zöller, Günter. 2004. "Ancilla sensus communis. K. L. Reinhold über die Metaphysik und ihre Fortschritte." In *Philosophie ohne Beinamen: System, Freiheit und Geschichte im Denken K. L. Reinholds*, edited by Martin Bondeli and Alessandro Lazzari, 347–69. Basel: Schwabe.

Part Three

Anthropology

Aesthetics as Apolaustic: Baumgarten and the Controversy over Sensitive Pleasures

Alessandro Nannini

1. Introduction

By the middle of the nineteenth century, when the noun "aesthetics" was well rooted in European languages, the Scottish metaphysician Sir William Hamilton put forward a different term to indicate the domain of aesthetics. While Hegel notoriously proposes the name "callistic" in the introduction to his *Lectures on Aesthetics*, which mostly draws on the aspect of beauty, Hamilton emphasizes pleasure:

> It is nearly a century since Baumgarten, a celebrated philosopher of the Leibnitio-Wolfian School, first applied the term "Aesthetic" to the doctrine which we vaguely and periphrastically denominate the Philosophy of Taste, the theory of the Fine Arts, the science of the Beautiful and Sublime, etc., and this term is now in general acceptation not only in Germany but throughout the other countries of Europe. The term "Apolaustic" (from the Greek, to enjoy) would have been a more appropriate designation.
>
> (Hamilton 1859, 124)

Although Hamilton's suggestion fell on deaf ears, it certainly touched upon a seminal dimension, which belongs to Baumgarten's own concept of aesthetics.

At the outset of the first volume of his 1750 *Aesthetica* (AE), Alexander Gottlieb Baumgarten (1714–62) defines aesthetics as "the science of sensitive knowledge" (AE, §1). Before discussing his conception of aesthetics more precisely, Baumgarten lists a series of possible objections that the newly born discipline might arouse. Some are more general and concern the status of aesthetics (e.g., whether aesthetics is to be considered an art or a science). Others are concerned with the relationship with poetics and rhetoric. Two of these objections focus on the desirability of the cultivation of sensibility that aesthetics intends to achieve. The first criticism comes from the intellectualist camp, which accuses aesthetics of dealing with things that are unworthy of a philosopher (sensibility, for instance) (AE, §6). The second criticism states that the lower faculties of the soul, such as the senses, the imagination, and wit, should be repressed rather than cultivated. In fact, so runs the objection: the lower faculties are linked with the flesh; therefore, aesthetics is a noxious discipline (AE, §12) that strengthens sensitive desires (K, 12). While the objection is evidently polemical in its purpose, it is undoubtedly true that aesthetics must come to terms with the appetitive and pleasing dimension of sensibility and not just with its epistemic dimension alone.

During the early eighteenth century in Germany, sensitive or sensual pleasures and desires[1] were often discussed within the framework of a thorny controversy between orthodox Lutherans and Pietists over the "adiaphora" or "indifferents," things neither commanded nor forbidden by God. The discussion about the legitimacy of sensitive pleasures, however, did not remain limited to theology, but also involved the philosophy of the time. My goal in this chapter is to analyze, for the first time, Baumgarten's philosophical answer to this controversy and the consequences that this position entails for the invention of aesthetics.

In what follows, I briefly outline the Pietist stance in the debate, examining the theological requirement to crucify one's flesh and its link with the renunciation of the pleasures of the senses. I then turn to Baumgarten's position in this regard. First of all, I explore his philosophical approach in understanding the crucifixion of the flesh and self-abnegation. On this basis, I analyze Baumgarten's specific way of dealing with sensitive pleasures, focusing on a few examples that were the main targets of Pietist attacks: epithalamia, toasts, jokes, and leisure activities in general. This will contribute to the demonstration that Baumgarten, while not breaking with the Pietist conceptual framework in which he was educated, radically changes its meaning in multiple respects. Finally, I aim to examine the relationship between flesh and sensibility in Baumgarten as well as the role aesthetics can play in the correct cultivation of sensibility and sensitive pleasures. In this manner, I will draw attention to a polemical dimension of Baumgarten's relationship with Pietism, which has heretofore escaped the attention of commentators. Moreover, I will cast new light on the hedonistic stake of nascent aesthetics, which for the most part remains a blind spot of research.

2. The Objection to Aesthetics

Here is the aforementioned objection to aesthetics, in the way Baumgarten formulates it:

> One could object: the lower faculties and the flesh must be subjugated rather than awakened and strengthened. I respond: a) the lower faculties require mastery, not tyranny. b) To this end, to the extent that it can be achieved naturally, aesthetics leads us by the hand. c) The lower faculties, insofar as they are corrupted, are not supposed to be awakened and strengthened by the aesthetician. Rather they must be guided by him, so that they are not corrupted even more by misuse, and so that we are not deprived of a God given talent under the lazy pretext that we must avoid misusing them.
>
> (AE, §12)

Who hides behind the phrase "One could object" (*obiici posset*)? If we consider how the objection is stated, the controversy appears to have a theological background. An analysis of §12 of Baumgarten's *Lectures on Aesthetics* confirms this hypothesis:

> They say that the Scripture dictates crucifying the flesh, that is, the corrupted lower powers of the mind, rather than improving it. But in this case, they mistake the repression of what is sinful in them for the complete eradication of the sensitive. This would mean to deprive oneself of one's human nature, and the Christian religion never imposes such a thing; it just wants us to rule over this confused cognition. Further, aesthetics does not strengthen sensitive desires, but it makes its contribution to the fear of God. It teaches us how to execrate as awful the thoughts that are contrary to it. If they say that I must be prepared for the fear of God supernaturally and not through the arts, they do not ponder enough that some degrees of improvement can be attained through the human arts and do not happen supernaturally. As we still have some remnants of the image of God, we can distinguish them more clearly and better understand them by means of aesthetics.
>
> (K, §12)

Although Baumgarten does not say it overtly, in the 1740s and 1750s, those who argued for the crucifixion of the flesh in the sense of a rejection of sensibility and its desires were often identified with the Pietists, considered to be the offspring of the ancient anchorites.[2] Hence, it is to the Pietist conception that we have to turn to gain deeper insight into this objection.

3. The Pietist Crucifixion of the Flesh and Sensual Pleasures

As is known, at the basis of the Pietist condemnation of earthly pleasures and desires lies the rejection of the so-called "indifferents" (*adiaphora* or *Mitteldinge*), those things that are neither commanded nor forbidden by God. The orthodox Lutherans tended to admit the existence of indifferent actions *in abstracto*; only in their concrete use are voluntary actions submitted to the divine law, hence to a moral judgment.[3] Dancing might be an indifferent action in itself, but if I dance with lustful intentions, the action is sinful. For their part, the Pietists proved to be much more radical in denying the very existence of adiaphora, in both concrete and abstract, hence also without any reference to an individual agent nor to specific circumstances.[4] In fact, for the Pietists any voluntary action is either taken to serve the glory of God or it is doomed to fall prey to sin, according to Paul's dictum: "Everything that does not come from faith is sin" (Rom. 14:23).

This is also true of sensual pleasures. In the controversial debate over pleasure with the Lutheran preacher Albrecht Christian Rotth (1651–1701), the Pietist pedagogue Gottfried Vockerodt (1665–1727), closely linked with the founder of Halle Pietism August Hermann Francke (1663–1727), rejects every pleasure that does not come from God.[5] Vockerodt maintains that there are only two internal principles of action for our soul and body, namely spirit and flesh:

Before the conversion the flesh predominates; after the conversion the spirit fights against the flesh. Therefore, what a person does is an impulse and an effect either of the flesh or of the spirit. Hence, every pleasure of a person can only be of two types: sinful or holy. [...] No pleasure is left that is indifferent, hence neither sinful nor holy.

(Vockerodt 1699, 144)[6]

The biblical reference for this doctrine is Gal. 5:16-26, where the desires and works of the flesh are opposed to the desires and fruits of the spirit. Commenting on this passage, the Pietist Johann Jakob Rambach (1693-1735) writes that the spirit is here "the *nova indoles*, which the Holy Spirit achieves in a person with the rebirth." To walk by the spirit thus means to direct "their [of the Galatians] inner and outer *actiones* according to the good impulsion of God's Spirit." By contrast, flesh designates "the corrupted sinful nature, which is opposed to the spirit" (Rambach 1739, 307).[7] More precisely, σάρξ is the scriptural word to indicate what is termed "original sin" in the theological language, hence the corruption of human nature, and refers both to the will, as is shown by sexual immorality, impurity, debauchery, fits of rage, etc., and to the intellect, as in the case of heresy.[8] In order to walk by the spirit, it is therefore necessary to crucify one's flesh in both of these faculties: "Those who belong to Christ Jesus have crucified the flesh with its passions and desires" (Gal. 5:24).

For Rambach, the crucifixion of the flesh entails three stages, on the model of the crucifixion of Christ: deprivation of freedom, withholding of food, and slow agony. The same stages must feature in moral crucifixion: the flesh must be deprived of the freedom to rule over a person, then it must be deprived of the satiation of evil desires, which requires that one avoid arousing them. Thus, a lustful person who truly intends to crucify his flesh must distract his gaze from obscene images and books, while also avoiding drunkenness and the amiable conversation with women who might induce him to sin. Eventually, the old Adam must be progressively bled and weakened with *exercitia poenitentiae et pietatis*, through acts that include prayer, work, moderation, the zealous contemplation of Christ's sufferings, and fasting.[9]

As Vockerodt points out, it is a fact that the inclination to evil and people's fallibility express themselves first and foremost in sensual perception and its cognate pleasures (Vockerodt 1697, 30-1; 133). It does not come as a surprise that precisely in this historical period the German word for "pleasure" *Wollust* (or *Lust*), which at the time was a neutral term, gained a pejorative nuance owing to its constant link with the flesh.[10] Unlike the Stoics, however, the Pietists did not endorse apathy or anhedonia[11] but aimed to make pleasure serve a higher goal. According to Rambach, for example, pleasure, whether in earthly or in spiritual things, is good and permitted (*gute und erlaubte Lust*) if the one who experiences it is reborn in the spirit and views in the object of enjoyment a ladder to God. Conversely, pleasure is evil (*böse Lust*) if the object of enjoyment is the ultimate goal of pleasure, since in this case pleasure is necessarily inspired by the flesh.[12]

On the one hand, this position parts ways with the rigidity of the Augustinian distinction between *uti* and *frui*. According to Augustine, it is never permitted to enjoy the world, but only to use it in order to return as fast as possible to our heavenly homeland. By contrast, for Rambach the enjoyment of creatures is in a certain measure justified if the enjoyment elicits a feeling of gratitude and praise to God as Creator.[13]

On the other hand, Rambach's position is neatly different from Christian Wolff's. In his *German Politics*, Wolff states that sensual pleasures can be innocent and also useful to society if one avoids abuses and misuses, whence the social importance of music, theater, and leisure gardens (Wolff 1721, §389-93).[14] Thus, while Rambach distinguishes good and evil pleasures on the basis of their compliance with God's intentions and law, Wolff distinguishes innocent and noxious sensual pleasures on the basis of the law of nature, hence on the basis of their contribution to our self-perfection. In sum, for Wolff the innocence of sensual pleasures does not depend on the spiritual condition of those who experience them or on the transitivity of the pleasure from the concrete object to God, but only on their conformity to reason.

4. Baumgarten on the Crucifixion of the Flesh

Baumgarten introduces the concept of pleasure in the section of his *Metaphysica* (M) (Metaphysics, 1739) on empirical psychology, drawing on Wolff's conception. While Wolff defines pleasure as the "intuition of a perfection" (Wolff 1732, §511),[15] Baumgarten defines it as the state of the soul deriving from the intuition of a perfection (M §655).[16] For both Baumgarten and Wolff, pleasure can be either true or apparent, depending on whether it is prompted by the intuition of truly good things or not (Wolff 1732, §514; M §655).[17] In relation to the epistemic dimension from which pleasure arises, Baumgarten identifies three categories of pleasure: the pleasure deriving from a sensitive intuition (sensitive pleasure),[18] the pleasure deriving from a sensual intuition (pleasure of the senses), and the pleasure deriving from distinct intuition (rational or intellectual pleasure) (M, §656).[19] In Baumgarten, pleasure is related to desire, albeit with a different emphasis compared to Wolff. The recasting of the "law of desire" in a conative sense[20]—a sense that Wolff brought to the fore in rational psychology rather than in empirical psychology—causes Baumgarten to identify the driving force of desire not in a current pleasure, but in the foresight of a future pleasure.[21] A stronger desire or aversion, Baumgarten states, is affect (M, §678); the desire originating from a stronger sensitive pleasure is thus an agreeable affect (M, §679) or joy (M, §682).

What is the legitimacy of the pleasures of the senses from an ethical point of view? Should they be sacrificed according to the biblical command to crucify one's flesh? Baumgarten is well aware of the issue given his Pietist background, and he addresses it directly in the chapter of his *Ethica philosophica* (E) (Philosophical Ethics, 1740) devoted to the care of the body, in the particular context of the duties concerning food and fasting (E, §262).[22] As we have seen above, fasting was precisely one of the penitential exercises Rambach had recommended for the crucifixion of one's flesh.

Baumgarten's point of departure is philosophical death, that is, the set of "telestic" exercises whereby the ancients intended to rid the soul of the bonds of the body. The reference is clearly to the Pythagorean and Platonic sects, which attached importance to everyday *meditatio mortis*.[23] In this context, the body was considered to be the root of all evil, whence the necessity to conceive the practices of self-improvement through both the repression of the somatic dimension and the elevation of the soul.[24]

If philosophical death is understood in the sense of a progressive destruction of the interaction between the soul and the body, Baumgarten comments, then this doctrine belongs to a deceptive kind of ethics since we are actually obliged to preserve that tie as long as possible (E, §262). However, this doctrine can also be understood in the sense of a *disciplina corporis* (*castigatio*; *mortificatio*), that is, in German, *Casteyung* or *Creutzigung des Fleisches*, chastisement or crucifixion of the flesh. Such a link between philosophical *meditatio mortis* and the New Testament *crucifixio carnis* had already been discussed in the Church Fathers, for example in Ambrose's *De bono mortis* (Death as a Good) (387–9), and it was well known in the early modern age.[25] In light of this link, the crucifixion of the flesh is seen by Baumgarten as a form of self-mastery on the basis of which one gives up a number of goods that are pleasing to the external senses, insofar as they are hindrances to nobler actions (E, §262). For Baumgarten the crucifixion of the flesh is therefore framed in the doctrine of self-abnegation.

Abnegation was a key aspect of Pietist ethics starting with Philipp Jakob Spener (1635–1705), and had already been a battleground in the controversy over decorum ignited by Christian Thomasius (1655–1728).[26] According to the Pietists, since natural human beings after the Fall, and partly also the reborn, are subject to a kind of natural and disordered self-love, it is necessary to repress and mortify one's deceiving *philautia* on the basis of Matt. 16:24: "Whoever wants to be my disciple must deny themselves and take up their cross and follow me."[27]

For his part, Baumgarten does not understand abnegation as a way of mortifying natural self-love as such, but as a principle regulating a hierarchical scale of goods within the natural plane. Abnegation is thus discussed as a philosophical, rather than a theological, subject.[28] In more detail, abnegation consists in the aversion to the goods that are hindrances to greater goods and in the desire for evils that can avert greater evils (E, §238). In this sense, abnegation is a significant aspect of the cure of the faculty of desire, and it is strictly linked with the capacity of mastering the intuition of pleasure and displeasure (E, §237). More precisely, abnegation becomes greater the more we like what we avert and the more we dislike what we desire (E, §238). The kind of abnegation in which one desires what is bad for them and averts what is good for them is termed "self-abnegation" (E, §239). In the route toward self-perfection, self-abnegation might well be required a number of times, but one should be wary of its risks, in particular its spurious version, such as when one incorrectly judges either the goods and evils or the ratio between the hindrances and the goods and evils one desires or averts (E, §241). Hence, the objects of abnegation are not considered to be goods and evils in themselves, but only in relation to greater goods and evils.[29] This philosophical and comparative approach has consequences for the doctrine of the crucifixion of the flesh as well.

As mentioned above, the crucifixion of the flesh is a form of self-abnegation whose specific objects of renunciation are sensual pleasures.[30] Given the philosophical take on abnegation, the crucifixion of the flesh, too, is not viewed through the lenses of the Christological and penitential tripartition of stages mentioned by Rambach, but according to the rational calculus of the greater goods. Although it is necessary in some cases to sacrifice what is pleasing to the external senses in the name of a good that contributes more to our perfection, this does not imply that the goods we sacrifice in the crucifixion of the flesh are sinful in themselves and that the evils we accept are desirable in themselves. In fact, while self-mastery (*dominium sui* or *enkrateia*) (E, §200; 262) requires a continuous check on the magnitude of the goods one pursues, it may never be mistaken for an unqualified uprooting of sensibility and passions (AE, §12), which would end up in an intellectualistic or moralistic tyranny over oneself.[31] Hence, the crucifixion of the flesh in its philosophical meaning is not always incompatible with the enjoyment of sensual pleasures.

5. Fun and Games: Baumgarten on Sensitive Pleasures

This conclusion makes it possible to justify the activities aimed at providing a sensitive delight (*delectatio sensitiva*), that is, "external recreations" (*deliciae externae*), including all the pleasing pastimes. While the Pietists condemned actions such as dances, jokes, walks without further purpose, comedies, and worldly music,[32] not least because of their immanent end and the transient (i.e., merely sensitive) pleasures they provide,[33] Baumgarten's position is much more balanced.

To start with, Baumgarten holds that the leisure activities that do not run against the principles of self-abnegation are innocent (E, §290; 226). Hence, recreations that provide gratification to the senses and the imagination must be practiced with temperance and must not disrupt the principles of industriousness, chastity, frugality, sobriety, and the like (E, §291). However, one should not consider all the leisure activities as evils under the pretext that every sensitive pleasure is allegedly illegitimate (E, §290).

Baumgarten is aware of being on dangerous ground; for if many elements of his ethics are influenced by Pietism, in which he was raised,[34] the approbation of sensitive pleasures draws him closer to the side of its opponents. In order to downplay the elements of discontinuity, Baumgarten justifies his position starting from a number of theses shared by Pietism. On the one hand, Baumgarten argues, it is undoubtedly true that the leisure activities are not morally indifferent.[35] The necessary criterion for determining the goodness of an action as well as of a sensual pleasure, which we have seen in Rambach, is the contribution of the action or pleasure to the glory of God.[36] On this precise aspect, Baumgarten intends to make an important remark. In fact, Baumgarten accepts the idea, strongly advocated by Pietism, that the end of all our actions must be the glory of God (E, §67; 102; and 290). However, this does not mean that the glory of God must also be the main proximate end of every action.

With this statement, Baumgarten neatly opposes Francke, who had rejected the distinction between the primary and secondary end of an action as a worldly sophism, which aims to justify what we do without serving the glory of God (Francke 1726, 728). Baumgarten here goes as far as to restate almost *verbatim*, albeit without any explicit reference, the position of the orthodox Lutheran Rotth, precisely for his stance in the controversy against the Pietist Vockerodt. In his *Höchstnöthiger Unterricht von so genanten Mittel-Dingen* (Highly Necessary Teaching about So-Called Middle

Things, 1699), Rotth claimed that it would be nonsensical if we wanted to answer the questions: "Why do you eat? Why do you drink? Why do you take a walk?", with the phrase: "For the glory of God." In fact, although this is what is stated in Scripture (1 Cor. 10:31: "So, whether you eat or drink or whatever you do, you should do it all for God's glory"), we are used to answering these questions with the proximate intention, not with the remote end (Rotth 1699, 86).[37] In the same way, Baumgarten argues, when we are asked about the reason of our leisure activities, it would be nonsensical ("incongruus," corresponding to the term "ungereimt" employed by Rotth) to answer that we do them "for the glory of God." But this does not mean that they are illegitimate. Likewise, it would be ridiculous to mention God *in physicis* when someone asks us about the proximate causes of a certain phenomenon, which nevertheless does not mean that we deny that the will of God is the ultimate cause of all phenomena (E, §292).[38] What follows, according to Baumgarten, is that we cannot reject a certain pleasure simply because it does not have the glory of God as its main immediate end. In a cunning argumentative move, when Baumgarten rejects the existence of adiaphora, he actually justifies their most important category, that is, leisure activities.[39] In the *Lust-Streit* between orthodox Lutherans and Pietists, Baumgarten, although formally sticking to the Pietist categories, actually sides with the orthodox Lutherans to a great extent.

While Rambach had loosened Augustine's sternness by defending the legitimacy of some sensual pleasures in earthly goods, provided that the enjoyment of them may immediately lead one to a feeling of gratitude and praise toward God, Baumgarten thus seems to further loosen the rigidity of the argument. Although sometimes (*nonnunquam*) sensitive pleasure can be submitted to religion as a proximate end (E, §290; 71),[40] the legitimacy of sensitive pleasure derived from leisure activities is not justified through the immediate reference to God alone. In fact, the criterion that guides us to prefer certain leisure activities over others is the pursuit of more ends at a time (E, §292), for example when we lightly activate more faculties of the soul as in the case of music (not necessarily holy music) and in readings, or when we associate sensitive pleasure to the movement of the body, as in hunting, journeys, or walks. The leisure activities condemned by Pietism on the theological level thus find a legitimation from a dietetic point of view.[41] To those who claim that these things are scandals, that is, in a technical sense, hindrances to piety, for example because the voluptuary subtracts time available for devotional acts,[42] Baumgarten responds that we must distinguish leisure activities from scandals. In particular, he cautiously adds that we cannot think that something is a scandal just because of the malevolent judgments of some people (E, §135; 292).[43] In this sense, Baumgarten explicitly suggests that gatherings with friends and chaste social interactions with persons of the other sex are legitimate pastimes (E, §292). Despite the mandatory temperance in libido, Baumgarten points out, we should not mistake chastity for the total omission of venereal acts, continence for the horror of all that looks like an invitation to them, and lasciviousness for gallant and courteous conversation with persons of the other sex (E, §274).[44] The distance from Joachim Lange, who had thundered precisely against the amiable conversation between boys and girls, seen as an "empty delight" (*vana delectatio*) arousing "perverse libido" (*prava libido*), is all the more evident.[45]

6. Epithalamia, Toasts, and Jokes

This divergent position with regard to Pietism also emerges in some of Baumgarten's *Philosophische Brieffe von Aletheophilus* (Philosophical Letters of Aletheophilus) of 1741, just a year after the publication of his *Ethica Philosophica*.

Baumgarten devotes the twenty-third issue of the journal to epithalamia (Baumgarten 1741, 89-92). The theme, apparently superficial, was actually divisive. In his preface to his spiritual poems, Rambach railed against this genre of poetry for the fact that poets, there, felt freer to indulge in scurrilities (Rambach 1727², §4). In the issue of Aletheophilus, Baumgarten introduces the theme with a fictitious letter by Musophilus, who starts out by asking whether Aletheophilus' acolytes themselves write epithalamia. The "friend of the Muses" states that he has collected some of these writings, and now he is sending them to Aletheophilus, the friend of truth (and of God), to urge him to think further about this problem. Musophilus' hope is that Aletheophilus may demonstrate, taking a cue from some passage of the texts, that a poet is also able to write epithalamia without scurrilities. The friend of truth does not reply. Yet, he publishes Musophilus' letter in his own journal along with some passages of the epithalamia received, evidently forwarding the invitation to reflect about the subject to his readers. Baumgarten's sign of approval toward Musophilus' position is even more patent if we consider the fact that one of the extracts being published by Baumgarten in this issue is drawn from a nuptial poem that Christoph Joseph Sucro (1718-56) had dedicated to Baumgarten himself.[46] In this poem, interpolated by Baumgarten without any indication either to the author or to the dedicatee (Baumgarten 1741, 91-2), Baumgarten's serene wisdom is opposed to the misanthropic seriousness of the Stoic sage—a Stoic who unsurprisingly had the features of a clergyman.[47]

The following issue of the journal is even more emblematic. The theme of Aletheopilus' letter is the act of toasting (Baumgarten 1741, 93-6), another subject that attracted much criticism from the Pietist ranks. To the unjustified surprise of the readers who are shocked upon discovering that, even in philosophical circles, people toast in someone's honor, Baumgarten resolutely replies:

> Do you believe that my friends blindly follow with me those morose lawmakers who want to prohibit everyone from having what is not suited to their venerable hair, wrinkled forehead, grim look, withered cheeks, toothless mouth, staid voice, grey beard, stern facial features, dark clothing, hunched back, and weak feet? I have already long distinguished what is a sin for everyone from what is unbecoming of someone.
>
> (ibid., 93)

In this passage, Baumgarten describes the "persona" of the surly moralist,[48] emphasizing the relation between his sullen character and his unattractive look, which will become a refrain in his pupil Georg Friedrich Meier (1718-77).[49] The last statement of the quotation is particularly important. Here, Baumgarten is tacitly parting ways with a principle—clearly stated by Francke's friend Johann Hieronymus Wiegleb (1664-1730) in the title of an essay against the worldly dances—that is, the equipollence between what is unbecoming of a Christian and what is sinful ("sündlich und Christen unanständig dasselbe") (Wiegleb 1697).[50] Against any attempt to relativize the condemnation, Francke himself contended that the worldly dances are a sin for any child of God "without distinction" (and not, for example, only for a preacher) (Francke 1697). Now, Baumgarten seems to argue in favor of this very distinction. On the one hand, as it is evident from the aforementioned discussion about the leisure activities, a certain act cannot be judged as sinful *erga omnes* only because it scandalizes someone. On the other hand, the fact that an act might be unbecoming of someone is not considered from a theological standpoint, but from the point of view of decorum. Decorum requires everyone, according to Horace's warning, to follow the behavioral patterns of one's age-group (*Ars poetica*, vv. 156–7). Thus, Baumgarten claims, a certain way of making oneself up and of dressing can be unbecoming of an old lady, just as a certain way of ogling a girl can be unbecoming of an old man. Yet, this does not make it sinful to powder one's face or to cast friendly looks at someone. Likewise, decorum depends on the social class, so that what is legitimate to someone can be unseemly or sinful to others.[51]

Despite his rejection of the adiaphora thesis, Baumgarten refuses to group all the actions that do not immediately stem from faith under the category of sin: "Some call indifferent the free actions that, on the basis of the circumstances, are sometimes good, sometimes bad. And in this sense, it is undoubtedly true that we should not regard the indifferents in bulk as sinful" (Baumgarten 1741, 94). To those who insist on an unqualified condemnation of the indifferents, Baumgarten replies with Catullus' verses: "Let us live, my Lesbia, and love,/and the rumors of rather stern old men/let us value all at just one penny!" (Carmen 5).

As far as the specific case of toasts is concerned, the main opponent of Baumgarten is Joachim Lange, who went as far as to claim that toasts are not only against divine law, but also against reason since nature requires that we only drink for thirst (Lange 1714, 78).[52] For his part, Baumgarten argues for the rationality of toasts (Baumgarten 1741, 93–6). The origin of toasts in the ritual libations on the occasion of a sacrifice does not make them condemnable. To be sure, it is necessary to avoid any excess in drinking, but today the number of toasts is diminished compared to the past. In any case, the quantity and magnitude are not an essential element of toasts. In conclusion, while for Lange toasts are both a sinful and an unreasonable act, for Baumgarten toasts are neither. To the contrary, toasts are an excellent occasion for observing the duties toward a guest, remembering those afar, and honoring the fatherland. It is difficult, Baumgarten concludes, to do better during a meal (Baumgarten 1741, 96).

In Lange, the rejection of toasts was framed in a wider condemnation of *actiones ludicrae* (playful actions) of those who are not reborn (*Wiedergeborene*), that is, of actions that are not commanded by natural, civil, nor divine law, but undertaken only out of pleasure (Lange 1709–11, vol. 2, 85–6). These actions had in conviviality, jokes, and laughter one of the most scandalous examples. On this point as well, Baumgarten takes exception to Lange, without mentioning him directly. The idea Baumgarten intends to reject is that Christianity is incompatible with jokes and jocular conversation. To do so, he takes issue with the "frowning foreheads" who seek to prove this incompatibility with the biblical passage Eph. 5:4: "Nor should there be obscenity, foolish talk or coarse joking [αἰσχρότης καὶ μωρολογία ἢ εὐτραπελία] which are out of place, but rather thanksgiving" (K, §376).

In condemning jokes, Lange had precisely commented on this passage. There are interpreters, Lange had stated, who mistake the condemnation of *eutrapelia* (jocular conversation) for the condemnation of scurrilities alone. According to Lange, this conception is wrong both for philological and for exegetical reasons. In fact, Paul rejects scurrilities with the words *aischrotes* (obscenity) and *morologia* (foolish talk). Therefore, Paul must explicitly condemn something else with the term *eutrapelia*, namely jocular conversation.[53] The fault of *eutrapelia*, even if it abstains from scurrilities and obscenities, precisely consists in its being a useless and vain speech ("sermo inutilis & vanus, vanae mentis interprete, & in aliis vanitatis affectum movente") and in the fact that it cannot occur "in timore Dei."[54]

To respond to the accusation, Baumgarten also aims to support his position through an interpretation of this biblical passage, which he discusses in his *Aesthetics* (AE, §376). When a joke is at the border between the elegant and witty jest and the licentious one, it is certainly advisable to restrain oneself, since the distinction between the two of them is perhaps easy in theory but much less in practice (not least for the speed with which a joke is pronounced) (AE, §377–80).[55] However, this does not change the fact that Christians are allowed to make use of witticisms. For when Paul condemns *eutrapelia*, Baumgarten argues, he just rejects the pleasantries that are against any decorum, especially Christian decorum (AE, §376; K, §376). From the second edition of his *Ethica philosophica* (1751), Baumgarten will reinforce the message, clearly stating that the speeches that have their proximate main purpose in the joyful conversation are not vain and useless, hence they should not be rejected as such (E, §378) ("non sunt vani, non inutiles, neque, ceu tales, reiiciendi"). Lange's argument, quoted almost *verbatim*, is therefore totally upended.

In light of this, Baumgarten not only endorses Anacreontic jocular poetry, but even dabbles in it himself.[56] As a matter of fact, the first treatise ever grounded on the principles of aesthetics will be devoted by Meier to the problem of jokes (Meier 1744).[57] Meier also evokes Anacreontic poetry at the beginning of his *Anfangsgründe aller schönen Wissenschaften* (First Principles of All the Beautiful Sciences, 1748–50). While reading about chaste love, kisses, and jokes, Meier writes, the standard audience is not usually brought to impure feelings. Instead, it experiences pleasure and the calming of the mind. Meier's implication is that it is rather the detractors who must feel an overwhelming urge to lust if they mistake these innocent actions for sins (Meier 1748, §22).[58] The fact that this remark is located in the prolegomena of Meier's treatise on aesthetics suggests that it is precisely aesthetics that must become the key to educate sensibility and the sensitive pleasures deriving from it.[59] It does not come as a surprise that for Meier, the aesthetic foundation of jokes provides the best defense against their possible excesses. In fact, it is for aesthetic reasons rather than for merely ethical ones that coarse joking should be rejected.[60]

7. Flesh and Sensibility

If the crucifixion of the flesh does not entail the elimination of sensual pleasures, we must now come to a better understanding of the link between flesh and sensibility. Baumgarten discusses the problem of the flesh from a theological point of view in his thoughts about Jesus' speeches, written as a personal meditation during his long-drawn-out illness (1751–62). Commenting on John 3:6, Baumgarten defines the flesh as "the corrupted representation of the world, insofar as it arouses aversions against the spiritual, that is, against what belongs to God's Spirit" (Baumgarten 1796, 59). For Baumgarten, the spirit is all that the Holy Spirit produces in the whole person through rebirth or regeneration rather than a part of man different from body and soul. The *vis repraesentativa* of the non-reborn represents the world in such an erroneous way that an enmity against God arises from it. Such enmity can be overcome only with the intervention of the Holy Spirit, which instills supernatural representations of truth concerning this world, thus guiding desires in a spiritual way. Accordingly, the reborn is at the same time flesh and spirit in this life, so that the spirit and the flesh fight against each other. The preponderance of the spirit will eventually be secured by God, whenever requested, with faith (Baumgarten 1796, 58–62).

In his lectures on dogmatic theology (1740s), posthumously published by Johann Salomo Semler (1773), the corruption of the representative force that constitutes the flesh is understood as "the state of corruption of the lower faculty, which either corrupts or wins over the higher faculty"[61]—a condition common to all of Adam's children (John 1:13 and 3:6). The link between the flesh and the lower faculty is made even more evident in the *Metaphysics*, where Baumgarten, starting from the second edition (1743), mentions the flesh in relation to the lower faculty of desire. The faculty of sensitive desires can in turn be split into a concupiscible faculty, concerning desires, and an irascible faculty, concerning aversions. In this regard, Baumgarten comments that the concupiscible and irascible faculties, along with the lower cognitive faculty, are sometimes called flesh (*caro*) (M, §676). Thus, Baumgarten also calls the fight between the lower and the higher faculty of desire (the will) "the fight between sensitive and rational desire," or "the fight between flesh and spirit" (M, §693). The association between lower faculties and flesh will be confirmed, as stated above, at AE §12.

While the theological reference to the fight between flesh and spirit was well present in Pietism, the way the idea is recorded in Baumgarten's *Metaphysics* is at odds with this conception. In fact, the Pietists diligently distinguished the fight between reason and sensual desire and the fight between spirit and flesh. We can turn to consider Rambach as an example. In the attempt to clarify the difference between these two fights, Rambach points out three elements of discontinuity: firstly, the conflicting parts. In the non-reborn (*Nicht-Wiedergeborene*), the fight is between reason and the coarsest sensual desires, which are patently sinful. By contrast, in the reborn, it is the spirit that turns against the flesh, fighting also against the smallest inclinations that diverge from God's law. Secondly, the weapons are different: in the former fight, these come from philosophy and rational representations; in the latter, from faith and prayer. Lastly, it is the outcome of the fight that changes. In fact, reason often succumbs to the affects, whereas the spirit in the reborn always wins (1 John 5:4).[62]

Compared to this position, Baumgarten shows more flexibility. According to Baumgarten, "flesh" is certainly a theological concept, and in this sense it concerns the whole person (including both the lower and the higher faculties of the soul). Yet, it can also be used in a philosophical sense. In this domain, the flesh does not refer to the whole person of the non-reborn, but is only synonymous with the lower faculties of the soul, the cognitive and the appetitive, insofar as they belong to post-lapsarian humans. Therefore, the flesh is not opposed to the spirit here, but to reason. The two meanings are not unrelated. In fact, it is precisely because the flesh in the theological sense is understood as "the state of corruption of the lower faculty, which either corrupts or wins over the higher faculty," that the flesh can indicate, in the philosophical context, the tendency of the lower faculties to gain supremacy over the higher ones.

The link between flesh and sensibility had already been clearly stated by the eldest of the Baumgarten brothers, the theologian Siegmund Jakob Baumgarten (1706–57). Commenting on Gal. 5:16-17, Siegmund wrote: "In the opposition against the spirit, the flesh is the natural corruption, the defective and confused condition of a person's mind, which is propagated through natural generation, consists in prepondering sensibility (*überwiegende Sinnlichkeit*), and is directed to the apparent goods of the corporal world which awaken the senses." The pleasing desires of the flesh (*Lust des Fleisches*) thus consist in the desires originating from "the disordered constitution of our nature and its sensibility" (Baumgarten 1767b, 129).[63] The link between flesh and sensibility does not imply any equivalence, though. In fact, the flesh does not consist in sensibility as such nor in sensitive desires, but in their undue supremacy. It is this supremacy and "ataxia" that was absent from Adam in the state of innocence, where the lower faculties "[were submitted] to the disposition and dominion of the intellect," since "these lower faculties, a person's sensibility, its imagination and sensitive desires and aversion could be ruled and determined as well as prompted by the higher faculties, the intellect and the will" (S.J. Baumgarten 1760, 453–4).

If such a conclusion is true, this also means that sensibility and confusion of knowledge also belonged to Adam before the Fall: "The confusion of human cognition [...] does not depend on natural corruption in itself, but it is necessary in contingent beings and depends on their essential finitude" (ibid., 570). In a footnote of his polemical theology, Siegmund Baumgarten explains: "We concede the presence of sensibility [in Adam], as it took place in Christ's humanity; it will not be eliminated even in the eternal life, because no finite spirit, not even angels, can be conceived as devoid of all the lower faculties and their use" (S.J. Baumgarten 1763, 385).[64] This position is also embraced by his brother Alexander in his lectures on dogmatic theology. In outlining the nature of Adam in the pre-lapsarian condition, Alexander Baumgarten argues that the original humans had both a cognitive and an appetitive faculty. Baumgarten adds: "Both of [these faculties] were also inferior, but they were not corrupted or flesh" (Baumgarten 1773, §290).[65] Hence, for Alexander Baumgarten as well, sensibility does not derive from a fault, but is rather the mark of human nature as a finite nature (M, §798).

Meier will point out this aspect with great clarity. Commenting upon the alleged carnal dimension of aesthetics, Meier accuses the critics raising this objection of being morose and Cato-like moralists who cannot tolerate smiles and joy. The archetype of these moralists is implicitly identified in none less than Qohelet, whom Meier quotes, without mentioning the source: "I said of laughter, 'It is folly!' and of pleasure, 'What does it accomplish?'" (Qoh. 2:2). Against Qohelet, as well as against Francke, who condemned laughing at jokes as a sin,[66] Meier appeals to more reasonable moralists, in whom it is not difficult to acknowledge the silhouette of the Baumgarten brothers, his masters: "The friendly and reasonable moralists know well that sensibility in general is different from the original sin—what the Spirit of God calls flesh—[...] and that Adam in the innocent state sweetly loved Eve" (Meier 1748, §22).[67] The same thought also occurs in preacher Johann Samuel Patzke (1727–87), the student who had taken the notes on which Baumgarten's extant *Lectures on Aesthetics* are based[68]: "A human can never be without sensitive desires, without a craving for pleasure. To make it a pure spirit, abstracted from all its senses, means to forget it is human" (Patzke 1768, 89).[69]

From these remarks, it is clear that sensibility is part of human nature, a remnant of the original image of God in us,[70] so that we are by no means allowed to annihilate it. Siegmund Baumgarten claims: "The effort towards a complete repression or elimination of sensibility (*Sinlichkeit*) or towards the whole insensibility (*Unempfindlichkeit*) is not only useless in itself, but also illegitimate, and connected with a severe loss in the increase of the union with God" (S.J. Baumgarten 1738, §306). His brother Alexander fully endorses this statement: "[To eradicate sensibility] would mean to deprive oneself of one's human nature, and the Christian religion never requires such a thing" (K, §12).

Instead of weeding out sensibility, it is rather necessary to emendate and cultivate it. Siegmund Baumgarten outspokenly contends: "Christians are bound to take care of the improvement and the increase of all their faculties and all their natural and supernatural abilities as far as possible" (S.J. Baumgarten 1738, §125).[71] Spener, the initiator of Pietism, had already affirmed that Christians must cultivate their intellect as a gift of God (Spener 1692, 433–4).[72] With similar words, Alexander Baumgarten explicitly extends this requirement to sensibility itself: "The lower faculties, in so far as they are corrupted, are not supposed to be awakened and strengthened by the aesthetician. Rather they must be guided by him, so that they are not corrupted even more by misuse, and so that we are not deprived of a God-given talent under the lazy pretext that we must avoid misusing them" (AE, §12). Like his brother Siegmund (S.J. Baumgarten 1738, §306),[73] Alexander believes that such an emendation cannot be lazily expected from God's grace, but must be partially achieved through a process of natural emendation:

> If they [the theological critics of aesthetics] say that I must be prepared for the fear of God supernaturally and not through arts, they do not ponder enough that some degrees of improvement can be attained through human arts and do not happen supernaturally. As we still have some remnants of the image of God, we can distinguish them more clearly and better understand them by means of aesthetics.
> (K, §12)

The consequences of this statement are momentous. In fact, since it is possible to partially amend the human nature corrupted by original sin on a natural level, it is evident that the flesh itself, which is but the scriptural pendant of original sin, can be partially countered on a natural level.[74] It is for this reason that the weapons against the flesh, hence against preponding sensibility, are no longer exclusively theological as in Rambach, but can also be philosophical. As we have seen, these weapons are, on the one hand, philosophical abnegation, which subordinates the lesser to the greater goods without condemning the former as such, and on the other hand, they are the cultivation of sensibility,[75] both in its epistemic and in its hedonistic dimension. While in the first case the treatment strategy of the flesh is ethical and omissive, which sometimes requires the renouncement of sensitive goods but not their condemnation, in the second case it is proactive, which requires the guidance of the lower faculties of the soul and the emendation of the knowledge attained by them. Such a treatment will be provided not by ethics, but by aesthetics.[76]

Aesthetics, as Baumgarten declares (AE, §12), leads us by the hand insofar as the mastery over the lower faculties can be achieved naturally. Then, it is implicit, the improvement of man and his mastery over himself will be brought forward with the supernatural weapons granted by the spirit in its fight against the flesh (now in a theological sense) (Baumgarten 1796, 61–2). Aesthetics thus takes part in the process of the general improvement of sensitive cognition, hence in the fight against the flesh, along a route that is eventually accomplished by means of divine grace.

8. Conclusion

In the present chapter, I have reconstructed Baumgarten's position in the controversy over sensitive pleasures, with special regard to its ethical and aesthetic consequences. I have first examined the relationship between Pietism and the sensual pleasure of earthly goods. While Pietism was often caricatured as an anhedonic strand of thought, the Pietist position on *hedonè* proves to be more nuanced. For the Pietist Rambach, for example, it is legitimate to take sensual pleasure in the creatures, at least for those who are regenerate, if this leads them to praise God. What is categorically rejected in the name of the crucifixion of the flesh is the set of all those actions that do not immediately serve the glory of God, such as dances, jokes, toasts, and nuptial poems.

The functionalization of sensual and sensitive pleasure in the view of religion is certainly also present in Baumgarten. Yet on his view, this no longer rules out the legitimacy of worldly leisure. In fact, Baumgarten also looks at Wolff, who understood the innocence of sensual pleasures in a philosophical rather than in a theological way, as a compliance with the law of nature and reason. On the one hand, the result is that Baumgarten, in his ethical conceptions of leisure, resorts to a number of concepts dear to Pietism, including the glory of God, the idea of self-abnegation, of scandal, and the rejection of *adiaphora*. On the other, he reinterprets their meaning. More specifically, Baumgarten distinguishes the primary end from the secondary end of actions, so as to also justify actions that are not immediately taken to serve the glory of God, parting ways from Francke. He additionally adopts a philosophical concept of abnegation that legitimizes sensitive pleasures, stipulating that in the case where they are not immediately related to religion, they are legitimized whenever they do not conflict with the rational calculus of goods and evils. He criticizes the arbitrary use of the category of scandal made by certain moralizers. Lastly, he does not subscribe to the equivalence, advocated by the Pietists, between what is sinful and what is unbecoming of Christians. This brings Baumgarten to a latent disagreement with the Pietists of the older generation concerning the leisure activities and the sensitive pleasure they produce. As a consequence, Baumgarten comes to discard the unqualified condemnation of epithalamia (against Rambach), of jokes, toasts and *eutrapelia* (against Joachim Lange), as well as of sensual worldly pleasures (against Vockerodt).

One of the key elements is the reinterpretation of the concept of flesh. While the Pietists used to consider the flesh as an exclusively theological category that opposes the spirit, Baumgarten believes that the flesh (the corruption of human nature) can be countered, at least partially, with philosophical strategies. Now, since the flesh is the proclivity of the lower faculties to prevaricate over the higher faculties, the philosophical fight against the flesh should be fought not only with the abnegation of sensual pleasures, but also with the discipline that emendates sensibility and the desires connected with it, namely, aesthetics. In sum, in order to crucify the flesh without crippling human nature, the education of sensibility is to be preferred over its total annihilation. Hence, aesthetics not only does not excite the flesh, but it turns out to be a seminal instrument that counteracts its supremacy.

Such a conclusion paves the way to a broader reflection about the nature of nascent aesthetics. Aesthetics is defined by Baumgarten as the science of sensitive knowledge that aims to achieve beauty, the perfection of sensitive knowledge. Because of this statement, Baumgarten's aesthetics has often been interpreted as a merely epistemological enterprise, not least with the aim of pitting it against Kant's aesthetic conception in the third Critique. However, beauty in Baumgarten is never neutral with regard to pleasure, since its enjoyment always sets the soul in a more or less pleasant condition. Unsurprisingly, Baumgarten discusses beauty in the chapter of his *Metaphysics* on pleasure and displeasure.[77] The very term *Sinnlichkeit*, on which Baumgarten builds his aesthetics, contains in itself an ambiguity between cognitive sensibility and seducing sensuality that will be pointed out by Marcuse (Marcuse 1998, 182).[78] It is precisely this hedonistic aspect of sensibility that increases the subversive potential of nascent aesthetics: while in the eyes of the intellectualists, aesthetics is suspicious for its relationship with the dark regions of the soul as well as with the appearance of phenomena, for rigoristic theologians, aesthetics is also (if not chiefly) dangerous for its link with the sources of pleasure.

In spite of the fact that he does not deny the bond between sensibility and pleasure, Baumgarten is no apologist for unbridled hedonism. He instead argues that the excesses of sensibility must be regulated from within sensibility itself. In fact, insofar as aesthetics intends to offer a special care to the lower faculties of the soul, its concrete practice entails not only a qualitative intensification of *aisthesis*, in its epistemic dimension, but also a training and molding of the pleasures originating from it. Rather than mere gnoseology, aesthetics also arises as apolaustic.[79]

Abbreviations

AE   Baumgarten, Alexander Gottlieb. 1750. *Aesthetica*. Frankfurt/Oder: Kleyb.

E   Baumgarten, Alexander Gottlieb. (1740) 1763³. *Ethica philosophica*. Halle: Hemmerde.

K	Baumgarten, Alexander Gottlieb. 1907. "Kollegium über die Ästhetik." In Bernhard Poppe, *Alexander Gottlieb Baumgarten. Seine Bedeutung und Stellung in der Leibniz-Wolffischen Philosophie und seine Beziehungen zu Kant. Nebst Veröffentlichung einer bisher unbekannten Handschrift der Ästhetik Baumgartens*, PhD diss., 65–258. Borna-Leipzig: Noske.
M	Baumgarten, Alexander Gottlieb. (1739; 1757^4) 2014. *Metaphysics: A Critical Translation with Kant's Elucidations, Selected Notes, and Related Materials*, edited by Courtney Fugate and John Hymers. London: Bloomsbury.

Notes

1. In Baumgarten's lexicon, "sensitive" refers to all the lower faculties of the soul and their representations, while "sensual" only refers to the knowledge attained by the senses. Where relevant, I will preserve this terminological distinction in the essay, in particular with regard to pleasure.
2. See, for example, the more or less veiled satirical attacks against Pietists' ethics in Lange 1748; von Loën 1751, 49.
3. See Wels 2009, 533–6, or in general, Martens 1989 and Sdzuj 2005.
4. See the Pietist key text in the controversy over adiaphora against orthodox Lutherans, Lange 1709–11, in particular vol. 2, 82: "Omnis non renatorum voluntaria actio est moraliter mala, non solum in concreto, seu speciatim, sed etiam in abstracto, seu generatim considerata."
5. See Scheitler 2009, 517.
6. On the controversy between Vockerodt and Rotth, see Sdzuj 2005, 265–81.
7. See also Francke März 1695, 257. On the concept of flesh, see Rambach 1738, 105–7 and 202.
8. Rambach 1739, 315.
9. Ibid., 325–6. See also Francke Januar 1695, 82–9, where Francke claims that the crucifixion of the flesh consists in two stages: conversion, which is the actual crucifixion, and everyday renovation, which is a kind of vigil over the crucified flesh to prevent it from getting rid of the nails. See also Spener 1706, 29–35.
10. See Scheitler 2009, 518.
11. As Zelle rightly remarks, Stoics and Pietists were seen as the expression of the same rigoristic normative horizon in the eyes of nascent aesthetics, see Zelle 2010, 80. Yet, this does not mean that the Stoic and the Pietist position concerning the affects can be viewed as similar. See, for example, Rambach's attack against Stoic apathy, Rambach 1738, 1083. On the role of the affects in Rambach, see Heigel 2014, chapter 2.
12. See Rambach 1851, 195.
13. Augustine, *De doctrina christiana*, I, 4, 4. On Rambach's distance from Augustine, see Rambach 1738, 660–1 and 796–7.
14. See Schwarz 2022, part 3, chapter 1.
15. See on this Schwaiger 1995, 51–66 and 120–89; Vesper 2008.
16. For this change, it is possible that Baumgarten takes into account Walch's critical influence. In his philosophical dictionary, Walch criticizes Wolff's definition of pleasure for mistaking the thing for its ground: to claim that a pleasure is the

intuition of a perfection does not say what pleasure is, but at best where pleasure comes from. Hence, Baumgarten more cautiously claims that pleasure is the condition of the soul stemming from the intuition of a perfection. See Walch 1726, columns 1686–9, "Lust."
17   More precisely, Baumgarten holds that true pleasure originates from a true intuition. He then concludes that true pleasure derives from the intuition of true perfection and goods (M, §655).
18   Baumgarten introduces the concept of beauty in relation to sensitive pleasure. Since beauty is phenomenal perfection, or perfection insofar as it is observable by taste in the broad sense, beauty arouses pleasure in those who intuit it (M, §662). The positive judgment of taste is therefore able to arouse sensitive pleasure. On the pleasure-beauty relation and its dietetic consequences in Baumgarten, see Nannini 2022b, 142–4. On the dietetic meaning of pleasure and beauty in Kant's aesthetics, see Nannini 2022c, chapter 5.
19   On the concept of intuitive cognition in Baumgarten, see Schwaiger 2011, 71–8.
20   M, §665: "This is the law of the faculty of desire: *I make an effort to produce those things that I foresee as pleasing and I anticipate will exist through my effort. I desire the opposite of those things that I foresee as displeasing and I anticipate to be impeded through my effort.*"
21   Cf. Schwaiger 2011, 83–4; Di Giulio 2019, 24–5.
22   See also Meier 1756, §690.
23   This issue was often discussed in that period. See Thomasius 1693; Cudworth 1733, 1034–5.
24   See also the remarks made by Baumgarten's brother, Lutheran theologian Siegmund Jakob (S.J. Baumgarten 1738, §306; S.J. Baumgarten 1767a, 29 and 1563–5), where Siegmund warns against the excesses of apathy and quietism. It is significant that Siegmund points out the gradual dimension of goods and evils, as his brother Alexander will also do with regard to abnegation. Both Siegmund and Alexander criticize these rigoristic theses for the neglect they foster of our duties toward external things (Baumgarten 1767a, 29; E, §276).
25   See for example Thomasius 1693, 136–7 and *passim*.
26   See for example Sträter 1995, 58.
27   Spener 1692, 354–71; Spener 1696, 489–503. See in general Langen 1954, 223, 435, 437, and 466.
28   The philosophical meaning of abnegation was divisive in Baumgarten's time. In a dissertation devoted to philosophical abnegation and presided by Baumgarten, it is clearly stated that the notion of abnegation is all too often wrongly considered as merely theological. See Baumgarten and Goldbeck 1742, §1. See also Meier 1756, §623, in which Meier takes exception to those theologians who think that reason, when left to its own devices, does not know anything about abnegation.
29   In his philosophical ethics, Baumgarten uses the term "sin" in a moral sense, indicating, in general, any action against a duty. See, for example, E, §151.
30   The kind of ethics that is too lenient in relation to sensitive motives and goods is called "ethica blandiens"; the kind of ethics that hardly shows lenience toward them is called "ethica rigoristica" (E, §5–6). Baumgarten considers them both as imperfect kinds of ethics. For a comment on the kinds of ethics in Baumgarten, see Schwaiger 2016.

31 See Meier 1756, §690. In this sense, it is important to point out that for Baumgarten the crucifixion of the flesh does not imply any enmity toward the body. On Baumgarten's conception of the body, see Nannini 2022d.
32 For a detailed list of the false indifferents, see Lange 1709-11, vol. 2, 87-121.
33 See Vockerodt 1698.
34 For an overview, Schwaiger 2011, 27-9.
35 See also A.G. Baumgarten 1760, §72; A.G. Baumgarten 1763, §25.
36 In general, the morality of an action determined by the law of God is expressed not only in the object of the action, but also in its form, hence in its motivation (faith) and its end (the glory of God). See Walch 1733, 373-4. Walch discusses the controversy over the indifferents in detail. See Walch 1733, 357-95 in particular.
37 The same argument will be repeated and clarified in Rotth 1701, 145. Baumgarten must have looked at Rotth also for the conceptions of secondary ends, which the latter tackles from 124 onwards.
38 See also Meier 1756, §753.
39 See *Grosses vollständiges Universal-Lexicon*, vol. 21, (1739), entry "Mitteldinge," where "Leibes—und Gemüths-Ergötzlichkeiten" are recognized as one of the main categories of the indifferents.
40 Meier takes issue with the moralists who oppose religion to "any pleasure of the senses, any use of earthly goods." See Meier 1749, 102-4. Not only are sensual pleasures innocent in themselves, but the beauties of the world can lead one to feel divine perfection (Meier 1749, 38). Hence, religion is not against pleasure: "So laßt uns denn, um der Religion willen, so vergnügt leben, als es möglich ist. [...] Die Religion selbst, wenn sie rechter Art ist, erfüllt alle Kräfte der Seele mit dem aller-süssesten Vergnügen" (Meier 1749, 106-7). See also Meier 1765. Despite the polemical approach against the moralistic theologians, we have seen that even the Pietist Rambach admitted the legitimacy of sensual pleasures in specific cases. On Meier's joyful Christianity, see Fritz 2016.
41 The list provided by Baumgarten ("motio corporis, politio ingenii, quales musica, lectio, venatio, obambulatio, itinera, commercium cum personis alterius sexus pudicum, amicorum sobria convivia," E, §292) is almost the same as the list of strategies to preserve one's mind serene provided by physician Friedrich Hoffmann in his dietetics: "a pleasant conversation with funny and joking people, graceful music, a game, a good glass of wine, riding, travelling, and pure and healthy air" (Hoffmann 1715, 115-16). On this, see Zelle 2008. The rehabilitation of these leisure activities goes hand in hand with the theological rehabilitation of fine literature made by Siegmund Jakob Baumgarten in his preface to the German translation of David's Odes. I discussed this aspect with further bibliography in Nannini 2013, §3.
42 Baumgarten devotes a dissertation to the issue of "continuous prayers," where "continuous" should be understood as "every time the occasion arises" (Baumgarten and Diterich 1742, §29).
43 See also Meier 1753, §256; Meier 1756, §753.
44 Meier mentions hand-kissing and hand-holding as examples (Meier 1756, §716).
45 Lange 1709-11, vol. 2, 114-15: "Mali sunt lusus reliqui, speciatim convivantium, & inprimis juvenum ac virginum jocosi."

46 Sucro's integral version can be read in Sucro 1747, 36–9, "Der Stoicker. An Hrn. Prof. Baumgarten in Franckfurt an der Oder. 1740." Baumgarten marries Luisa Wilhelmina Alemann on April 18, 1741, in Berlin.
47 On epithalamia, see also K, §185.
48 See the criticism levied against the excessive moralism and the lack of decorum of the Pietist fanatic in a textbook for conversation, *Die Manier*, 1724, 168–9.
49 On the relationship between Baumgarten and Meier in the founding of aesthetics, see Nannini 2021. On Baumgarten's approach to the cosmetic care of the body, see Nannini 2022a.
50 On Pietist criticism against worldly dances, see Eissner 2016.
51 The Pietists as well believed that it is the circumstances to make an action sinful. However, they claimed, it is impossible to think of circumstances under which certain actions are innocuous (in the case of dances, the possible exception of the holy dance practiced by King David, Francke pointed out, no longer exists in the eighteenth century, hence it cannot serve as a counterexample). See Francke 1697.
52 See also Lange 1709–11, vol. 2, 117–19.
53 Lange 1714, 71–5; Lange 1709–11, vol. 2, 115–17 ("Mala sunt non renatorum εὐτραπελία seu modus conversandi ac colloquendi jocularis"). Lange explains: "Per εὐτραπελίαν intelligo eum loquendi modum, qui & ab *ingenioso sapientum*, & a *turpi scurrarum*, sermone discrepat, &, in horum quasi medio positus, deprehenditur plerumque apud homines, natura aliquanto ingeniosiores, at judicio imbecilles, & consistit in affectatis jocis atque facetiis, nec non paradoxis & ridiculis historiolis, vel ipso usu, vel ex peculiaribus libellis, cum mentis vanitate placendique ac inaniter alios delectandi studio ac fine, studiose collectis ac prolatis." See also Walch 1733, 393–5.
54 Lange 1709–11, vol. 2, 117.
55 Baumgarten here makes reference to the excursus "de ridiculis" by Cicero (*De oratore*, II, 216–90).
56 Gleim claims he received "a graceful Anacreontic ode" from Baumgarten in a letter to Uz on the 12th of August 1745 (*Briefwechsel* 1899, 80).
57 On this, see Mauser 2000a. See, also, the contributions in Lacher ed., 2019.
58 See also Meier 1744, §2, for an attack against those who condemn jokes as sins just because they mistake their sadness for a consequence of virtue.
59 On the link between Anacreontic poetry and dietetics, see the classical Mauser 2000b. On the relationship between Anacreontic poetry and aesthetics, see also Verweyen 1989. Verweyen dealt with this issue also in other important essays that cannot be mentioned here.
60 Meier 1744, §35: "Ich will nich sagen, daß diese abgeschmackten Zoten viel zu schmutzig sind, als daß sie einem ehrbaren Menschen solten anständig seyn. Ich sage nur, daß derjenige einen sehr armseeligen Witz blicken läßt, der mit Schertzen aufgezogen kommt die unter den Pöbel im Schwange gehen, und davon man Millionen ähnliche und gantz gleiche Schertze antrifft." For Lange, it was "sapientia" and "vera pietas" that had to set limitations to witticisms. See Lange 1709–11, vol. 2, 116.
61 Baumgarten 1773, §341. See also Baumgarten 1773, §352.
62 Rambach 1738, 1095–7.
63 See also Baumgarten 1767b, 209, on Eph. 2:3. Siegmund Jakob Baumgarten also warns us not to mistake the fight between flesh and spirit for the fight against sensitive and rational desire, because the flesh entails not only the violence of sensibility, but also the weakness of reason. Furthermore, a certain fight between

sensitive and rational desire was also possible in the state of innocence. See S.J. Baumgarten 1763, 385.
64 For a similar statement about angels in his brother Alexander, see Kliche 2002.
65 For the Lutheran theological context, in particular concerning the momentous change in the doctrine of original sin between the seventeenth and eighteenth centuries, see Schubert 2002. For the consequences of this change in Baumgarten, see Borchers 2011, 137–56.
66 See Francke 1696, 15–16: "Insonderheit wenn andere über Schertz und Narrentheidung lachen /so hüte dich /daß du nicht mit lachest. [...] Lachest du /so hast du mit gesündiget."
67 See also Meier 1753, §22. Meier might also have thought of Stiebritz, one of Wolff's followers, who set out to demonstrate the sinfulness of pleasure on the basis of rational (non-Scriptural) arguments. On this topic, see Stiebritz 1742. Among other aspects, Stiebritz clearly articulated the connection between original sin and pleasure, understood in the sense of an inclination toward a bad thing that is confusedly represented as good.
68 The manuscript published by Poppe in 1907 and that went missing after the Second World War (Schochow 2003, 160–5) had the following signature in the Berlin Royal Library: MS NIC 249 (see Tedesco 1998, 21). Hence, it was part of Friedrich Nicolai's collection. In his autobiography, Nicolai claims that he had asked for the notes of Baumgarten's lectures on aesthetics to his friend Patzke (along with the notes on Baumgarten's lectures on logic and metaphysics). He also claims that he had transcribed a great deal of it. See Nicolai 1799, 27–8.
69 While admitting the legitimacy of sensitive pleasures, Patzke is stricter than Baumgarten in drawing the line of their legitimacy (for instance, reading is fine if the book is "useful," or a conversation with a friend is fine if the friend is pious).
70 Insofar as the sin is an accident, and not a change of substance (Baumgarten 1773, §350), the natural faculties belonging to Adam's soul before the Fall are still present after the Fall, despite their corruption, in the form of "remnants," §384. See also K, §12.
71 See also S.J. Baumgarten 1767a, 689–94.
72 Spener's remark concerned the reborn.
73 See also S.J. Baumgarten 1767a, 1563–5, where Siegmund indicates a series of exercises to repress disordered sensibility, that is, disordered sensitive desires (the investigation of one's sensitive desires and the careful distinction between good and sinful ones; constant watchfulness against sinful desires; the acquisition of control over one's sensibility; the arousal of oppositive good sensitive desires against the bad ones, so on). In Alexander, these exercises, insofar as they can be practiced in a natural way, will lie at the convergence between philosophical ethics and aesthetics.
74 In fact, the admission of the philosophical notion of "flesh" in Baumgarten's *Metaphysics* already went in this direction.
75 For the necessity to mold the flesh as a result of a new conception of this issue, see Zelle 2010, 83.
76 The description of the strategies to attain this goes beyond the scope of this chapter.
77 See Nannini 2022b.
78 See also Welsch 1997, 12.
79 This text was written with support of the grant PCE 105/2021 (PNCDI III) funded by the Romanian Ministry of Research, Innovation and Digitization, CNCS/CCCDI-UEFISCDI.

Bibliography

Anon. 1724. *Die Manier, wie man sich in der Conversation [...] verhalten möge*. Nürnberg/Leipzig: In dem Felßeckerischen Buch-Laden.

Baumgarten, Alexander Gottlieb. (1739; 1757⁴) 2014. *Metaphysics: A Critical Translation with Kant's Elucidations, Selected Notes, and Related Materials*, edited by Courtney Fugate and John Hymers. London: Bloomsbury.

Baumgarten, Alexander Gottlieb. (1740) 1763³. *Ethica philosophica*. Halle: Hemmerde.

Baumgarten, Alexander Gottlieb. 1741. *Philosophische Brieffe von Aletheophilus*. Frankfurt.

Baumgarten, Alexander Gottlieb. 1750. *Aesthetica*. Frankfurt/Oder: Kleyb.

Baumgarten, Alexander Gottlieb. 1760. *Initia philosophiae practicae primae acromatice*. Halle: Hemmerde.

Baumgarten, Alexander Gottlieb. 1763. *Ius naturae*. Halle: Hemmerde.

Baumgarten, Alexander Gottlieb. 1773. *Praelectiones theologiae dogmaticae*, edited by Johann Salomo Semler. Halle: Hemmerde.

Baumgarten, Alexander Gottlieb. 1796. *Gedanken über die Reden Jesu nach dem Inhalt der evangelischen Geschichte*, vol. 1, edited by Friedrich Gottlob Scheltz and Anton Bernhard Thiele. Pförten: Brükner.

Baumgarten, Alexander Gottlieb. 1907. "Kollegium über die Ästhetik." In Bernhard Poppe, *Alexander Gottlieb Baumgarten. Seine Bedeutung und Stellung in der Leibniz-Wolffischen Philosophie und seine Beziehungen zu Kant. Nebst Veröffentlichung einer bisher unbekannten Handschrift der Ästhetik Baumgartens*. PhD diss., 65–258. Borna-Leipzig: Noske.

Baumgarten, Siegmund Jakob. 1738. *Unterricht vom rechtmäßigen Verhalten eines Christen, oder Theologische Moral*. Halle: Bauer.

Baumgarten, Siegmund Jakob. 1760. *Evangelische Glaubenslehre*, vol. 2, edited by Johann Salomo Semler. Halle: Gebauer.

Baumgarten, Siegmund Jakob. 1763. *Untersuchung theologischer Streitigkeiten*, vol. 2, edited by Johann Salomo Semler. Halle: Gebauer.

Baumgarten, Siegmund Jakob. 1767a. *Ausführlicher Vortrag der theologischen Moral*. Halle: Gebauer.

Baumgarten, Siegmund Jakob. 1767b. *Auslegung der Briefe Pauli an die Galater, Epheser, Philipper, Colosser, Philemon und Thessalonicher*, edited by Johann Salomo Semler. Halle: Gebauer.

Borchers, Stefan. 2011. *Die Erzeugung des "ganzen Menschen." Zur Entstehung von Anthropologie und Ästhetik an der Universität Halle im 18. Jahrhundert*. Berlin/Boston: De Gruyter.

Cudworth, Ralph. (1678) 1733. *Systema intellectuale huius universi* Latin commented edition, edited by Johann Lorenz Mosheim. Jena: Meyer.

Di Giulio, Sara. 2019. "Handlungstheorie und Anwendbarkeit der Ethik. Ein Vergleich zwischen Kant und Baumgarten." PhD diss., Tübingen University.

Diterich, Johann Samuel. 1742. "Cogitationes philosophicae de precibus continuis." PhD diss., presided by Alexander Gottlieb Baumgarten. Frankfurt/Oder: Hubner.

Eissner, Daniel. 2016. "*Heydnische Tantz-Greuel*—Zur pietistischen Auseinandersetzung mit dem Tanz." *Pietismus und Neuzeit*, 42, 87–115.

Francke, August Hermann. Januar 1695. *Observationes biblicae*. Halle: Salfeld.

Francke, August Hermann. März 1695. *Observationes biblicae*. Halle: Salfeld.

Francke, August Hermann. 1696. *Schrifftmässige Lebens-Regeln*. Wesseln: Bremen.

Francke, August Hermann. 1697. "Vorrede." In *Günd—und ausführliche Erklärung Der Frage: Was von dem Weltüblichen Tanzen zu halten sey?* Halle: Wetterkampff.

Francke, August Hermann. 1726. *Predigten über die Sonn—und Fest-Tags-Episteln*. Halle: Verlegung des Wäysen-Hauses.
Fritz, Martin. 2016. "Aufklärung als religiöser Stimmungswandel. Georg Friedrich Meiers Ideal eines 'vergnügten Christentums.'" In *Religion und Aufklärung*, edited by Albrecht Beutel and Martha Nooke, 647–59. Tübingen: Mohr Siebeck.
Goldbeck, Johann Friedrich. 1742. "De abnegatione philosophica." PhD diss., presided by Alexander Gottlieb Baumgarten. Frankfurt/Oder: Literis Alexianis.
Hamilton, William. 1859. *Lectures on Metaphysics and Logic*, vol. 1. Edinburgh and London: Blackwood and Sons.
Heigel, Julian. 2014. *Vergnügen und Erbauung. Johann Jakob Rambachs Kantatentexte und ihre Vertonungen*. Halle: Franckesche Stiftungen.
Hoffmann, Friedrich. 1715. *Gründliche Anweisung, wie ein Mensch vor dem frühzeitigen Tod [...] sich verwahren könne*, vol. 1. Halle: Renger.
Kliche, Dieter. 2002. "'Ich glaube selbst Engel können nicht ohne Sinnlichkeit sein'. Über einen Fund aus der Frühgeschichte der Ästhetik im Werner-Krauss-Archiv." In *Genuss und Egoismus. Zur Kritik ihrer geschichtlichen Verknüpfung*, edited by Wolfgang Klein and Ernst Müller, 54–61. Berlin: De Gruyter.
Lacher, Reimar F. (ed.). 2019. *Scherz. Die heitere Seite der Aufklärung*. Göttingen: Wallstein.
Lange, Joachim. 1709–11. *Antibarbarus Orthodoxiae Dogmatico-Hermeneuticus*, 2 vols. Berlin: Meyer.
Lange, Joachim. 1714. *Die richtige Mittel-Straße*, vol. 4. Halle: Renger.
Lange, Samuel Gotthold. 1748. "Von der Gesellschaft der Samariter." *Der Gesellige*, 1, 5, 41–8.
Langen, August. 1954. *Der Wortschatz des deutschen Pietismus*. Tübingen: Niemeyer.
Marcuse, Herbert. (1955) 1998. *Eros and Civilization*. London: Routledge.
Martens, Wolfgang. 1989. *Literatur und Frömmigkeit in der Zeit der frühen Aufklärung*. Tübingen: Niemeyer.
Mauser, Wolfram. 2000a. "Geselliges Lachen als 'patriotische Tat'. Georg Friedrich Meiers Apologie des Scherzens." In *Konzepte aufgeklärter Lebensführung*, edited by Wolfram Mauser, 346–58. Würzburg: Königshausen & Neumann.
Mauser, Wolfram. 2000b. "Anakreon als Therapie? Zur medizinisch-diätetischen Begründung der Rokokodichtung." In *Konzepte aufgeklärter Lebensführung*, edited by Wolfram Mauser, 301–29. Würzburg: Königshausen & Neumann.
Meier, Georg Friedrich. 1744. *Gedancken von Schertzen*. Halle: Hemmerde.
Meier, Georg Friedrich. 1748. *Anfangsgründe aller schönen Wissenschaften*, vol. 1. Halle: Hemmerde.
Meier, Georg Friedrich. 1749. *Gedancken von der Religion*. Halle: Hemmerde.
Meier, Georg Friedrich. 1753. *Philosophische Sittenlehre*, vol. 1. Halle: Hemmerde.
Meier, Georg Friedrich. 1756. *Philosophische Sittenlehre*, vol. 3. Halle: Hemmerde.
Meier, Georg Friedrich. 1765. *Von dem unschuldigen Gebrauche der Welt*. Halle: Hemmerde.
Nannini, Alessandro. 2013. "Da Baumgarten a Baumgarten. Siegmund Jakob Baumgarten e la fondazione dell'estetica moderna." In *Premio nuova estetica*, edited by Luigi Russo, 67–90. Palermo: Aesthetica.
Nannini, Alessandro. 2021. "The Cofounding of Aesthetics: Baumgarten and Meier." In *Baumgarten's Aesthetics*, edited by Colin McQuillan, 171–92. Lanham: Rowman & Littlefield.
Nannini, Alessandro. 2022a. "Baumgarten the Beautician. The Origins of Cosmetics as an Aesthetic Discourse." *Aesthetica Preprint*, 120, 159–72.

Nannini, Alessandro. 2022b. "La dieta di Baumgarten. Esercizio fisico, salute e bellezza." *Aisthesis. Pratiche, linguaggi e saperi dell'estetico*, 15, 2, 137–46.

Nannini, Alessandro. 2022c. *Al di qua del logos. Logica delle idee estetiche tra Baumgarten e Kant*. Milano: Mimesis.

Nannini, Alessandro. 2022d. "Somaesthetics in Baumgarten? The Founding of Aesthetics and the Body." *Estetika. The European Journal of Aesthetics*, 59, 2, 103–18.

Nicolai, Friedrich. 1799. *Über meine gelehrte Bildung*. Berlin and Stettin: Nicolai.

Patzke, Johann Samuel. 1768. "Von dem Vergnügen der Sinne und den sinnlichen Ergetzlicheiten." In *Betrachtungen über die wichtigsten Angelegenheiten des Menschen*, edited by Johann Samuel Patzke, 84–89. Helmstedt/Magdeburg: Hechtel.

Rambach, Johann Jakob. (1723) 1727². "Vorrede von dem Mißbrauch und rechtem [sic] Gebrauch der Poesie." In *Poetische Fest-Gedancken*, edited by Johann Jakob Rambach. Jena: Ritter.

Rambach, Johann Jakob. 1738. *Moral-Theologie oder Christliche Sittenlehre*, edited by Joachim Lange. Frankfurt/Main: Sand.

Rambach, Johann Jakob. 1739. *Exegetische und porismatische Erklärung der Ep. Pauli an die Galater und an den Titum*. Giessen: Krieger.

Rambach, Johann Jakob. 1851. *Erbauliche Betrachtungen über die heiligen zehn Gebote*. Schaffhausen: Schalch & Wölfflin.

Rotth, Albrecht Christian. 1699. *Höchstnöthiger Unterricht von so genanten Mittel-Dingen*. Leipzig: Friedr. Lanckischens sel. Erben.

Rotth, Albrecht Christian. 1701. *Wiederholter und ferner ausgeführter Unterricht von Mittel-Dingen*. Leipzig: Friedr. Lanckischens sel. Erben.

Scheitler, Irmgard. 2009. "Menschenbild und Musikauffassung bei Gottfried Vockerodt und seinen Gegnern." In *Alter Adam und Neue Kreatur*, edited by Udo Sträter, 513–30. Tübingen: Niemeyer.

Schochow, Werner. 2003. *Bücherschicksale. Die Verlagerungsgeschichte der Preußischen Staatsbibliothek*. Berlin: De Gruyter.

Schubert, Anselm. 2002. *Das Ende der Sünde: Anthropologie und Erbsünde zwischen Reformation und Aufklärung*. Göttingen: Vandenhoeck & Ruprecht.

Schüddekopf, Carl (ed.). 1899. *Briefwechsel zwischen Gleim und Uz*. Tübingen: Litterar. Verein in Stuttgart.

Schwaiger, Clemens. 1995. *Das Problem des Glücks im Denken Christian Wolffs*. Stuttgart-Bad Cannstatt: Frommann-Holzboog.

Schwaiger, Clemens. 2011. *Alexander Gottlieb Baumgarten—ein intellektuelles Porträt*. Stuttgart-Bad Cannstatt: Frommann-Holzboog.

Schwaiger, Clemens. 2016. "Zwischen Laxismus und Rigorismus. Möglichkeiten und Grenzen philosophischer Ethik nach Alexander Gottlieb Baumgarten." In *Schönes Denken. A. G. Baumgarten im Spannungsfeld zwischen Ästhetik, Logik und Ethik*, edited by Andrea Allerkamp and Dagmar Mirbach, 255–70. Hamburg: Meiner.

Schwarz, Olga Katharina. 2022. *Rationalistische Sinnlichkeit. Zur philosophischen Grundlegung der Kunsttheorie 1700 bis 1760. Leibniz, Wolff, Gottsched, Baumgarten*. Berlin/Boston: De Gruyter.

Sdzuj, Reimund. 2005. *Adiaphorie und Kunst. Studien zur Genealogie ästhetischen Denkens*. Tübingen: Niemeyer.

Spener, Philipp Jakob. 1692. *Die Evangelische [sic] Lebens-Pflichten*, vol. 2. Frankfurt/Main: Zunner.

Spener, Philipp Jakob. 1696. *Der hochwichtige Articul von der Wiedergeburt*. Frankfurt/Main: Zunner.

Spener, Philipp Jakob. 1706. *Predigten über des seeligen Johann Arnds Geistreiche Bücher vom Wahren Christenthum*. Frankfurt/Main: Zunner.

Stiebritz, Johann Friedrich. 1742. "Gründlicher Beweis, daß die Lust Sünde sey." In *Der Prüfenden Gesellschaft zu Halle Fortgesetzte, zur Gelehrsamkeit gehörige, Bemühungen*, 5. Stück, 420-40. Halle and Leipzig: Schuster.

Sträter, Udo. 1995. "Aufklärung und Pietismus—das Beispiel Halle." In *Universitäten und Aufklärung*, edited by Notker Hammerstein, 49-61. Göttingen: Wallstein.

Sucro, Christoph Joseph. 1747. *Versuche in Lehrgedichten und Fabeln*. Halle: Hemmerde.

Tedesco, Salvatore. 1998. "Avvertenza del curatore." In *Lezioni di estetica*, edited by Salvatore Tedesco, 21-2. Palermo: Aesthetica.

Thomasius, Jakob. (1653) 1693. "Programma XIV. Philosophiam esse meditationem mortis." In *Dissertationes LXIII*, edited by Jakob Thomasius, 124-47. Halle: Zeitler.

Verweyen, Theodor. 1989. "'Halle, die Hochburg des Pietismus, die Wiege der Anakreontik'. Über das Konfliktpotential der anakreontischen Poesie als Kunst der 'sinnlichen Erkenntnis.'" In *Zentren der Aufklärung I: Halle*, edited by Norbert Hinske, 209-38. Heidelberg: Schneider.

Vesper, Achim. 2008. "Lust als 'cognitio intuitiva perfectionis': Vollkommenheitsästhetik bei Wolff und ihre Kritik durch Kant." In *Christian Wolff und die Europäische Aufklärung*, vol. 4, edited by Jürgen Stolzenberg and Oliver-Pierre Rudolph, 283-96. Hildesheim: Olms.

Vockerodt, Gottfried. 1697. *Mißbrauch der freyen Künste*. Frankfurt: Zauner.

Vockerodt, Gottfried. 1698. *Ad orationes publicas de voluptate concessa*. Gotha: Litteris Reyherianis.

Vockerodt, Gottfried. 1699. *Erleuterte Auffdeckung des Betrugs und Aergernisses*. Halle: Waysenhaus.

Von Loën, Johann Michael. 1751. "Epikureische Sittenlehre die beste." In *Gesammelte kleine Schriften*, vol. 3, edited by Johann Michael Von Loën 45-56. Frankfurt/Leipzig: Hutter.

Walch, Johann Georg. 1726. *Philosophisches Lexicon*. Leipzig: Gleditschens seel. Sohn.

Walch, Johann Georg. 1733. *Historische und Theologische Einleitung in die Religionsstreitigkeiten*. 5 Teile (1733-1739), Anderer Theil. Jena: Meyer.

Wels, Ulrike. 2009. "Die anthropologische Bestimmung der Geselligkeit im Zweiten Adiaphoristischen Streit und ihr Einfluss auf das protestantische Schultheater." In *Alter Adam und Neue Kreatur*, edited by Udo Sträter, 531-44. Tübingen: Niemeyer.

Welsch, Wolfgang. 1997. *Undoing Aesthetics*. London: Sage Publications.

Wiegleb, Johann Hieronymus. 1697. "Anderer Tractat, Darinnen die gantze Sache vom Weltüblichen Tanzen als in einem Begriff verfasset/und aus dem wahren Grunde des Christenthumbs recht eigentlich gezeiget wird/wie sündlich und Christen unanständig dasselbe sey." In Johann K. Kessler, Johann H. Wiegleb, *Gründ—und ausführliche Erklärung Der Frage: Was von dem Weltüblichen Tanzen zu halten sey?*, 115-66. Halle: Wetterkampff.

Wolff, Christian. 1721. *Vernünftige Gedanken von dem gesellschaftlichen Leben der Menschen*. Halle: Renger.

Wolff, Christian. 1732. *Psychologia empirica*. Frankfurt/Leipzig: Renger.

Zedler, Johann Heinrich (ed.). 1739. *Grosses vollständiges Universal-Lexicon*, vol. 21, columns 589-92. Leipzig/Halle: s.v. "Mitteldinge."

Zelle, Carsten. 2008. "Klopstock Diät—das Erhabene und die Anthropologie um 1750." In *Wort und Schrift—das Werk Friedrich Gottlieb Klopstocks*, edited by Kevin Hilliard and Katrin Kohl, 101-27. Tübingen: Niemeyer.

Zelle, Carsten. 2010. "Klopstocks Reitkur. Zur Konkurrenz christlicher Lebensordnung und weltlicher Diät um 1750." In *Aufklärung und Religion—Neue Perspektiven*, edited by Michael Hofmann and Carsten Zelle, 65-84. Hannover: Wehrhahn.

8

Drives, Inclinations, and Perfectibility: Leonhard Cochius' Response to the 1768 Prize Question

Tinca Prunea-Bretonnet

1. Introduction

In 1768, Leonhard Cochius (1718–79) was awarded the prize of the Berlin Academy for a noteworthy essay devoted to the problem of inclinations titled "Untersuchung über die Neigungen" ("Inquiry Concerning the Inclinations").[1] The question for the academic competition, initially announced for 1767, read: "Is it possible to uproot inclinations coming from Nature or to generate inclinations that are not produced by it? And what are the means to fortify the inclinations that are good and weaken those that are bad [if we] suppose that the latter are invincible?"[2] On Adolph von Harnack's account, the *Preisfrage* was praised for focusing on pressing concerns of the time and regarded as particularly significant since it engaged the foundations of ethics.[3] Four essays were short-listed and after some deliberation, Cochius' dissertation was finally awarded the prize.[4] It was published in 1769 alongside the responses of Christian Garve and Christoph Meiners.

In this chapter, I argue that Cochius' prize essay marks a significant moment in the Enlightenment's treatment of inclinations, and of drives in general, given that crucial ethical principles are overshadowed by—if not entirely disregarded in favor of—concerns of a more psychological and pedagogical nature. I believe that Cochius radicalizes an already discernible psychological shift in practical philosophy, initiated by the post-Wolffian school, and gives it a novel, comprehensive philosophical expression in his essay. Therefore, I will examine Cochius' response within a larger philosophical context shaped by four central issues: the controversy over the fundamental powers or faculties of the soul, which dates back to the 1720s debate between Wolff and the so-called Thomasian-Pietist school[5]; the more recent and pressing controversy regarding the reception of Jean-Jacques Rousseau's views in Germany, with an emphasis on his concept of perfectibility; the revived reception of Leibniz's thought after the publication of the *New Essays* in 1765; and finally, the problem of the "depth" of the soul (*Tiefe der Seele*) that became crucial for the psychological turn in ethics during the second half of the eighteenth century. I contend that Cochius' position, elaborated in a rigorous and insightful way in the prize essay, can be properly understood only when read against the backdrop of these debates, to which it decisively contributed.[6]

To show this, I will first detail Cochius' general views on inclinations in Section 2. I will then examine his conception of the soul as an active force (Section 3) and the innate character of inclinations (Section 4). I then turn to what I consider the central concept of his essay, namely the "depth of the soul" (Section 5) and determine the sense in which it can be called "groundless" (Section 6). In Section 7, I examine Cochius' reception of Rousseau's notion of perfectibility and show that he redefines it with the help of the Leibnizian and Wolffian notion of perfection. Finally, in Section 8, I present Cochius' answer to the main concern of the prize question, namely whether it is possible to alter our inclinations.

2. Cochius and the Problem of Inclinations

Leonhard Cochius studied theology in his hometown, Königsberg, and went on to study philosophy and mathematics in Marburg with Christian Wolff in 1737. After moving to Berlin, he held positions as tutor and college professor before being named court and garrison preacher in Potsdam in 1749. The success of his 1768 prize essay on inclinations ensured his entrance to the Berlin Academy in 1770, where he became a member of the speculative philosophy class. His declining health prevented him from making a substantial contribution to the publications of the Academy, but he nevertheless established a solid reputation as a fervent admirer of Leibniz, as well as an accomplished composer and Latinist.[7]

His acceptance address at the Academy, pronounced in Latin and published in a translated and abridged version in the proceedings for the year 1772,[8] was dedicated to Leibniz. In this writing, he argues for the necessity of a single fundamental principle in the investigation of the soul and endorses Leibniz's analysis of ideas (Cochius 1774, 39). He also states his anthropological conviction that the human being is a unity composed of a soul and a body, the latter playing the role of a "musical instrument" (Cochius 1774, 40). Cochius insists that Leibniz should be praised for having enabled the coming of age of philosophy and paved the way for all philosophers to follow.

This is precisely what Cochius himself had put into practice in 1768: his prize essay on inclinations was written in a Leibnizian vein and its explicit aim was to address contemporary issues by appealing to Leibnizian theses such as the definition of the soul as an active force, the presence of *petites perceptions* in the human mind, and the Leibnizian treatment of perfection and happiness. As I argue in this chapter, Cochius' conception should be inscribed in the larger revival of Leibnizian thought that took center-stage in the aftermath of the publication of the *New Essays* in 1765.

It is important to note here that in 1766 the class of *belles-lettres* of the Berlin Academy announced a prize question titled "*Éloge de Leibniz*" to be awarded in 1768. In spite of the ambiguity of the term "*éloge*" in French—standing for both praise and a funeral speech—we can undisputedly speak about an authentic and enthusiastic revival of Leibniz's philosophy in the second half of the 1760s that went beyond a mere reassessment of his influence on the early Enlightenment. The Academy actively contributed to this revival. So did Cochius, who, albeit being conversant with Wolff's views since his student years and taking up clear Wolffian elements, explicitly aims for a return to Leibniz's own standpoint. A further significant influence on Cochius' conception of the nature and operations of the soul is undoubtedly Johann Georg Sulzer, who had elaborated his perspective across several academic memoirs since the 1750s as well as in his book *Kurzer Begriff aller Wißenschaften* (Compendium of All Sciences).[9]

Cochius' *Inquiry Concerning the Inclinations* is divided into three sections that are devoted (1) to inclinations in general, (2) to specific (*bestimmt*) inclinations, and (3) to the modification of inclinations. From the outset, he states that the essence of the soul is simple. By endorsing this Wolffian standpoint recently taken up by Sulzer in several influential essays and rearticulated within a similar metaphysical *and* psychological context,[10] Cochius insists throughout the essay that experience and introspection are legitimate tools for the investigation of the nature and the operations of the soul. They must, however, be accompanied, he argues, by a metaphysical consideration of the soul in the lineage of past doctrines, such as those of Leibniz and Wolff. When one tries to scrutinize the changes that are observable in the soul, one realizes their obscure character and the fact that they do not seem to admit of any explanation (UN, 17–8). On his account, the weaknesses and imperfections of past and competing treatments of the soul are either due to an abstract and general approach to the metaphysics of the soul or to the symmetrical, but equally faulty, approach that pays exclusive attention to experience and specific causes, thus preventing one from addressing the existence of a common cause or the question of the origin of the modifications occurring in the soul.

Regarding inclinations as such, Cochius argues that we should distinguish between, on the one hand, an active (if indetermined) principle of the soul, called "the elastic force of the soul" (UE, 18), and, on the other hand, the objects that offer it the occasion to determine itself in a specific way. He understands the principle as a force aiming to constantly acquire new representations and sensations or to perfect those that the soul already has. This force attempts to constantly increase the evidence and vividness of representations (UE, 20), of which the principles of contradiction and identity are the first. These two principles, alongside the natural elastic drive of the soul, suffice, on his account, to explain all the changes occurring in the soul. All inclinations are founded on the harmony (*Übereinstimmung*) between the elastic drive and the object, this drive being innate while objects are not. He argues that "secret motivations" (*geheime Triebfedern*) are at work in our soul,[11] that is, secret driving forces which direct us toward specific objects and are grounded on numerous obscure representations and sensations that we are not conscious of.[12]

3. The Soul as a Fundamental Elastic Force

Relying on both the metaphysics of the soul and empirical psychology, Cochius wishes to offer a clear and novel account of the genesis of inclinations that reaches back to their first "source" (*Quelle*) and analyzes the elements composing these inclinations. In opposition to both the Wolffian and the Thomasian-Crusian tradition, he argues that it is not enough to deduce inclinations from a fundamental drive, because fundamental drives are inclinations too, albeit very general ones (UN, §1). This brief reference invokes an enduring controversy from the first half of the eighteenth century, one that opposed thinkers defending the existence of two or more fundamental drives grounded on the two fundamental faculties of the soul (the will and the understanding)[13] to the Leibnizian-Wolffian position arguing for a single fundamental drive (the drive to perfection) based on the representative faculty of the soul.[14] Both schools of thought held that the fundamental drive is imprinted in the soul by God and, if correctly employed, can direct it toward the acquisition of virtue. Cochius distances himself from both these stances. As we will come to see, he substantially changes the frame and the goals of his analysis, renouncing not only the reference to the fallen human being (and thus to sin) but also that to a virtuous, happy life. He aims to go "deeper" than the Leibnizian-Wolffian tradition, insisting on several occasions on its "unaccomplished" character, while nonetheless situating his own contribution in this lineage.

On Cochius account, all inclinations consist of three elements. In a Leibnizian vein, he first identifies an active (*wirkend*) and *formal* principle, also called an "active force" or "striving" of the soul (UN, 20). He adds a second principle, namely the determining or ordering *material* principle that is constituted by the object of the inclination. The third element is the direction taken by the active force toward the object. This direction, Cochius claims, makes it possible to explain how an inclination is produced. Experience and observation encourage him to argue for the central role of the object in this process: we notice that inclinations vary; if they depended solely on the essence of the soul, they would be identical; consequently, inclinations must also depend on external objects, and we should distinguish between their formal and material aspects. Moreover, Cochius argues, if determined inclinations depended strictly on the active force, they would be necessary and not contingent.

In line with Wolff, Cochius maintains that the simplicity of the soul admits of only one fundamental or original force (*Grundkraft* or *Urkraft*), which is defined as a force of representation:

> The sole original force of the soul, its sole basic drive [*Grundtrieb*], is thus this, to enlarge its representations, through new concepts, new relations; or to raise them to more evidence or vividness. In general, to expand oneself towards all the areas of the domain of representations.
>
> (UN, 24)

This elastic character, already mentioned in the Preface (UN, 18), is "essential" to the soul and cannot be further reduced—this is why we must assume that it represents the active principle of inclinations. When the representation of an object is added to this basic drive and confers a specific orientation to it, inclinations become specific or determined (UN, §4). Because we can conceive of representations without inclinations, but not of inclinations without a representation, representations are more fundamental and constitute the ground on which inclinations are formed. Cochius reaches this conclusion by appealing to the analytical method and claims that representations precede the formation of inclinations, for which further elements are needed. Thus, on his account, we could say that "the soul itself [is] the general undetermined basic drive" that searches for (representations of) objects (UN, 25).

In §4, Cochius provides further details on how the object and the desire (*Begierde*) interact in the formation of inclinations. Desire is less attracted to an object as such, but rather to the relationship (*Beziehung*) this object has with us. An inclination can also be brought about through a relationship with a particular feature or quality of an object, and this even if we are not aware of the totality of the characteristics of the object or if we dislike some of them. This explains why we sometimes choose to do something that is disagreeable, evil, or dangerous: a particular feature of the object creates a specific and lively desire, and this relationship obscures opposing or incompatible relationships to other features of the same object, which therefore do not reach reflection (UN, 25-6). This observation announces a crucial element of Cochius' analysis, namely the problem of inclinations that escape our control. However, further elements are needed before this aspect is fully considered in Section 2 of his essay.

The specific way in which the elastic force deploys itself is examined in §5. On Cochius' account, the essential drive or elasticity of the soul expands in a way that is similar to either movement (*Bewegung*) or extension (*Ausdehnung*). In a movement, the soul passes from one representation to another, it merely exchanges (without retaining) acquired representations for new ones. This cannot be considered a proper extension, he argues, and therefore cannot be regarded as specific to the essence of the soul (UN, 27). Nevertheless, because of the finite character of our faculties, which cannot expand indefinitely, and because some objects or relations exert a stronger attraction that either obscures or chases previous representations, it can safely be claimed that this is what sometimes happens with respect to representations. The second type of deployment of the elastic force is analogous to extension and is said to be truly specific to the soul: in it, the soul embraces and "incorporates" increasingly more representations or renders previously achieved ones clearer or more vivid (ibid.).

Expansion (*Erweiterung*)—often identified with extension—applies to all representations, Cochius claims, though in a different manner according to whether representations have "a relation" (*Beziehung*) to us or not (UN, 28). Those that do not bear any relation to us are called the *theoretical* part of the soul or knowledge (*Erkenntnis*). If they correspond to our already acquired representations and do not contradict them, they are said to be true; if they contradict any representation that we have, wish to have, or are about to have, they are said to be untrue and cannot be taken up. Cochius calls the representations that do have a relation to us the *practical* part of the soul and considers them a part of inclinations as such.[15] If the former contain contradictions, they are rejected by the soul; if they do not, they are taken up and classified as either active or feasible (*thunlig*), or as passive and bearable (*leidlich*) (UN, 29). Cochius insists that both types of representations, theoretical and practical, are founded on the one and only fundamental force of the soul. The practical capacity is on his account a mere phenomenon created by the combination of the elastic force of the soul with an object that is related to our state.

The elastic force of the soul is "ruled" by the drive to perfection defined as a general drive, that is, an immediate consequence (*Folge*) of the nature of the soul. Against

Wolff's standpoint,[16] however, Cochius argues that this drive cannot be considered an active principle of inclinations nor a first indecomposable principle because it can be divided into two further elements: the original power of the soul to acquire new representations and the absence of contradictions. According to Cochius, what is truly active and efficient is the elastic force of the soul: "The so-called fundamental drives are applications of our essential force to a very general object" (UN, 30).

4. Are Inclinations Innate?

It is in §7 of the *Inquiry* that Cochius directly addresses the first part of the prize question: are there inclinations "coming from Nature," that is, innate ones?[17] On his account, only the force of the soul can be said to be innate (it belongs to the essence of the soul), but not inclinations as such because the objects or relations to objects—one of the three components of inclinations, as we have seen—come from the outside and thus cannot be innate. The third element, namely the law according to which the force is directed toward the object, defined in §6 (UE, 30) as the drive to perfection, can also be regarded as innate since it flows from the essence of the soul, without, however, being fundamental.

Cochius includes a very significant exception here: "when we think about ourselves, and observe in ourselves the essential drive to expansion, there is an object in our representations that is innate to us, namely this elasticity of the soul" (UN, 31). All that opposes its extension produces aversion (*Abneigung*), and we resent any form of constraint or obstruction. This is why, Cochius claims, we should consider the inclination to (inner) freedom to be innate: it is essential (*wesentlich*) and inseparable from ourselves. He demarcates inner freedom from outer freedom, arguing that the former has primacy over the latter, as can be witnessed in those who choose to be enslaved or imprisoned for a greater cause. Despite a prevailing consensus, he holds that the drive to our own existence is not essential to the soul (UN, 32). We can easily conceive of a soul that is merely possible (by which he means: not yet existing), but not of a soul that has no elastic drive. Therefore, on Cochius' account, only this last drive is essential to the soul and not the drive to existence. Once we exist, another drive can be regarded as immutable and inseparable from the soul, namely the drive to perfect oneself. On this point, Cochius' position seems to integrate what Wolff considered to be the fundamental human drive (and what Crusius listed among the three fundamental drives, too),[18] that is, the drive to perfect one's state, without, however, considering external objects.

Cochius confers a particular and intermediate status to inclinations. They are said to be more than mere possibilities, but less than actualities: they are "virtualities" (*Virtualitäten*) (UN, 33). This third status is given by the innateness of two of their components and by the fact that the (representation of the) object is a mere occasion that imprints a specific direction to the active force. In order to illustrate this intermediate modality, Cochius mentions the "inflammable" character of inclinations: he compares them to glowing coal that only needs some air to be set ablaze (UE, 34). In line with Leibniz, he calls them "dispositions" waiting to be actualized.[19]

The distinction between that which is innate to our soul (*innatum*) and that which is born with us (*connatum*) brings further nuance to Cochius' analysis (UE, 34). The *innatum* is unchangeable and inseparable from the soul. In contrast, the *connatum* is founded on the *innatum*, and its characteristics require closer examination. It is once again our experience that teaches us that humans are born with specific inclinations: no one could exist with mere essential determinations, Cochius argues, thereby endorsing a standpoint that will allow him to account for Rousseau's influential notion of perfectibility. Even contingent qualities (*Beschaffenheiten*) must be determined in an individual. These latter inclinations may be obscure, weak, or unconscious, but they are present from the first instant of our existence. On Cochius' account, the cry of the new-born testifies to the presence of aversions and inclinations, to the fact that the new-born "brings them into the world" (UN, 34). The second part of the *Inquiry* is devoted to the analysis of these dispositions.

5. The Depth of the Soul

The law according to which the elastic force of the soul expresses itself maintains that it "seizes" (*ergreift*) anything "that is in harmony with the natural drive to expansion and to our state" (UE, 35). Cochius thereby offers a reformulation of Wolff's "natural law" and of the definition of perfection,[20] aligning it with his own disposition to lean toward a more psychological rather than ethical analysis. The main task of the second section of the *Inquiry* is to examine the origin of the diversity of inclinations, which cannot reside in the essential elements because the latter are the same for everyone. Three questions guide his approach: (1) the inquiry into the emergence of specific inclinations, (2) the analysis of the driving forces of pleasure and enjoyment as well as their origin, and (3) the discussion about the intensity and the degrees of the vividness of inclinations.

The scrutiny of the genesis and development of inclinations is based on the crucial concepts of the "depth" (*Tiefe*) or the "abyss" (*Abgrund*) of the soul. Cochius indifferently uses these concepts in order to render the idea of what was called before him (by Wolff, Israel Gottlieb Canz, Alexander Baumgarten, and Sulzer among others) the *fundus animae* or the "ground" of the soul. As Alessandro Nannini has shown, this concept had a long theological history prior to its endorsement by Leibniz and to its renaissance within the Wolffian school, where it acquired a growing psychological significance.[21] Sulzer's treatment of the notion was particularly influential at the time, and Cochius' views are certainly indebted to his essays as well as to the renewed interest in this concept owing to Leibniz's *New Essays*, where the central role of the *fundus animae* is established within the first chapter of Book I.[22]

We should note that in line with Sulzer, Cochius prefers the concept "*Tiefe der Seele*" to "*Grund der Seele*."[23] He understands it as a "dark" region of the soul that escapes consciousness but determines the human being from birth onward. In the *Inquiry*, the notions "depth" and "abyss" are associated with and occasionally replaced by concepts like "night" (*Nacht*) or "darkness" (*Dunkelheit*), and usually determined by the adjective "deepest" (*tiefste*) (UN, 36–7, 53). On Cochius' account, the depth of the soul has chronological, motivational, and thus behavioral priority. It is "inhabited" by infinitely many and infinitely small representations that are preconscious—and thus pre-reflexive, too—of which some never get to become conscious (UN, 36-7). He understands this region both as the origin of all representations and knowledge (theoretical *and* practical) and as the container of acquired but forgotten representations.

It is again experience that allows him to infer the existence of such "first representations" and guides him through most of the developments in this section, which can thus be assigned to empirical psychology: Cochius argues that by comparing a child to an adult and by progressively reducing the number and the degree of consciousness and of vividness in the representations of the adult, one can conclude that the force of the soul is initially (at birth) active in a first, unconscious, and weak representation. One should necessarily assume the existence of such a first representation, even if it is infinitely small and no longer displayable (*unanzeigbar*) through the analysis he advances, "because nothing can spring from nothing" (UN, 38).

The development described here by Cochius starts from this first unconscious representation, which is said to be in "the deepest darkness" (*tiefsten Dunkelheit*) (UN, 36). It imperceptibly grows through "infinitely small steps" toward clarity, distinctness, and vividness until it becomes conscious and observable (*merklich*). On Cochius' account, all representations, inclinations, and capacities (*Fertigkeiten*) find their origin in this first unconscious representation (UN, 37). He calls it the "main representation" (*Hauptvorstellung*) that is always accompanied by a multitude of other representations. Indeed, even if we have to postulate this first state of the soul, "a representation is never completely alone in us" (UN, 37). Owing to the restlessness of the active force of the soul and to the kinship among representations, the elastic force, immediately after acquiring a representation, seizes the one next to it. All changes in the soul are based on this infinitely small representation that in an unexplainable way also generates the main inclination giving the character of a person.[24] For Cochius, the main feature (*Hauptzug*) of one's character is formed during very early childhood and proves particularly difficult, if ever possible, to alter later on: "The main inclinations that form our character are lost to the first instant in which, with infinitely small effects, the force started to manifest itself" (UN, 39).

According to Cochius, we can retrace the development of inclinations as follows: as we have seen, the first representations are not conscious. They are said to dwell in the "deepest darkness" of the depth of the soul. Originally mere "virtualities" or "distant predispositions" (*Anlagen*), they become "dispositions" (*Dispositionen*) when they attain the level of the general and weak (*schwach*) representations of the possibility to feel enjoyment (UN, 41). Gradually, they gain further intensity (*Stärke*) and determination, thus "coming from the deepest night into a twilight [*Dämmerung*]" and becoming inclinations. They progressively acquire more "light" and steadily become more determined and vivid (*lebhaft*), thereby reaching the level of desires (*Begierde*). This progression takes place in "infinitely small steps," through imperceptible nuances (UN, 43).

A similar development can be traced for all inclinations, and not only for the main one: the active principle lies in the soul; its means of expanding are attention, opportunity, and the object. It is through pleasure and enjoyment that the object attracts the soul (UN, 43). On Cochius' account, since this process starts at birth, the formation of inclinations in very young children is of the outmost importance. If the first objects of their inclinations are conservation and vital necessities (UN, 40), the formation of further, more complex inclinations can be influenced by adults who are able to cultivate either pleasure as the ruling principle or the acceptance of rational rules guiding (and overpowering) desires (UN, 43). This is a crucial point in Cochius' essay because it involves the formation of the moral character and offers the principle of "rational education" (ibid.). This topic is discussed at length in Section 3 ("On the modification of inclinations"), which goes beyond the scope of this chapter. However, three important aspects should be mentioned here.

The first point is that reason has a certain power over inclinations according to Cochius, especially if it is encouraged and established as a guiding faculty very early on. Therefore, the *Inquiry* does not endorse the common standpoint of the time, which promotes the powerlessness of reason over passions and prejudice, its capitulation when confronted with the "hidden forces" of the soul.[25] Cochius advances a nuanced, if prudent, answer to the academic question on the possibility to change or at least bend previously formed inclinations. On his account, it is possible to acquire new inclinations through reflection and distinct knowledge, and thus to subdue or "push down" (*niederdrücken*) the main inclination. This dynamic accounts for the possibility of changes in character. Therefore, Cochius believes that reason cannot successfully influence or modify inclinations if it addresses them directly, but it can do so by creating opposing or competing inclinations that eventually overshadow previous main inclinations (UN, 46). In §6, Cochius argues that our conscience (*Gewissen*) can advance "counter-representations" able to prevent an inclination from becoming the driving force of an action, even if this inclination is neither displaced nor diminished (UN, 31).[26]

The second important aspect regarding the modification of inclinations is given by the mention of "rational education" (*vernünftige Erziehung*). It testifies to the authentic aim of the essay: Cochius is mainly concerned with advancing tools and strategies to help educators and teachers. His psychological analysis serves a pedagogical goal. To be sure, ethical or moral concerns seem almost absent from his essay, and they undoubtedly do not constitute the driving force of his account. In this respect, we can certainly argue for his significant departure from Wolff and even Sulzer, and even more so from the theory of affects that was developed by the Thomasian school.[27]

The third point mentioned in the reconstruction of the genesis of inclinations in young children gives us an essential feature of the depth of the soul. Cochius claims that in this region, we find not only pre-conscious representations, but also representations that have at some point been conscious and are now forgotten (UN, 42). The latter can easily be recalled into consciousness and are said to rapidly retrieve their vividness and determination when brought to light. Thus, the depth of the soul represents both the origin of representations and the region where (temporarily or permanently) forgotten representations return.

6. Is the Soul a "Groundless Abyss"?

In §13, Cochius advances a further clarification regarding the depth of the soul. He addresses the problem of sensation (*Empfindung*) by elaborating two main arguments from a Leibnizian and Wolffian perspective: he first argues for the reduction of all sensations to representations; then he posits the existence of "small sensations," an equivalent of Leibniz's *petites perceptions*. On his account, everything that is present in the (conscious or unconscious) human mind is reducible to representation, even that which seems to be a sensation or a sentiment (*Gefühl*). Pointing to "recent foreign writers," he contends that it would be an error to distinguish a "thinking soul" from a "feeling spirit [*Gemüth*]" because they are one and the same (UN, 47). If we wish to provide a consistent and truthful analysis of the soul, we must understand that what we take to be a sensation is in fact a multitude of obscure (*dunkel*) representations that have "flown into one" (ibid.). Sensations can be brought to light or woken up (*erweckt*) by our senses (UN, 54–5), but they are no different from the sensations produced by thoughts (*Gedanken*)—both are representations. They obey the same rules and follow a similar "ascent" through imperceptibly small steps from the depth of the soul to the light of consciousness.[28] Like representations, Cochius claims, sensations are infinitely numerous, unconscious at first, and no finite spirit (such as the human one) can exist without them (UN, 55). If there is no contradiction with previous sensations and no constraint on the elastic force of the soul is exerted, the sensation is enjoyable. As soon as a relation to us is observed in the sensation, an inclination is formed.

Two further elements regarding the depth of the soul are discussed in this context. It is here that Cochius employs the concept of "abyss" of the soul and qualifies it as "groundless" (*bodenloser Abgrund*) (UN, 53). He refers to the darkness and the lack of consciousness which reign as we go deeper and deeper into the *Tiefe der Seele*, where sensations decrease in determination, and the representations that form them become mere virtualities. Cochius compares them to the roots of a tree and employs this analogy to illustrate his conception of inclinations in general. He starts from already formed inclinations and uses the analytical approach:

> Inclinations arise from sensations like the trunk of the tree [arises] from the main root; the latter takes the nourishment from the secondary roots, which [in turn] lose themselves in innumerable hair-like roots [*Haar-Wurzeln*] that direct the sap to the tree and each contributes to the trunk.
>
> (UN, 53)

There is, however, an important difference for Cochius: the smallest roots of a tree are finite in number and their ends can be seen. This is not the case with sensations because individual sensations are imperceptible since they are the effect of numerous convergent representations originating from the darkest and deepest, and therefore "groundless," region of the soul.

However, this abyss appears groundless only to our human faculties. We are in fact unable to grasp the true origin of inclinations, unable to infer the first inclination from present representations. In other words, we are incapable of bringing them all to the light of consciousness through complete determination and vividness. On Cochius' account, these representations are innumerable, infinitely small, imperceptible, and unconscious only with respect to our faculties. As we have seen, the active or elastic force of the soul cannot expand indefinitely and thus sometimes "moves" from one representation to another without being able to retain all that it seizes or attempts to seize.[29] In calling the depth of the soul a "groundless abyss," Cochius endorses the human point of view, namely the one offered by observation and experimental inquiry, which is the perspective he espouses throughout the essay in his attempt to provide the mapping of our soul. It is here that the psychological description seems to distance itself from the metaphysics of the soul.

7. Perfection and Perfectibility

I mentioned in the Introduction Rousseau's notion of perfectibility; while Cochius does not use this term in the *Inquiry*, I believe that this notion plays an important role in his argument. Moreover, I argue that its interplay with the concept of "depth of the soul" makes possible the articulation of a central thesis in this essay.

On several occasions, Cochius insists on the incomplete character of the Wolffian treatment of the drive to perfection (although he does not always mention Wolff's name). As we have seen, he argues that the drive to perfection is not fundamental but should be regarded as the most general drive among those founded on the drive to indefinitely expand the representations of the soul. He goes further and claims, against Wolff's conviction, that this drive does not bring us enjoyment as such: "the sensation of enjoyment does not arise from the mere perfection that lays within a thing [*Sache*]" (UN, 52). Enjoyment arises instead from the fact that perfection increases within the thing: "an imperfect thing, that progresses [in perfection], produces more sensation than a perfect one that remains what it is" (ibid.). The drive to expand one's representations goes beyond the drive to perfection; it has a broader scope than the drive to "seize" the representation of a perfect thing. Appealing to a Leibnizian distinction, Cochius calls the perfection residing in a thing "a dead force" when it is understood as a mere (or static) harmony (*Übereinstimmung*) among the components of a thing. Perfection, however, becomes "a living force" when it takes the thing and our drive "further," that is, when it increases progressively and corresponds to the essential drive for the constant expansion of the soul.

Despite his rejection of the Wolffian definition of the "natural law," Cochius retrieves the latter's definition of happiness as a never-ending progress toward perfection.[30] In line with Leibniz as well, he argues that "there is no tranquility" in the soul, that enjoyment and happiness are not static but dynamic states.[31] This is why we are attracted to novelty and not to habit, why we lose interest in the most perfect things once we know them. In my view, the drive to expand one's representations, understood as a drive to perfection with the restrictions that we have seen, constitutes Cochius' redefinition of Rousseau's theory of perfectibility within the Wolffian tradition. Unlike some of his contemporaries, such as Reimarus,[32] who engages in an open debate with the views advanced by Rousseau in his *Second Discourse*,[33] Cochius does not reject the latter's conception directly, even if he probably alludes to Rousseau when he mentions foreign thinkers using "tropical expressions" (UN, 62).

On Cochius' account, the drive to expand one's representations has the crucial function of bringing into consciousness the unconscious representations dwelling in the depth of the soul. He therefore calls it the "essential drive to heighten the representation of the soul" (UN, 54). Precisely because the soul is an active force, it never ceases to be active. Therefore, we may infer that the representations from the depth of the soul all aim at eventually reaching consciousness, so to speak. They may lack consciousness but "only for a while" (UN, 54) – for a longer or shorter while, but not forever. Thus, the soul does not rest until it brings to consciousness its own preconscious. This thesis allows Cochius to allude to the fact that the soul remains active even after "what we call" death, although he does not elaborate this point.

As we have seen, the effect of the essential force on representations is to make them conscious. The "distant dispositions," completely indeterminate and general at first, brought by the human being into the world at birth, need to reach consciousness in order to gain determination and vividness. This is the reason why Cochius encourages introspection and the analysis of the soul, despite its seemingly "groundless" depth. In this way he takes up and reformulates Rousseau's notion of perfectibility[34] without mentioning the latter's specific views nor appealing to the comparison between humans and animals. Moreover, the ethical aspect of the drive to perfection that could be found in Wolff or Reimarus, among others, is here overshadowed by Cochius' focus on the psychological dimension of the soul, and this despite the pedagogical concern displayed in the final chapters of the *Inquiry*.[35]

8. Can Inclinations Be Changed?

Cochius answers the second part of the prize question in the third Section of the *Inquiry*. The developments regarding the role of vividness (*Lebhaftigkeit*) and its interplay with distinctness constitute the main arguments of his response. He discriminates between an increase in distinctness and an increase in vividness or light (UN, 57). The more distinct a representation becomes, he claims, the less vivid it is. And the more vivid it is, the more it touches our heart, a dynamic particularly important for preachers. Citing Leibniz, Cochius argues that too much distinctness and too much rigor (*Gründlichkeit*) do not motivate nor move[36]; too little of both does not give food for thought when the sensation and the "bright light" of conviction have faded away (UN, 59). Vividness comes either from a bright representation of the object that presents many sides to us, or from our mind when we pay attention to the object, thereby excluding secondary representations (UN, 60). On his account, it is very important to cultivate reflection, as well as the slow, thorough consideration of things, lest an attention that is too vividly focused on a single thing turns inclinations into desires, passions, and eventually wildness.

These developments allow Cochius to detail a twofold means to weaken and modify inclinations: persuasion. In this context, persuasion is achieved either when the mind is enlightened or when the heart is touched. Both are needed if the alteration is to be successful. The more determined an inclination, the easier it is to modify or bend it. Of course, on Cochius' account, the drive to expand one's representations is immutable. The best way to uproot the inclinations we want to modify is to pursue the already recommended strategy: not to attack them directly, but to create opposite inclinations, render them vivid and thus overshadow the inclinations we want to fight against. In the last part of the *Inquiry* (UN, 82–90), Cochius offers practical advice and concrete examples that are aimed at teachers, parents, and preachers, and addresses pressing pedagogical concerns of his time.[37]

9. Conclusion

I hope to have shown in this chapter how Cochius elaborates the main arguments of his prize essay on inclinations in relation to the main controversies of its time. He explicitly quotes Leibniz and inscribes his endeavor within a tradition that aims to revive the Leibnizian legacy in the 1760s. In this respect, Cochius thus actively participates in a more general reappraisal of Leibnizian thought in the wake of the publication of the *New Essays*. Moreover, Wolff's ethical standpoint is partially taken up as well with respect to specific theses such as the drive to perfection. This endorsement, however, is not extended to Wolff's non-Leibnizian convictions. Sulzer's writings on empirical psychology undoubtedly played a crucial role in Cochius' developments on unconscious representations, the formation of inclinations, and on his appeal to observation and introspection. These various influences, rearticulated in a coherent view, allow Cochius to propose a specific understanding of the concept of perfectibility and to redefine the central notion of the depth of the soul with the help of a novel treatment of the drive to perfection. While metaphysical and ethical considerations do not take center-stage in the *Inquiry*, Cochius' pedagogical goal and psychological analysis of the origin and function of inclinations testify to his understanding of and contribution to the philosophical tendencies of the time. Thus, his 1768 prize essay offers a nuanced and consistent response to the twofold question of the Berlin Academy, an institution that, once again, proved it could grasp the main concerns and the acute problems of the Enlightenment—and this not only in the *Preisfragen* it proposed to European scholars, but also in the writings of its members.[38]

Abbreviation

UN   Cochius, Leonhard. 1769. *Untersuchung über die Neigungen, welche von der königlichen Akademie der Wissenschaften zu Berlin für das Jahr 1767 ausgesetzten Preis erhalten hat. Nebst andern dahin einschlagenden Abhandlungen*, 15–90. Berlin: Haude und Spener.

Notes

1. The full title is "Untersuchung über die Neigungen, welche von der königlichen Akademie der Wissenschaften zu Berlin für das Jahr 1767 ausgesetzten Preis erhalten hat" (hereafter abbreviated as UN).
2. "Peut-on détruire les penchans qui viennent de la Nature, ou en faire naître qu'elle n'ait pas produits? Et quels sont les moyens de fortifier les penchans lorqu'ils sont bons, ou de les affoiblir lorsqu'ils sont mauvais, supposé qu'ils soient invincibles?"; see Harnack 1900, vol. 2, 307.
3. See Harnack 1900, vol. 1.1, 412–13.
4. See the "Protokoll" of the June 2, 1768, session of the Berlin Academy: Sitzungsprotokoll der königlich preußischen Akademie der Wissenschaften zu Berlin vom 2. Juni 1768 (bbaw.de).
5. On the prize competition devoted to the basic faculty of the soul in 1773/1775, see Daniel Dumouchel's chapter in this volume and Falduto 2014, 15–24.
6. I hereby side with Mogens Laerke's claim that contextually internal perspectives, which take into account the active part played by texts in the controversies of their time, are particularly relevant for the interpretation of a philosophical work. On historical perspectivism and actualism, see Laerke 2013. Contrast this approach with the "detective method" advanced (and illustrated in the sixth chapter of the present volume) by Ursula Goldenbaum (Goldenbaum 2013, 75), who, "distrusting" the authors' statements about their intentions, "look[s] for possible philosophical intentions" that motivated the writings and standpoints of past authors. On Goldenbaum's account, the detective method establishes a parallel between the approach of the historian of philosophy and the criminal investigator, as well as between authors and wrongdoers, and aims to assess the "sincerity" of authors and "discover their options." To this end, philosophical controversies are particularly interesting for Goldenbaum who writes: "The way in which philosophers argue with their opponents during such philosophical controversies is far more illuminating in respect to their intentions as well as their logical strengths than any preface of their works could ever be" (Goldenbaum 2013, 76). Obviously, the authors "under investigation" (Goldenbaum 2013, 75) do not have the capacity to claim nor prove their innocence, if we were to keep the detective metaphor.
7. See Bartholmèss 1851, 123. According to Bartholmèss, Cochius "was the most correct and elegant Latin writer within the Academy. He was one the most respectful disciples of Leibniz, one of those who tried to justify their master's idealism through the results of experience."
8. See Cochius 1774.
9. Sulzer 1759; Sulzer 1765; Sulzer 1766a; Sulzer 1766b.
10. See Nannini 2022.
11. UN, 20. On the concept of *Triebfeder* (and drive) before Kant, see Buchenau 2002.
12. See Leibniz 1981, 166.
13. Crusius 1999, §1–14. See also Hahmann 2021.
14. Wolff 1976, §12, 40–4.
15. On this, see Baumgarten 2014, §669 and §671. See also Nannini, forthcoming.
16. See Wolff 1976, §12.
17. Contrast with Klemme 2010 who claims, probably influenced by Mendelssohn's reading (Mendelssohn 1843, 104), that Cochius does not respond to this question. In

fact, Cochius devotes the long §7 to arguing that inclinations as such are not innate (with one exception), even if two of their components can be regarded as innate.
18 On Crusius' account, there are three basic drives: the drive to perfection, the drive to be unified with what we perceive as perfect, and the drive to conscience; see Crusius 1999, §111–37.
19 On this, see Wilson 2022, 19.
20 Wolff 1999, §12.
21 On the history of this concept, see Nannini 2021. The author addresses the theological roots of the concept and revises the familiar narrative according to which Baumgarten invented this concept or was the first to apply it to psychology. The analysis of Canz's contribution is particularly important (Nannini 2021, 60–72).
22 On this, see Wilson 2022, 20-1.
23 See, for instance, *Kurzer Begriff* (Sulzer 2014, 141), where Sulzer uses the plural "*Tiefen*." See also Sulzer's 1759 essay "Explication d'un paradoxe psychologique" devoted to the "hidden forces" and to the "obscure regions" of the soul, an essay in which he explicitly quotes Leibniz's *petites perceptions*, (Sulzer 1766, 439). On Sulzer's redefinition of the *Tiefen der Seele*, see Dumouchel 2018.
24 "The active force of the soul manifests itself from this first instant through infinitely small effects [Wirkungen]" (UN, 39).
25 See Sulzer 1766, 439 and 447.
26 "Man kann eine Neigung haben, seine Güther zu vermehren, die man in keinem Falle ausführen wird, wo das Gewissen Gegenvorstellungen machet; und man würde, bey der Neigung reich zu werden, allezeit vorsätzlich arm bleiben, wenn es keine Fälle gäbe, es ohne Vorwürfe des Gewissens zu werden," UN, 37.
27 On Thomasius' *Affektenlehre*, see Schneiders 1971, 310–15.
28 See UN, 55: "Man muß sich bey den sinnlichen Empfindungen begnügen, überzeugt zu seyn, daß sie ein Phänomen sind, welches aus vielen, kleinen, und unbemerkten Empfindungen entsteht; daß jede hievon etwas ganz anders, als die aus ihrem Zusammenfluß entstandene Haupt-Empfindung ist; daß sie endlich in einzelne Vorstellungen, als ihre wahre Elemente, zurück gehen; daß wir aber so wenig uns derselben bewust seyn, als einen ersten Grad ihrer Stärke angeben können."
29 See also UN, 27.
30 Wolff 1976, §44.
31 Cochius alludes here to the *New Essays*, see Leibniz (1981, 188).
32 For an explicit rejection of Rousseau's conception of perfectibility, see Reimarus 1755, chapter 7.
33 On the critical reception of Rousseau in Germany, see Hourcade et al. 2022.
34 Bartholmèss (1851, 124) notes with respect to Cochius' standpoint: "En concevant toutes les inclinations humaines comme autant de formes, souvent dégradées, du besoin de perfection, de l'amour du progrès, Cochius dut plaire à une génération dont la principale croyance était l'infinie perfectibilité de l'espèce humaine."
35 Despite the very influential theory of the drives of Hermann Samuel Reimarus at the time, I believe that Cochius does not endorse its main features, such as its teleological and hierarchical organization nor the reference to God's design. On Reimarus, see Wilson 2022 and Zammito 2022.
36 Cochius exemplifies the distinction between distinctness and vividness by referring to Wolff's style: "Zu einer Probe hiervon kann das Urtheil vieler Leser über die Psychologie, sonderlich in dem Theil von dem praktischen Vermögen der Seele,

dienen, die der Herr von Wolf deutlich und gründlich, folglich ohne Lebhaftigheit, erkläret; und darüber einige auswertige Schriftsteller, durch die Hülfe tropischer Ausdrücke, und eingestreuter Blume, mit vieler Lebhaftigkeit schreiben" (UN, 62).
37 On this, see Schneiders 1971, 314.
38 This text was written with support of the grant PCE 105/2021 (PNCDI III) funded by the Ministry of Research, Innovation and Digitization, CNCS/CCCDI—UEFISCDI.

Bibliography

Bartholmèss, Christian. 1851. *Histoire philosophique de l'Académie de Prusse*, vol. 2. Paris: Ducloux.
Baumgarten, Alexander Gottlieb. (1739; 1757⁴) 2014. *Metaphysics: A Critical Translation with Kant's Elucidations, Selected Notes, and Related Materials*, edited by Courtney Fugate and John Hymers. London: Bloomsbury.
Buchenau, Stefanie. 2002. "Trieb, Antrieb, Triebfeder dans la philosophie morale prékantienne." *Revue germanique internationale*, 18, 11–24.
Cochius, Leonhard. 1769. *Untersuchung über die Neigungen, welche von der königlichen Akademie der Wissenschaften zu Berlin für das Jahr 1767 ausgesetzten Preis erhalten hat. Nebst andern dahin einschlagenden Abhandlungen*. Berlin: Haude und Spener, 15–90.
Cochius, Leonhard. 1774. "Sur divers objets appartenans à la Philosophie, et particulièrement à celle de Leibniz" (1772). In *Nouveaux Mémoires de l'Académie Royale des Sciences et Belles-Lettres*, 36–42. Berlin: Voss.
Crusius, Christian August. 1999. *Anweisung vernünftig zu leben*. Hildesheim: Olms.
Dumouchel, Daniel. 2018. "Tiefen der Seele. Veränderte Zustände und psychologische Paradoxe. Die empirische Psychologie bei J. G. Sulzer." In *Johann Georg Sulzer—Aufklärung im Umbruch*, edited by Elisabeth Décultot, Philipp Kampa and Jana Kittelmann, 14–35. Berlin: De Gruyter.
Falduto, Antonino. 2014. *The Faculties of the Human Mind and the Case of Moral Feeling in Kant's Philosophy*. Berlin/Boston: De Gruyter.
Goldenbaum, Ursula. 2013. "Understanding the Argument through Then-Current Public Debates or My Detective Method of History of Philosophy." In *Philosophy and Its History. Aims and Methods in the Study of Early Modern Philosophy*, edited by Mogens Laerke, Justin E. Smith, and Eric Schliesser, 71–90. Oxford: Oxford University Press.
Harnack, Adolph von. 1900. *Geschichte der Königlich Preussischen Akademie der Wissenschaften zu Berlin*, 3 vols. Berlin: Reichsverlag.
Hourcade, Emmanuel, Charlotte Morel, and Ayşe Yuva (eds.). 2022. *La perfectibilité de l'homme. Les Lumières allemandes contre Rousseau*. Paris: Classiques Garnier.
Klemme, Heiner. 2010. "Cochius, Leonhard (1728-79)." In *The Dictionary of Eighteenth-Century German Philosophers*, edited by Heiner F. Klemme and Manfred Kuehn, 139–40. Oxford: Oxford University Press.
Laerke, Mogens. 2013. "The Antropological Analogy and the Constitution of Historical Perspectivism." In *Philosophy and Its History. Aims and Methods in the Study of Early Modern Philosophy*, edited by Mogens Laerke, Justin E. Smithy, and Eric Schliesser, 7–29. Oxford: Oxford University Press.

Leibniz, Gottfried Wilhelm. 1981. *New Essays on Human Understanding*, translated and edited by Peter Remnant and Jonathan Bennet. Cambridge: Cambridge University Press.

Mendelssohn, Moses. 1843. "Zu Cochius Über die Neigungen." In *Moses Mendelssohns Gesammelte Schriften*, vol. 4.1, edited by Georg B. Mendelssohn, 102–5. Leipzig: Brockhaus.

Nannini, Alessandro. 2021. "At the Bottom of the Soul: The Psychologization of the 'Fundus Animae' between Leibniz and Sulzer." *Journal of the History of Ideas*, 82, 1, 51–72.

Nannini, Alessandro. 2022. "Origins of the Arts, Origins of Man in Sulzer's Academic Essays." In *The Berlin Academy in the Reign of Frederick the Great: Philosophy and Science*, edited by Tinca Prunea-Bretonnet and Peter R. Anstey, Oxford University Studies in the Enlightenment, 205–31. Liverpool: Liverpool University Press.

Nannini, Alessandro. Forthcoming. "*Impetus aestheticus*: Baumgarten on Physics and Aesthetics." In *Perspectives on Science*.

Reimarus, Hermann Samuel. 1755. *Abhandlungen von den vornehmsten Wahrheiten der natürlichen Religion*. Hamburg: Bohn.

Schneiders, Werner. 1971. *Naturrecht und Liebesethik. Zur Geschichte der praktischen Philosophie im Hinblick auf Christian Thomasius*. Hildesheim: Olms.

Sulzer, Johann Georg. 1759. *Kurzer Begriff aller Wißenschaften und andern Theile der Gelehrsamkeit, worin jeder nach seinem Inhalt, Nutzen und Vollkommenheit kürzlich beschrieben wird*, 2nd edition. Leipzig: Langenheim.

Sulzer, Johann Georg. 1765. "Analyse de la raison." In *Histoire de l'Académie Royale des Sciences et Belles-Lettres* (1758), 414–32. Berlin: Haude and Spener.

Sulzer, Johann Georg. 1766a. "Explication d'un paradoxe psychologique; Que non seulement l'homme agit et juge quelquefois sans motifs et sans raisons apparentes, mais même malgré des motifs pressans et des raisons convainquantes." In *Histoire de l'Académie Royale des Sciences et Belles-Lettres* (1759), 433–50. Berlin: Haude and Spener.

Sulzer, Johann Georg. 1766b. "Sur l'apperception et son influence sur nos jugemens." In *Histoire de l'Académie Royale des Sciences et Belles-Lettres* (1764), 415–34. Berlin: Haude and Spener.

Wilson, Catherine. 2022. "The Theory of Drive: The Dual Legacy of Leibniz's Theory of Appetition." In *The Concept of Drive in Classical German Philosophy*, edited by Manja Kisner and Jörg Noller, 11–37. Cham: Palgrave Macmillan.

Wolff, Christian. 1976. *Vernünfftige Gedancken von der Menschen Thun und Lassen, zu Beförderung ihrer Glückseeligkeit* [German Ethics]. In *Gesammelte Werke*, series I, vol. 4, edited by Jean École et al. Hildesheim: Olms.

Zammito, John. 2022. "Between Reimarus and Kant: Blumenbach's Concept of Trieb." In *The Concept of Drive in Classical German Philosophy*, edited by Manja Kisner and Jörg Noller, 139–60. Cham: Palgrave Macmillan.

The Origin of Language as an Anthropological Topic: The 1769/1771 Prize Question of the Berlin Academy

Gualtiero Lorini

1. Introduction

It is difficult to identify a specific moment in the history of philosophy that can be said to have inaugurated the philosophical reflection on the nature of language. Certainly, Plato's *Cratylus* might well be, and historically has been regarded as, the starting point. Beyond the theories outlined therein, one could indeed note that the positions presented in this dialogue, with some variations, repeatedly confronted each other over the following centuries under the labels of "naturalistic" and "conventionalist" theories. Against the backdrop of this macro-debate, one can isolate a further and more specific topic, namely, the role that language plays in defining the human being. Philosophical anthropology began to search for this definition as an independent discipline—detached from theology and medicine, as well as from both empirical and rational psychology—during the Enlightenment. In this regard, we can frame some prevailing trends in recent scholarship, which we will constantly have in mind throughout this discussion.

We have convincing historical overviews, such as that offered by Hans Aarsleff (1982), which provides a dynamic picture of the lively debate concerning language, its nature, and its relation to thought, beginning in the modern age and reaching up to the dawn of contemporary linguistics. Then there are works that, endorsing a similar historical scope, specifically concentrate on the topic of the origin of language that was occasioned by the 1769–71 prize question of the Berlin Academy of Sciences (Neis 2003). Cordula Neis collects and compares the recurring topics among the essays sent to the Academy and provides a useful analysis of manuscripts that have long remained in the shadows. More recently, Avi Lifschitz effectively deals with the debates that occurred within the Berlin Academy to argue for their significant contribution to the emergence and consolidation of certain methodological instances that were central to the Enlightenment. From this perspective, he pointed out that the inquiry into the "origin" of certain core phenomena of human life, including language, fostered the Enlightenment adoption of research practices such as "conjectural history" (Lifschitz 2012), a tool that, in various forms, will frequently recur throughout our analyses. Finally, we need to mention some important studies that were particularly devoted to pivotal figures of Enlightenment research on the origin of language, such as Condillac (Tiercelin 2002; Charrak 2003) and Herder (Gesche 1993; DeSouza 2012; Waldow-DeSouza 2017), to which we will refer in the attempt to add nuance to the mainstream opinions on central issues, especially with respect to Herder.

Despite the attention that the topic has received, we currently lack any study that systematically relates the contribution of the debate on the origin of language to the search for the proper methodological lines of philosophical anthropology, a domain that from the 1770s onward (especially thanks to Kant) emerged as a philosophical discipline in its own right. The most appropriate historical contingency to address this topic is precisely the 1769 essay prize that the Berlin Academy dedicated to the origin of language because it is immediately prior to the 1770s, during which Kant introduced anthropology as an independent discipline within the didactic curriculum of the University of Königsberg.

In this chapter, however, we will have to set our sights a little earlier than the *Preisfrage* and reach further than the Academy. Indeed, we will begin by presenting the naturalism-conventionalism distinction and by exploring the views of Leibniz and Locke concerning the origin of language. We will then analyze the pivotal figure of Condillac, whose positions were partly developed and popularized by Rousseau. Condillac adheres to Lockean positions but from different assumptions. In fact, in his reflection on the origin of language, the *a priori* and *a posteriori* perspectives implicate each other, and we will take this co-implication as a fruitful common thread between the views of Leibniz, Locke, and Condillac. We will subsequently turn our attention to the Berlin Academy and the direction its research took under Maupertuis' leadership in the early 1740s. This will enable us to grasp the emergence of the theme of language in its multifarious denotations as a central topic, which is well exemplified by the prize question of 1759. Next, we will be able to address the *Preisfrage* of 1769, exploring the salient lines of Herder's winning essay and the *topoi* shared by many manuscripts. This analysis will allow us to recognize the increasingly consistent methodological trend called "hypothetical empiricism." In the last part of the essay, we will show how this "hypothetical empiricism" actually corresponds, in many respects, to the methodological needs of philosophical anthropology, thereby characterizing this discipline as the natural place for the research on the origin of language.

2. The Roots of the Prize Question

2.1. Locke and Leibniz

In an essay published in the first volume of the *Miscellanea Berolinensia* (1710), the memoirs of the Berlin Academy of Sciences, the "Brevis designatio meditationum de originibus gentium, ductis potissimum ex indicio linguarum" (A Short Outline of Reflections on the Origins of Nations, Drawn Chiefly from the Evidences of Language),

Leibniz, who had founded the Academy under the patronage of Frederick I in 1700, focuses on the theme of language and specifically on its origin. Interestingly enough, this short text is in line with an earlier fragment, which remained unpublished until 1903,[1] with the unfinished "Epistolica dissertatio" (Epistolary Dissertation) (1712), as well as with the well-known theses contained in the third book of the *New Essays*. In the context of this well-established Leibnizian interest in language, some statements from the "Brevis designatio" seem particularly relevant for our analysis. There Leibniz claims that:

> Languages have neither arisen by convention, nor as if they were established by law (*quasi lege conditae*), but have come into being by some natural impulse of men who adapted the sounds to the affections and motions of the soul [...] in languages born gradually the words have arisen accidentally from the analogy of the voice with the affections of the soul that accompanied the sensation of the thing; I tend to believe that the way Adam gave names to things did not differ from this.
> (Leibniz 1710, 2)[2]

On the one hand, Leibniz's intuition is astonishing, since he once again seems to be ahead of his time when he refers to the way in which the phonetic structure of words is mimetic with respect to the inner path that generates them (what would be labeled as "linguistic iconism" today).[3] On the other hand, considering the debate that Leibniz very likely had in mind while writing this essay, we need to notice the incredible concentration of themes converging in these few lines. Namely, both a biblical and a secular reference to the origin of language lay intertwined.[4] The first biblical element refers, albeit indirectly, to chapters 10 and 11 of Genesis. The first alludes to an ethnical-geographical origin of languages, to be traced to Noah's descendants after the Flood, who are said to have spread over the lands "every one after his tongue, after their families, in their nations" (Gen. 10: 5-6). The second describes the confusion of languages that God brings down on humans as a punishment for the sin of *hubris* and the attempt to build the Tower of Babel.[5]

Yet, by rejecting the conventional origin of language—which at the time was attributed with some imprecision to Aristotle[6]—Leibniz rather adheres to the secular-naturalistic tradition, which refers back to Epicurus' *Letter to Herodotus*. The latter maintains that the names of things have not been established by agreement, but that different groups of human beings emitted air from the phonatory organ in a manner corresponding to the particular affections they underwent and that produce certain representations (Epicurus 1925, 605; see also Gensini 2012, 187). Certainly, there are elements shared with the historicization of nature proposed in Genesis 11, but any element of sacredness is now completely absent. In the same vein, Leibniz emphasizes these affections as a prevailing component of the original human and therefore of Adam himself, who is thereby regarded as a sort of Vician beast. The original human being is in fact dominated by the passions and placed in a "rude barbarism," having "in itself more impulses than reasoning" (Leibniz 1710, 2).

We must note that Leibniz does not expressly refer to Epicurus, whose linguistic materialism had been widely diffused in the Christian tradition by Gassendi.

Nevertheless, in the *Epistolica dissertatio*[7] (ED), he defends views that come very close to Epicurus' positions. For instance, he argues for the non-conventional character of natural-historical languages. Furthermore, although leveraging Plato's *Cratylus* in an anti-conventionalist way, Leibniz agrees with Epicurus that "the drive to onomatopoeia does not come from rational choice, but from *affectus*, which is determined by randomness, the partiality of viewpoints (*respectus*), and immediate advantage (*commoditas*)" (Gensini 2020, 25; see ED §§14–5, 22). The *commoditas* mentioned here is a key term for the Epicurean interpretation. The idea that there are primitive roots common to all languages, deduced from the way in which the speaker's expressive effort responds to the sensitive stimuli of need, and that these roots would later be modified and mixed with occasional elements, is largely addressed in the *New Essays*, where Leibniz provides many examples in this regard (Leibniz 1996, 281–5).[8]

It is well known that the *New Essays* is a chapter by chapter response to Locke's *Essay*. Furthermore, if, on the one hand, the *New Essays* remained unpublished until 1765, when the Berlin Academy debate had already taken the path leading to the *Preisfrage* of 1769/1771, on the other hand, their drafting dates back to the period when the other Leibnizian texts on language discussed so far were written. Thus, it seems likely that since the "Brevis designatio", Leibniz thought of Locke (who is nevertheless not mentioned in this essay) as his main target when endorsing the naturalistic origin of language and rejecting the conventional (synonymous here with arbitrary) origin. The comparison between Leibniz's and Locke's conceptions of language is beyond the scope of our chapter, as is the analysis of book III of the *Essay* and of the corresponding book in the *New Essays*. Let us simply recall the vehemence with which, from the beginning of this book, Locke excludes any natural origin for language, unreservedly advocating its conventional origin (Locke 1975, 424–5). The polemic against any form of naturalism is substantiated as follows: "Because *Men* would not be thought to talk *barely* of their own Imaginations, but of Things as really they are; therefore, they *often suppose their Words to stand also for the reality of Things*" (Locke 1975, 407). The Leibnizian Theophilus responds: "I know that the Scholastics and everyone else are given to saying that the significations of words are arbitrary (*ex instituto*), and it is true they are not settled by natural necessity; but they are settled by reasons—sometimes natural ones in which chance plays some part, sometimes moral ones which involve choice" (Leibniz 1996, 278). He then proceeds with the etymological considerations mentioned above in an attempt to save language from the Lockean theory by arguing that words "*signify* only Men's peculiar *Ideas* [...] *by a perfectly arbitrary imposition*" (Locke 1975, 408).

Beyond the notable and more general divisions between the philosophies of Locke and Leibniz, their considerations on the origin of language reveal their conception of the relationship between language and thought. Locke is interested in language from a procedural point of view: he aims to reconstruct the process by which science refers to its contents in order to avoid errors and misunderstandings, whereas Leibniz regards language as an intrinsic component that cannot be detached from the essential structure of our reason, and thus of our thought. Despite the late publication of the *New Essays*, as we have seen, Leibniz's naturalistic position was known owing to other publications. Nevertheless, the French *philosophes* of the mid-eighteenth century were decidedly more attracted to the Lockean approach, which—as stated in Locke's *Epistle to the Reader* (Locke 1975, 8–10)—was not intended to provide universal models.

We thus face the following paradox: "Locke's *Essay* throughout the eighteenth century exercised an influence on language study which [...] was as foreign to his intentions as it would, with certain important qualifications, have been proper to those of Leibniz" (Aarsleff 1982, 69). In order to better assess the impact of these debates on the Berlin Academy, we need to go back a few years and move to France.

2.2. Coming Closer: Condillac and Rousseau

In the background to the debate on language, as it was to be addressed by the Berlin Academy during the mid-century, is Condillac's *Essay on the Origin of Human Knowledge* (1746). There, Condillac elaborates a naturalistic conception of language that is in many ways inspired by Locke's viewpoint, which Condillac tries to further develop.

For Condillac, investigating the origin of language means investigating the nature of human understanding as it expresses itself through knowledge because "the progress of the human mind depends entirely on the skill we bring to the use of language" (Condillac 2001, 69). His most relevant methodological contribution in the essay consists in an essentially semiotic consideration of knowledge, according to which signs are to be understood as a sensible artifact that allows the fulfillment of cognitive processes. In order to understand how such a view influences the research on the origin of language, we need to consider a thought experiment that was very common at the time among those who dealt with the origin of language and whose construction was basically designed to avoid conflicts with the religious authorities. Unwilling to accept that language was originally given by God to humankind, it was customary to imagine the couple who survived the universal flood. The flood would have wiped out all previous knowledge and skills in these two individuals, who then found themselves having to reacquire them from scratch.

Faced with such a scenario, Condillac asks how the children of the primordial couple began to communicate. He first identifies a strictly expressive phase: "their mutual discourse made them connect the cries of each passion to the perceptions of which they were the natural signs" (Condillac 2001, 114). These are the so-called *cris de la nature* (natural cries) that these children "usually accompanied [...] with some movement, gesture, or action that made the expression more striking" (ibid.). At this point, Condillac introduces a fundamental bodily component, namely, the so-called *language d'action* (action language): "he who suffered by not having an object his needs demanded would not merely cry out; he made as if an effort to obtain it, moved his head, his arms, and all parts of his body" (ibid.). The driving force in these passages is undoubtedly represented by need, which, similarly to the situation described by Leibniz, manifests itself gradually through a certain kind of language.[9] Habit gradually leads to the semantization of these gestures: "little by little they succeeded in doing by reflection what they had formerly done only by instinct" (Condillac 2001, 115). Thus, imagination, triggered by sign-behavior, makes it possible for "the use of signs" to have "gradually extend[ed] the exercise of the operations of the soul, and they in turn, as they gained more exercise, improved the signs and made them more familiar. Our experience shows that those two things mutually assist each other" (ibid.).

The Lockean echo, especially in reference to the role of reflection, is evident. But it should not be forgotten that the epistemic framework in which Condillac's treatment is set—namely, research into the origin of language—is foreign to Locke's perspective. This also means that the arbitrary nature of signs acquires even more weight in Condillac and poses problems that do not occur in Locke. In this regard, Condillac identifies three types of signs (Condillac 2001, 36) in his *Essai*: first, the accidental signs, which are independent of communicative purposes and refer to mere association with an object that some particular circumstance linked to a feeling. Second, the natural signs, namely the cries that are linked to a feeling of joy, fear, or pain and have a communicative purpose since they pass between two individuals who have a common "ground for their ideas" *(fonds de leurs idées)*. Finally, the instituted signs *(signes d'institution)*, the only ones that characterize human verbal language and differentiate it from the animal one. However, since this analysis of the origin of language is part of a more general consideration of human cognitive faculties, the passage from natural to arbitrary signs remains problematic. On the one hand, this passage implies the priority of reflection over signs; on the other, if the exercise of reflection is to be gradual, a different solution must be found. Opting for the latter, Condillac tries to solve the cognitive problem of the institution of arbitrary signs by advancing a consideration that relates to the communicative level: it is the practice of *commercium* among individuals that settles the use of the sign.

This is not the place to delve into Condillac's strategies aimed at avoiding the risk of a vicious circle that he foresees in these passages, strategies that would lead to the *Traité des sensations* (Treatise on the Sensations) and *La Grammaire* (Grammar).[10] For our purposes, it suffices to emphasize that the *Essai* could be considered the main common, if often critical, thread running through the essays sent to the Berlin Academy for the *Preisfrage* of 1769-71 because it conflates the two main research-lines concerning the *origin* of language. On the one hand, this topic suggests an empirical approach that aims to reconstruct the processes through which the cognitive endowments of the human being are fundamentally complemented by the emergence of a linguistic expression. This viewpoint excludes, first of all, the miraculous origin of language as a divine gift, a theme often criticized by the participants in the Academy competition. On the other hand, one cannot avoid asking about the preconditions allowing human beings to take certain steps that are not available to animals. The question is whether these prerequisites are innate faculties, qualitatively different from those possessed by animals, or whether they are aptitudes originally acquired through practices that humans are able to perform to a degree that is only quantitatively higher than the capacities of animals.

In order to understand this problem, we must overcome the classical opposition between the rationalist *a priori* approach and the empiricist *a posteriori* one. This is discernable in the naturalist position defended, rather unexpectedly, by Leibniz as well as in some Lockean pronouncements, which on the contrary seem akin to a rationalist view. On this last point, it is worth mentioning what Locke declares in a note to Burnett's *Third Remark* (1699): "I never deny'd such a power to be innate, but that which I deny'd was that any Ideas or connection of Ideas was innate" (Yolton 1956, 8).[11] The theme of the origin of language thus blurs the boundaries between these somewhat reassuring categories and, in this sense, Condillac's *Essai* is an ideal entry-point into this speculative dimension. Within it, the abstract and timeless theme of the search for a universal grammar is methodologically intertwined with a historicized hypothesis concerning the origin of language. Moreover, the structural link between the more strictly gnoseological research and its tracing back to the expressive-communicative (or social) level aroused the interest of those who, like Rousseau, have in turn attempted to reconstruct an original state of humankind, in which language plays a central role, such as the origin of inequality.

Although Rousseau devotes an essay (composed between 1754 and 1761) to the origin of languages, it was published posthumously in 1781. Therefore, we need to examine his *Discourse on the Origins of Inequality* (1755), which was repeatedly called into question by the protagonists of the debate on the origin of language in the second half of the eighteenth century. There, Rousseau openly takes his cue from Condillac: "May I be allowed to consider for an instant the obstacles to the origin of Languages. I could be satisfied to cite or repeat here the researches that the Abbé de Condillac has made on this matter, which all fully confirm my sentiment, and which perhaps gave me the first idea of it" (Rousseau 1992, 29). The core problem that Rousseau faces in this regard exemplifies, and in some ways enriches socially, the epistemological problems emerging from Condillac's *Essai*. Rousseau imagines humans as "having neither houses, nor huts, nor property of any kind, [...] Males and females united fortuitously, depending on encounter, occasion, and desire, without speech being a very necessary interpreter of the things they had to say to each other" (Rousseau 1992, 30). Yet despite admitting that "men needed speech in order to learn to think, they had even greater need of knowing how to think in order to discover the art of speech" (ibid.). Here Rousseau faces the most pressing problem, namely: "Which was most necessary, previously formed society for the institution of languages; or previously invented languages for the establishment of society?"—a question that he leaves "to whomever would undertake it" (ibid., 33). However, when Rousseau comes back to the issue in the second part of the text, he considers the emergence of language as dependent upon a rudimentary form of social organization, thereby adopting a solution similar to that explored by Condillac. Indeed, need gave the primitive human being "some crude idea of mutual engagements" (ibid., 45), so that he or she developed "some sort of reflection, or rather a mechanical prudence that indicated to him the precautions most necessary for his safety" (ibid., 44).

By admitting some form of proto-society, and hence proto-communication driven by need, Rousseau is embracing Condillac's hypothesis. The fact that such positions were often exclusively attributed to Rousseau in the German debate of the mid-eighteenth century, and also within the Berlin Academy, may be due to the fact that while Rousseau's *Discourse on the Origins of Inequality* was translated into German in 1756, Condillac's *Essai* was not translated until 1780 (Aarsleff 1982, 156). However, Rousseau's considerations should be taken with due care, the same carefulness that orients his assumption about the state of nature: "The Philosophers who have examined the foundations of society [...] speaking continually of need, avarice, oppression, desires, and pride, have carried over to the state of nature ideas they had acquired in society: they spoke about savage man and they described Civil man" (Rousseau 1992, 18–9).

The debate could therefore focus on the natural endowment we are willing to grant human beings in the state of nature. Indeed, even if communication—and thus language—were a primordial need, it may have gradually become a derived need, one that stems from the need to cooperate in order to guarantee the minimal conditions of security that each individual has agreed to uphold. This issue therefore requires, once again, that we carefully move between the *a priori* and the *a posteriori* in order to avoid oversimplifications. And here as well, the convergence between Locke and Condillac provides some interesting elements. For however vivid the debate about the characteristics and needs of humans in the state of nature proved to be, it was obvious that this was a conjectural model. The manner in which Condillac uses this working-hypothesis in the linguistic domain is very reminiscent of Locke's use of it in the *Second Treatise on Government*, that is, with a clear political goal in mind. The anthropological background—often nourished by reports of journeys to exotic places and primitive people—that Locke's construction of the political state of nature shares with Condillac's linguistic state of nature has rightly been regarded as belonging to comparative anthropology (Aarsleff 1982, 161–2). In this respect, in order to clarify some of the questions we have encountered so far, we should include the treatment of the origin of language in the field of philosophical anthropology, whose methodology emerged during these same years.

3. The Prize Question of 1769/1771

3.1. Back to Berlin

This complex epistemic picture found an ideal development in Prussia starting in the 1740s, when Frederick the Great—whose Francophilia is well known—invited Maupertuis to preside over the Academy of Sciences and Belles-Lettres. Maupertuis was very interested in the debate on the origin of language, was familiar with Condillac's *Essai*, and dedicated at least two important works to the topic. In the "Réflexions philosophiques sur l'origine des langues et la signification des mots" (Philosophical Reflections on the Origin of Languages and the Signification of Words),[12] he criticized the arbitrary assignment of linguistic signs for not considering the possible errors deriving from the use of words, while in the "Dissertation sur les différents moyens dont les hommes se sont servis pour exprimer leurs idées" (Dissertation on the Different Means that Men Have Used to Express their Ideas) (Engl, 1756), he explored the general principles that led each people to form its own language.[13] Owing to his position, Maupertuis promoted this perspective in Berlin. Two essays read by J.P. Süssmilch, a respected demographer, at the Academy on October 7 and 14, 1756, should be interpreted in this context.[14] These texts were published in 1766 under the title "Attempt to Prove That the First Language Did Not Originate from Man, but from the Creator Alone."[15] The title reveals Süssmilch's main thesis, but it simultaneously contains the premises of a misunderstanding that frequently accompanied its reception, primarily within the Academy.

Süssmilch's intention is indeed not to demonstrate that language is a divine product that is given to human beings by God, nor to explain how this transmission came about. Rather, he aims to demonstrate the impossibility of an origin of language deriving from human invention through a "mere philosophical" (*bloss philosophisch*) procedure (Süssmilch 1766, Pref., 5). In an appendix to his text, in which he confronts Rousseau's *Discourse on the Origins of Inequality*, he admits that he has not read Condillac's *Essai* (ibid., 118n). He nevertheless seems to go against Condillac's position—probably known to him through Maupertuis—when he rejects the idea that humans originally possessed some pre-verbal rational capacity that would have allowed them to gradually rise above the animal ways of communication. While sharing the fundamental idea of a structural relationship between language and thought, and therefore between language and reason with the main protagonists of the debate, Süssmilch considers it inadmissible that the perfection and order (*Vollkommenheit und Ordnung*) characteristic of human languages could have been achieved gradually, since the exercise of reason that is necessary to this achievement would have required a fully developed language (ibid., 33–4). Süssmilch thus frames "the reciprocal development of language and reason identified by Condillac" in a more limited treatment, aimed at studying how human beings have historically used language as an instrument of reason (Kieffer 1978, 102). However, the origin of language must be excluded from a strictly philosophical consideration. In this regard, although one can only opt for a non-philosophical path, the fact that this path is in harmony with Scripture does not mean that it invokes Scripture as the authoritative foundation of any rational justification. As we shall see, this *fideistic* reading of Süssmilch's essay was quite diffuse.

Such a lively discussion drove the Academy to propose a prize question related to this topic in the public assembly of June 9, 1757, which formalized a question that was not yet focused on the origin of language, but that prepared the ground for the later prize essay. The text read: *What Is the Reciprocal Influence of People's Opinions on Language and of Language on Opinions?*[16] In 1759, the winner was announced as the distinguished orientalist Johann David Michaelis with the essay "Answering the Question of the Influence of Opinions on Language, and Language on Opinions."[17] This text reflects a very rich understanding of the debate developed in the French Enlightenment and, through the analysis of the positive and negative effects of language on thought, argues for an inescapable determination of the latter by the former.[18] Of particular interest for our analysis is the wish expressed by Michaelis at the end of his essay. He hopes that attention will be paid to the following issue: "How would a language come into being at first among men who previously had none, and how would it gradually reach its present perfection and elaboration?" (Michaelis 1760, 78) Within a decade, the Academy accepted this invitation and published a question which seemed to indicate that the way in which the problem should be addressed should programmatically exclude the idea of a divine origin of language. The text of the *Preisfrage* of 1769 reads: "Assuming that men are left to their natural faculties, are they in a condition to invent language? And by what means will they arrive at this invention of their own accord? A hypothesis is required which would explain the thing clearly, and which would satisfy all the difficulties."

3.2. The Winning Essay and the Honorable Mentions

Herder won the competition with a text titled "Treatise on the Origin of Language" (Abhandlung über den Ursprung der Sprache). Although he later openly declared his dissatisfaction with the text,[19] Herder's essay was considered a real watershed in the history of the reflection on language for a long time. This judgment was attenuated in many quarters in the last few years, for reasons that we will briefly outline below.

Herder argues for the intrinsically linguistic nature of the human being as a rational being and he clearly differentiates the human being from animals insofar as man "has no such uniform and narrow sphere where only a single sort of work awaits him; a world of occupations and destinies surrounds him. His senses and organization are not sharpened for a single thing; he has senses for everything and hence naturally for each particular thing weaker and duller senses" (Herder 2002, 79). The human being does not have any mechanical instinct, to which the origin of language might be attributable: "*What language [...] does the human being possess as instinctively as each animal species possesses its language in, and in accordance with, its own sphere? The answer is short: none! [...] The bee hums just as it sucks, the bird sings just as it makes a nest ... But how does the human being speak by nature? Not at all!*" (ibid., 80). The human being compensates for this instinctual deficiency by means of an ability called "awareness" (*Besonnenheit*): "In the whole ocean of sensations which floods the soul through all the senses," this awareness allows the human being to "separate off, stop, and pay attention to a single wave, and be conscious of its own attentiveness" (Herder 2002, 87). Such a *Besonnenheit* is an essential characteristic of the human species, and through its exercise, reflection develops as a rational activity,[20] so that "the invention of language is hence as natural for him as is his being a human being!" (ibid., 87). The sense in which this invention can be defined as "natural" thus rests upon a meaning of "nature" that is completely different from that which humans might share with animals.[21] Humans develop a plastic and creative tool such as language precisely because they cannot rely on the safe, if mechanical, guidance of the instincts that govern animal behavior:

> If the human being had animal *senses*, then he would have no *reason*; for precisely his senses' strong susceptibility to stimulation, precisely the representations mightily pressing on him through them, would inevitably choke all cold awareness [*Besonnenheit*].
>
> (Herder 2002, 84)

Besonnenheit allows us to look at the lamb without being driven by the hunger of the wolf, nor by the sexual desire of the ram: "Not so to the human being! As soon as he develops a need to become acquainted with the sheep, no instinct disturbs him, no sense tears him too close to the sheep or away from it; it stands there exactly as it expresses itself to his senses" (Herder 2002, 88). Human beings indeed have a cognitive approach to reality. They try to organize their experience, so they look for "an inward characteristic word" (*innerliches Merkwort*) (ibid., 89), which they identify with the sheep's bleating: "this was a *grasped sign* on the occasion of *which the soul distinctly recalled to awareness an idea*. What else is that but a word?" (ibid.).

The peculiar human understanding of nature and of animality makes Herder claim during the opening of his essay that "Already as an animal, the human being has language" (Herder 2002, 65). This claim allows Bruce Kiefer to contend that "Süssmilch and Herder alike assert that man had language from the beginning of his existence as man: Süssmilch out of a belief in divine necessity [...] Herder out of a belief in natural necessity" (Kiefer 1978, 102). Although their assumptions are different, Herder's violent criticisms of Süssmilch go beyond a mere divergence of premises. He openly accuses Süssmilch of leaving the origin of language entirely to "divine instruction" (Herder 2002, 91) and attributes such a position that he rejects to Süssmilch. He thereby misses the essence of Süssmilch's position, as described above.[22]

Something similar happens with Herder's main polemical target, Condillac.[23] Herder does not accept Condillac's idea of a gradual transition from the action language (*language d'action*) to the articulate verbal language, and he vehemently contests what he regards as an Epicurean-style naturalness. He denies that the genesis of human language can be reconstructed starting from a gradual emergence of the human being from a condition similar to that of animals, and in this passage regards the work of the understanding as the intentional organizer of the cry of nature (*cris de la nature*) as essential.[24] Aarsleff argues that Herder refers only to the second part of Condillac's *Essai* without taking into account that in the first the French philosopher dwells on the role of reflection, which allows us to more adequately contextualize the second part on the origin of language within a more general investigation of human knowledge. The paradoxical result of Herder's lacuna is that, in order to challenge Condillac, he ends up reconstructing the second part of the *Essai* in the *Abhandlung*, showing that he is unfamiliar with it (see Aarsleff 1982, 198). It thus becomes apparent that Herder picks up and reworks topics that were already in the air—above all the structural relationship between language and thought in the human being in a particularly lively style. He identifies the genesis of language with the capacity, qualitatively peculiar to man, through which human beings imprint a characteristic mark of the activity of taking-awareness on their consciousness.

When Herder criticizes Condillac, he often pairs the French philosopher with Rousseau.[25] However, Herder's polemic against Rousseau depends less on a misinterpretation of the latter's positions than in the cases of Süssmilch and Condillac. At the core of Herder's criticism of Rousseau lays an anthropological conception that strongly questions Rousseau's historical pessimism. For Herder, even the most savage child remains a human being and, in this sense, education—which is necessary for instinctually poorly endowed beings—does not corrupt the individual but rather makes him or her authentically human. This holds true, paradigmatically so, for language (Herder 2002, 145). Thus, on the one hand, Herder often distorts the positions of the authors he aims to attack. On the other, as his remarks are not particularly original when compared with those of the other contestants, as we shall see, it is likely that his brilliant style played a decisive role in his success in the competition. An excellent example of Herder's overconfidence is his acknowledgment that he transgressed the second part of the Academy's request, since in contrast with the "philosophical novel—*Rousseau's, Condillac's*, and others," he claims to not need hypotheses, to have rather collected "firm data" (Herder 2002, 164) concerning the question at stake.

In response to the prize question, the Academy received thirty-one essays.[26] many of which impressed the judges by their sharpness and depth. Johann Bernhard Merian's report, for instance, emphasizes the difficulty of the choice due to the high value of several essays. This is confirmed by the high number of *accessits* (honorable mentions): six as opposed to the usual one or two. These essays were presented anonymously, so most of their authors remain unknown to us today. The authorship of only one *accessit* essay can be established with certainty, namely that of the Latin empirically oriented contribution of the Italian Francesco Soave (M666).[27] Three further essays, submitted in German, should be mentioned. One of them (M667) was criticized by the judges for not dealing with the topic, while nevertheless being awarded an *accessit* for reasons that are still debated by scholars (Neis 2003, 107). Another essay (M672) presents an erudite and well-documented discussion based on sensuous premises that expands on the language-thought relationship, as well as a comparison between human language and animal forms of communication. The third essay (M683) is notable for the original research devoted to native languages (including Chinese and Coptic). Finally, there is a further essay written in Latin that was awarded an *accessit* (M674). It is mainly epistemological in nature and argues for the dependence of thought on language, on the basis of Wolff's *Psychologia rationalis* (Rational Psychology).[28]

3.3. The Common Topics

Neis' careful scrutiny of the essays revealed the recurrence of certain topics. While we cannot exhaustively analyze them here, the main topics are worth mentioning: the language of animals, of infants and toddlers; the problem of "wild boys" and "woodsmen"; the case of exotic peoples, and deaf-mutes; as well as the relationship between thought and language,[29] and between thought and society. One fundamental methodological assumption of these essays is the possibility of reconstructing linguistic phylogeny through a study of ontogeny, which leads us to consider the topic of infants and toddlers and to grasp its frequent connection with that of feral children and woodsmen. This already emerges in Soave's essay which, referring to Condillac, sketches an anthropological picture of the state of nature that is modeled on the family. Through the valorization of the affective mother-child relationship, he develops a counter-model of the isolationism that characterizes Rousseau's state of nature (M666, 7 and 10). For Soave, the child is driven by need toward its parents to make intentional use of vocal signs. An important source of the genesis and development of these sounds is Charles De Brosses (1765), whom Soave explicitly quotes regarding the universality of the sound inventory that leads all children to articulate the words "mum" and "dad" first (M666, 61).

The author of M672 (88–9) admits, in partial agreement with Rousseau, that as children grow up, they can leave their mother. However, he does not exclude the possibility of a longer stay of the child within the family and this allows the author—in line with Condillac and Soave—to trace the origin of language back to need (*besoin*).

M686 attributes an important role to onomatopoiesis through which children initially name things. A case study similar to the one described in this essay is recalled by M675, who attributes a great importance to children in the investigation of the origin of language. The author, however, first criticizes the isolationist view of the Rousseauian state of nature, and then considers a single child as a possible example of the first nomothete, taking its lullabies and natural tendency to monologue as proof of the fact that, although society can contribute to the development and maintenance of language, it is not necessary for its emergence (M675, 13). Hereby, the author dismisses Rousseau's dilemma concerning the anteriority of either language or society, limiting himself to the example of a single ideal child who (contrary to Condillac and Rousseau) cannot actually be nomothetic, because in the archaic societies to which these authors refer, the despotism of the *pater familias* is still in force. It follows that "both the child and the parents must have contributed to some extent to the invention of language" (M675, 33).

The participants in the prize essay contest are divided regarding the primacy of parents or children in the invention of language. The author of M678 refers to the numerous nonsensical words that children invent at home, which they must (learn to) abandon as they grow up, with the help of their parents: "Our children should neither enrich the language nor form a new one" (M678, 17). In contrast, Michaelis—in line with the author of M683—attaches great importance to the contribution of children not only for their enrichment of language, but also for its emergence. In this sense, the imitative impulse of children, which distinguishes them from animals, is fundamental. The particular plasticity of this capacity in infants and young children means that, unlike adults, they have a spontaneous and hedonistic use of the organs of articulation, to the point that Michaelis sees a kind of automatic mechanism between the organs of hearing and those of voice production. He argues that "human nature has an impulse to speak [*ein Trieb zu reden*]" (Michaelis 1760, 19), a claim founded on personal observational evidence. In this regard, and against Rousseau, Michaelis values the child's emotional relationship with the mother (ibid., 39–40). Moreover, the author does not consider the observations on feral children to be conclusive, as they lack an important component for language development, namely the acoustic model of a spoken language, which they can only encounter in a civilized environment (ibid., 18–9).

These observations intersect with two other important topics. The first, which we will not delve into, is that of deaf-mutes, considered within a broader investigation into the possibility of inventing language by individuals who are characterized by some kind of deficiency. The second, which is part of this broader framework, concerns feral children, who can be compared to infants, with the difference that the deficiencies that infants overcome with growth remain in feral children. A further development in this vein is the research on "woodsmen."[30] A text that is interesting in this respect is M667, which, in the wake of Rousseau's thought, regards the child as possessing an instinctual endowment that is useful for understanding what primitive humans were like. The author claims that education reduces this endowment, but recognizes that the human being's instinctual resources are still less rich than those of animals, as can be seen by observing "woodsmen" (M667, 9–10). Although this essay does not directly deal with the origin of language, it calls for the need to cross-reference different themes that address the problem of language from an essentially anthropological point of view.[31]

The authors also disagree regarding the relevance of the case studies about "savages." Like Michaelis, but for different reasons, the author of M667 rejects the idea that savages can serve as an example of the original human condition because strictly speaking, on his account, they are not human. Nor is it possible for a child, even if left to its own devices, to engage in a behavior that is typical for savages. In this sense, the author of the manuscript also rejects the widespread idea that exotic peoples can be regarded as savages because an individual raised in a culture that is different than that of the observer's cannot be equated with an individual raised in the wild, whose very humanity can be questioned (M667, 2). The essay M674, for instance, considers the topic from a gnoseological point of view and examines the cognitive faculties that are naturally present in the human being in order to understand whether one could have developed something as complex as human language if left on one's own. The essay combines an empirical reading with an interpretation of Genesis, according to which the Creator bestows a linguistic capacity – and not a language – on humans. Yet, if language is a "denotation of ideas" (*denotatio idearum*) (M674, 13), the problem of how to arrive at "simple ideas" (*ideae simplices*) remains open. On Locke's account, we arrive at these simple ideas through observation from experience, that is, through sensation (*sensation*), perception (*perception*), and attention (*attention*). Consciousness arises between *sensatio* and *perceptio*, while *attentio* exercises that prelinguistic selective capacity that characterizes the human being and reminds us of Condillac's *attention* as well as of Herder's *Besonnenheit*. Now, the perception observed in humans, understood as the first step toward conscious representation and therefore toward knowledge, is considered to be an endowment that is independent from language to the extent that it is also observed in domestic animals recognizing their masters. Yet, some evidence shows, the author argues, that feral children who are lacking language have no knowledge at all, as if in their case perception were language dependent. The author solves the problem by contending that perception and attention are natural, not because they are innate, but because they are original acquisitions (*acquisitiones originariae*) (M674, 26).[32] These elements should suffice for the examination of the methodological constants with which the recurrent themes are treated and made to interact with each other.

4. Emerging Methodological Characters

4.1. The Isolation Experiment

One of the most widespread methodological strategies of the prize essays is a thought experiment already encountered in Condillac. It consists in studying the linguistic development of children who are imagined to have grown up in conditions of total isolation from society. The source of these thought experiments is the so-called "Psammetichus" experiment, narrated by Herodotus. Aiming to find out if there existed peoples more ancient than the Egyptians through the study of languages, the Egyptian king Psammetichus I (seventh century BC) ordered a shepherd to raise two children in complete isolation, feeding them with the milk of his goats and never letting them hear a word. After two years, these children began to pronounce the sound "bekos" at the sight of the goats and the king. Upon verifying that the Phrygians refer to bread in a similar way, he concluded that Phrygian was the oldest language of humankind.

This experiment has undergone an innumerable series of transformations in the course of history, but beyond its obvious evidential limitations, it is interesting to note the different attitudes endorsed by the participants of the 1769 prize question. Without going into the ethical reservations regarding the admissibility of this experiment, doubts about its feasibility and reliability are raised by M683 (M683, 3). Similarly, for M667, the "small induction" of mental experiments does not tell us whether and why things would actually take this direction: in the case of Psammetichus' experiment, for example, it seems that children do not achieve a (proto) language except in the presence of some form of sociality (for instance, when the shepherd arrives with the goats). Therefore, they conclude, it seems necessary instead to "question nature directly" (M667, 4).

A similar position is held by essay M668, which prefers Condillac's account that analyzes two children of both sexes on an island. The author of this manuscript considers it plausible that the children would have been raised by wild animals in such a context, on the basis of some travel accounts and of the myth of the Capitoline twins.[33] Furthermore, he considers Psammetichus' experiment as artificial because of its rejection of the social egalitarianism promoted by Rousseau's state of nature. For the author of this manuscript, it is impossible for relations of domination and subordination to not arise immediately in a large social group, and this would distort the neutrality and therefore the reliability of the experiment. It is interesting that the artificiality of Psammetichus' experiment is also asserted by those who, like the author of M681, hold a view of the state of nature that is similar to Rousseau's. Although he draws on the Lucretian idea that "convenience produced the names of things" (*utilitas expressit nomina rerum*), he contends that this does not apply to this experiment because the children are provided with everything they need to survive. By denying that these children have a motivation to develop language, the author seems to agree with Süssmilch, who rejects the Lucretian conception of the state of nature. Whereas Süssmilch, himself, concluded that language must come from God, the author of this manuscript argues that it arises when humans associate to safeguard themselves (M681, 66).

4.2. Hypothetical Empiricism

Beyond the intrinsic interest of each of the theses, their common thread is the attempt to access a dimension that cannot be directly documented through an empirical-observational approach, such as the original scenario in which humanity—and with it language—arose. Abbot Copineau (M673, 5-6), who also refers to Psammetichus with Condillacian accents, precisely insists on the way in which the observer must behave in order to ensure the best conditions for the experiment. The need for observation and thus the search for the modalities of a correct observation are indeed inescapable aspects to be taken into account in order to at least approximate an origin that, in itself, unavoidably remains conjectural. As it becomes increasingly clear, this methodological approach implies an inextricable interweaving of induction and deduction. The observation of individuals in certain developmental stages (infants and toddlers, for example) or social (savages) situations was often enriched by narratives and reports that were very popular during the eighteenth century, such as chronicles of exploration in exotic countries where, for example, explorers had come into contact with 'native' populations. These kinds of texts were widely circulated in the eighteenth century and were exposed to distortions.

Such elements represent the prerequisites for the elaboration of thought experiments, of which Psammetichus is the most striking example. The extension of ontogenetic observation to the phylogenetic hypothesis needs a ground-casuistry and the reservoir of empirical observations provided by the travel literature responds precisely to this need. The construction of numerous variants of Psammetichus' experiment is based on the observations made on wild children, enriched by the comparison with the development of children in civilized contexts, on the one hand, and by the reports of explorers returning from exotic lands, on the other. This state of affairs determined the rise of what has been perspicuously defined as "hypothetical empiricism" (Neis 2003, 231).[34] Such expression effectively summarizes some of the methodological characteristics of the discipline that, owing to Kant, acquired its own defined philosophical and academic status during this period: anthropology. Indeed, the analysis of the manuscripts sent to the Academy shows an amplification of the difficulties encountered by Condillac and by all those who followed in his footsteps in their investigation of the origin of language. The problem essentially consists in the fact that, by questioning the origin of language, we cannot completely maintain either a strict empiricism or rationalism. Condillac is in explicit continuity with Locke regarding the centrality of the conventional-arbitrary element in his theory, while at the same time, he also endorses Leibnizian elements, such as the idea that the sign-process grounds human thought as well as the idea that the determination of signs corresponding to experiences unfolds gradually. Leibniz concedes a lot to the Epicurean viewpoint on these topics in turn, albeit without explicitly identifying them as Epicurean. In sum, it is important, if not essential, for us to understand how the method of the rising philosophical anthropology was influenced by the need to effectively deal with the tensions characterizing the investigation of the origin of language.

5. Beyond the Academy Prize Question: Language as an Anthropological Issue

Not long after the French and German discussions on the question of the origin of language, James Burnett's (Lord Monboddo's) *Of the Origin and Progress of Language* (1773) was published in England. Monboddo's proposal is radically empiricist and, to some extent, reminiscent of the conclusions advanced by the essay M674. He admits of two natures in the human being: one strictly animal and one that led humans to rise from the former. This second nature is completely acquired, being the result of a spirit of adaptability that is not dissimilar to Herder's *Besonnenheit* but which does not allow the identification of any specific *a priori* feature of human nature. By virtue of this characteristic of our species, we "*make* ourselves, as it were, over again, so that the *original* nature in us can hardly be seen; and it is with the greatest difficulty that we can distinguish it from the *acquired*" (Monboddo 1773, 24–5). According to Monboddo, both thought and language belong to our acquired nature. This applies to the material component of language (the voice, for instance) that individuals suffering from communication deficiencies are unable to develop, as well as to the formal and logical component, based on the abstraction and the conceptual universalization required by science.[35] These brief indications serve to show us that, even beyond the continental debate, the question of the origin of language was increasingly discussed within the context of a broader consideration of human beings in their complexity, a complexity for which the rigid opposition between *a priori* and *a posteriori* proved to be inadequate. The investigation into the origin of language constantly confronts us with an essential question that can be formulated as follows: should we focus on the *a priori* adaptability that allows humans to shape language in accordance with their needs, or should we examine the concrete *a posteriori* ways in which language is actually structured?

It seems impossible to strictly retain only one alternative without losing a central component of human nature. Significantly, very similar conclusions to those of Monboddo's are drawn roughly thirty years later by Jean Itard, the physician who studied and tried to educate Victor d'Aveyron, the famous savage child.[36] For Itard, too, "the finest prerogative" of the human species consists in "the capacity to develop its intelligence by the force of imitation under the influence of the society in which it is placed" (Itard 1994, 3). It is perhaps no coincidence that such similar results are obtained in this thirty-year period in philosophy and medicine. It is at the crossroads of these two disciplines that anthropology comes to its own strictly philosophical determination in the eighteenth century, owing to Kant, who begins to teach the new discipline called anthropology in the early 1770s.[37]

The absence of an extensive thematization of language by Kant has often and rightfully been emphasized. However, it is significant that one of the few places where he addresses this topic is precisely his *Anthropology*, where we immediately encounter some of the mentioned theses. Kant characterizes the relation between language and thought by defining "all language" as "a signification of thought […,] the best way of signifying thought," because "thinking is *speaking* with oneself" (AA 7: 192; Louden 2007, 300). In this regard, he provides two examples of exotic peoples and of individuals with communication deficits. The first example refers to "the Indians of Tahiti," who "call thinking 'speech in the belly.'" In the second example, Kant claims that "[t]o the man born deaf, his speaking is a feeling of the play of his lips, tongue, and jaw; and it is hardly possible to imagine that he does anything more by his speaking than carry on a play with physical feelings, without having and thinking real concepts" (ibid.). Beyond these specific, relatively isolated references, the very conception of a philosophical anthropology requires the methodological elements brought to the fore as inescapable by the investigation of the origin of language. Above all was the observational approach: in a letter to Markus Herz about the introduction of anthropology among his academic lectures, Kant defines anthropology as an observational doctrine (*Beobachtungslehre*).[38]

This approach is identical to the one elaborated in 1764 in his *Observations on the Feeling of the Beautiful and Sublime*, which anticipates themes dealt with in the lectures on anthropology. On Kant's account, such topics must be considered "more with the eye of an observer than of the philosopher" (BGSE 2, 207; Guyer 2007, 23).

Furthermore, at the heart of the most original part of Kant's anthropology, the *Anthropological Characteristic*, there is a definition of "character" as a "way of thinking" (*Denkungsart*), which means "that property of the will by which the subject binds himself to definite practical principles that he has prescribed to himself irrevocably by his own reason" (AA 7: 291–2; 389–90). In this framework, "it does not depend on what nature makes of the human being, but of what the human being *makes of himself*" (ibid., 390). If we take into consideration the way in which, in the debate on the origin of language, the adaptability of the human being imposed itself as a decisive component that explains the emergence from mere animality, these passages from Kant's *Anthropology* do sound familiar. Indeed, on the one hand, human adaptability is certainly stimulated by the need to survive, but on the other hand, it requires the ability to identify effective norms for the success of the adaptation process and, more so, the strength to freely elevate these norms to laws. This free self-imposition of a behavioral norm constitutes the human being's character as a "way of thinking." In this pivotal notion of Kant's anthropology, we thus find a necessary co-implication of *a priori* and *a posteriori* elements. Such a mutual interaction reminds us of the need to reconceive the boundaries between these crucial perspectives, a need that constantly emerged in the foregoing debates on the origin of language. This issue mirrors and amplifies the problematic transition we started from, namely the interplay between the human natural linguistic endowment and the enrichment of language.

The foundations of Kant's philosophical conception of anthropology thus seem to share many salient methodological features with the discussion about the origin of language during the mid-eighteenth century. This should not be surprising considering Kant's openness to the most heated debates of his time, debates that were often either directly prompted or otherwise revived by the Berlin Academy.[39] Despite the fact that Kant did not directly engage with the question concerning the origin of language, the methodological needs uncovered by this discussion shaped some pivotal notions of his anthropology, such as the understanding of human character as *Denkungsart*. We can verify this reading by assessing Kant's proximity to one of the major contributions to the development of later anthropology that can be credited to the eighteenth-century discussion of the origin of language. As Lia Formigari has argued, in the panorama of Enlightenment anthropology, "Monboddo is, perhaps with Herder, the only one who traces the origins of language to the praxis of associated work, avoiding the error that Engels, describing in the *Dialectic of Nature* the process of humanization of the ape, still reproaches the anthropology of his time, that of explaining activity by thought instead of by needs" (Formigari 1972, 32). On the one hand, with respect to this evaluation, Kant does not cease to consider thought as the human core characteristic, the background against which language must be understood and studied. Yet on the other hand, Kant's anthropology brings the need for mutual interaction between the *a priori* and *a posteriori* perspective in the investigation of the human being to its most acute and systematic expression, thereby valuing such a complex debate as the origin of language, with all its social implications. This becomes evident in Kant's *Anthropological Characteristic*, in which he defends the idea that humanity achieves and expresses its authentic character not in the individual, but only in the species (AA 7: 321–33). This leads to a cosmopolitan perspective, where the individual's *a priori* endowment (reason) confronts them with the inadequacy of the means to achieve their moral destination individually, thereby revealing association as the pragmatic way to reach that goal. This state of affairs puts the onus on the human being to empirically identify effective strategies for achieving the best model of coexistence.

Although language is not at the center of Kant's reflections on these fundamental anthropological dynamics, we can easily identify many of the crucial topics dealt with in the prize essays of 1769–71 here, as well as in Monboddo's texts, such as the drives and structures of human relations,[40] the socialization of knowledge, and the role of education. Therefore, it is fair to conclude that thanks to the problems highlighted by the investigation on the origin of language, philosophical anthropology acquired a growing self-awareness of its distinctive methodological approach during these crucial years.

Notes

1   The fragment was published by Couturat (Leibniz 1903).
2   Unless otherwise indicated, all translations are mine.
3   The central idea, promoted by C.S. Peirce, is that language is not reducible to its symbolic-arbitrary component, but contains an intrinsically imitative character of non-linguistic realities. For instance, see Wescott 1971.
4   Besides the reference to Adam's language, Leibniz, while explaining that he does not want to deal with artificial languages, points out: "such, also, will have been the language that God taught men, if He did so" (Leibniz 1710, 2).
5   The idea that originally all humanity spoke the same language is variously attested to in the Western intellectual tradition. A perspicuous example is Dante's *De vulgari eloquentia* (I, 388–405), in which it is assumed that the original language was Hebrew. In the transition from this treatise to the *Commedia* (Pd, XXVI, 130–2), Dante grants greater autonomy to human beings in the development of language.
6   The traditional reference in this sense is Aristotle's *De interpretatione*, 16a20. Notoriously, the mediation of Boethius contributes to the reception of Aristotle's position on the origin of language.
7   Attention to this text was first drawn by Schulenburg 1973.
8   In these pages, Leibniz also recalls the limits of etymology and philology in an attempt to thoroughly reconstruct these roots. Lifschitz 2012, chapter 3, rightly insists on the problem—which arises here but will become particularly urgent in Condillac and his critics—of the transition between the original-natural and the acquired-artificial levels of language. We will come back to this issue.
9   "The use of signs *gradually* extended the exercise of the operations of the soul, and they in turn, as they gained more exercise, improved the signs and made them more familiar" (Condillac 2001, 115; emphasis added).
10 On this topic see: Duchesneau 1974; Pichevin 1978; Trabant 1986; Pécharman 1999; Tiercelin 2002; Charrak 2003, 95–116; and Coratelli 2014. Among the most

recent reconstructions, Lifschitz (2012, 28–9) is particularly accurate in relating the problem of reconciling the natural origin of language with later conventional acquisitions as it is encountered in Condillac. Lifschitz (2012, 29) stresses Condillac's transition from "'arbitrary' (in 1746) to 'artificial' (in 1775)" signs, a distinction "meant to address the apparent incommensurability between natural sounds on the one hand, and manmade, instituted signs on the other."

11 "Locke was much more than the *Essay*, and something quite different from the sort of empiricist he has later [...] been made out to have been. In our terms Locke was, like Descartes, a rationalist" (Aarsleff 1982, 160).

12 The text was translated into English in 1748. Beeson 1987 questioned the dating of the *Réflexions* in 1748 and proposed 1740 instead, but his arguments, although robust, are still debated.

13 There is also further evidence of Maupertuis' linguistic interests, such as the dissertation presented at the Academy on June 18, 1750, on "Les devoirs de l'académicien" (The Duties of the Academician) or the 1752 "Lettre sur le progrès des sciences" (Letter on the Progress of the Sciences).

14 At the outset of the preface (Süssmilch 1766, Pref., 3–4), Süssmilch states that he became interested in the subject after hearing an essay by Maupertuis, which was none other than the *Dissertation*.

15 *Versuch eines Beweises, daß die erste Sprache ihren Ursprung nicht vom Menschen, sondern allein vom Schöpfer erhalten habe.*

16 *Quelle est l'influence réciproque des opinions du peuple sur le langage et du langage sur les opinions?*

17 *Beantwortung der Frage von dem Einfluss der Meinungen in die Sprache, und der Sprache in die Meinungen.* The text was published in 1760, but its success was ensured by its translation into French: "De l'influence de l'opinion sur le langage, et du langage sur l'opinion" (1762). For a more detailed discussion of this text, see Smith 1976 and Haßler-Neis 2009, 415–17.

18 See particularly Sections 2, 3, and 4. Cf. Lifschitz 2012, 91–4, who interestingly highlights Prémontval's role in the choice of the theme for the 1759 *Preisfrage*.

19 Herder himself reports that he wrote the essay in great haste and sent it shortly before the deadline. These circumstances are partially the cause of his later dissatisfaction with the text. For instance, see the letter to Nicolai of February 1772, in Düntzer-Herder 1861, 328.

20 On this, see also Lifschitz 2012, 184, who renders *Besonnenheit* as "active reflection."

21 This feature is highlighted by Waldow 2017, 153.

22 We cannot go into more detail here about Herder's remarkable misinterpretations of Süssmilch. See Kieffer 1978, 102–4, who also deals with the inadequate rendering of Süssmilch's text in Herder's *Abhandlung*.

23 In the wake of the works of Gesche 1993 and DeSouza 2012, Zammito 2017 emphasizes that, beyond Herder's polemic with Süssmilch and Condillac, central to Herder's "effort to develop a naturalistic yet distinctive theory of the origin of human language, by drawing a new conception of the animal-human boundary," was his engagement with H.S. Reimarus and the theory of animal instinct (Zammito 2017, 128).

24 To provide just one of many available examples: "But I cannot conceal my astonishment that philosophers, that is, people who seek distinct concepts, were ever able to arrive at the idea of explaining the origin of human language from this cry of the sensations. For is human language not obviously something completely different?

[...] The Abbé *Condillac* is among these people. Either he has from the first page of his book presupposed the whole thing, language, as already invented, or I find on each page things that could not have happened at all in the ordering of a formative [*bildenden*] language" (Herder 2002, 74–5). See also Liftschitz 2012, 185.

25 For instance, see Herder 2002, 76–7.
26 Of these texts, we still have eleven manuscripts in German, ten in French and three in Latin. In addition to these twenty-four manuscripts from the Berlin Academy's archive, there is one manuscript that was mistakenly included among the prize essays. Thus, there are six essays missing, which, according to Neis, were requested back by the authors and in some cases published. Neis 2003, 110–14, convincingly identified the authors of three of these manuscripts as G.C. Füchsel 1773; J.N. Tetens 1772 (translated in 2022); and J.D. Michaelis (Cod. Michaelis 71, the original manuscripts are in Göttingen: see Neis 2003, 508).
27 Hereafter, manuscripts will be indicated by the letter "M" followed by the number under which they are catalogued in the archive of the Berlin Academy.
28 In addition to the *accessits*, many other essays are of interest both intrinsically and comparatively. After an initial survey of the Berlin collection containing these manuscripts carried out by Megill 1974, Neis' work (2003) offers an entrée into this fascinating debate.
29 See for instance: "experience teaches us that the progress of reason is always linked to that of language" (M665, 24).
30 As Formigari (1972, 12) points out, during the eighteenth century, the cases of children found after having been abandoned and reduced to a feral state became more frequent and even suspicious. Condillac, Rousseau, Linnaeus, Monboddo, Herder, and Tetens, among others, wrote about them. A very famous case is that of Victor d'Aveyron. See, for instance, Itard 1994.
31 This essay also perspicuously links considerations about children to considerations about the relationship between thought and language. For instance, see M667, 3 and 14.
32 For this reconstruction, see Neis 2003, 301–4.
33 This is one of the myths of the founding of Rome, according to which the twins Romulus and Remus were suckled by a she-wolf (symbol of the city) and, once grown up, came to be at odds with each other. Romulus founded the city of Rome, of which he was the first king, after killing his brother Remus. Tetens also reflects on the implications of animals nurturing children (Tetens 2022, 153–6). He concludes that in the absence of a society, the natural capacities of humans are developed individually and do not allow the individual to actually shift from the animal to the human condition. A similar position is held by M665: "That language cannot subsist without society is proved by its very definition: it is the art by which one man passes his present thought into the mind of another, by means of common sounds, that is, equally understood by the speaker and the listener" (M665, 9).
34 We can trace hypothetical empiricism back to the widespread Enlightenment use of "conjectural history" mentioned in the introduction.
35 See Monboddo 1773, Part I, Book I, chapter 3, pages 11, 13, and 15; Book II, chapter 6, pages 8 and 12; and Book III, chapter 2, pages 4–7. For these references, see Formigari 1972, 28, n. 25.
36 It is the child, about ten/twelve years old, who was found in the woods of central France at the end of the eighteenth century. After an unsuccessful period in an institution for the deaf-mutes, the boy was placed in the care of the physician J. Itard,

who studied him and tried to help him reach a level of sociality that would enable him to become integrated.
37 As is well known, this teaching activity culminated in 1798 with the publication of the *Anthropology from a Pragmatic Point of View*.
38 Kant, Br, 10, 146; Kim 1994, 98.
39 Notoriously, Kant directly participated in the Berlin Academy's *Preisfragen* on several occasions.
40 See, in this sense, the fundamental dynamic of the "unsocial sociability" (AA 8, 21), which lies in the background of the cosmopolitan outcomes of Kant's anthropology.

Bibliography

Aarsleff, Hans. 1982. *From Locke to Saussure: Essays on the Study of Language and Intellectual History*. Minneapolis: Minnesota University Press.
Alighieri, Dante. 1983. "De vulgari eloquentia." In *Opere minori*, vol. 1, edited by Giorgio Barberi Squarotti, Sergio Cecchin, Angelo Jacomuzzi, and Maria Gabriella Stassi, 353–533. Torino: UTET.
Alighieri, Dante. 1996. *Divina commedia*, vol. 3, edited by Vittorio Sermonti. Milano: Bruno Mondadori.
Beeson, David. 1987. "Maupertuis at the Crossroads: Dating the Réflexions philosophiques." *Studies on Voltaire and the Eighteenth Century*, 249, 241–50.
Burnet, James [Lord Monboddo]. 1773. *Of the Origin and Progress of Language*. Edinburgh, Balfour, London: Cadell.
Charrak, André. 2003. *Empirisme et métaphysique. L'*Essai sur l'origine des connaissances humaines *de Condillac*. Paris: Vrin.
Condillac, Etienne Bonnot de. 2001. *Essay on the Origin of Human Knowledge*, translated and edited by Hans Aarsleff. Cambridge: Cambridge University Press.
Coratelli, Giorgio. 2014. "Dal segno arbitrario al tatto. Condillac e l'origine naturale del linguaggio umano." *Filosofi(e) Semiotiche*, 1, 1, 1–11.
De Brosses, Charles. 1765. *Traité de la formation mécanique des langues*. Paris: Saillant.
DeSouza, Nigel. 2012. "Language, Reason, and Sociability: Herder's Critique of Rousseau." *Intellectual History Review*, 22, 2, 221–40.
Duchesneau, François. 1974. "Condillac critique de Locke." *International Studies in Philosophy*, 6, 77–98.
Düntzer, Heinrich-Herder and Ferdinand Gottfried von. 1861. *Von und an Herder. Ungedruckte Briefe aus Herders Nachlaß*. Leipzig: Dyk'sche Buchhandlung.
Epicurus. 1925. *Letter to Herodotus*. In Diogenes Laertius, *Lives of Eminent Philosophers*, vol. 2, translated by Robert Drew Hicks, 565–613. London/New York: Heinemann, Putnam's Sons.
Formigari, Lia. 1972. *Linguistica e antropologia nel secondo Settecento*. Messina: La Libra.
Füchsel, Georg Christian. 1773. *Entwurf zu der ältesten Erd- und Menschengeschichte, nebst einem Versuch, den Ursprung der Sprache zu finden*. Frankfurt and Leipzig. https://www.digitale-sammlungen.de/en/view/bsb11256240?page=4,5
Gensini, Stefano. 1991. *Il naturale e il simbolico. Saggio su Leibniz*. Roma: Bulzoni.
Gensini, Stefano. 2012. "Secolarizzare le origini: Leibniz e il dibattito linguistico seicentesco." In *Sulle origini del linguaggio. Immaginazione, Espressione, Simbolo*, edited by Amerini Fabrizio-Messori Rita, 173–90. Pisa: ETS.

Gensini, Stefano. 2020. "Le radici naturali del linguaggio secondo G.W. Leibniz." *BLITYRI*, 9, 1, 11–34.
Gesche, Astrid. 1993. *Johann Gottfried Herder: Sprache und die Natur des Menschen*. Würzburg: Königshausen & Neumann.
Haßler, Gerda and Cordula Neis. 2009. *Lexikon sprachtheoretischer Grundbegriffe des 17. und 18. Jahrhunderts*. Berlin: De Gruyter.
Herder, Johann Gottfried. 2002. "Treatise on the Origin of Language." In *Philosophical Writings*, edited by Michael N. Forster, 65–164. Cambridge: Cambridge University Press.
Itard, Jean. 1994. *Victor de L'Aveyron*. Paris: Allias.
Kant, Immanuel. 1999. *Correspondence*, edited by Arnulf Zweig. Cambridge: Cambridge University Press.
Kant, Immanuel. 2007a. "Observations on the Feeling of the Beautiful and Sublime." In *Anthropology, History, and Education*, translated by Paul Guyer, edited by Robert B. Louden and Günter Zöller, 18–62. Cambridge: Cambridge University Press.
Kant, Immanuel. 2007b. "Anthropology from a Pragmatic Point of View." In *Anthropology, History, and Education*, translated by Paul Guyer, edited by Robert B. Louden and Günter Zöller, 227–429. Cambridge: Cambridge University Press.
Kieffer, Bruce. 1978. "Herder's Treatment of Süssmilch's Theory of the Origin of Language in the *Abhandlung über den Ursprung der Sprache*: A Re-Evaluation." *Germanic Review*, 53, 3, 96–105.
Kim, Soo Bae. 1994. *Die Entstehung der Kantischen Anthropologie und ihre Beziehung zur empirischen Psychologie der Wolffschen Schule*. Frankfurt a. M.: Peter Lang.
Leibniz, Gottfried Wilhelm. 1710. "Brevis designatio meditationum de originibus gentium, ductis potissimum ex indicio linguarum." In *Miscellanea Berolinensia*, 1–16. Berlin: Papen.
Leibniz, Gottfried Wilhelm. 1712. "Epistolica de historia etymologica dissertatio." In Stefano Gensini, 1991, *Il naturale e il simbolico. Saggio su Leibniz*, 191–271. Roma: Bulzoni.
Leibniz, Gottfried Wilhelm. 1903. "De linguarum origine (1677–1678)." In *Opuscules et fragments inédits*, edited by Louis Couturat, 151–2. Paris: Alcan.
Leibniz, Gottfried Wilhelm. 1996. *New Essays on Human Understanding*, translated and edited by Peter Remnant and Jonathan Bennett. Cambridge: Cambridge University Press.
Lifschitz, Avi. 2012. *Language and Enlightenment: The Berlin Debates of the Eighteenth Century*. Oxford: Oxford University Press.
Locke, John. 1975. *An Essay Concerning Human Understanding*, edited by Peter H. Nidditch. Oxford: Clarendon Press.
Megill, Allen Dickson. 1974. *The Enlightenment Debate on the Origin of Language*. New York: Columbia.
Michaelis, Johann David. 1760. *Beantwortung der Frage von dem Einfluss der Meinungen in die Sprache, und der Sprache in die Meinungen*. Berlin: Haude und Spener.
Neis, Cordula. 2003. *Anthropologie im Sprachdenken des 18. Jahrhunderts. Die Berliner Preisfrage nach dem Ursprung der Sprache (1771)*. Berlin: De Gruyter.
Pécharman, Martine. 1999. "Signification et langage dans l'*Essai* de Condillac." *Revue de métaphysique et de morale*, 1, 81–103.
Pichevin, Claude. 1978. "Remarques sur le statut des signes et du langage dans le système de Condillac." In *Systèmes symboliques, science et philosophie*, edited by Gilles-Gaston Granger, 33–59. Paris: CNRS.
Rousseau, Jean-Jacques. 1992. *Discourse on the Origins of Inequality*, edited by Roger D. Masters and Christopher Kelly. Hanover (NH): University Press of New England.

Schulenburg, Siegrid von der. 1973. *Leibniz als Sprachforscher*. Frankfurt a.M.: Klostermann.
Smith, Raoul N. 1976. "The Sociology of Language in Johann David Michaelis' Dissertation of 1760." *Journal of the History of Behavioral Sciences*, 12, 338–46.
Süssmilch, Johann Peter. 1766. *Versuch eines Beweises, daß die erste Sprache ihren Ursprung nicht vom Menschen, sondern allein vom Schöpfer erhalten habe*. Berlin: Buchladen der Realschule.
Tetens, Johann Nikolaus. 2022. "On the Origin of Languages and Writing." In *Tetens's Writings of Method, Language, and Anthropology*, edited by Courtney D. Fugate, Scott Stapleford, and Curtis Sommerlatte, 153–94. London: Bloomsbury.
Tiercelin, Claudine. 2002. "Dans quel mesure le langage peut-il être naturel?" In *Condillac. L'origine du langage*, edited by Bertrand Aliénor, 19–56. Paris: Puf.
Trabant, Jürgen. 1986. "La critique de l'arbitraire du signe chez Condillac et Humboldt." In *Les Idéologues. Sémiotique, théories et politiques linguistiques pendant la Révolution française*, edited by Busse Winfried and Trabant Jürgen, 73–96. Amsterdam: John Benjamins.
Waldow, Anik. 2017. "Between History and Nature: Herder's Human Being and the Naturalization of Reason." In *Herder: Philosophy and Anthropology*, edited by Anik Waldow and Nigel DeSouza, 147–65. Oxford: Oxford University Press.
Wescott, Roger W. 1971. "Linguistic Iconism." *Language*, 47, 2, 416–28.
Yolton, John W. 1956. *John Locke and the Way of Ideas*. Oxford: Clarendon Press.
Zammito, John. 2017. "Herder and the Problem of an Animal-Human Boundary." In *Herder: Philosophy and Anthropology*, edited by Anik Waldow and Nigel DeSouza, 127–47. Oxford: Oxford University Press.

10

The Philosophical Context of the 1773/1775 *Preisfrage*: Johann Georg Sulzer on Knowledge and Sensibility

Daniel Dumouchel

1. The 1773/1775 *Preisfrage* and Sulzer's Psychology

In the report of the public assemblies, published alongside the *mémoires* of the Berlin Academy of 1773, one finds the announcement for the 1775 prize competition in speculative philosophy. The question deserves to be quoted in its entirety:

> The soul has two primitive faculties that form the basis of all its operations: the faculty of knowing and the faculty of feeling.
>
> When exercising the first, the soul is occupied with an object that it considers to be outside itself and about which it is curious: it seems, then, that its activity only tends to see well. By exercising the other, it is occupied with itself and its state, being affected for good or for evil. Then its activity seems only determined to change its state when it is unpleasantly affected or to enjoy when it is pleasantly affected. This assumed, we ask for:

1. An exact development of the original determinations of these two faculties and the general laws they follow.
2. A thorough examination of the reciprocal dependence of these faculties and of the way in which one influences the other.
3. Principles that show how the genius and character of a man depend on the degree of strength and vivacity and progress of the one and the other of these faculties, and on the proportion that is found between them.[1]

The same announcement specifies that the contestants must submit their essays by the 1st of January 1775 and that the Academy's judgment will be delivered on the 31st of May 1775. In 1775, the Academy found that it had received several submissions, some of which contained "very good things." However, as the purpose of the competition was "to occasion original research and genuine discoveries that would circumscribe the limits of our knowledge," the Academy suggested that the authors further reflect upon these themes, therefore deferring its adjudication of the prize. They then invited the candidates to submit either a new essay or an *addendum* to their existing one before the 1st of January 1776. The refined criteria of the newly imposed rubric were the following:

> It invites them [i.e., the authors who submitted *mémoires*] to shed light on the following subjects. 1. Regarding the first question, what are the conditions under which a perception affects only the faculty of feeling; and of what order, on the contrary, are the perceptions that only interest curiosity and only occupy the faculty of knowing? In both cases, it will be seen that these conditions depend partly on the perception, or on the object itself, and partly on the state of the soul, at the moment when it experiences the perception. 2. Regarding the second question, the Academy would like a clear and satisfactory explanation of the psychological phenomenon that is usually indicated by saying that *the mind is the dupe of the heart*; and of that other phenomenon, which is observed in certain speculative people, that is, that they feel only weakly. 3. With respect to the third question, we ask what conditions are required for a man to be more disposed to exercise the faculty of knowing than that of feeling, and what conditions result in the opposite case.[2]

As is known, it was the *Allgemeine Theorie des Denkens und Empfindens* by Johann August Eberhard, a future adversary of Kant, that won the prize in 1776. But anyone acquainted with the thought of Johann Georg Sulzer cannot help but notice, in the very question itself, not only the stamp of his terminology but also the essential character of his philosophical program, at least with respect to his psychology. Sulzer's psychology, developed since 1751 in numerous essays presented to the Academy,[3] was eventually published in 1773 in German in his *Vermischte philosophische Schriften* (Miscellaneous Philosophical Writings). By the time this question was presented to the European public, Sulzer himself had provided detailed answers to most of the questions and requests for clarification about the *Preisfrage*, and his efforts were largely directed toward the great project of the *Allgemeine Theorie der schönen Künste* (General Theory of the Fine Arts), the first edition of which occupied him from 1771 to 1774. During the period of the prize competition on knowledge and sensibility, from the publication of the question (1773) until the awarding of the prize (1776), the "metaphysical" *mémoires* that Sulzer presented to the Academy focused on the refutation of materialism and on the immortality of the soul. One may therefore wonder why Sulzer insisted on bringing a question so intimately tied to preoccupations that no longer seemed to him of total topicality to the attention of scholars.

Nonetheless, the insistence on coming up with "genuine discoveries" that "push back the boundaries of knowledge" is in line with one of the cardinal ideas of Sulzer's thinking, namely the need for psychological research in order to shed new light on the "depths of the soul." In §206 of the *Kurzer Begriff aller Wissenschaften und andern Theile der Gelehrsamkeit* (Compendium of All Sciences and Other Branches of Learning) of 1759, Sulzer recommends that psychology, which he considers "the noblest part of philosophy," should "give the most precise attention to the obscure regions of the soul (if you will permit me the expression), where it acts by means of very indistinct and obscure concepts" (Kurzer Begriff, §206).[4] And for him it goes without saying that sensibility and its effects on our knowledge and desires belong to this area of the mind that is based on confused or obscure representations.

Sulzer's efforts focus on broadening and deepening empirical psychology. But this empirical pursuit is always conducted with a view to enrich the metaphysical theory of the soul by espousing a methodology that moves back and forth between the essence of the soul and the explanation of particular observations. The *Kurzer Begriff* shows that Sulzer never abandons the prospect of realizing an "explanatory psychology" (*erklärende Psychologie*), which would correspond to Wolff's "rational psychology" (*psychologia rationalis*). It is useful to specify Sulzer's way of proceeding in the *Kurzer Begriff* here:

> Psychology is the science of the human soul. It examines its nature, its essence, its forces and faculties, its particularities, and its modifications [...]. It consists of two main parts, which Wolff distinguished under the name of *Psychologia empirica* and *Psychologia rationalis*. The empirical psychology contains a precise and distinct definition of everything we know about the soul by means of experience. The various effects of the soul are described in the most precise manner and divided up, so to speak; then, based on the most precise observation, the most distinct explanations of the effects, the faculties and the properties of the soul are proposed; one proceeds here as for the corporeal things in physics, which one learns to know by means of experiments and tests. We could therefore call this part of psychology the experimental physics of the soul [...] The empirical psychology based on observation is followed by the explanatory psychology [*erklärende*] (*Psychologia rationalis*). It aims, by means of the resolution [*Auflösung*] of the events ascertained in the first part, to discover the essence and the fundamental properties of the soul, and then, from these, by a reverse path, to explain the other properties and modifications of the soul.
>
> (Kurzer Begriff, §§204 and 208)

Two points should be noted. (1) Sulzer constantly insists on the importance of experience, of "facts" and observations in psychology, and on the necessity and the utility of research that aims to explore the "obscure parts of the soul" (Kurzer Begriff, §206). Although Sulzer constantly acknowledges Wolff's pioneering role, he considers the excellence of his psychology to be limited to having described the effects of the understanding on our *distinct* knowledge of things. Sulzer's work aims to provide more than a mere "filling in" of the areas left fallow by Wolff. It is a question of broadening psychology and directing it toward "extraordinary" cases and phenomena that do not seem "to be decomposable [*zergliedern*] from the known properties of the soul."[5] "One cannot deduce all of the particularities of the soul from its essence," argues Sulzer, "and some of them are perhaps not even yet known" (Kurzer Begriff, §210).

What best characterizes Sulzer's approach is his desire to shed light on the function of lesser-known dimensions of the human soul by studying its extreme, even pathological, states. Sulzer shows a sustained interest in the exceptional states of the soul, such as cases of weak self-apperception (dreaming, intense meditation, and waking-up); cases of insufficient attention, daydreaming, or distraction; premonitions; loss of consciousness (fainting, head trauma, temporary bodily "failure"); violent passions; cases of "weakness of the will"[6]; madness and temporary delirium; and physical insensitivity of individuals absorbed in intellectual attention or dominated by a single passion (to which the serenity of martyrs testifies, as well as the tolerance for torture of the American Indians).

This interest and method also explain Sulzer's way of writing—and perhaps of thinking. The argument of the *mémoires* is constantly interrupted by detours and digressions, which stand as attempts to dwell on certain unusual aspects of the experience of the soul. Sulzer's originality is not found in the general framework of his thought, which is not always clearly distinguished from Wolff's empirical psychology, as much as it is in these explanatory detours, which sometimes bring his method closer to that of the classical "moralists." It is generally in such moments of argumentative rupture that Sulzer reminds his readers that it is not enough to look in order to see: "To observe the soul in its most secret operations" (Paradoxe, 1766, 445) requires "great acuity in one's observations and a sustained attention to everything that happens in the soul" (Kurzer Begriff, §205). For the "facts," from whence our observations spring, are varied and fleeting. Some of the effects of the soul are manifest, but others are obscure and "occur so suddenly that they easily escape attention." Other effects only manifest themselves indirectly, through the traces that they leave on other "still more remote modifications of the soul, upon which they depend" (ibid.).

(2) A second preliminary remark is necessary. The question proposed by the Academy overlooks the possibility of reducing these two primitive faculties of the soul to one original power of the soul. It is the whole outlook on the relations between explanatory psychology and descriptive psychology that becomes modified. The 1773 and 1775 question is therefore formulated in the terms of the famous *mémoire* of 1763,[7] "Observations sur les divers états où l'âme se trouve en exerçant ses facultés primitives, celle d'apercevoir et celle de sentir" (Observations of the Diverse States in Which the Soul Finds Itself by Exercising Its Primitive Faculties of Apperception and Sensation). As early as the *mémoire* of 1751 on agreeable and disagreeable sentiments, Sulzer understood "the essence of the soul," following Wolff, as an "active substance" that naturally acts "to produce, or if one wishes, to receive ideas, and to compare them, that is to say, to think."[8] It is on this basis that one can think about the unity of psychic phenomena: "[…] the essence of our soul, the principle from whence are born all our enduring desires, is a powerful drive to produce or to receive ideas" (Observations, 1770, 60). The "Analyse du génie" (Analysis of Genius) of 1757 goes in the same direction, arguing that all faculties of the soul can be traced back to this primitive force which, in accordance with the Leibnizian tradition, constitutes the essence of all substance and particularly that of the soul: "[i]t is this active force, which is more easily sensed within oneself than defined, that produces all ideas, or *at least* which continually prompts us to develop and to multiply them" (Génie, 1759, 394; emphasis added).[9] The "Analyse de la raison" (Analysis of Reason) of 1758 defines the

principal property of the soul, always referring to the Leibnizian and Wolffian origin of this concept as a *representative power* or as a "principle of activity that drives us, and in a certain way forces us, to give ourselves to impressions excited in us by the senses" (Raison, 1765, 416). It is this power that "seems *to produce all the changes that occur in the interior of substances*" (Raison, 1765, 416; emphasis added). Each of these definitions raises many questions, but I will limit myself here to emphasize that the 1763 *mémoire* seems to distance itself from this "continuist" background. Apperception—*Vorstellen* in German—and *sensibility* are put forward as two primary faculties that engender different "states," but do not seem to share any common root. Sensibility is even presented on two occasions as deprived of exteriority, insofar as in the act of feeling, the soul is supposed to be concerned only with itself. The influential 1769 *mémoire* entitled "Considérations psychologiques sur l'homme moral" (Psychological Considerations of the Moral Man) employs the same language: there are two mental "acts," knowing and feeling, and it is only in virtue of sensibility that truths can be transformed into motives for desire and action (Considérations, 1771, 369). This is complicated, however, by the fact that a 1771 *mémoire* entitled "Observations sur quelques propriétés de l'âme comparées à celles de la matière: pour servir à l'examen du matérialisme" (Observations on Some Properties of the Soul Compared to Those of Matter: To Serve for the Examination of Materialism), presents, in the context of a refutation of materialism, the fundamental activity of the soul as an *effort* that is irreducible to the mere modification of bodily organs. It presents this effort as that in virtue of which the soul "takes interest in the impressions that it receives, either to enjoy them, or to resist the effects that they might have" (Observations sur quelques propriétés de l'âme, 1773, 393). The efforts of the soul, through which our perceptions are modified, seem to be directed by what today we would call a hedonic valence, which constantly works to adapt our perceptions to practical use. The soul is not passive in its reception of impressions, insofar as it "enjoys certain ones but resists others" (Observations sur quelques propriétés de l'âme, 1773, 395). Here we find ourselves once more on the pathway that Wolff forged in his psychology.

2. Principles, Faculties, States: The *Mémoire* of 1763 on Apperception and Sensibility

The *mémoire* of 1763 seems to ignore the possibility of reducing the expressions of the soul to a fundamental activity, that of representation, and emphasizes instead the dichotomy between two *primary* faculties: "One is the faculty of *apperception*, or knowing the qualities of things; the other, that of *sensibility*, or being affected agreeably or disagreeably" (Observations, 1770, 407).[10] Sulzer makes clear that despite the apparent diversity of operations in the soul, "they are all reducible to the exercise of two faculties, which are the *sources* of all its affections" (ibid.; emphasis added). Moreover, "in the exercise of these two faculties, the soul *seems so different from itself*" (ibid.; emphasis added) that one is tempted to believe, as the ancient philosophers did, that there are *two* souls in human beings and not just one. One is presented here with the crucial question of a possible evolution, or even a profound transformation, of the theory of agreeable sentiments elaborated in the "Recherches" (Investigations) of 1751 and 1752. The very title of the *mémoire* would seem to suggest that Sulzer called into question the possibility of explaining all phenomena of the mind in virtue of a single principle, and that he recognized from then on two primary irreducible faculties, even if certain passages suggest instead to see in it rather two orientations of the soul's activity. If Sulzer did modify his explanation of psychological phenomena to emphasize the dichotomy between sensibility and knowledge, which are elevated to the status of "faculties," we must recognize that the *mémoire* of 1763 constitutes a pivotal moment in this process. The traditional interpretation, as well as certain recent interpretations, would tend to see at work there a rupture with the rationalist psychology of the first *mémoires* and the establishment of the autonomy of the feeling of pleasure and pain from the intellectual faculties of the soul. Such an idea might have had an influence on the philosophy of Kant.[11] By contrast, some recent interpreters have strongly contested this thesis, emphasizing that up to the end—that is, to the *Allgemeine Theorie*—Sulzer remained faithful to the main principles of his theory of agreeable and disagreeable sentiments developed as early as 1751.[12]

It seems appropriate in my view to distinguish, in Sulzer's thought, between *principle* (the activity of the soul as willingness to produce or receive representations), *primary faculties* ("those of apperception and sensibility"[13]), and the *states* of the soul expressed in the exercise of these two faculties: the state of *meditation*, the state of *sensibility*, and the intermediary state of *contemplation*.

The notion of *apperception* should be clarified. Sulzer generally understands apperception as doubly orientated toward the perception of an object of thought (exterior to the self) and toward self-consciousness. It is the objective orientation that is preserved in 1763; the German version of 1763 will eliminate the fundamental ambiguity in the term "apperception" in Sulzer's thought by translating it as *Vorstellen* (representation) (*Vermischte philosophische Schriften*, 225). But it is the second meaning, the apperception of one's own existence, that is preserved, for example, in the 1756 *mémoire*, "Sur l'aperception et son influence sur nos jugements"[14] (On Apperception and Its Influence on Our Judgments). Here, the German translation will be taken to be decisive in its rendition of apperception as *Bewusstsein*.

Sulzer successively examines the three *states* of the soul: the state of meditation, that of sensibility, and that of contemplation. The first two are occasional, even *extreme* states; they are not in the least representative of the ordinary state of the mind and even constitute, in certain respects, pathological states of the soul:

> Ordinarily the soul exercises these two faculties at the same time; there are, however, cases in which one or the other predominates to the point that it seems to entirely occupy all the activity of the soul.
>
> (Observations, 1770, 407)[15]

The two extreme states, namely the complete meditative immersion in a particular object to the detriment of the capacity for action or global comprehension of situations, on the one hand, and the total withdrawal into the feeling of oneself at the expense of intellectual clarity, on the other hand, are neither desirable nor sustainable.

These cases offer, to an accurate observer, facts and circumstances suitable to shed light on several very important psychological questions. This is what I propose to show in this *Mémoire*.

(Observations, 1770, 407)[16]

We see that it is the analytic approach to empirical psychology that justifies Sulzer's project in this text, more so than the desire to set forth a new hypothesis on the dichotomy of the soul. The intense exercise of both faculties produces "facts" that need to be analyzed. As for the state of contemplation, it is grounded in an "ordinary" activity of the mind, which allows for a back-and-forth movement between meditation and sensibility.

The faculty of *apperception* aims to produce distinct knowledge by fixing one's attention on an object or on one of its parts. The more one's conception of a partial aspect of the object becomes clear, the more the object as a whole becomes obscured. One could say that the state of *meditation*, which is characterized by the concentration of our intellectual activity on a single point, naturally tends toward *distraction*. The soul forgets itself in order to immerse itself in its object of interest (Observations, 1770, 407). The state of *sensibility*, on the other hand, is the complete opposite of intellectual penetration. Sulzer refers to *sensibility* as the agreeable or disagreeable character of a perception or its capacity to produce either desire or aversion (ibid., 410). In the state of sensibility, the soul "is occupied only with itself," whereas in deep meditation sensations are often weakened or even suspended. Sulzer argues that the force of sensibility is "proportionate to the degree of confusion that reigns in the perceptions" (ibid., 411).[17] The more confused the perception, the more vivid the sensation, insofar as the object that produces it disappears completely and we feel only its effect. As for the third state of the soul, the state of contemplation, it is defined as the result of a continuous and rapid transition between the two other states. Contemplation occurs "without effort"; impressions only scratch the surface of the soul, without deepening the ideas of the things perceived. Sulzer compares the *ease* and tranquility of the soul's activity to the peaceful flow of a river across a plain. The state of contemplation therefore never leads us to the excesses of the passions or of meditation but maintains us in a kind of superficial and quiet pleasure.

Let us make a brief digression. Meditative distraction is an extreme state that corresponds to intellectual concentration on a distinct object. One will recall that the *Preisfrage* of 1775 asked the competitors to reflect on "this other phenomenon that one observes in some speculative people, [that is] that they feel only weakly." This phenomenon, which is actually a kind of paradox, had long interested Sulzer. In his *mémoire* of 1756, Sulzer treats it as a particular case of faint self-apperception. And in the *mémoire* of 1759, he opposes the state of distraction—a temporary deficit in attention—to "the state of perfect alertness" (*état d'éveil parfait*) that our faculties of knowledge must aim at in the implementation of human reason. The weakness of self-apperception in distraction is compatible with the deep examination of abstract materials and highly complex forms of reasoning. One is presented here with the paradox of the individual who exercises his reason and constructs precise and profound arguments but who seems, at the same time, to be a madman and an imbecile—the classic example of this situation being the judgment that his contemporaries made on Democritus, according to a letter that we attribute to Hippocrates. The seeming madness and idiocy of these engrossed thinkers are founded on a rather incomplete idea that we have of ourselves when we are thus captivated. In other words, it is founded on a defect in apperception, where the individual idea that we have of ourselves almost becomes a general one. Sulzer likens this sort of incompleteness in apperception to a wakeful reverie (a type of distraction) and to dreaming. Daydreaming is a distraction that can be explained by the properties of the imagination, which makes us persist in a certain idea—Sulzer speaks of imaginary ideas—as long as another one does not oppose it.[18] The state of being engrossed, or distracted, can nevertheless be interrupted by a sensation that arouses a new association of ideas. Thus, a louder sound may draw our attention to a local circumstance, which has the effect of pulling us out of our reverie. Sulzer draws two conclusions from this. (1) First and foremost, we tend to make the content of our imaginations manifest, and this sort of illusion happens whenever, while distracted, we receive a clear impression caused by a sensation that is not very detailed or, in other words, not very determined by the spatial and temporal circumstances in which our body is placed. The "vision" of the anchorite consumed by his spiritual meditations, for example, can be explained in the same way. But this is also the case with dreams. One must recognize that while perceptions are not deprived of clarity or intensity in dreams—to the extent that they are sometimes confused with those of the waking state—they are nevertheless deprived of the spatio-temporal markers that are essential to the clarity of self-apperception, which requires one to receive sensations through one's own body. However, our tendency to make our imaginations real implies that, when the sensations relative to the spatio-temporal present are lacking, we will believe that we are in the place and time to which belong the very clear perceptions we have.[19] (2) Second, Sulzer believes that "it is therefore only by means of continuous and diversified sensations that we preserve our common sense, relative to the reality of our external situation." As the meditative state and the distraction that accompanies it show, we can very well judge and reason about ideal things, while we think and act in a disordered way in relation to real objects and to our situation in the world. Sulzer does not hesitate to conclude that the purely intellectual operations of the mind, those which result from its capacity to conceive and reason *distinctly*, depend neither on the senses nor on the organization of the body, but derive from the very essence of the soul. As soon as it is a question of orienting ourselves among existing things, we require sensations. Therefore, if we only had these negligibly detailed sensations, such as in the case of purely distinct knowledge, we would only perceive our existence *generally*, and our whole life would be nothing but an endless dream.

It seems to me that Sulzer's true position can be summarized by the idea that "in the state of sensibility, the soul apperceives clearly its state and fixes its attention there, but [...] apperceives obscurely the object that produces it, and takes no notice of it" (Observations, 1770, 413).[20] It is the will to distinguish the specific aspects of these two extreme states of the soul that compels Sulzer to emphasize the irreducible "subjectivity" of sensibility, while in fact, in this relation of the soul to itself, it always keeps a confused idea of the object that occasions the sentiment. Therefore, "the most perfect state that the soul can find itself in" is neither that of blind sentiment, nor that of distracted meditation, but that of "free movement from one of these acts of the mind to another," which also characterizes the "geniuses equally suitable for speculation and for practice" (Observations, 1770, 414). It is indeed the characteristic of the "practical ideas"—or those that structure our desires and our actions—that "we apperceive them only with the feeling of ourselves which accompanies their perception" (ibid.). Sulzer summarizes the three states of the soul as follows:

> Here are the various states in which the soul necessarily finds itself whenever the exercise of its faculties is accompanied by apperception. For we are not speaking here of sleep, nor of other states in which the soul has only an obscure knowledge of itself or of its operations. It follows from these observations that there is a state in which man sees very clearly and feels nothing; another in which he feels strongly and sees nothing; a third in which he sees and feels clearly enough to take cognizance of what is outside him and what is within him.
> (Observations, 1770, 417)[21]

I would like to suggest that the thesis of a radical rupture between the Wolffian theoretical framework that presided over the theory of sentiments in 1751 and 1752 and the conception developed by the *Observations* is not proven, even if the insistence on the autonomy of our sensibility from objective representation or knowledge seems to bring the theory about the unity of the soul almost to breaking point. Thus, in the *Considérations sur l'homme moral*, Sulzer wishes to oppose a "moral genius" to the simple knowledge of theoretical precepts in morality (Considérations, 1769, 362). He emphasizes the distance between the "knowledge of a truth" and the "way of apperceiving it which gives it an active power over the soul" (ibid., 369). He then distinguishes truth, which is grounded in the act of knowing, from *motive*, which presupposes the *act of sensibility*. It does not suffice *to see* a moral truth—one must also *feel* it, so that it is transformed into a *motive* capable of producing a *desire* in the soul. On two occasions in this *mémoire*, Sulzer employs the following formula: "To know first, and then to feel" (ibid., 374-5). In a *mémoire* titled "Réflexions sur l'utilité de la poésie dramatique" (Reflections on the Utility of Dramatic Poetry) read in 1760, Sulzer reaffirms that "the truth that is merely rooted in the superior part of the soul, or the understanding, exerts no power over us" (Réflexions, 1767, 334). The *mémoire* of 1765 "De l'énergie dans les ouvrages des beaux-arts" (Of the Energy in the Works of the Fine Arts) goes so far as to claim that "the understanding does not provide any active force to the soul" (Énergie, 1767, 483). It seems hard to deny that the *mémoire* of 1763 highlights what can be called an *opacification*—both sensual and moral—of sensibility, which thereby acquires a certain autonomy from the faculty of representation, that is to say from the activity of the soul oriented toward knowledge. What "interests" us no longer seems to have its source in the cognitive activity of the mind. In other words, Sulzer comes to place greater emphasis on the receptive dimension of the soul in the production of sentiments and insists on the *passivity* of sensibility: "It is not the object that one feels, but oneself" (Observations, 1770, 410).

However, we have some good reasons to claim that there is no radical change in Sulzer's thought. (1) A first reason can be found in the *Observations sur quelques propriétés de l'âme comparées à celles de la matière* of 1771, a title that was cited at the outset, where it is clear that the essence of the soul as power of representation continues to play an essential metaphysical role.

(2) The second reason can be found in one of the main arguments defended in the *mémoire* of 1763. Even when Sulzer argues that sensibility is "non-objective," insofar as the subject senses himself, it remains clear that this perception is never entirely detached from the activity of the soul. When he highlights the fact that there are "cases in which one or the other [of these two faculties] predominates to such an extent that it alone seems to occupy all the activity of the soul" (Observations, 1770, 407), he nonetheless continues to consider these two expressions of the soul, which seem so opposed, as two branches of the same stock. One grasps the ambivalence of the Sulzerian conception of sensibility when he presents it as "an act of the soul that has nothing in common with the object that produces it, or which occasions it," and in which "the soul is occupied only with itself" (ibid., 410). Sulzer advances two ideas here that are difficult to reconcile: on the one hand, it is the activity of the soul, given its capacity for representation, that produces a "sentiment" of either pleasure or pain. On the other, this "subjective" response, which draws the mind within itself, has no essential relation to the "content" of the experience that excites it. One might wonder whether it was partly under the influence of David Hume[22] that Sulzer came to believe that reason is by itself morally "inert," that it is powerless to give rise to desires and actions. Concerning the tension between the mental "action" of sensibility and its passive dimension, Sulzer will claim that "sentiments and the immediate effects that they have, are *involuntary* acts of the mind" (Observations, 1770, 420). The activity of the mind can be either intentional (as in the activity of distinct theoretical representation) or dependent on an "ordinary attentiveness" (ibid., 418) and carried out "without effort" (ibid., 416) (as in the state of contemplation), or involuntary (as in sensible pleasure or in the production of passions). In other words, it does not seem possible to deprive the feeling of any objective reference. The activity of the soul necessarily relies on a minimum of objective qualities that can support and maintain it. When the soul is only concerned with itself, it fixes its attention on the state that it apperceives *clearly* but apperceives at the same time *obscurely* the object that produces it (Observations, 1770, 411; 413-4). Pleasure is therefore not devoid of cognitive elements.

(3) The third reason concerns the fact that Sulzer designated sensibility a mental "act," and passion an "involuntary act" of the soul (Observations, 1770, 420).[23] Certain psychological phenomena, such as passions, good and bad moods, and the paradoxes of a weak will or poor judgment, reveal to us that the soul is active even below the threshold of apperception.[24] To clarify such phenomena, Sulzer has recourse to *obscure* perceptions. We must therefore penetrate more deeply into the "hidden" dimension and into the "dark side" of the human soul. This grounding in obscure representations does not only concern ideas, but also judgments, sentiments, desires, and aversions—that is, the whole of the "acts" of the soul (Paradoxe, 1766, 440).[25] In his words, they are "the *je ne sais quoi* that everyone sometimes feels" (ibid.). The example of good and bad moods, the effects of which one notices without perceiving their "obscure" causes, is quoted by Sulzer—in the *mémoire* of 1759 as well as in the one of 1758 on reason—in support of this theory on the causality of obscure perceptions and affects in the realm of consciousness; in this case, indeed, "one senses, one judges, one desires or one abhors

some object that one only represents to oneself obscurely" (Paradoxe, 1766, 440). A mood is then not a simple "physical" state, but the result of the unperceived actions of the soul. For him, it is therefore "demonstrated," based on his analysis of a multitude of experiences and observations, that all faculties of the soul can be exercised in two ways: a clear way, which we perceive and can account for, and the other obscure, which escapes our attention. In order to understand what the famous paradoxes of the will and judgment consist in more precisely, we must grasp the coexistence and simultaneous action of two desires or two judgments that act as contradictory forces. In this respect, the "declared passions," where sentiments contrary to reason "are not entirely obscure," are less worrisome than the affections that are "so obscure that it is not possible to know them" (Paradoxe, 1766, 441).

There are therefore, on Sulzer's account, judgments, sentiments, passions, desires, and aversions that we are not—or no longer—conscious of, but which remain active in our beliefs, sentiments, and decisions, even though we are not conscious of their causes. These obscure motivations can also attach themselves to distant events in the individual's past[26]: the memory of an object or an event carries with it evaluations and beliefs that are "incorporated," so to speak, into the history of the individual, and the "causality" occasioned by such representations is not a physical "causality." It is a sort of "biographical causality" that will soon find expression in psychopathology and in the novel.[27] To the "physiological" *sub-conscious* (or infra-conscious), which concerns the analogy between the human body's sensory system and perceptions of the soul, is added a "biographical" *unconscious*, which testifies to an activity of the soul that escapes apperception while producing real effects on sensibility. Without going further into the details of Sulzer's analyses, I would like to argue that such obscure perceptions, far from demonstrating the dichotomy of knowledge and sensibility, attest to the continuity of psychic phenomena in Sulzer's thought given that numerous sentiments are explained in virtue of the constant activity of the soul, which mobilizes the interiorized lived experiences of the individual. The case of prejudices is particularly interesting. Each new situation, by involuntarily recalling judgments, sentiments, and desires, which are so to speak "incorporated" in the memory—or even the history—of the individual, can occasion a response that is contrary to the conscious efforts of the soul and that prevents reflection. The judgments to which we have been exposed before the age of reason and which concern those things that "have become so familiar to us that every time one of these things recurs to us," especially when we are confronted with the same situation, "the judgment we heard made comes back at the same time, and this happens so quickly that the whole perception seems to be an inner sensation" (Paradoxe, 1766, 441). Judgment is a felt effect, but the *causes* are obscure. This is why what appears to us as paradoxes or aberrations in the practices, opinions, and customs of individuals, sects, and peoples becomes more comprehensible if one recalls that what one sees and hears as a child penetrates the mind unhindered.[28] By recalling these words or these meaningless propositions that fill the imagination, our memory rekindles at the same time, whether obscurely or *unconsciously*, the feeling of truth that initially accompanied them. "We acted," Sulzer argues, "long before reason had the time to develop its arguments" (Paradoxe, 1766, 448).

To establish a radical dichotomy between knowledge and sensibility, one must *first* successfully argue that they do not derive from the same power or primary faculty, and *secondly*, show that our sentiments are determined in complete independence from our cognitive representations. It would be prudent to conclude that Sulzer goes in the direction of the second thesis,[29] but he never goes so far as to defend the first. If we recall the distinction proposed above between the *principle*, the *faculties*, and the *states* of the soul, we can draw the conclusion that there is no contradiction between the metaphysical affirmation of the unity of the soul's activity and the psychological investigation of its two main faculties, which was the main issue of the 1773 *Preisfrage*. Indeed, the demand for such deepening was in the very spirit of psychological research as Sulzer defined it in his *Kurzer Begriff* of 1759. Moreover, since the dichotomy between knowledge and sensibility, for Sulzer, is essentially linked to the motivation of our actions, it is perhaps, in the end, a mere "shortcut" that he employs in his writings that are more directly *practical* in nature, as is the case with his considerations of the moral human being and of the function of the fine arts. Despite the probable influence of empiricist tendencies on his thinking, it is reasonable to conclude that Sulzer's psychology remains in the wake of Wolff's philosophy.

Abbreviations

Apperception	Sulzer, Johann Georg. (1756) 1766. "Sur l'apperception et son influence sur nos jugements." In *Histoire de l'Académie Royale des Sciences et des Belles-Lettres de Berlin*. Berlin: Haude und Spener.
Considérations	Sulzer, Johann Georg. (1769) 1771. "Considérations psychologiques sur l'homme moral." In *Histoire de l'Académie Royale des Sciences et des Belles-Lettres de Berlin*. Berlin: Haude und Spener.
Énergie	Sulzer, Johann Georg. (1765) 1767. "De l'énergie dans les ouvrages des beaux-arts." In *Histoire de l'Académie Royale des Sciences et des Belles-Lettres de Berlin*. Berlin: Haude und Spener.
Génie	Sulzer, Johann Georg. (1757) 1759. "Analyse du génie." In *Histoire de l'Académie Royale des Sciences et des Belles-Lettres de Berlin*. Berlin: Haude und Spener.
Kurzer Begriff	Sulzer, Johann Georg. 1759. *Kurzer Begriff aller Wissenschaften und andern Theile der Gelehrsamkeit*. Leipzig: Johann Christian Langenheim.
Observations	Sulzer, Johann Georg. (1763) 1770. "Observations sur les divers états où l'âme se trouve en exerçant ses facultés primitives, celle d'apercevoir et celle de sentir." In *Histoire de l'Académie Royale des Sciences et des Belles-Lettres de Berlin*. Berlin: Haude und Spener.

Raison	Sulzer, Johann Georg. 1758 (1765). "Analyse de la raison." In *Histoire de l'Académie Royale des Sciences et des Belles-Lettres de Berlin*. Berlin: Haude und Spener.
Recherches	Sulzer, Johann Georg. (1751) 1753. "Recherches sur l'origine des sentiments agréables et désagréables, Premier mémoire: Théorie générale du plaisir." In *Histoire de l'Académie Royale des Sciences et des Belles-Lettres de Berlin*. Berlin: Haude und Spener.

Notes

1 "L'âme possède deux facultés primitives qui forment la base de toutes ses opérations; la *faculté de connaître* et la *faculté de sentir*. En exerçant la première, l'âme est occupée d'un objet qu'elle regarde comme une chose hors d'elle et pour lequel elle a de la curiosité: son activité paraît alors ne tendre qu'à bien voir. En exerçant l'autre, elle s'occupe d'elle-même et de son état, étant affectée *en bien ou en mal*. Alors son activité semble uniquement déterminée à changer d'état, lorsqu'elle se trouve désagréablement affectée, ou à jouir, lorsqu'elle est agréablement affectée. Cela supposé, on demande:
    1. *Un développement exact des déterminations originaires de ces deux facultés et les lois générales qu'elles suivent.*
    2. *Un examen approfondi de la dépendance réciproque de ces facultés et de la manière dont l'une influe sur l'autre.*
    3. *Des principes qui servent à faire voir comment le génie et le caractère d'un homme dépendent du degré de force et de vivacité et des progrès de l'une et de l'autre de ces facultés, et de la proportion qui se trouve entre elles.*"

2 "Elle les [i.e. les auteurs ayant remis des mémoires] invite à répandre du jour sur les objets suivants. 1. Par rapport à la première question; quelles sont les conditions sous lesquelles une perception n'affecte que la faculté de sentir; et de quel ordre au contraire sont les perceptions qui n'intéressent que la curiosité et n'occupent que la faculté de connaître? Dans l'un et l'autre cas, on s'apercevra que ces conditions dépendent en partie de la perception, ou de l'objet même, et en partie de l'état de l'âme, au moment où elle éprouve la perception. 2. Par rapport à la seconde question, l'Académie souhaite une explication claire et satisfaisante du phénomène psychologique qu'on a coutume d'indiquer en disant que *l'esprit est la dupe du cœur*; et de cet autre phénomène qu'on observe chez certains spéculatifs, c'est [sic] qu'ils ne sentent que faiblement. 3. Par rapport à la troisième question, on demande les conditions requises pour qu'un homme soit plus disposé à exercer la faculté de connaître que celle de sentir, et celles d'où résulte le cas contraire."

3 Sulzer's essays are published in two series of publications of the Academy: *Histoire de l'Académie Royale des Sciences et des Belles-Lettres de Berlin* (for the *mémoires* read between 1745 and 1769) and *Nouveaux Mémoires de l'Académie Royale des Sciences et Belles-Lettres* (for the *mémoires* presented from 1770 onwards). I will refer to Sulzer's memoirs by the year of their presentation to the Academy and by the original pagination.

4   See the recent scientific edition of this text: *Gesammelte Schriften. Kommentierte Ausgabe, Band 1: Kurzer Begriff aller Wissenschaften*, edited by Hans Adler and Élisabeth Décultot, 2014, 141.
5   Thus, Sulzer calls for a description of the different types of madness that is analogous to the one that doctors make of the different types of diseases. On this point, it is Louis de Beausobre who will try to meet Sulzer's request, with the five *mémoires* that he presents to the Academy in 1759 and 1760: "Sur la nature et les causes de la folie" (On the Nature and Causes of Madness).
6   To which the *mémoire* of 1759 is dedicated: "Explication d'un paradoxe psychologique; que non seulement l'homme agit et juge quelquefois sans motifs et sans raisons apparentes, mais même malgré des motifs pressants et des raisons convaincantes" ("Explanation of a Psychological Paradox; that not Only does Man Sometimes Act and Judge without Motives and Apparent Reasons, but even Despite Pressing Motives and Convincing Reasons"; cited as: Paradoxe), published in 1766.
7   The 1763 memoir, which was presented to the Academy in 1770, will simply be referred to as "Observations."
8   "Recherches sur l'origine des sentiments agréables et désagréables" (Research on the Origin of Pleasant and Unpleasant Feelings; cited as Recherches), I, 1751; Sulzer 1753, 60.
9   "C'est cette force active, qu'il est plus facile de sentir au-dedans de soi-même que de définir, qui produit toutes les idées, ou qui *du moins* nous engage continuellement à les développer et à les multiplier." Sulzer also adds that any man who "pays attention to himself, feels in himself something which prompts him continuously to think."
10 "L'une est la faculté *d'apercevoir*, ou de connaître les qualités des choses; l'autre, celle de *sentir*, ou d'être affectée agréablement ou désagréablement."
11 Cf. in particular: Anton Palme, *J.G. Sulzers Psychologie und die Anfänge der Dreivermögenslehre* (Berlin, 1905); Élisabeth Décultot, "Métaphysique ou physiologie du beau? La théorie des plaisirs de Johann Georg Sulzer (1751–1752)," in "Esthétiques de l'Aufklärung," ed. S. Buchenau and É. Décultot, *Revue germanique internationale*, no. 4 (Paris: PUF, 2006): 93–106.
12 Cf. Euler 2011, 101–35; Heinz 2011, 83–99.
13 Observations, 1770, 407.
14 Published in 1766, with the *mémoires* of the year 1764.
15 "Ordinairement l'âme exerce ces deux facultés à la fois; il y a cependant des cas dans lesquels l'une ou l'autre prédomine au point qu'elle paraît occuper seule toute l'activité de l'âme."
16 "Ces cas offrent à un observateur exact, des faits et des circonstances propres à répandre du jour sur plusieurs questions psychologiques très importantes. C'est ce que je me propose de faire voir dans ce Mémoire."
17 In accordance with what he argued about sensible pleasures and pains in 1752.
18 Sulzer's theory is reminiscent, in some respects, to Spinoza's theory of imagination in the second part of the *Ethics*.
19 Note the similarity of this approach to imagination with the one Beausobre uses to account for madness. For Beausobre, there is "madness" when an imagination is taken for a sensation—when one transposes one's reveries into the physical world (First *Mémoire*, 396). The "madness" rests on this capacity of the imagination to make the perceptions it produces more vivid than the sensations (Second *Mémoire*, 406).
20 "[…] dans l'état du sentiment, l'âme aperçoit clairement son état et y fixe son attention, mais […] aperçoit obscurément l'objet qui la produit, et n'y prend pas garde."

21 "Voilà les divers états dans l'un desquels l'âme se trouve nécessairement toutes les fois que l'exercice de ses facultés est accompagné de l'aperception. Car nous ne parlons ici, ni du sommeil, ni des autres états où l'âme n'a qu'une connaissance obscure d'elle-même ou de ses opérations. Il résulte de ces observations qu'il y a un état où l'homme voit très distinctement et ne sent rien; un autre où il sent fortement et ne voit rien; un troisième où il voit et sent assez clairement pour prendre connaissance de ce qui est hors de lui et de ce qui est en lui." One will note in this passage a return to the double meaning of apperception (as consciousness of something and consciousness of oneself).
22 Sulzer contributed to the German translation of Hume's works from 1755 onwards.
23 See also "Sur un paradoxe psychologique."
24 I cannot go into the details of Sulzer's analysis here, which includes his favorite concept, that of the "physics of the soul."
25 The *mémoire* of 1763 also insists that obscure—unperceived—feelings, desires, and passions are acts of the soul. In itself, the notion of unperceived perception may have seemed problematic to most empiricists: Jean Bernard Merian devotes a significant part of his remarks to it. But the idea of an obscure "passion" may seem even more difficult to grasp.
26 Cf. Paradoxe, 1766, 442.
27 The two preoccupations come together in Karl Philip Moritz, author of the famous autobiographical novel *Anton Reiser* (1785) and editor, since 1783, of the *Magazin zur Erfahrungsseelenkunde*.
28 On this question, it seems that Sulzer tries to renew a typically Cartesian theme, that of the lasting acquisition of certain prejudices in childhood—with a Leibnizian conceptual apparatus.
29 As early as the *mémoire* of 1756 "Sur l'apperception, et son influence sur nos jugemens" (On Apperception and Its Influence on Our Judgments): "no distinct idea can produce feeling" (Apperception, 1766, 426).

Bibliography

Beausobre, Louis de. (1759) 1766. "Réflexions sur la nature et les causes de la folie, Premier, second et troisième mémoires." In *Histoire de l'Académie Royale des Sciences et des Belles-Lettres de Berlin*. Berlin: Haude und Spener.
Beausobre, Louis de. (1760) 1767. "Réflexions sur la nature et les causes de la folie, Quatrième et cinquième mémoires." In *Histoire de l'Académie Royale des Sciences et des Belles-Lettres de Berlin*. Berlin: Haude und Spener.
Décultot, Élisabeth. 2006. "Métaphysique ou physiologie du beau? La théorie des plaisirs de Johann Georg Sulzer (1751–1752)." In "Esthétiques de l'Aufklärung," edited by S. Buchenau and É. Décultot, *Revue germanique internationale*, no. 4, 93–106. Paris: PUF.
Euler, Werner. 2011. "Die Idee des Schönen in Sulzers allgemeiner Theorie des Vergnügens." In *Johann Georg Sulzer (1720–1779). Aufklärung zwischen Christian Wolff und David Hume*, edited by Frank Grunert and Gideon Stiening, 101–35. Baden-Baden: Akademie Verlag.
Heinz, Marion. 2011. "J. G. Sulzer und die Anfänge der Dreivermögenslehre bei Kant." In *Johann Georg Sulzer (1720–1779). Aufklärung zwischen Christian Wolff und David Hume*, edited by Frank Grunert and Gideon Stiening, 83–9. Baden-Baden: Akademie Verlag.

Moritz, Karl Philipp. 1783–93. *Magazin zur Erfahrungsseelenkunde*, edited by Sheila Dickson and Christof Wingertszahn. http://telota.bbaw.de/mze/

Palme, Anton. 1905. "J. G. Sulzers Psychologie und die Anfänge der Dreivermögenslehre." PhD diss. Berlin: Friedrich Wilhelms-Universität.

Riedel, Wolfgang. 1994. "Erkennen und Empfinden. Anthropologische Achsendrehung und Wende zur Ästhetik bei Johann Georg Sulzer." In *Der ganze Mensch. Anthropologie und Literatur im 18. Jahrhundert*, edited by Hans-Jürgen Schings, 410–39. Stuttgart: Weimar.

Sulzer, Johann Georg. (1751) 1753. "Recherches sur l'origine des sentiments agréables et désagréables, Premier mémoire: Théorie générale du plaisir." In *Histoire de l'Académie Royale des Sciences et des Belles-Lettres de Berlin*, 57–75. Berlin: Haude und Spener.

Sulzer, Johann Georg. (1756) 1766. "Sur l'apperception et son influence sur nos jugements." In *Histoire de l'Académie Royale des Sciences et des Belles-Lettres de Berlin*, 415–34. Berlin: Haude und Spener.

Sulzer, Johann Georg. (1757) 1759. "Analyse du génie." In *Histoire de l'Académie Royale des Sciences et des Belles-Lettres de Berlin*, 393–404. Berlin: Haude und Spener.

Sulzer, Johann Georg. 1758. (1765). "Analyse de la raison." In *Histoire de l'Académie Royale des Sciences et des Belles-Lettres de Berlin*, 414–32. Berlin: Haude und Spener.

Sulzer, Johann Georg. 1759. *Kurzer Begriff aller Wissenschaften und andern Theile der Gelehrsamkeit*. Leipzig: Johann Christian Langenheim.

Sulzer, Johann Georg. (1759) 1766. "Explication d'un paradoxe psychologique; que non seulement l'homme agit et juge quelquefois sans motifs et sans raisons apparentes, mais même malgré des motifs pressants et des raisons convaincantes." In *Histoire de l'Académie Royale des Sciences et des Belles-Lettres de Berlin*, 433–50. Berlin: Haude und Spener.

Sulzer, Johann Georg. (1760) 1767. "Réflexions sur l'utilité de la poésie dramatique." In *Histoire de l'Académie Royale des Sciences et des Belles-Lettres de Berlin*, 326–39. Berlin: Haude und Spener.

Sulzer, Johann Georg. (1763) 1770. "Observations sur les divers états où l'âme se trouve en exerçant ses facultés primitives, celle d'apercevoir et celle de sentir." In *Histoire de l'Académie Royale des Sciences et des Belles-Lettres de Berlin*, 407–20. Berlin: Haude und Spener.

Sulzer, Johann Georg. (1765) 1767. "De l'énergie dans les ouvrages des beaux-arts." In *Histoire de l'Académie Royale des Sciences et des Belles-Lettres de Berlin*, 475–92. Berlin: Haude und Spener.

Sulzer, Johann Georg. (1769) 1771. "Considérations psychologiques sur l'homme moral." In *Histoire de l'Académie Royale des Sciences et des Belles-Lettres de Berlin*, 361–80. Berlin: Haude und Spener.

Sulzer, Johann Georg. (1771) 1773. "Observations sur quelques propriétés de l'âme comparées à celles de la matière: pour servir à l'examen du matérialisme." In *Nouveaux Mémoires de l'Académie Royale des Sciences et Belles-Lettres*, 390–410. Berlin: Voss.

Sulzer, Johann Georg. 1773. *Vermischte philosophische Schriften*. Leipzig: Weidmanns Erben und Reich.

Sulzer, Johann Georg. 2014. *Gesammelte Schriften. Kommentierte Ausgabe, Band 1: Kurzer Begriff aller Wissenschaften*, edited by Hans von Adler and Élisabeth Décultot. Zürich: Schwabe.

Note on the Contributors

Andreas Blank holds a Research Position funded by the Austrian Science Fund at the Alpen-Adria Universität Klagenfurt, Austria. Previously, he has been Visiting Associate Professor at the University of Hamburg and Bard College Berlin, as well as Visiting Fellow at the Center for Philosophy of Science (University of Pittsburgh), the Cohn Institute for the History and Philosophy of Science (Tel Aviv University), and the Istituto per il Lessico Intellettuale Europeo (CNR, Rome). He has published some eighty articles on early modern philosophy and science in collective volumes and journals such as *British Journal for the History of Philosophy*, *Journal of Modern Philosophy*, *History of Philosophy Quarterly*, *Journal of the History of Ideas*, *Intellectual History Review*, *History of European Ideas*, *Journal of Early Modern Studies*, *Studia Leibnitiana*, *Perspectives on Science*, *Annals of Science*, *Science in Context*, and *Early Science and Medicine*.

Daniel Dumouchel is Professor in the Department of Philosophy at the Université de Montréal, where he has taught the history of modern philosophy and philosophical aesthetics since 1993. After devoting much of his work to Kant's aesthetics (*Kant et la genèse de la subjectivité esthétique*, 1999), his research has focused on Enlightenment philosophy in general, the history of aesthetic thought, the philosophy of the passions, and the use of fiction in philosophy. He recently edited *Philosophie spéculative à l'Académie de Berlin. Mémoires 1745-1769* (2022, with F. Duchesneau, A. Ferraro and Ch. Leduc).

Ursula Goldenbaum is Professor emerita at the Department of Philosophy at Emory University where she taught since 2004. Previously, she held academic positions at research institutions in Berlin and Potsdam in Germany. Her subject of research is the history of early modern philosophy and science. She has published monographs on Spinoza (1993), the controversy between Maupertuis and Euler with Samuel König and Voltaire about the principle of least action (2002 and 2016), and two volumes on the public debates in the German Enlightenment (2004). She has published more than 100 articles and book chapters, and has edited a German translation of G. W. Leibniz's writings and letters (1991), as well as M. Mendelssohn's translation of J.-J. Rousseau's *Treatise on the Origin of Inequality* (2000), *Infinitesimal Differences* (2008, with D. Jesseph), and *Doing without Free Will* (2015, with Ch. Kluz).

Stephen Howard is a Research Fellow at KU Leuven, Belgium. He is the author of *Kant's Late Philosophy of Nature: The Opus postumum* (2023) and various articles on early modern and modern natural philosophy and metaphysics, including "The Cosmological Ideas in Kant's Critical Philosophy: Their Unique Status and Twofold

Regulative Use" (*Southern Journal of Philosophy*, 2023), "Kant on Limits, Boundaries, and the Positive Function of Ideas" (*European Journal of Philosophy*, 2022), and "Why Did Leibniz Fail to Complete His Dynamics?" (*British Journal for the History of Philosophy*, 2017).

Christian Leduc is Professor of Philosophy at the University of Montreal. His research focuses on Leibniz and the German and French Enlightenment, more specifically on metaphysics of nature, natural teleology, and speculative philosophy at the Berlin Academy. He is the author of *Substance, individu et connaissance chez Leibniz* (2009) and has edited several volumes and special issues, among which are *Leibniz and Natural Teleology in the 18th century* (*Studia Leibnitiana*, 2018, with R. Andrault) and *Philosophie spéculative à l'Académie de Berlin. Mémoires 1745–1769* (2022, with F. Duchesneau et al.).

Gualtiero Lorini is Assistant Professor of Philosophy at the Catholic University of Milan and an Alexander von Humboldt-Alumnus. His main research interests concern Kant's philosophy, its German sources and reception. His most recent publications include the edited volume *Knowledge, Morals and Practice in Kant's Anthropology* (2018, with Robert B. Louden); the articles "'Diversa Theologiae Naturalis Systemata'. Christian Wolff's Ways to God" (*Rivista di Storia della Filosofia*, 2021) and "Bewusstsein und innerer Sinn bei Baumgarten: ein Beitrag zu Kants Begriff der Apperzeption?" (in *Kant's Transcendental Deduction and the Theory of Apperception. New Interpretations*, ed. by G. Motta, D. Schulting, and U. Thiel, 2022); as well as the monograph *Die anthropologische Normativität bei Kant* (2023).

Alessandro Nannini is Researcher in philosophy at the Martin Luther University, Halle-Wittenberg. His academic work mainly concerns the aesthetics and the intellectual history of the German eighteenth century. His recently published volumes include *Christian Garve e l'estetica dell'interessante* (2020); *Al di qua del logos. Logica delle idee estetiche tra Baumgarten e Kant* (2022); *Il segno e l'immagine. Estetica e semiotica delle arti da Du Bos a Lessing* (2023). He edited the new Italian edition of Baumgarten's *Aesthetica* (Aesthetica Preprint Supplementa, 2020, with S. Tedesco) and the volume *Schriften zu Psychologie und Ästhetik* as part of the critical edition of J. G. Sulzer's *Gesammelte Schriften* (2023, with É. Décultot).

Tinca Prunea-Bretonnet is Researcher at the Institute for Philosophy and Psychology of the Romanian Academy and at the University of Bucharest. Her work focuses on Kant and the German Enlightenment, as well as on the French Enlightenment and the reception of Kant's philosophy in the twentieth century. Her recent publications include the monograph *L'avènement de la métaphysique kantienne. Prémises et enjeux d'une réception au XXe siècle* (2023) and the edited volumes *The Berlin Academy in the Reign of Frederick the Great: Philosophy and Science* (2022, with P. R. Anstey) and *The Experiential Turn in Eighteenth-Century German Philosophy* (2021, with K. de Boer).

Pavel Reichl is Assistant Professor of Philosophy at the University of Groningen. His research interests are primarily in Kant and post-Kantian philosophy. His publications include the articles "Kant's Response to Hume on Natural Theology: Dogmatic Anthropomorphism, Analogical Inference, and Symbolic Representation" (*Journal of the History of Philosophy*, 2023), "The Role of the First Principle in Fichte's Philosophy of History" (*Fichte-Studien*, 2021), and "Making History Philosophical: Kant, Maimon, and the Evolution of the Historiography of Philosophy in the Critical Period" (*British Journal for the History of Philosophy*, 2020).

Lloyd Strickland is Professor of Philosophy and Intellectual History at Manchester Metropolitan University (UK). Much of his research concerns the thought and reception of Gottfried Wilhelm Leibniz, on which he recently co-authored a book with Harry Lewis (Harvard University) entitled *Leibniz on Binary: The Invention of Computer Arithmetic* (2022). Among Lloyd Strickland's other books are *Leibniz's Monadology* (2014), *The Philosophical Writings of Prémontval* (2018), and *Leibniz's Key Philosophical Writings: A Guide* (2020, with P. Lodge).

Gesa Wellmann is Junior Professor for History of Philosophy at the University of Oldenburg (Germany). She obtained her PhD from the KU Leuven (Belgium) in 2018. Her scholarship draws upon Kant, German Idealism, and decolonial theory. The main focus of her research is the investigation of the problem of history, systematicity, and method on which she published several articles and book chapters, among which the most recent are "Kritik und Philosophie als Wissenschaft. Das Verhältnis der Wissenschaftslehre zu Kants kritischer Metaphysik" (in *Philosophie als Wissenschaft. Wissenschaftsbegriffe in den philosophischen Systemen des deutschen Idealismus*, edited by N. Schleich, 2022), and "'The Subsequent Delivery of the Deduction'—Fichte's Transformation of Kant's Deduction of the Categories" (*Fichte-Studien*, 2021).

Index

Aarsleff, Hans 183, 193
Abicht, Johann Heinrich 4, 114–15, 117–20, 122–3, 125–6, 128–9
Adam 142, 150–2, 185
Adiaphora/indifference 140–2, 146, 148, 153
Adolfus Frederick IV 69
Aesthetics 3–5, 116–17, 139–54
Alciato, Andrea 13, 18
Anne of Orange, Princess 92, 95–6
Anthropology 3, 5, 183–4, 190, 198–201
Aristotle 1, 117, 119, 126, 185
Arnauld, Antoine 56
Attention 17, 173, 176, 192, 196, 209–10, 213–14, 216–17
Augustine of Hippo 142, 146
Aversion 24, 143–4, 150–1, 170–1, 213, 216–17

Babel, Tower of 185
Baumgarten, Alexander Gottlieb 4–5, 139–54, 171
Baumgarten, Siegmund Jacob 151–2
Béguelin, Nicolas 69, 71
Bernoulli, Daniel 93
Bernoulli, Johann I 93
Bernoulli, Johann II 93–4
Bernoulli, Nicolaus 93
Body 56–63, 141, 143–4, 146, 150, 166, 187, 214, 217
Boirac, Émile 81
Bongie, Laurence 52
Bonne, Rigobert 36
Bouillier, Francisque 81–2
Burnett, James (Lord Monboddo) 188, 198–201

Calinger, Ronald 72
Calvin, Jean 80
Calvinism 80
Canz, Israel Gottlieb 171
Categories 119, 127

Châtelet, Émilie (Marquise du) 62, 93
Cheneval, Francis 12–14, 16
Civitas maxima 3, 11–16, 19–21, 24–5
Clairaut, Alexis 97
Clarke, Samuel 62
Cochius, Leonhard 5, 165–77
Colonialism 3, 32, 34, 37–40
Condillac, Étienne Bonnot de 4, 51–65, 184, 187–91, 192–8
Consciousness 58, 171–6, 193, 196, 210, 212, 216
Contemplation 142, 212–13, 216
Controversy 1–5, 11–3, 25, 32, 33, 89–90, 92, 99–100, 140–1, 144–6, 153, 165, 168
Copernicus 113
Copineau, Abbot 197
Cosmology 4, 52–4, 58, 60, 64–5, 102, 113, 119, 124–6, 128
Cosmopolitanism 3, 11–16, 20–2, 24–5
Cramer, Gabriel 65, 93
Cravetta, Aimone de 18
Crusius, Christian August 116, 170

De Brosses, Charles 194
De Pauw, Cornelius 35
Democritus 214
Denina, Carlo Giovanni Maria 32–3, 40
Descartes, René 1, 59, 82, 92
Desire 140–4, 146, 150–2, 169, 172–3, 176, 189–90, 192, 209–11, 213, 215–17
Di Giovanni, George 119
Diderot, Denis 31, 37–8
Divisibility 4, 56–8, 63–4
Dogmatism 118, 120–1, 125–8
Domitius Ulpianus 23
Dohm, Christoph Wilhelm 35
Drive 5, 165, 167–71, 175–7, 210
  to perfection 168–70, 175–7
Dualism 121

Index

Eberhard, Johann August 114–15, 123, 208
Empiricism 39, 52–3, 64–5, 120–1, 188, 198, 218
  hypothetical empiricism 184, 197–8
End/Final cause 38–9, 74, 77–8, 80, 146, 153
Engels, Friedrich 200
Enlightenment 2–4, 33, 35, 52
Epicurus 185–6
Euler, Leonhard 51, 57, 62, 89, 90–103
Eve 152
Experience 34–5, 38, 55–6, 59–63, 118, 121, 167–8, 172, 196, 198, 209–10, 216–17
  possible experience 123–4, 128

Feder, Johann Georg H. 120
Feral children 187, 193–9
Fermat, Pierre de 92
Fiction 3, 11–15, 22, 24–5
Flesh 140–3, 144–5, 149–54
Fontenelle, Bernard Le Bouyer de 56
Force 51, 53–5, 60, 65, 94, 166–7, 171, 173, 209–11, 217
  see also *vis viva*
Formey, Johann Heinrich Samuel 51, 69–71, 73–4, 91, 99–100
Formigari, Lia 200
Francke, August Hermann 141, 145, 147–8, 151, 153
Frederick I 185
Frederick II / the Great 2, 4, 32, 34, 39, 51, 89–90, 93, 95, 100–2, 190
Frederick Wilhelm II 32
Freedom of speech 89–90, 96, 100, 103–4

Garve, Christian 165
Gassendi, Pierre 185
God 54, 61–2, 64, 73–81, 92, 119, 129, 140–3, 145–9, 150, 152–3, 168, 185, 187, 191, 197
Gottsched, Johann Christoph 98, 100, 102, 104

Haller, Albrecht von 93, 95, 97–8
Hamilton, William 139
Hanov, Michael Christoph 3, 12
Harmony 60–2, 65, 167, 171, 175
  pre-established harmony 61–2, 65
Harnack, Adolf 72, 89–90, 165
Hegel, Georg Wilhelm Friedrich 139

Heinius, Johann Philipp 69–72
Hellwig, Marion 72
Henzi, Samuel 91, 93–4, 99–100
Heraclitus 118
Herder, Johann Gottfried 33, 184, 192–4, 196, 198, 199–200
Hermann, Jacob 93
Herodotus 196
Hertzberg, Ewald Friedrich 3–4, 32–40
Herz, Markus 199
Hippocrates 214
Hirzel, Ludwig 72
Historiography 1–2, 33–7, 39
History 2–3, 32–40, 184, 197
Holbach, Paul-Henry Thiry d' 31
Horace 148
Hume, David 62, 116–17, 126–7, 216

Idealism 52, 58–9, 121
Imagination 57–8, 139, 145, 151, 186–7, 214, 217
Inclination 5, 165–77
Innate Ideas 119, 121, 171, 188–9
Instinct 187, 192–3, 195
Iselin, Isaak 40
Israel, Jonathan 102
Itard, Jean 199

Jacobi, Friedrich Heinrich 2
Javary, Louis Auguste 81
Jesus of Nazareth 142, 150–1
Joachim of Fiore 80
Jussieu, Antoine-Laurent 36
Justi, Johann Heinrich Gottlob von 51

Kahrel, Hermann Friedrich 3, 12–13, 15–17, 19–25
Kant, Immanuel 2–4, 11, 33, 40, 74, 113–20, 122–130, 154, 184, 198–201, 208, 212
Kästner, Abraham Gotthelf 92, 98, 101
Kiefer, Bruce 193
Kiesewetter, Johann Gottfried K. C. 123–4
König, Samuel 4, 89–104
Künzli, Martin 70–2, 74

Laerke, Mogens 1
Lambert, Johann Heinrich 116, 120
Lange, Joachim 146, 148–9, 154

Language 2–3, 5, 54, 183–201
Leibniz, Gottfried Wilhelm 1–5, 51–8, 60–5, 70–4, 77–8, 82, 89–96, 98–101, 104, 113–17, 119–20, 122, 126–7, 129, 165–71, 174–7, 184–8, 198
Leibniz(ian)-Wolffian 51–3, 70–1, 100–1, 114, 116–17, 120, 127, 168
Lessing, Gotthold Ephraim 2, 98
Lifschitz, Avi 183–4
Locke, John 38, 53–6, 59, 62, 184, 186–8, 190, 196, 198
Lutheran 4, 80, 140–1, 145–6

Maimon, Solomon 113–14
Malebranche, Nicolas 77, 82
Marcuse, Herbert 154
Materialism 121, 185, 208, 211
Mathematics 2, 89, 91, 93, 101, 166
Maupertuis, Pierre-Louis Moreau de 4, 70–3, 89–103, 184, 190–1
Mechanics 101
Medicine 183, 199
Meditation 143–4, 150, 210, 212–14
Meier, Georg Friedrich 116, 147, 149, 151–2
Meiners, Christoph 165
Meliorism 70, 77, 79–82
Mendelssohn Moses 2, 74, 116
Menochio, Jacopo 18–19
Merian, Jean-Bernard 69, 71–2, 91, 97–8, 101, 194
Metaphysics 1–2, 4–5, 52–3, 55, 58–60, 99, 113–30, 167, 175
Michaelis, Johann David 191, 195–6
Monad 2, 4, 51–65, 116, 121
Monboddo, Lord *see* Burnett, James
Mylius Christlob 97–8, 101–3

Naigeon, Jacques-André 31
Nannini, Alessandro 4–5, 171
Natural Law 3, 12–18, 22–4, 39, 93
Naturalism vs Conventionalism 184, 186
Neis, Cordula 183, 194, 198
Newton, Isaac 62–4, 70, 90, 93–4, 104
Nicole, Pierre 56
Noah 185

Ontology 52–3, 57–9, 124–7
Optimism 2, 4, 51, 69–82
Order 4, 53, 59–65, 76, 80, 115–17, 191

Pain 188, 212, 216
Pantheism 2, 121
Pascal, Blaise 1
Patzke, Johann Samuel 152
Paul the Apostle 141, 149
Perception 53–4, 58–61, 63, 65, 142, 166, 174, 187, 196, 208, 211–17
  apperception 119, 210–17
  petites perceptions 166, 174
Perfectibility 80, 165–6, 171, 175–77
Perfection 3, 11, 24, 60, 64, 69, 74, 77, 80–1, 117, 125, 143–5, 154, 166, 168–71, 175–7, 191
Philosophy, critical 113–19, 121–30
  of history 3–4, 32, 34
  practical 15, 24, 119, 165
  speculative 2, 40, 129, 166, 207
Pietism 4, 140–7, 150, 152–4
Plagiarism 90, 94–5, 99
Plato 76–7, 126, 183, 186
Platonism 143
Plattner, Ernst 120
Pleasure 5, 139–47, 148–9, 153–4, 171, 173, 212–13, 216
Ploucquet, Gottfried 51
Pope, Alexander 69, 73
Possible worlds 74–8, 81
Prémontval, André-Pierre Le Guay de 4, 69–82
Presumption of goodness 3, 12–25
Principle, of conservation 94
  of contradiction 167
  of identity 167
  of least action 2, 4, 89–90, 92, 94–5, 99, 101, 103
  of sufficient reason 54, 71, 115
Prize competition 2–5, 31–2, 40, 51–2, 64, 78, 113, 115, 122–3, 165, 188, 192–3, 207–8
Progress 4, 5, 80–1, 91, 93, 165–6, 172, 175, 187, 207
  of metaphysics 113–30
Psammetichus I 196–8
Psychology 5, 53–4, 116, 124, 128, 143, 183, 206–13, 218
  empirical 5, 54, 116, 143, 167, 172, 177, 183, 188, 209–10, 213
  rational 54, 124, 183
Public debate 4, 89–104

Pyrrhonism 80, 126
Pythagoreanism 143

Quasi-contract 12, 14–15, 22

Rambach, Johann Jakob 142–7, 150, 152–4
Raphson, Joseph 62
Rationalism 70, 116, 120–1, 188, 198
Raynal, Guillaume 3–4, 31–8, 40
Réaumur, René Antoine 93
Reflection 56, 169, 173, 176, 187–9, 192–3, 217
Reimarus, Hermann Samuel 2, 175–6
Reinhard, Adolf Friedrich 69–75, 77–8
Reinhold, Karl Leonhard 4, 114–15, 118, 120–3, 126, 128–9
Representation 39, 118–21, 150, 167–77, 185, 192, 196, 209, 211–12, 215–18
Rink, Friedrich Theodor 114, 122, 125
Rotth, Albrecht Christian 141, 145–6
Rousseau, Jean-Jacques 5, 31, 165–6, 171, 175–6, 184, 187, 189–91, 193–5, 197

Savage 40, 190, 193, 196, 198–9
Schultz, Johann 116
Schwab, Johann Christoph 4, 114–17, 119–20, 123, 126–7, 129
Semler, Johann Salomo 150
Sensation 4, 18, 52–7, 59–65, 167, 174–6, 185, 192, 196, 213–14, 217
Sensibility/Sensitive 5, 116, 139–41, 143, 145–6, 149–54, 207–9, 211–18
Signs 16–17, 54, 187–8, 190, 193–4, 198
Sin 141–2, 145, 147–53, 168, 185
Skepticism 57, 116–17, 120–1, 125–8
Slavery 38
Soave, Francesco 194
Socrates 115
Soul 5, 37, 58, 60–2, 141, 143–4, 150–1, 165–77
    depth of the soul 5, 165–6, 171–7
    faculties/operations 118–19, 139, 143, 146, 150–1, 153–4, 165–77, 185, 187, 192–3, 207–18
    immortality of 118–19, 208–10, 218
Space 4, 53, 60, 62–4, 93, 119
Spener, Philipp Jacob 144, 152

Spinoza, Baruch 1–2
Stoic 142, 147
Substance 52–7, 59–62, 64–5, 73, 118, 121, 210–11
Sucro, Christoph Joseph 147
Sulzer, Johann Georg 5, 69–73, 91, 95–6, 167, 171, 173, 177, 207–18
Supersensible 123–5, 127–9
Süssmilch, Johann Peter 190–1, 193, 197
System 51–3, 65, 69–70
    Kantian 122–5, 127–8
    metaphysical 114–18, 120, 122, 124–6, 128

Teleology 92, 129
Testimony 34–6
Tetens, Johann Nikolaus 116
Theology 2, 5, 12, 53, 76, 82, 119, 124–6, 128, 140, 144, 146, 148–53, 166, 183
Thomasian 165, 168, 173
Thomasius, Christian 144
Thomism 1
Timaeus of Locri 76–7
Turgot, Anne Robert Jacques 40

Vattel, Emer de 3, 12
Victor d'Aveyron 199
Vis viva 94–5, 99
Vockerodt, Gottfried 141–2, 145, 154
Volition/Will 12–17, 20–1, 23–5, 74, 76, 78, 80–1, 118–19, 121, 142, 146, 150–1, 168, 200, 210, 216–17
Voltaire 4, 31, 89–90, 93, 100–3

Wiegleb, Johann Hieronymus 147
Wieland, Christoph Martin 71
Will see *volition*
William Charles Friso of Orange, Prince 93
Wolff, Christian 2–5, 11–16, 21–5, 51, 53–5, 57–8, 60, 62, 70–3, 80, 91, 93, 113–17, 122, 126, 129, 139, 143, 153, 165–71, 173, 175–7, 194, 209–11, 218
Wundt, Max 3

Zimermann, Johann Georg Richter 71

www.ingramcontent.com/pod-product-compliance
Lightning Source LLC
Chambersburg PA
CBHW071832300426
44116CB00009B/1525